The Positive Hero in Russian Literature

Rufus W. Mathewson, Jr.

NORTHWESTERN UNIVERSITY PRESS / EVANSTON, ILLINOIS

Northwestern University Press
Evanston, Illinois 60208-4210

First edition published 1958 by Stanford University Press; second edition published 1975 by Stanford University Press. Copyright © 1958, 1975 by the Board of Trustees of the Leland Stanford Junior University. Northwestern University Press paperback edition published 2000 by arrangement with Ruth M. Mathewson. All rights reserved.

Printed in the United States of America

ISBN 0-8101-1716-9

1 0 0 3 2 4 5 5 8 9

Library of Congress Cataloging-in-Publication Data

Mathewson, Rufus W.
    The positive hero in Russian literature / Rufus W. Mathewson, Jr.—2d. ed.
        p. cm. — (Studies in Russian literature and theory)
    2d ed. originally published: Stanford, Calif. : Stanford University Press, 1975.
    Includes bibliographical references and index.
    ISBN 0-8101-1716-9 (paper : alk. paper)
    1. Russian literature—History and criticism. 2. Heroes in literature. I. Title. II. Series.

PG2989.H4 M3 1999
891.73'409352—dc21   99-049407

For Murray, Tom, Kevin, and Judy

Contents

Preface to the Second Edition

꿏꿏꿏

When this study first appeared in 1958, I had hoped to establish the hypothesis that the true continuity in Russian prose, joining the nineteenth and twentieth centuries, was to be found in a persistent conflict between two contrary views of the true nature and proper uses of literature—one prescriptive, controlled, and social, the other open, autonomous, and broadly human. Much had happened on the literary scene in the five years between Stalin's death in 1953 and the appearance of my first edition: the rhythm of "thaw" and "freeze" had occurred twice; there was evidence of restlessness beneath the surface, of cries for "sincerity" in literature, and obvious impulses to replace official writing with more candid, better-written texts. But I concluded then that although much had happened, little had really changed in the long view. The new literature was well-intentioned but crude— novels like Ehrenburg's *Thaw*, Dudintsev's *Not by Bread Alone*. No genuine critical debate was sustained; the socialist realists still occupied "the commanding heights" of literature. I saw no gain in reviewing the touching but melancholy and unproductive record between 1946 and 1958—all the dreary protocols of meetings and conferences, the decrees, resolutions, editorials, and recantations which marked the victory of the antiliterary literary party over this fledgling movement. I concluded then and still hold that nothing had happened by 1958 to end the sway of the basic doctrine initially laid down by Andrei Zhdanov, whose suffocating strictures were quoted for years after Stalin's death.

On socialist realism, I wrote in the Preface to my earlier edition
that its power was maintained by two massive traditions—Leninist
Marxism and the utilitarian aesthetic of the Russian radical democrats—and that it expressed "the vested interests of a unitary state,
unused to criticism, hostile to pluralism, and untroubled about the
larger ends of existence." To dismantle it or remove it seemed inconceivable—with one possible exception: "a series of brilliant new literary
works, provided they were allowed to see daylight, might suddenly
render the entire structure of socialist realism obsolete, another monument to Russia's agony and servitude." This is precisely what has
happened—or has been happening—since 1958. Genuine Russian writing has reappeared, generated in the underground, smuggled to "daylight," astonishing the world with its reach and vitality. If socialist
realism is still standing, it has been discredited and outflanked, and
is held in place by the police apparatus, which has taken over the
function of "criticism," and by the swarm of literary officials in the
Gogolian writers union, which has expelled most of its genuine writers *because* they are genuine writers. A significant renewal of the
moribund doctrine seems blocked forever by its own internal contradictions. Andrei Sinyavsky has said that it is impossible to present
a true psychological portrait according to the socialist realist canon
without producing a parody. In his fiercely mocking essay "On Socialist Realism," he has traced this self-defeating process to a flaw in the
doctrine's foundation—the doomed effort to fuse a "realist" with a "religious" mode of expression.[1] The bastard neoclassical literature that
issues from this unnatural coupling is guaranteed to fail by its own
contradictory nature.

[1] This remarkable essay was smuggled out of the Soviet Union and first published
in *Esprit* in 1959 under the pseudonym Abram Tertz. We did not know that Tertz was
Sinyavsky until his arrest in September 1965. "Chto takoe sotsialisticheskii realizm," in
Fantasticheskii mir Abrama Tertsa (New York, 1966); Abram Tertz [pseud.], *"The
Trial Begins" and "On Socialist Realism,"* trans. Max Hayward ("Trial") and George
Dennis ("Realism") (New York, 1965).
A companion essay to this one has recently appeared, bringing Sinyavsky's thought
up to date on the perilous situation of the writer in Russia, whom he sees as an outcast,
"a Jew," his ostracism bearing witness to the genuineness of his commitment. He presents several ironic excuses for the Russian people's profound hostility to the writer-
scapegoat: the written word is so vital to Russians that the challenger of the handed-
down language becomes an insupportable presence among them; their anti-Semitism
becomes explicable as the efforts Russians make to attribute the evil in themselves to
ill-intentioned outsiders. Writers join the Jews at this point as honorable scapegoats,
and the current emigration of Jews from the Soviet Union is exactly analogous to the

Rendered obsolete by its own failures, eclipsed by the work of its victims, it fights for its life from a position which is as strong externally as it is weak internally. This battle, I came to understand, marks a renewal in another form of the literary war I had already traced in the century from the later Belinsky (in the 1840s) to the Zhdanov blackout in 1946. It was this discovery that persuaded me to add a new section to my record of this divided and warring tradition, a new chapter in a deep-laid continuity. Solzhenitsyn has described the terrain of Soviet culture as a shell-ravaged forest in which a few trees had miraculously survived. The antagonists became defined for me as the literary establishment, expressing the interests of an all-powerful state, and a handful of individual writers, free and alive only by accident, armed with no more than their art and their personal courage. Unevenly matched in all ways but one, the writers compensate through their talent and moral authority for the weakness of their situation ("How many divisions does the Pope have?") in a way and to a degree that validates Solzhenitsyn's oft-quoted aphorism: "A great writer in a country is like a second government."

Three prose writers—Pasternak, Solzhenitsyn, and Sinyavsky— nominated themselves as the principal combatants in the traditional fight against the materialist determinists, a fight waged once against menacing, if powerless, radical journalists; latterly against the absolute governors of a Communist empire. The relative positions of the antagonists have drastically changed in a hundred years, but the issue between them, I discovered, has remained nearly identical—an argument about the nature and uses of literature which merged with other arguments about history, morality, and the nature of man. The very appearance of their work is an aggressive assertion of their right to exist; beyond that, their work *internalizes* the full range of issues in dispute by translating them into dramatic terms. Thus I decided to bring the new edition up to date by concentrating entirely on the new dissident literature, since the resurrection of the great Russian prose tradition is by far the most significant literary event in the years after 1946. I felt free to say no more about the socialist realist position in the new section because I had presented its arguments fully in my

---

clandestine export of manuscripts. We may also take this as a final explanation of his own Jewish pseudonym, Abram Tertz, with which he signs this essay, "The Literary Process in Russia" (*Kontinent*, No. 1, 1974).

earlier text, and it has not undergone significant modification since. And there seemed little to learn from the maneuvers of literary politics, the mind-numbing repetition of formulae, and the orchestrated techniques of repression. To conclude with a "rebuttal" would be true to the rhythm already established in the book, would correct the gross imbalance of the Zhdanov victory, and would do dramatic justice with respect to the outcome, to date, of a conflict in which I have never pretended to be neutral. The new section, "Rebuttal III: The Dissident Vision," is one-sided yet true to the essential facts and to the merits of the case.

It is a property of the great Russian tradition that each individual work argues for its right to exist by casting as evil the ideas—determinist views of historical progress, theories of the social genesis of consciousness, scientific assumptions about the rational bases of human behavior, ideological definitions of art and morality—that destroy the very ground of civilization in which literature has its being. This destructive family of ideas is as visibly present in *War and Peace*, *Crime and Punishment*, and *Fathers and Sons* as it is in *Doctor Zhivago*, *First Circle*, and *Lyubimov*. Herein, then, is the bedrock continuity I hope to bring to light by analyzing the structure of dramatized argument realized through character in the dissident writers' critical vision of their world.

I tested my assumption that this connection had survived for a century by applying the formula that worked so well in the nineteenth century: in the radical critics' view of literature, character was a function of ideology; in the classical writers' view, ideology was always a function of character. Thus the character of Chernyshevsky's Rakhmetov was entirely contained in and expressed by his revolutionary ideology. Raskolnikov's Napoleonic nihilism usurped his moral sense and released the most destructive elements in his character, but when his moral sense reasserted itself, through his own inner resources, the ideology's hold on him dissolved. In the dissidents' vision, a similar ideology has usurped the nation's moral sense, and lonely individuals cast off its disfiguring ideas only by discovering their own humanity —as Rubin, for example, has begun to do in *First Circle*. The universally human, anchored in art and morality, attempts to assert its primacy over social ideology derived from closed systems of thought; two realms contest for supremacy, seek to eclipse or envelop each other, in the literature of both periods. And there is a common urgency of commitment. The writers of both periods ask for freedom not merely to explore new and unknown reaches of experience, but to defend the rights of human beings to lead full human lives, in touch with the real sources of being, outside the confines of reductive ideologies. I became convinced that the new literature in Russia continues to exemplify and to defend this position.

I have been aware that the dissident writers—Solzhenitsyn in particular—have immensely widened the audience of those interested in contemporary Russian literature. New readers need not follow every twist and turn of the debate I have traced in order to understand that the work of these writers constitutes a rebuttal to the claims of a contending tradition—not simply a local tyranny. The chapters Rebuttal I and Rebuttal II (6 and 7) will, I hope, set the terms for the new section I have called Rebuttal III.

In that section, to represent the upsurge of creative vitality between 1958 and 1974 I have chosen Pasternak's *Doctor Zhivago* and the main corpus of Solzhenitsyn's novels to date. I have drawn selectively on Andrei Sinyavsky's fiction and essays to help me organize my conclusions, and on my own (unpublished) essay "Trapped in History: The Mind of Andrei Sinyavsky" (1968). I cannot say here all I would like to say about this extraordinary writer and scholar, but readers may consult Margaret Dalton's very able analysis of his work.[2]

Specialists will understand, I hope, that I have relied on the relevance and coherence of the argument itself in deciding to make minimal changes in the 1958 text. I find it reassuring that a number of excellent studies since 1958 provide support for my argument, fill in gaps, or supply beneficial corrections. Robert Maguire's *Red Virgin Soil* and Peter Demetz's *Marx, Engels, and the Poets* are representative of many such works that concentrate on aspects of the problem which I treat only briefly, but still leave my argument standing.[3] In Andrei Sinyavsky's brilliant essay "On Socialist Realism" I have found heartening confirmation of many of my ideas, and I would be happy to think that if he has chanced upon my work in the years since his own essay appeared, he may have recognized affinities be-

---

[2] Margaret Dalton, *Andrei Siniavskii and Julii Daniel': Two Soviet "Heretical" Writers* (Würzburg, 1973).

[3] Robert A. Maguire, *Red Virgin Soil: Soviet Literature in the 1920's* (Princeton, N.J., 1966); Peter Demetz, *Marx, Engels, and the Poets: Origins of Marxist Literary Criticism* (Chicago, 1967).

tween his work and my own more pedestrian treatment of the same phenomena.

I have restrained the impulse to add many new details to the original discussion, convinced that an argument sufficient to an earlier time has remained sufficient to our own, the more so since it is borne out by subsequent events. I have eliminated the old bibliography, however, as obsolete; footnotes and index together should convey in trimmer form my actual working bibliography. I have discarded a glossary of socialist realist definitions as no longer necessary to illustrate that well-known and threadbare doctrine. I have replaced the old Preface with this one, added Part 4 on the grounds I have explained, and sectioned the earlier text accordingly.

All these changes—including the key change from intellectual history (in Parts 1–3) to textual analysis (in Part 4)—suggest to me that over the years, this study, first put together as an original scholarly investigation, has become an essay on a special Russian literary problem, calling attention to its reflections rather than its research.

Though I have not felt the need to keep the historical record of minor alterations in a moribund doctrine, one change cannot pass unremarked: the disappearance of the positive hero himself. Given the nature of the society, one should seek the controlling reason for such changes in considerations of political expediency. The deflation of the Cult of Personality presumably let the air out, too, of the cult of heroes, who take on the aspect, in retrospect, of idealized mini-Stalins. This reflects a change in the style of political leadership, narrowing the distance, perhaps, between leader and led, and altering the quality of this relationship. But as a phenomenon which is primarily political, it has only marginal consequences for literature, representing a rearrangement in the facade of slogans, but not diminishing the pressure on writers, who are still required to be optimistic, instructive, and politically responsible in the decreed way. Of course, there were literary reasons too for this change (whether or not they influenced the decision), which I touch on in my introductory words to Part 4.

I do feel obliged to take corrective note of two points touching the essence of the literary argument. I have insisted on the heavy contribution Belinsky, Dobrolyubov, and Chernyshevsky made to the genesis of socialist realism. I still think this is so, but the way out does not necessarily follow the way in. These Russian progenitors have all but faded from view in the aspect this body of thought presents to its articulate victims today. In the fiction of Pasternak, Solzhenitsyn, and Sinyavsky they are not mentioned. The name of the adversary is Marxism—with all its variant isms—and the native radical democrats are included by implication only when it is pointed out that Marxism is the latest of a family of closed systems of thought, born in Western Europe, which rest on "scientific" theories of historical progress. Nor is it the scattered and often contradictory utterances Marx and Engels made about literature that these Russian writers have in mind. It is rather the chief premises of Marxist theory, seen as the controlling ideas of an order specially designed to fulfill human needs which has gone wildly awry, producing something very nearly the opposite of what it had promised.

The first correction concerns the new writers' perception of their own past. The second concerns a necessary change in my own perception of the literary problem. In the earlier edition I had built much of my argument on opposing views of the hero: the exemplary positive hero, clearheadedly acting out and validating beneficial social theories (sometimes by dying for them), stood against the traditional hero, whose life is lived out existentially and ends tragically, its mistaken course illuminated only in the moments before it ceases. The new Russian writing has altered the existential-tragic formula in a significant way. "Existential" still describes the lonely individual living out his life in permanent collision with adversity, constantly forging his identity against hostile circumstances; but "tragic" no longer describes the dramatic outcome of the collision. Terrence des Pres has ably defined the step beyond tragedy which he has discovered in modern writing—above all in *l'univers concentrationnaire*, and quintessentially in the work of Solzhenitsyn.[4] In a world in which the individual—and the race—are daily threatened with extinction, the hero's death can serve no end nor teach us anything we want to know. Now the victim gives way to the man who survives, intact in soul if not always in body. The pathos is in the monumental unevenness of the struggle, in the miracle of his staying alive, to preserve, as Des Pres says, "the living seeds of existence as a human being." This formulation is remarkably in point; it illuminates the lives of Solzhenitsyn's *zeks*, of the wretched writer-personae in most of Sinyavsky's fiction, and of Zhivago, too, who dies alone but "sur-

---

[4] Terrence des Pres, "The Survivor: On the Ethos of Survival in Extremity," *Encounter*, September 1971, pp. 3–19.

vives" in his children, in the minds of his friends, and in the novel itself.

Seen in this perspective, the "small" act of staying morally alive becomes heroic; the hero is spiritually unbreakable, successful in his stance of opposition, true to his mission, an example for others. Are we not circling back, then, to the notion of positive heroes? On a certain plane of abstraction, it would seem to be so, but the differences between the Soviet official hero and the battered survivor in the dissident literature lie in the particular circumstances of their situation. The Soviet model hero lives and acts within the confines of an infallible doctrine promising certain success in the public domain, whatever the private cost. The survivor-hero generates his moral strength out of his own personal resources in conditions of solitude and unrelenting adversity. Stretched to the limit in his suffering, he searches out and formulates ideas, but they are ideas born of experience; he is never their puppet or their prisoner. His personal "ideology" is a function of his character, not vice versa. He is more humanly recognizable, and for this reason, if for no other, is more aesthetically acceptable. What resemblances there are between the two kinds of hero may arise from the absolute oppositions, with extremity set as the norm, that characterize the totalitarian world. For the working writer, this world permits no traffic between good and evil, no areas of ambivalence where difficult choices are made. Mistakes are not interesting because they are not tolerated. In this world the official hero wins by exterminating evil wherever he finds it; the survivor triumphs by defining it and holding it at bay. Seized with this idea, the new Russian literature has survived as the literature of survival.

It has not been easy to write in the "curl" of the headlines. Since I began to put together this edition, Sinyavsky has chosen exile in Paris and has published his letters from prison, *A Voice from the Choir.* Solzhenitsyn has been forced into exile in Zurich, and has released his monumental *Gulag Archipelago* and published his "Letter to the Leaders" in the London *Sunday Times.*[5] In a final attempt

---

[5] Abram Tertz [pseud.], *Golos iz khora* (London, 1973); Aleksandr I. Solzhenitsyn, *Arkhipelag Gulag, 1918–1956: Opyt khudozhestvennogo issledovaniya,* 1–2 (Paris, 1973), published in a translation by Thomas P. Whitney as *The Gulag Archipelago, 1918–1956: An Experiment in Literary Investigation* (New York, 1974). The second volume of *Gulag,* Parts 3 and 4, appeared under the same title in Paris in 1974 but is not yet available in English. Solzhenitsyn's letter has been published as a book, *Letter to the Soviet Leaders* (New York, 1974).

to keep up with Solzhenitsyn's pronouncements from Zurich, I must also take note of his disclosure, in December 1974, that the published texts of all his smuggled works as we now read them were cut, re-arranged, and, in his words (spoken in English), "softened down" in the hope of gaining Soviet acceptance for publication.[6] At this writing previously cut chapters and full variants are in process of appearing. My interpretations of some of these works are immediately rendered tentative by such information; the critic can only hope that what he has found to be implicit in a text he did not know was incomplete will be made more explicit by the writer in his final version.

A first reading of Solzhenitsyn's latest work encourages me to think that my analysis of the earlier smuggled fiction holds. I had earlier teased out of Solzhenitsyn's literary texts the notion that Marxism itself was the principal—the foreground—enemy, the source of all evil in the Soviet world, but was in turn only one of a family of theories—wholist, rational, determinist, "scientifically" historical, born in the West—which Dostoevsky, Tolstoy, and Turgenev had done battle with in their time. Solzhenitsyn's plain name for this evil in *Gulag* and "Letter" is *ideology*—always printed in the italics of sarcasm. It has led his country to the brink of ruin at home and abroad, and killed the nation's conscience and imagination. In *Gulag* he notes his opposition in terms I have explored at length in my analysis of his novels, and extends his definition of ideology to include all theories which justify evil as good or as dictated by higher truths. "Thus the Inquisitors fortified themselves with Christianity, conquerors with the greater glory of the Motherland, colonizers with civilization, Jacobins (early and late) with equality, fraternity and the happiness of future generations."[7] And the governors of the prison society, he demonstrates at great length, have justified it with the scientific certainties of Marxism and Leninism.

In literature the great evil-doers either know they are evil and act

---

[6] "Solzhenitsyn Reveals Self-Censorship," interview with Hedrick Smith, *New York Times*, December 4, 1974. From this account and from other sources we now know that nine chapters were cut from *First Circle*, that *Cancer Ward* was rearranged, and that a chapter on Lenin was omitted from *August 1914*—to mention only the works discussed at length in this study. Of all this revised matter, I have been able to read only one of the nine chapters cut from *First Circle* (see footnote 9, p. 291, for my comments), the chapter published in the journal *Kontinent* (No. 1, 1974), the Western voice of Soviet dissidence, including among its staff and contributors distinguished exiles—Sinyavsky, Solzhenitsyn, Brodsky, Golomshtok—and others, like Andrei Sakharov, who have remained in the Soviet Union.

[7] Solzhenitsyn, *Arkhipelag Gulag*, 1–2: 181; *The Gulag Archipelago*, p. 174.

accordingly, or lack an adequate justifying theory and succumb to conscience. "Macbeth's justifications were weak and his conscience tore him to bits.... The imagination and spiritual forces of Shakespeare's evil-doers drew up short at a dozen corpses. Because they had no *ideology*." Literature and morality belonged together in Macbeth's kind of moral tragedy, which ideology has made impossible. By licensing evil in the world, ideology kills the literary rendering of it. We see how precisely the issue is joined and how visible it is to both sides in a sample of official criticism. Pomerantsev, whose tormented cry for "sincerity" in literature marked the emotional high point of the first thaw, is the target of this resolution of the Union of Soviet Writers:

Pomerantsev elevated the quality of sincerity to the rank of a prime fundamental criterion in evaluating a literary work, thereby substituting a moral criterion unrelated to any specific time or society for the ideological, class-social judgment universally recognized in our literature.... He demoted literature from its high position as educator of the feelings and character of communism's builders to the role of "confessional" recording of the "direct impressions" of an individual, writing in detachment from the struggles and constructive labor of society.[8]

Thus ideology confronts and reduces a morally committed literature. For the wholly politicized critic, a zero ideology is itself an ideology, representing an attitude toward the inescapable forces of history. But if ideology is seen as a closed system of belief in, and action toward, an abstractly defined end, the Russian writer's counterstatement to this kind of claim has always been to open up the closed system of thought, to pluralize the possibilities of belief, to question the absoluteness of the absolute, and to show the harm promised or accomplished by action toward the questionable end. Openness, pluralism, uncertainty, relativism, the entertainment of mystery may constitute an ideology for some, but it is of a totally different kind, free of dogmatic certainties or political imperatives.

Beyond achieving this revival of the Russian literary tradition, these dissident writers have attempted to raise the question of the bankruptcy of Marxism, not as an apparatus of historical analysis or as a guide to revolutionary action—as non-Soviet intellectuals tend to

---

[8] "Ob oshibkakh zhurnala *Novyi Mir*," *Literaturnaya gazeta*, August 17, 1954, p. 3, as quoted in Edith Belle Rogovin, "*Novyi Mir*: A Case Study in the Politics of Literature," unpublished dissertation, Columbia University, 1974.

regard it—but as the matrix of a humane and livable civilization. Since in Solzhenitsyn's view the history of this failure is recorded in the minds and bodies of actual human beings, this story can be told one way in novels and another way in historical documentaries, all focusing on the police-prison system as the actual and symbolic center of the Soviet world. All three dissident writers not only restore to us the voice of the Russian literary imagination; they tell us their versions of subjective history, of how it has felt to be a Russian, filling in that page of mankind's record long left blank.

This, then, is why I have chosen to re-present this argument about the vital center of the Russian prose tradition. In the accumulated efforts over the years I have been helped by so many that I can only name the category and hope that each individual will place his name under the appropriate heading. I have been helped by librarians, editors, research assistants, and typists. The American Council of Learned Societies, the Guggenheim Foundation, and my own Russian Institute at Columbia have provided support at important moments. Students who talked back in class or in conference or researched beyond the limits of my own knowledge deserve my deep gratitude for their help, patience, and admirable intolerance for sloppy thinking. The wider circle of colleagues who have responded to me at lectures and in arguments over beer may discover echoes of their own thoughts, for which I thank them herewith. My family has contributed not only warm support but useful insights and perspectives. My son Tom has drawn on his training in logic to help me distinguish *seq* from *non seq*. My wife, Ruth Murray Mathewson, has frequently set aside her own work to edit my words and to clarify my ideas. It was her suggestion to title my final section Rebuttal III, an idea which has given the book its final shape.

Rufus W. Mathewson, Jr.

Columbia University, 1974

Acknowledgments

Acknowledgment is extended to Pantheon Books, a Division of Random House, Inc., for permission to quote from *Doctor Zhivago*, by Boris Pasternak, translated by Max Hayward, Manya Harari, and Bernard Guilbert Guerney. Copyright © 1958 by William Collins & Co., Ltd. Copyright © 1958 by Pantheon Books, Inc.

Acknowledgment is extended to Harper & Row, Publishers, Inc., for permission to quote from *The First Circle*, by Aleksandr I. Solzhenitsyn, translated from the Russian by Thomas P. Whitney. Copyright © 1968 by Harper & Row, Publishers, Inc. English translation copyright © 1968 by Harper & Row, Publishers, Inc.

Acknowledgment is extended to Farrar, Straus & Giroux, Inc., for permission to quote from *Cancer Ward*, by Alexander Solzhenitsyn, translated by Nicholas Bethell and David Burg. Translation copyright © 1968, 1969 by The Bodley Head, Ltd.

Acknowledgment is extended to Farrar, Straus & Giroux, Inc., for permission to quote from *August 1914*, by Alexander Solzhenitsyn, translated by Michael Glenny. Translation copyright © 1972 by Michael Glenny.

The Positive Hero
in Russian Literature

*For the History of the World occupies a higher ground
than that on which morality has properly its position;
which is personal character—the conscience of individuals.
... What the absolute aim of spirit requires and
accomplishes—what Providence does—transcends
obligations,... and the ascription of good or bad motives.*

· · ·

*A World-historical individual is not so unwise as to
indulge in a variety of wishes to divide his regards. He is
devoted to the One Aim, regardless of all else. It is even
possible that such men may treat other great, even sacred
interests, inconsiderately.... But so mighty a form
must trample down many an innocent flower—crush to
pieces many an object in its path.*

HEGEL, Introduction to *The Philosophy of History*

*But the highest passion in a man is faith, and here no
generation begins at any other point than did the preceding
generation, every generation begins all over again, the
subsequent generation gets no further than the foregoing.
... If the generation would only concern itself about its
task, which is the highest thing it can do, it cannot grow
weary, for the task is always sufficient for a human life.*

KIERKEGAARD, *Fear and Trembling*

We hate poetry that has a palpable design upon us.

KEATS, *Letters*

CHAPTER I

Introduction

Perhaps it is a commonplace, by now, to mention the unique intimacy of politics, morality, and literature in the Russian tradition. We know that in the nineteenth century, where this study begins, writers were constantly enjoined to treat political issues; that literature was charged in very specific ways with the responsibility to oppose serfdom and the autocracy and to further political measures which challenged the status quo. The writers themselves often shared the social and economic grievances of the politically minded, while differing as to methods. Moreover, the very assertion of a free literature's right to exist was a kind of political act and further grounds for identification with radicalism. The radicals, in their turn, made heavy demands on literature because they saw it as one of the few outlets of expression, "Aesopian" or not, for the great social issues.

These relationships are well established. Less can be taken for granted, however, about the durable compatibilities such shared sympathies might suggest. The conventional view, echoed by Edmund Wilson, for example, in his essay "The Historical Interpretation of Literature," that writer and radical critic in Russia coexisted in some form of loose, untroubled alliance based on their shared opposition to the status quo, must yield to a new understanding of what bound them together and what finally separated them. Their association more nearly resembles an alliance in which the grounds for communion between them were undermined by deeper disagreements, under stresses which have now, through acquaintance with other kinds of "Popular

Fronts," become familiar to us. In 1860 there was a crucial separation, which established a fundamental polarity in thinking about literature. Other conventional formulations of the division—"pure" vs. "utilitarian" as these terms were used in the nineteenth century, or "sociological" vs. "aesthetic," or "Marxist" vs. "formalist" as it is sometimes described in the USSR—do not comprehend the real terms of the opposition which has existed largely, as it seems to me, within the realm of realist fiction. We shall find, too, that after the revolution, these contentions were waged inside the confines of Marxism, and that each faction found ammunition in that armory.

In this debate, and in the continued association, free or enforced, of art and politics in the Soviet era, there is a clear continuity of tradition across the October Revolution. It is manifested particularly in the reappearance in the Soviet era of the nineteenth-century concept of "positive" literary heroes, that is, of emblematically virtuous images of political men. Beginning in 1932 there prevailed in the USSR a cult of heroism embracing education, psychology, literature, and the fine arts. It came to be one of the principal means of indoctrination and exhortation throughout the society, and one of the most important propaganda instruments of Party and government. It is, of course, an obvious propaganda technique, and if it were only that, if the Soviet hero were represented only in the newspaper portraits of Stakhanovites, or the statues of war heroes in public squares, there would be little to say on the subject. But the Soviet cult goes far beyond these conventional occasions for iconology. The Soviet hero rested on a theory which is both intricate and ancient. From this arsenal of ideas he was fitted out with the rudimentary elements of an inner life, and with an ethical code which guided him surely and inflexibly.

Literature has a key role in publicizing this fabricated individual, who may have resembled real Soviet types, but who, when he appeared in fiction, tended to conform to the lineaments drawn by the official moralists. Writers were told where to look for him, what his loyalties would be, and the destiny he would have. Writers were then expected to document this blueprint, to discover bright, persuasive instances of the prescribed type.

My interest in the subject of this book was not at first directed toward the problem of continuity, although I was aware of it from the outset. I had thought, rather, to concentrate on the Soviet version of the positive hero, hoping, first, to gain insight into the moral condition of the Soviet Communist and, second, to define one of the literary archetypes of our time. It soon became apparent that these lines of investigation were barren. The Soviet positive hero is too much the instrument of Party policy and too little a product of the literary imagination to bear comparison with the hero-types of other literatures. These problems were not dropped entirely, but were made a part of the main effort.

It became clear to me that the central ideas on the hero in literature had been transmitted very nearly intact, in the form of a continuous controversy, from the middle decades of the nineteenth century to the Soviet present. Finally, it became clear that the concept of the positive hero had been developed as a weapon of argument in the pivotal debate in the 1860s about the nature and function of literature. The debaters were, on the one hand, political radicals who advanced a systematic aesthetic in which the positive hero was central; and on the other, the classical writers who rejected any suggestion that they devote themselves merely to the celebration of political virtue in literature, and who defended their art as an autonomous kind of exploration, concerned with politics but finally independent of any political claims made upon it. The essential conflict in the debate—between a free and a controlled art, conducted sometimes in the open, sometimes not—endured for nearly a century. On later occasions the participants were not always aware of the sources of their ideas. A Soviet novel which slipped by the censors might suddenly revive the argument by evoking central ideas from the classical heritage. But sometimes in the ensuing argument neither the writer nor the critics would recognize that they were repeating the basic terms of the argument between Turgenev and Chernyshevsky. When Stalin coined his repellent description of the writer as "an engineer of the human soul," he may not have known of its origins in the manipulative aesthetic theory of the radical democratic critics in the mid-nineteenth century.

The positive hero, then, is important as a characteristic element in the thinking of one group of contestants in the long war for control of Russian realism. The debate was ended in complete victory for the political utilitarians and the partisans of positive heroes, with A. A. Zhdanov's assertion in 1946 of total Party dominion over the literary imagination. This melancholy conclusion may prompt the student of literature to wonder what profit he may expect to draw from this account of the decline of a great national tradition. Too often it may seem that we are concerned with attitudes bleakly hostile to the literary imagination, or with the thankless critical task of explaining why bad novels are, indeed, bad. It should be pointed out, however, that the whole strand of continuity we are following is a controversy about the nature of literature itself, and it is to be hoped that we will touch repeatedly on questions of general interest.

If the art form under discussion were the icon we should not be so apologetic. But the novelist's obligation to reveal the whole of man in all his meaningful relations runs full tilt against any pressure to advocate or to celebrate virtue in fiction. For this reason we shall frequently be involved with assumptions about the very nature of human experience. Can it be believed that man can live wholly, successfully, in an exemplary way, within such a rigid code of political virtue? Or would it not be better to accept a commitment from the outset, in company with the great Russian writers, to the proposition that one of the distinguishing marks of man's humanity is his fallibility, that weakness, compromise, and defeat are elements of all men's lives, and that a novelist's failure to say so represents a degrading kind of falsification?

II

These political attitudes, literary ideas, and moral values are, of course, not peculiar to Russia, although the intensity with which they were expressed, the particular emphases put on them, and the final configuration they were to assume have not been duplicated elsewhere. Western European, North American, and other cultures have known moments of economic crisis and political urgency as great as Russia's, and have at times been called upon to deal with fanatical codes of political virtue and obnoxious doctrines for the "proper" uses of literature. Since the Renaissance the West has generally rejected them or outgrown them, or contained them within a pluralist framework. Russia's inability to rid herself of them has its sources deep in her history, and may be seen more recently as the outcome of a bitter, complex struggle in Russian thought between Western and Eastern, between libertarian and authoritarian approaches to man and society.

The two antagonistic traditions measure the value and efficacy of ideas in sharply contrasting ways. It may be said, in general, that the Western tradition is more used to consider ideas for their larger applications, as they relate man's momentary needs to his permanent condition. The Eastern European tradition tends to value ideas for their local utility (against a background of dogmatic absolutism) as defined by the governors (or the subverters) of the society, usually in a situation of extreme social tension. When the critic Belinsky steeped himself in the Hegelian system, its most important consequence for him was the effect it had on his attitude toward the Tsarist regime. Intoxicated by the formula "what is, is what ought to be," Belinsky lived at perfect peace with the autocracy. But when the left-Hegelians showed him the contrary tendency in Hegel's thought, that "what is" is constantly evolving into "what ought to be," that history never stands still, he became a revolutionary overnight. Belinsky's conversion illustrates an attitude toward ideas which is both passionate and myopic, which responds to them on the basis of their immediate relevances alone, and inevitably reduces them to tools. Belinsky's reading of Hegel is certainly duplicated in Lenin's reading of Marx.

This habit of reduction is partly to be explained by Russia's special situation on the fringe of Europe, and by the enormous appetites stimulated in the one who lags behind. The contradictory needs to exclude Europe and to become like her have again and again generated a spirit of urgency that is hostile to the free exercise of thought and imagination. Earlier iron curtains, we remember, excluded every great movement of European thought before 1700 in the name of national integrity and a sterile Byzantine orthodoxy. It might be said that Russia has never recovered from her success in excluding the "harmful" effects of the Renaissance in the name of the "Third Rome." But Western ideas could not be permanently kept out. The governors of the regime needed technology, military skills, administrative techniques; the opponents of the regime needed arguments to support their cry for social justice. Once begun, the flood could not be turned back. But the opposition between the Western and Eastern approaches reproduced itself in the interpretation of these imported ideas. Much of the intellectual history of the nineteenth century may be read in the light of the struggle between those who were concerned with the larger implications of the ideas and those who would convert them immediately into social levers. Here investigation, speculation, and experiment stand in opposition to rationalization, persuasion, and exhortation. Wonder confronts certainty. Theory and ideology challenge each other as mutually exclusive modes of thought.

The situation of literature in this contest is clear, I think. The major writers found and staked out an area of leisure and equilibrium in which they could examine the deeper meanings of their countrymen's suffering. It was a troubled, precarious kind of leisure, to be sure, encroached upon by the government censor from one side and by the revolutionary critic from the other, and kept clear, as it sometimes seemed, only as a kind of no-man's-land in the savage war between the two forces. Tolstoy deserted this position and organized his own campaign to harness the free imagination. More than once the area appeared to have been engulfed, only to manifest itself again in the form of new and compelling works of art. At the risk of simplifying a very complex process, it might be said that the struggle ended, on the level of critical theory, when Soviet Marxists established the devastating proposition—as Marx never did—that literature is a form of class consciousness, and ended, in fact, when Zhdanov converted the proposition into an enforceable statute in 1946. His victory over the creative imagination may be read as the formal, certainly the official, defeat in Russia of the Western way of taking experience.

Utility as a criterion of artistic value is not unknown, of course, in other societies, including our own. Extraneous claims on literature have taken many forms: writers have been asked to refrain from undermining many kinds of decorum, many views of morality, many attitudes of belief. When Flaubert is dragged into court by the French police, when books are banned in Jersey City or Boston, when Pushkin's work is put under the surveillance of the Tsar, when Dickens reports the enormous pressure on him of Victorian expectations, we are in the presence of the police sergeant's fear of literature as a profound disturber of the peace. This kind of negative claim is more common than the step beyond it which solicits the writer's active support of a given code of values. Albert Camus has noted both attitudes in a brief review of the question in *The Rebel*,[1] but he does not distinguish sufficiently, I believe, between the ignorant hostility toward art which would tame it or silence it, and the more sophisticated contempt for art which would keep it alive in order to use it. He cites extreme examples of the censorious attitude among the Russians: Tolstoy in the mood of *What Is Art?* and Pisarev, the nihilist, who advocated the abolition of literature. In the West he names the Saint-Simonians and Victor Hugo as advocates of an art that would serve progress by stimulating healthy social forces. Actually there are many

[1] Albert Camus, *The Rebel* (New York, 1954), pp. 222–24.

more of both kinds in both East and West, but no one, I think, has duplicated the effort made by the Russian radicals to gain control of the literary imagination. Successive generations sought to establish a definition of literature's function and value that would proclaim as good writing only those works that advocated *their* program of social change, and would proscribe all else. In the West, partisan claims on literature from all species of bigot to produce "edifying" works have somehow been resisted; literature survives, at least, if it does not always flourish. But in Russia the claims were so urgent, backed, as it often seemed to the guilt-ridden intellectuals and writers, by the massive grievances of the Russian populace; and the habits of thought resisting them were so precariously grounded, that the eventual victory of the utilitarians seems foreordained. Art was frivolous, many Russians, including Tolstoy, were prepared to agree, unless it humbled itself before the needs and expectations of the disinherited majority and actively set forth models of behavior that promised a better life in the future for the entire nation.

We return finally to the question of the hero and of his place in literature. In the West, the French have been most preoccupied with this problem. Discussing our chances for survival, André Malraux said in an interview: "It is not certain that our civilization can rediscover the heroes and found on them its exemplary image of man."[2] Apart from the roles heroes do or do not play in the fate of cultures, it seems pertinent to inquire whether or not it is proper for the "exemplary image" to appear in literary works. Camus may be completing Malraux's thought when he says that the aim of the world's great literature

seems to be to create a closed universe or a perfect type. The West, in its great creative works, does not limit itself to retracing the steps of its daily life. It ceaselessly presents magnificently conceived images which inflame its imagination and sets off, hot foot, in pursuit of them.[3]

It is important to ask what is meant here. Has this really been the function of Western literature in the past? In what sense are Lear, Ahab, Julien Sorel, Emma Bovary, or Kyo Gisors "exemplary," that is to say, serving as a pattern or deserving imitation? What do we do when we overtake them in our "hot foot" pursuit? How do we identify with them? Do we admire them, pity them, learn from them, emulate them? Obviously there is no simple answer. The reader's identification

2 "Man's Quest," *Time*, 66.3 (July 18, 1955): 29.
3 Camus, *The Rebel*, p. 228.

with the hero may take many forms, but it must not, it seems to me, be complete or blindly subordinate. Reader and hero must meet in some sense as equals, and yet an essential distance between them must be maintained. It is this remove, preserved by Aristotle's catharsis, that permits tragedy, and frees the reader of the terrible burden of the hero's suffering. And it is precisely this remove that is absent from "official" Soviet writing. Even when the hero dies, no provision is made for the spectator's disengagement. The heroes of the world's great literature are not edifying in the copybook sense; homilies cannot be drawn from the examples of their lives. The Soviet hero, on the contrary, is primarily a model whose example is expected to give rise to admiration and emulation. He stands in an authoritarian relationship to the reader. He is the representative of official virtue, and the certified model for behavior.

Homo sovieticus and his ancestor, the Russian revolutionary, considered as human types for a moment, not as literary constructs, must be recognized as members of the family of man—of a special and exotic branch, perhaps—and not as agents of the devil. He has an historical pedigree, and he is not the first of his kind to plague mankind. Roundheads, Jacobins, and Abolitionists, to name only his most familiar relatives, knew as surely as the Bolsheviks did that their version of the truth was the only one that could save mankind. The Russian differs from his predecessors, however, in one important particular: power to impose his truth on a nation fell into his hands and he managed to hold onto it. The earlier political brotherhoods, for all the mark they left on history, were kept from the prolonged exercise of power. The societies that nurtured them found slower, less direct, and less painful ways to move toward the goals which the absolutists hoped to reach without delay, compromise, or pausing to count the costs. In many ways the Russian revolutionary is a tougher, deadlier specimen. Bred over a century in a world of absolute denial and absolute assertion, he was psychically armed for no-quarter struggle, prepared for expediency, deception, and violence, and well equipped with ideologies and strategies.

He might seem at first glance to make a poor candidate for literary portraiture. But Turgenev, Dostoevsky, Conrad, and others have found, on the contrary, that he was indeed an excellent subject, provided he was kept at a distance, and shown in all his dimensions. He had energy, passion, courage, and principle, he lived dangerously, and his life was full of pain, deprivation, and defeat. He was often dis-figured in his collisions with life, and was, as a result, badly flawed in a human or moral sense. As such he became a fitting subject for tragic investigation, as Dostoevsky, above all others, found out. But when the artist's detachment is lost, when, in effect, the hero writes immodestly about himself, pity is impossible; his tragic appeal is blotted out by his oppressive sense of his mission. This, in general, is the situation in Soviet literature.

Malraux's heroes in *Man's Fate* use the Shanghai workers' insurrection as an occasion to confront, in a total way, their condition as men. Though they remain true to their vision of the cause throughout, and though they hope that the example of their deaths will be efficacious, will, as Malraux says, create "the bloody legends from which the golden legends are made,"[4] in their moment of heroic agony they rise above the political scene and come face to face with the mystery of their presence on earth. They endeavor, in their extremity, to tran-scend the knowledge that men live in untouchable solitude, that life, itself, is empty and absurd, without love or meaning. Such questions are not allowed to trouble the Soviet hero. It is incidental to Malraux's novel that his revolutionaries rise to heroism in the act of defying Party orders, but in a Soviet novel such a contingency is unthinkable. Doctrinal truths contain the universe. All things are declared to be known, including history's final outcome, and the mysteries of ex-istence are kept by the society's Grand Inquisitors from troubling their subjects.

[4] André Malraux, *Man's Fate* (New York, 1936), p. 323.

PART ONE

The Divided Tradition

CHAPTER 2

The Hero and the Heritage

౾౾౾

Russian imaginative literature—perhaps more than any of the world's great literatures—has been concerned with the celebration of emblematic literary heroes. The source of this tradition is lost in remote antiquity. Early Russian literature, both oral and written, has held up numerous images of virtuous men, for the comfort, instruction, or inspiration of its audience: the *bogatyr* (hero of the oral epic), the martyred saint, the Cossack bandit-revolutionary, the peasant-fool, the neoclassic *raisonneur*, and the benevolent (or terrible) tsar-despot have served at various times as symbols which were intended to give meaning and purpose to experience. The propagation of the image of virtue, too, whatever its human guise, has served many interests, religious, social, moral, and political—and in all these areas, tendencies both conformist and subversive.

Of course, similar types have served similar purposes in other literatures. What really distinguishes the Russian tradition before the nineteenth century is the absence of other approaches, notably of the indirect, exploratory mode of tragedy. In general, Russian literary heroes were conceived as attractive and uncomplicated representatives of specific points of view, that is, as teachers by their beneficent—rather than by their terrible or pitiable—example.[1]

---

[1] *The Lay of the Host of Igor*, the first great work of Russian literature, written, it is now believed, at the end of the twelfth century, contains elements of a primitive tragic drama. The hero, Prince Igor, in search of personal glory, endangers the security of

In the shift to a more recognizable human type during the nineteenth century, the requirements of realism reduced the hero's dimensions, and the writers' predominantly tragic view of experience muted the note of affirmation which had prevailed in the earlier, less sophisticated literary forms. The search for hero images continued, nevertheless. The question of the nature and the destiny of the literary protagonist was foremost among the thematic preoccupations of the century. And the degree to which nineteenth-century Russians read their own spiritual history in the lives of their literary heroes is a unique feature of the whole national literary experience.

The solemn Russian novel of character, with its rudimentary plot structure, was peculiarly well designed to focus attention on the moral responsibilities of individuals. Russian literature was hero-centered, if not heroic in the conventional sense, from the earliest moments of the realist epoch. Pushkin's Onegin, the hero of his novel in verse, *Eugene Onegin*, and Lermontov's Pechorin, the central figure of his novel, *A Hero of Our Time*, established a pedigree for the literary protagonist in the early decades of the nineteenth century which persisted to the point of becoming a stereotype. Dostoevsky's Myshkin, Raskolnikov, the Karamazovs, Tolstoy's Pierre, Prince Andrei, Levin, Turgenev's gallery of faltering heroes—to name only the most prominent—all demonstrate an intensive effort to center the novelists' moral quest in the figure of the protagonist. In his fate are contained the novelist's generalizations—hopeful or despairing—about human experience.

Of the critical controversies that nourished the literature of the century none was more intense than discussion about the *kind* of significance that should be invested in the figure of the literary hero. The politically minded critics, Belinsky, Dobrolyubov, and Chernyshevsky, who made specific, insistent, and programmatic demands on literature, devoted a large part of their energies to the matter of effecting a fundamental change in the image of the hero. In calling for a literature which would serve social change they had first to isolate and define the characteristics of the hero they wanted to replace. In generalizations

---

Kievan society by leading an irresponsible attack on neighboring pagan nomads. He is thoroughly beaten by them, but then is miraculously rescued from the consequences of his vain and unpatriotic acts, and is brought home in triumph. Solzhenitsyn's convicts "try" Igor under the Soviet penal code and find him guilty of treason. See below, p. 286.

they made about "Oblomovism"[2] and "the superfluous man" they attacked the single characteristic of the dominant hero-type which they most hoped to change—his overwhelming predilection for defeat. The reasons for the emphasis on failure might be sought, they felt, in various hypotheses: that life offered no other significant types; that tragedy was somehow rooted in the nature of the novel form; that the celebration of fallibility, the "worship of sorrow," were basic to the tradition of European literature and to the world-view of the writers themselves. None of these justifications seemed to the radical critics to be valid deterrents to the creation of a more effective and more successful literary hero.

Seen as a type which dominated Russian literature for a century, the kind of hero they opposed is a complex figure, apart from his habit of failure. The men without hope—Pechorin, Stravrogin (Dostoevsky's *The Possessed*), and Prince Andrei (Tolstoy's *War and Peace*) —are successful in their rebellious search for annihilation. The men of hope and good intentions fail, in spite of themselves, to live as they plan to, or to fulfill the apparent promise of their lives. Such are Turgenev's ego-centered heroes *manqués*, each with his special personality failure—Rudin's fatal eloquence, Lavretsky's weakness disguised as scruple, Bazarov's narcissistic arrogance.[3] Both these types are characterized by a disastrous alienation from other human beings and from purposeful activity. For the radical critics it was the inactivity resulting from this maladjustment which linked all these figures, disparate though they were in character and in motivation.

These types were given a label, "the superfluous men," taken from Turgenev's short story "The Diary of a Superfluous Man" (1850). Though it became one of the most durable clichés of Russian literary criticism, there is a curious ambiguity about the term's actual meaning. It is not clear in many cases to whom the superfluous man is unnecessary or by whom he is unwanted, or, indeed, that it is he who has been rejected. Lermontov's Pechorin, for example, cannot be consid-

---

[2] See N. A. Dobrolyubov, "What Is Oblomovshchina?" in *Selected Philosophical Essays* (Moscow, 1948), pp. 174–217. This article, which first appeared in *Otechestvennyie zapiski*, Nos. 1–4, 1859, is the most striking effort to find a lowest common denominator in the behavior and the destinies of Russian literary heroes. Although this is not the first discussion of the subject, it may be said to have initiated the major phase of the hero controversy.

[3] Rudin is the hero of *Rudin* (1856), Lavretsky of *A Nest of Gentlefolk* (1859), and Bazarov of *Fathers and Sons* (1862).

ered a pathetic castoff from society; he himself took the initiative, with some foreknowledge of its tragic consequences, in revolting against a way of life he considered contemptible. The modern concept of "the alienated man" accounts more comprehensively and more precisely for the process of interaction between individual and society which resulted in the individual's final condition of aloneness, defeat, or death. In flat contrast, then, we may speak of the revolutionary hero sought by the radicals as the "integrated man"—integrated, that is, with the "scientific" promises and the ethical sanctions of his ideology of dissent, or, after 1917, with the values and goals of the new society. The superfluous man, it must be kept in mind, does not represent retrogressive values; rather, he opposes them inadequately; he is their victim, not their advocate.

Scattered references throughout the century suggest that the need to develop affirmative ideological heroes was deeply felt by others, but that the obstacles to its imaginative realization were enormous. The Decembrists, the most authentic and dramatic symbols of political protest, apparently defied artistic re-creation. Pushkin, in a variant conclusion to *Eugene Onegin*, considered having his hero join the Decembrist conspiracy at the end of the novel. With the Eugene Onegin we know, the artistic cost of such a conversion seems exorbitant; Pushkin, we must assume, had the good taste, as well as the political prudence, not to attempt it. The long detour Tolstoy made around the same problem—that of incorporating the Decembrist movement in fiction—when he was beginning *War and Peace*, suggests the strength and the multiplicity of the pressures opposing the representation of this kind of political virtue in art.[4] There is no doubt that a good part of the difficulty lay in the creative problems attendant on the reproduction of a plausible, active, and successful image of ideological virtue.

It might seem that Tolstoy's "blundering" heroes, Pierre Bezukhov in *War and Peace* and Levin in *Anna Karenina*, qualify as affirmative figures. But the modest lesson they affirm—that life, defined in terms of love, family, and work, is somehow preferable to death—lacks the combative spirit and the specifically social orientation sought by the radical critics. Apart from these dogmatic objections there are literary

---

[4] See Kathryn Feuer, "The Genesis of *War and Peace*" (unpublished diss., Columbia University, 1965), for a quite different version of the origins of this novel, stressing, for example, the impact of Tocqueville's *L'Ancien Régime* on Tolstoy's early versions.

grounds, as well, on which to question the success with which this Tolstoyan truth is presented. E. M. Forster, for example, offers a persuasive interpretation of the concluding mood of *War and Peace* which casts doubt on the modest note of affirmation that seems to have been intended:

Tolstoy, like Bennett, has the courage to show us people getting old—the partial decay of Nicolay and Natasha is really more sinister than the complete decay of Constance and Sophia [in Arnold Bennett's *The Old Wives' Tale*]: more of our own youth seems to have perished in it.[5]

The same sense of the destructive effect of time's passage surrounds Levin's final discovery of "the meaning of life," which has the quality of a desperate assertion shot through with uncertainty, not of a statement of unqualified belief. Hindsight, of course, confirms these impressions: to the extent that Bezukhov and Levin are autobiographical figures, they must be presumed to contain the seeds of Tolstoy's impending spiritual crisis, in the course of which despair at the approach of death came close to gaining supremacy in his system of values.

Gogol had made an earlier effort to personify a specific concept of virtue in Volume II of *Dead Souls*. In the confusion of the last few pages of the novel, two shadowy figures suddenly appear, the wise and forgiving man of wealth, Murazov, and the unnamed Prince, a high bureaucrat of great pride and rectitude. It is their joint function to restore order and morality after the unrelieved wickedness that has gone before. The magnitude of their task—which includes the reform of Chichikov—is too much for them, and, inferentially, for Gogol's unique imaginative powers. He was clearly unable to solve the moral problem by persuasive literary means, arbitrarily, that is, to alter the vividly established moral nature of his central character, or abruptly to assume a tone of high moral earnestness, in contrast to the sly and ribald cynicism which dominated the earlier sections of the novel. Actually Gogol has turned to an earlier tradition for his affirmative spokesmen. The images of his dual heroes, and their *ex machina* appearance on the scene, are reminiscent of the *raisonneurs* of neoclassic drama, the omniscient representatives of virtue who correct the malefactors and draw the moral for the spectators. This abstract personification of good, it should be pointed out, was no more satisfactory to the radical critics of the nineteenth century than it is to the modern

[5] E. M. Forster, *Aspects of the Novel* (New York, 1927), p. 63.

reader or, if we may judge by his attempt to destroy the manuscript, than it was to Gogol himself.[6]

In Dostoevsky's work the problem of the hero, as it reflects the controversies of the sixties, assumes an importance which invites a more extensive investigation than is possible here. Dostoevsky reacted strongly, at first, against the radical prescription for the hero, then attempted to adapt the purely literary formula to his own diametrically opposite views about politics and society. The "antihero" of *Notes from Underground* (1864) is intended as a polemical counterstatement to the roseate vision of heroism in Nikolai Chernyshevsky's *What Is to Be Done?*[7] The attack on his radical position is thorough and deadly. Dostoevsky's view of human nature as weak, unstable, governed by caprice, given to irrational acts of rebellion, is used to challenge the radicals' untroubled identification of reason with progress, and of happiness with the satisfaction of material needs.

Having ridiculed the concept of the rationally virtuous revolutionary hero, and every premise on which he stood, Dostoevsky set about in *Crime and Punishment*, two years later, to convert him. Raskolnikov is the first Dostoevskyan version of the revolutionary "new man," the proud, active, Western-oriented rationalist who imagines that he is independent of all codes of morality. Raskolnikov acts decisively— by committing two murders—and his act is shown to have symbolic meaning in many spheres of human activity and belief. It is then Dostoevsky's intention to strip away successive layers of rationalization and show that in all spheres this kind of "reasoned" act is evil and insane. Raskolnikov's controversial conversion in Siberia to Sonya's ethic of submissive and limitless love for mankind, although it strains credibility to the limit, is meant to conclude his journey from evil to good, from a rebellious individualism in which "all is permitted," to a pious acquiescence in the way things are, however painful and unjust.

Dostoevsky's difficulties with the stubborn Raskolnikov suggest that the active, emblematic man was generally hard to handle in literary

[6] Gogol's concern with the virtuous moral agent receives a quite different statement in one of his comments on his comedy *The Inspector-General*: "I regret that no one noticed the honorable person who was in my play. Yes, there was one honorable, noble person acting in it through its entire length. This honorable, noble person was laughter." N. V. Gogol, *Polnoe sobranie sochinenii* (Moscow, 1949), 4: 169.

[7] Dostoevsky was quite explicit about his intention. See Ernest J. Simmons, *Dostoevski: The Making of a Novelist* (New York, 1940), p. 137, for a discussion of his state of mind at the time he planned the work. Both novels are primary documents in the great cultural crisis that split the liberals and the radicals during the years immediately preceding and following the emancipation of the serfs in 1861.

terms—as difficult to reclaim from his evil ways as he was to present sympathetically. Dostoevsky's solution invites comparison with Turgenev's treatment of Bazarov in *Fathers and Sons*. These two outsiders' views of the radical personality have much in common: both writers, the liberal Turgenev and the conservative Dostoevsky, admire his strength and fear his violence and irresponsibility. But while Turgenev pities his hero and allows him to die defeated but unreconstructed, Dostoevsky apparently felt that his must be brought to a complete reversal of attitude, however implausible it might seem in terms of character and motivation. While he was writing the novel, he considered suicide as an alternative end for Raskolnikov. It would have been neater, perhaps, and easier to bring off, but apparently it did not fulfill Dostoevsky's moral intention. In any case, it is not to be wondered at that the radicals, who, like most of their contemporaries, read the imaginative literature of their own time as a more or less literal transcript of experience, were pleased with neither portrait of their champion.

The only area open to reform is the individual human soul which, though fallible and perverse, is not immune to the example of selfless, all-forgiving love, as enacted by Dostoevsky's men of virtue. To act in any other sphere is to engage in self-centered and presumptuous lawlessness. Thus the radical challenge to society is contained, whether it proceeds from egocentric defiance or from an unselfish desire for social change. This, at least, is the *political* relevance Dostoevsky's novels bore to the contemporary scene.

In *The Idiot* (1868–69) and *The Brothers Karamazov* (1880) Dostoevsky tried to create a "conservative" positive hero. In the Christlike figure of Prince Myshkin a major note of affirmation was intended, although his personal defeat at the end of the novel is complete. Here the doctrine by which Myshkin tries to live is inadequately tested, since Myshkin certainly is a special case, unworldly and unwell, and not equipped to cope with the crushing knowledge of evil.

Myshkin's final madness is instructive, nevertheless, as a view of the destiny that awaits the saintly individual who is at the same time an incomplete, emasculated man. As though profiting by his experiment in *The Idiot*, Dostoevsky evolved a more robust standard-bearer a decade later in the figure of Alyosha Karamazov. He came closer, too, to solving the difficult problem of creating an active spokesman for an attitude which was passive toward many of the acknowledged causes of human maladjustment and suffering. Since the flaws in the social and political environment were excluded from the sphere of remedial action because man's reason is powerless to change them and he risks his moral integrity in daring to try, Alyosha relies on his belief in the responsiveness of the human heart to sustain him in his positive acts. Thus armed, he intervenes at many points in the passionate human entanglements around him, always in behalf of kindness, forgiveness, and a sense of personal justice between individuals. In his most impressive success he is instrumental in teaching Dmitri to respond to the regenerative forces in his own character. But final and complete vindication of his approach in the central conflict of values between Ivan, the unreclaimed rationalist, and himself, the Christian humanist, is denied him. His victory is permanently deferred because the destiny of his opponent, on which his own destiny finally depends, remains forever unresolved in the mists of Ivan's brain fever.

With Alyosha, Dostoevsky came as close to a successful image of the affirmative hero as any of the major writers of the century. Yet it is certain that the radical democrats, had they been active at the time, would have had less patience with Alyosha Karamazov than with his brother Ivan, who might have been catalogued as another in the long list of well-intentioned failures. Failure to validate an ideology of dissent would, we may be sure, have been preferred by Dobrolyubov or Chernyshevsky to the celebration of any attitude which seemed to counsel acquiescence in the social, political, and economic status quo.[8]

II

How can we begin to distinguish those aspects of this complicated hero-quest which are relevant to the Soviet period?

An overall dependence on the views of the radical democrats may

[8] M. A. Antonovich, who continued to apply the principles of the revolutionary democrats to literary matters in the seventies and eighties, tends to confirm this hypothesis in his angrily unfavorable review of *The Brothers Karamazov*, "Mistiko-asketicheskii roman" (*Izbrannye stati*, Leningrad, 1938, pp. 243–97), first published in 1881. Antonovich says of Alyosha: "The personality of Alyosha ... is extremely pale, unnatural, undefined, and incomprehensible, it is simply an invention of the author, a fantasy" (p. 252). Ivan, too, is "undefined, untypical, and unclear," but "his poem, 'The Grand Inquisitor,' presents the only poetic pages in the entire novel" and the "form" in which Ivan's doubts are expressed is "truly artistic" (pp. 266–67). Translating from the critical idiom of this school which identifies the "poetic" and the "artistic" with the true, and the true with the socially desirable, it is not difficult to read these opinions as judgments about the political significance of the two characters.

be asserted from the outset. This borrowing includes definitions of the nature and function of literature, of the proper relationship between literature and society, of the nature of value in literary judgment, and of the moral and social obligations of the writer. In this conglomerate, the positive hero is a focal point, where theory is translated into literary practice. Although they were held in respect, the radical democrats' influence is diffuse in the years just after the revolution and is seldom acknowledged. But the importance of the radical democrats was to receive more and more explicit statement in critical pronouncements after the First All-Union Congress of Soviet Writers in 1934, and to receive ultimate official sanction in the declaration of literary policy made by A. A. Zhdanov in his 1946 "Report on the Journals *Zvezda* and *Leningrad*." In it he establishes them as primary legislators of Soviet literary theory:

It follows that the finest aspect of Soviet literature is its carrying on of the best traditions of nineteenth-century Russian literature, traditions established by our great revolutionary democrats, Belinsky, Dobrolyubov, Chernyshevsky, and Saltykov-Shchedrin, continued by Plekhanov, and scientifically elaborated by Lenin and Stalin.[9]

Zhdanov's remarks might be read simply as a glib summoning of native Russia in the search for non-Western sources for Soviet attitudes, or a casual theft of ideas in the face of a widespread shortage. But they represent more than that. His report marks the culmination of a long process of intellectual development, the movement toward final ascendancy in the Soviet consciousness of the nineteenth-century utilitarian aesthetic. The tradition's continuity was eclipsed twice by other leftist theories of literature. The Narodniks' Mikhailovsky and the early Marxist Plekhanov developed distinctive approaches to prob-

---

[9] A. A. Zhdanov, "Doklad o zhurnalakh *Zvezda* i *Leningrad*," *Literaturnaya gazeta*, 39 (September 21, 1946): 3. In this legislative statement the names of Belinsky, Chernyshevsky, and Dobrolyubov are mentioned nineteen times, Lenin's seven times, Stalin's six times, and Marx's not at all. The only reference to Marxism further confirms the importance of the Russian radicals' ideas: "Marxist literary criticism, which carries on the great traditions of Belinsky, Chernyshevsky, and Dobrolyubov, has always supported realistic art with a social stand" (p. 3). Marxism still supplies the formal *arrière-plan* for most thinking about cultural matters. But the radical democrats in 1946 became primary authorities on all specifically literary matters. One of the most authoritative books on Soviet Marxist views—F. V. Konstantinov, ed., *Istoricheskii materializm* (Moscow, 1950)—admitted the Russian radicals into the tiny group of thinkers who are credited with designing the official cosmology. L. I. Timofeev's *Teoriya literatury* (Moscow, 1938) set forth the Soviet position in terms of traditional aesthetic theory. Though Timofeev has not always acknowledged his debt, this book makes it clear that by this time the radical democrats' ideas pervaded all aspects of Soviet thinking about literature.

lems of literary analysis and judgment. But a direct line of inheritance can be established nevertheless.

The relation of socialist realism's theorists to the Russian past is simplified by their abrupt rejection of all but a handful of men, and all but one body of ideas. Given this simplified view of cultural history, it is not surprising to find them siding with their champions in the decisive break between liberals and radicals in 1861. The split occurred along a basic fault in the uneasy alliance between the two groups which had had its origin in Belinsky's overbearing defense of Gogol during the forties, and ended in the wholesale rupture that accompanied the publication of *Fathers and Sons* in 1862. The occasion of the break was a disagreement about the means, the tempo, and the goals of social change, notably in the matter of freeing the serfs. But the break was so profound, so complete, and so clean that it divided them on a score of related issues—including most phases of art's relationship to life. In the forefront of the battle between the two factions stood the two competing hero images, the "new" and the "superfluous" men, who crystallized in the contrast between them most of the underlying doctrinal issues.

Soviet criticism has taken sides in this century-old conflict because of the radicals' uncompromising stand on social and economic matters, not because of the intrinsic validity of their views on art. In the Soviet view, the value of the second flows from the correctness of the first. For this reason, any follower of the radical approach is bound to find himself committed to the defense of a number of exposed positions which raise very awkward questions of literary judgment. As a result of their politically motivated assault the radicals managed to alienate every major writer of the century, with the exception of Nekrasov and Saltykov, from their own extreme position.[10] Soviet literary magistrates inherited—and had to make the most of—this costly distinction, which tended after 1932 to downgrade Turgenev, Tolstoy, Dostoevsky, and others as a source of primary guidance for modern writers. Scholars and critics rationalized this awkward choice by arranging the competing idea-systems in an evolutionary sequence, maintaining that the radical theory is a "higher," that is, a more advanced, a more profound, and a more useful, approach to the under-

---

[10] Nekrasov and Saltykov, it is worth noting, are the only two nineteenth-century writers who are favorably mentioned by Zhdanov in his report.

standing of the literary process, because it represents a later and "higher" stage of economic development. Terminology was then devised to account for this sweeping judgment: the intellectual assumptions and the literary practice—"world-view" and "method" in the Soviet vocabulary—of all the great classical writers have been classified under the heading "critical realism," and the theory that replaced it, first sketched out by the radical democrats, has, since 1932, been given the permanent designation "socialist realism," which Timofeev says flatly "is the highest stage in the development of art," "the fulfillment" of the history "of all art and literature."[11] Critical realism, although it was based on an imperfect understanding of society, served a beneficial function by exposing human suffering in Russia, and by challenging, however indirectly, the Tsarist status quo. But it was inferior (arrested, that is, on a lower level of the evolutionary scale) because it refused or was unable to point the way toward a better future in which the human agony the classical writers described so well would be done away with. The new literature, because of its doctrine of active intervention in the processes of social change, and because it reflected a new and higher form of social organization, deserved, according to the Soviet formula, *a priori* recognition as a qualitatively superior order of creation. The distinction between the two literatures was not made to exclude or suppress the older literature. Heeding Lenin's injunction to repossess the classical heritage for all, the Soviet leadership has made the work of the classical writers (with exceptions) available to readers on an enormous scale. But when Soviet writers and critics seek guidance from the past, they may well return to the precepts of the radical democrats, as Zhdanov did in 1946.

The problem of the hero has been central to the Soviet system of classification. Thus critical realism is distinguished by its unsuccessful

---

[11] Timofeev, *Teoriya literatury*, p. 7. Critical realism, which came into being under conditions of unresolved contradiction between objective, social reality and man's aspirations toward a better life, "set itself the task of revealing life's imperfections, the depiction of the crisis man and society were living through," hence its negative designation (*ibid.*, p. 306). Though the "most important step forward" is the transition from critical to socialist realism, one or more intermediate phases are distinguished in what Timofeev calls the literary "movement of liberation" (*ibid.*). The article "Realism" in the *Literary Encyclopedia* identifies them as "radical democratic realism" and "proletarian realism," citing Gorky's *Mother* as the outstanding example of the latter school. *Literaturnaya entsiklopediya*, 9: 573. Timofeev subsequently names "radical democratic realism" as a progressive mutation within the movement of critical realism but absorbs proletarian realism, and, with it, Gorky's *Mother*, into socialist realism.

effort to create a credible human spokesman for its positive moral content: "The search for him ... was expressed in the creation of heroes whose positive traits were limited, incomplete, or Utopian."[12]

Revolutionary democratic realism, by identifying itself with the "people's interests," "expressed itself in a much sharper criticism of the bases of bourgeois landowner society, and in the formation of the images of revolutionaries fighting against this order."[13] The "correct" representation of heroism, we were informed, was the first task of socialist realism and the surest measure of its superiority over all the literature that has preceded it.

Following Soviet historians back to the starting point of this absurdly simple, unilinear "dialectic process," through the hectic decade 1855–65, the trail ends finally with Belinsky. In the course of his "furious" career he laid down a number of operating principles that Soviet critics have made part of their own theories. The central notions that good literature exerts a kind of beneficent leverage in the process of social change and is good for that reason were his. The later assertion—that the emblematically virtuous hero was the most effective of literary levers—issued from Belinsky's premises.

[12] Timofeev, *Teoriya literatury*, p. 307.   [13] *Ibid.*, p. 308.

CHAPTER 3

Belinsky: "My Heroes Are the Destroyers"

~~~~

I cannot live without beliefs, warm and fanatical. BELINSKY

The history of Vissarion Belinsky's (1811–48) reputation in Russia is an immense subject, touching on nearly all major currents of thought and of imagination. He offered guidance and inspiration to successive generations of radical thinkers and activists, and his unquestioned purity of purpose won the respect of many who were indifferent or hostile to his ideas. Certainly in the decades after 1932 in Soviet literary councils his has been a most authoritative voice from the Russian past. The Soviet version of Belinsky's legacy is by no means true to the original on all counts. Soviet critics have drawn almost exclusively on his later (the post-Hegelian) period, and in deriving a coherent aesthetic from the whole body of his work have ignored all that does not serve their own needs.

It can be fairly said, I think, that to discover consistency in Belinsky is to distort him. Herbert Bowman has said of Belinsky's role in Russian literature: "He came not so much as its systematic analyst, but rather as its evangelist. His contribution to Russian criticism was less a gift of mind than a gift of soul."[1] It was a saving grace—and a characteristic of Belinsky's "method"—that by blurring distinctions, by entertaining ambiguities on crucial points, or simply by contradicting himself, he was able to escape the toils of his theory before it really became a system. But in the hands of less passionate, more orderly

[1] Herbert E. Bowman, *Vissarion Belinski, 1811–1848: A Study in the Origins of Social Criticism in Russia* (Cambridge, Mass., 1954), p. 14. This careful, literate study of Belinsky's thought proved indispensable as background to a study of the uses his successors have made of him.

men—"men of far duller and cruder minds," as Isaiah Berlin has characterized the generation of radical intellectuals following Belinsky[2]—who do not share his underlying reverence for literature itself, Belinsky's thought has been given the value of codified legislative utterance. This is not to say that what later interpreters, including contemporary Soviet commentators, claim to find there is not there. It is, but it is not all that is there. And by selecting only what they need, they have identified Belinsky with attitudes, values, and policies he very probably would have refused to endorse. He has been narrowed, rigidified, and made into a spokesman for a literature not of service to human welfare, which he advocated vigorously if intermittently, but of subservience to political dictatorship.

The key to the Soviet use of Belinsky is contained in a half-serious judgment Trotsky made in 1925:

Belinsky was not a literary critic; he was a socially-minded leader of his epoch. And if Vissarion could be transported alive into our time, he probably would be . . . a member of the Politburo.[3]

Trotsky, of course, knew the difference between a literary critic and a social theorist, an essential difference which has been forgotten by later Soviet commentators. His designation of Belinsky as a political forebear, an initiator of movements that culminated in the October Revolution, has been repeated by so many Soviet voices that it has become a permanent article of faith. Unquestionably this attitude is the real source of Belinsky's authority in the USSR, and literature is inevitably diminished in any such interpretation of Belinsky's legacy. Trotsky made his own contribution to this tendency when he wrote:

The historic role of the Belinskys was to open up a breathing-hole into social life by means of literature. Literary criticism took the place of politics and was a preparation for it. But that which was merely a hint for Belinsky and for the later representatives of radical publicism, has taken on in our day the flesh and blood of October and has become Soviet reality.[4]

In this view the line of descent includes a transition, it would appear, from a lower to a higher kind of concern. If literary criticism is but "a preparation for" political activity is it not subordinate to pol-

[2] Isaiah Berlin, "A Marvellous Decade," Encounter, 4.6 (June 1955): 37.
[3] Leon Trotsky, Literature and Revolution, trans. Rose Strunsky (New York, 1925), p. 210.
[4] Ibid., p. 209.

itics, is it not considered to have identical aims? For less cultivated men than Trotsky, who apparently knew that "radical publicism" was not really concerned with literary criticism at all, the temptation to demean literature was overwhelming. When it became necessary to subject imaginative literature to the purposes of the Soviet state, the literary magistrates turned to their politically certified ancestor and found the elements of a theory which unmistakably justified literature's subordination to social concerns. The Soviet reading of Belinsky, selective as it is, is not entirely implausible. The prescriptive aspect of Belinsky's thought is there for all to see. Its quality and the terms of its translation into Soviet doctrine are what engage our attention now.

Belinsky was in solicitous attendance at the birth of Russian realism. He welcomed it, nurtured it, and defended it against its detractors. In the course of this devoted work he expressed a number of attitudes toward literature, incorporating much that foreign philosophies had taught him, and much that social reformers and political radicals could find no other way to say in the Russia of Nicholas I. His defense of the new realism rested on larger notions about the nature of society and of history, which exerted constant pressure on his aesthetic theory and insistently shaped it to his extraliterary purposes. Having officiated at the birth of this promising new phenomenon, realism, he felt at times that it was a part of his own philosophy, and ventured to legislate its scope, function, and purpose and to chart its future development. These contradictory tendencies in his thought—toward the liberalizing of old standards and toward a new orthodoxy of his own making—characterize (and confuse) all he had to say about art.

As the champion of a new kind of writing Belinsky had first to challenge the attitudes he hoped to replace. Initially he set out to justify the use of subjects which were forbidden under the canons of neoclassicism and romanticism: in this he performed a service acknowledged by his friends and his enemies, opening literature to include the vulgar, the average, the topical, and the unpleasant, to make possible the candid exploration of the lives of average men. The new "truthfulness" of literature was an important step forward: in this light Belinsky's questionable judgment about Gogol, that he was "the first who looked boldly and directly at Russian reality,"[5] has a rele-

[5] V. G. Belinsky, *Selected Philosophical Works*, ed. M. T. Yovchuk (Moscow, 1948), p. 182. This postwar selection of his work for export is designed, according to a publisher's note, to show Belinsky's role as "a predecessor of Russian social democracy."

vance as an historical judgment that it lacks as a description of Gogol's imaginative vision. Similarly, Belinsky's enthusiastic description of *Eugene Onegin* as an "encyclopaedia of Russian life" was meant as high praise in its time, though it rings strangely to a modern reader who does not read the poem for the information it contains. These judgments, however, arise logically from his premise that Russian literature, henceforth, must concern itself with the contemporary, the topical, and the national, all of which he discovered in abundance in *Onegin* and *Dead Souls*.

His efforts to broaden the scope of fiction worked at the same time to reduce to life-size whatever, in the earlier genres, had been larger than life. In this leveling process the heroic stereotypes of the past were swept away with everything else that seemed to him false, conventional, lifeless, or overblown. So drastic was the purge that the heroic mold itself seemed at times to have been destroyed. But the contrary tendency in his thought, the prescriptive phase of his theory of realism, exerted a strong pressure in the opposite direction. Moving beyond his general injunction that literature engage itself with reality, Belinsky devised an intricate set of commitments within which literature, in his view, must function in order to acquire value. It is at this point that he engages the attention of his future disciples. His views of progress, of human nature, of the function of ideas, of the nature of society, of the relations between the individual and society, were brought to bear on the literary imagination in later years. They are essential ingredients of the literature of positive heroes.

II

It was the extra work literature was asked to perform that created the conditions of its servitude. In Belinsky's view, great works of art were freighted with intellectual and moral significance. When he repudiated neoclassicism he did not mean that art's obligation to convey moral ideas was abolished or that art was to become simply a recording apparatus. The special conditions of Russian intellectual life which tended to channel many extraliterary concerns into forms of imaginative expression influenced Belinsky's fundamental definition of the nature of art: "Art," he wrote, "is the immediate contemplation of truth, or a thinking in images."[6] Literature was thus broadly

6 *Ibid.*, p. 186. This formulation has survived to modern times. Plekhanov welcomed it as the most profound concept developed by the radical critics. Konstantinov cites a

and carelessly linked with any and all activities of the human mind, and the way was open for literature to serve as the vehicle for a whole range of ideas which were denied other outlets. It is easy to see how one proceeds from this close equivalence between the products of the literary imagination and of abstract thought to a condition in which art's truth is subordinated to other intellectual disciplines, to the truths of philosophy or social science, or to the half-truths of political ideology. Sometimes Belinsky seems to be saying that literature was intended to serve *primarily* as a means of transmitting ideas: "In it, and it alone, is contained the whole of our intellectual life."[7] And, further, "it is the vital spring from which all human sentiments and conceptions percolate into society."[8]

In assuming a responsibility to crystallize and disseminate all the fruits of his society's intellectual life, the writer is invited to derive comfort from the fact that he is a primary agent in a process of progressive historical change. "Life consists only in progress," Belinsky wrote, and progress is a steady movement in the minds of men, of nations, of humanity toward "self-cognizance."[9] Thus the importance of the "encyclopaedic" *Eugene Onegin* lay in the fact that it was "an act of consciousness for Russian society...a great step forward... after which there could no longer be any question of standing still."[10]

The national self-cognizance toward which history moves is only partly concerned with the search for the unique national identity, the nation's "soul," that is the usual preoccupation of theories of nationalism. It moves rather toward a double awareness: on the one hand, of correct and healthy principles of social justice, including full recognition of the inalienable rights of man, and on the other hand, of their daily violation, by serfdom and autocracy, in contemporary Russia.

---

similar definition by Belinsky as an amplification of the Marxian definition of art as "a form of social consciousness." It is worth quoting in full:

"The philosopher speaks in syllogisms, the poet in images and pictures, and they both say the same thing. The political economist armed with statistics, *proves*, by acting on the reason of his readers or listeners, that the condition of a certain class in society has greatly improved or worsened, as a result of certain causes. The poet, armed with a clear, living representation of reality, *shows* in a faithful picture, by acting on the imagination of his readers, that the condition of a certain class has improved or worsened for certain reasons. One *proves*, the other *shows*, and both *convince*, one by logical means, the other by pictures." Quoted by F. V. Konstantinov, ed., *Istoricheskii materializm* (Moscow, 1950), pp. 591–92 (Belinsky, *Selected Philosophical Works*, p. 432).

[7] Belinsky, *Selected Philosophical Works*, p. 333.   [8] *Ibid.*, p. 339.

[9] *Ibid.*, p. 308. The Hegelian source of this notion is obvious.

[10] *Ibid.*, p. 276.

The goal was a nation in which the natural rights of man were to be recognized by all and the individual human personality would be freed thereby of indignity and injustice. Then, presumably, Russia would be free to realize its unique identity. These are the terms of social morality, and in the Russian setting of that time they were controversial—even subversive—ideas. Literature is thus committed to an educational function which automatically places it in an advanced position of advocacy and partisanship.

The writer describes and forwards this process which goes on unceasingly in the world of ideas and in the minds of men. The form of advance is conflict in the familiar Hegelian pattern of forward movement through the clash of opposites, between progressive and retrogressive forces. These contending forces are not given fixed labels by Belinsky, but the definitions that emerge resemble the eighteenth-century opposition between reason and prejudice. Belinsky, after Hegel, has made the static opposition between good and evil a dynamic one, has given the process "lawful" regularity and set it in motion toward an assured goal. In the war for control of the society's governing moral ideas, eventual victory for the forces of progress is assured, but before that moment the issue is always in doubt, and the full collaboration of the already-convinced is the only means to its achievement.

Generally in this climate of conflict the obligation is as binding on the writer as it is on anyone else. It is on this point, of course, in all varieties of this approach, that literature's subordination to extraliterary concerns begins. The writer's enlistment in the service of a demanding but ultimately beneficent dialectical process, which he accelerates by reporting accurately, represents a crucial act of surrender. This definition of literature's obligatory service in the cause of human welfare needed to be changed only in particulars as it passed from the hands of one radical literary theorist to another, from Belinsky, finally to Zhdanov. The definition of the warring forces in the universe may be drastically and continuously altered without releasing literature from its fundamental obligation to serve the progressive current in history.

Belinsky has given his own version of the *terms* of its service in a sequence of definitions. He began, as we have seen, by opening literature to direct observation of everyday Russian experience. But the writer's entanglement in the dialectic of history introduces important restrictions affecting the selection and treatment of material. In order to focus the writer's perceptions, Belinsky paid particular attention to the standards of selectivity. In his optimistic view of the universe, with its implication that the contest between truth and error would, in the end, go well, the writer could not be indifferent toward experience nor was he free to write about any random or insignificant aspect of Russian life. Objectivity did not necessarily imply neutrality, nor did realism mean that the writer was freed of his obligation to select and evaluate his material. On the contrary, the writer could not fail to be passionate and committed—in Belinsky's term, "subjective"—about the world he lived in.

His essential connection with experience took place under the wholesome influence of a "vital idea," one which is close to the secret of the unfolding universe and is engaged therefore in mortal combat with the outworn regime of superstition and prejudice. In this way art performs its function of interpreting reality purposefully and, in effect, takes sides in the master conflict:

[Art] is no longer confined to a passive role—to mirror nature faithfully and dispassionately—but it brings into its reasonings a living, personal idea that imparts to them design and meaning.[11]

The writer's lively personal engagement with experience—the continuous action of his "subjectivity"—is a matter of the emotions and the nerves, an intuitive relationship with the dominant idea that gives meaning to the experience. Art might be a "thinking in images," but the transition from abstraction to image did not take place within the mind of the writer. His attachment to the "vital idea" depended not on its compelling logic but on its emotional power and its moral radiance. By its action on his imagination the moral idea automatically imparted a "healthy" tendency to all the material that passed through it. The reader presumably would respond to the tendency by feeling and thinking, and finally by acting differently. When this didactic function was properly performed some aspects of Belinsky's own social morality were certain to be transmitted. Literature, though it depended on life in all essentials ("poetry is life first and art afterward"), achieved in its concentrated and selective reproduction of experience a clarity and a power of evaluation that raw experience never offered: "A poetical conception is shorn of all the accidental and extraneous and depicts only the necessary and the significant."[12]

---

[11] *Ibid.*, p. 287.　　　　　　　　[12] *Ibid.*, p. 292.

Selectivity raises the problem of literature's capacity to generalize. How does a purposive, realistic literature achieve a level of general statement and preserve the liveliness of the particular image and the full effect of the didactic ingredient at the same time? Belinsky's solution was contained in the concept of "typicality."[13] The typical character and the typical circumstance, recorded in all their detail and color—their "realness"—would not, if they were properly selected, lose any of their broader meanings in the particularity of their representation. Belinsky thought that the genuinely typical character was endowed with energy, individuality, and significance by the same "vital idea" that informed the writer's view of experience. Writing of Gogol, who, he felt, had achieved a notably sound fusion of the particular and the general without falsely idealizing his characters, he said:

Here the crux of the matter is types, the ideal being understood not as an adornment (consequently a falsehood) but as the relations in which the author places the types he creates, in conformity with the idea which his work is intended to develop.[14]

The danger that the new realism would lose its verisimilitude and degenerate into a literature of moralistic abstractions preoccupied Belinsky, who sometimes sensed the contradictory tendencies in his own thought. To keep the general significance of the typical character from engulfing his concrete identity, Belinsky insisted on the wholeness and integrity of personal motivation within the narrative. Only in this way could the literary images of men achieve the unmistakable semblance of life. The documentation of their personal traits and of their public attitudes must be precise and voluminous, because literature had first of all to seem real. It must not be a clever fabrication but a representation of experience subject to verification by the reader. Only in this way could generalization, tendency, and instruction receive persuasive fictional statement. The highest value—indeed, the *sine qua non*—of literature, Belinsky never ceased to proclaim, was its "truthfulness." Any conflict between truth and instruction must be resolved in the light of this injunction. But the contradictory tendencies in his thought remain to plague him and all his followers, and the resolution is more often in the other direction. Belinsky never

[13] *Ibid.*, p. 413. This notion is not original, of course, with Belinsky.
[14] *Ibid.*

forgot that the documentation of an *a priori* attitude is not the same thing as the naked wrestling with experience that produces great works of art, but he was able at the same time to entertain ideas which were quite incompatible with the practice of a free art.[15] It is the prescriptive phase of his thinking which has been emphasized here because it is the source of the three principal concepts—optimism, service, and typicality—which constitute the legacy Soviet critics claim to inherit from Belinsky. They have had to set aside all that he said in favor of art's and the artist's independence. The real tragedy of Belinsky's legacy is that in his passionate *volte-faces* he managed to blur certain essential distinctions—notably between art and life, and between the language of art and the language of science and of doctrine—which made it easier for his successors to use him for purposes it is hard to imagine he could have supported. It is *not* easy, finally, to picture Belinsky as a member of the Politburo.

III

Two important questions arise for a literature which heeds Belinsky's direction to select, distill, and generalize. How does it render its service to human welfare within the system of the dialectic? And who, if anyone, is to play the role of virtue's conscious agent?

The radical critics devised two general answers to the first question: literature might hasten the disintegration of the old, retrogressive tendency by exposé or ridicule, or it might accelerate the progressive tendency by indicating its presence and by giving it favorable publicity. Belinsky was aware of these two possibilities, but all that he found in Russian life and literature persuaded him that the affirmative note would have to be postponed indefinitely in favor of a literature of criticism and negation. In this reluctant choice are found the answers to the second question, and the key to Belinsky's basic attitudes toward heroism.

In the contest between value systems the actual combatants in the field are individual men, and the partisans of truth are the virtuous agents of progress. Belinsky felt sure that they must exist—had there not always been heroes in the past?—but their identity, their function, and their relationship to literature in his time raised questions that were not easily answered. He found it easier to excoriate his enemies

---

[15] Bowman shows how Belinsky contradicted himself on these essential points until the end of his life. See Bowman, *Vissarion Belinski*, pp. 178–79 and p. 199.

than to celebrate his allies, and in this pugnacious, destructive mood his deepest attitudes toward heroes were formed. "My heroes," he wrote in a letter to Botkin, "are the destroyers of the old, Luther, Voltaire, the Encyclopaedists, the Terrorists, Byron ... and so on."[16]

In his own time Belinsky sought these exposers and destroyers among the men of thought and imagination; in Russia the likeliest candidates were the writers whose critique of the reigning order seemed to him to be doing history's work. The critic—in this case himself—could make his own contribution. In apologizing to Botkin for an article which he described as a "clumsy patchwork" of his own and Katkov's ideas, he says characteristically: "Never mind! If I will not supply a theory of poetry I will have killed the old ones, killed at one fell stroke all our rhetorics, poetics and aesthetics—and that is not to be sneezed at!"[17]

Clearly, he read both *Eugene Onegin* and *Dead Souls* as indictments of the social system. Neither work, it is true, offered a stirring heroic image or any sign of positive forces working for a better world, but their liberating destructiveness qualified their *authors* as agents of progress. Although they had performed this heroic task, they themselves were poor candidates for imitation: Pushkin was dead, and the unhappy Gogol drew back in horror from Belinsky's accolade. It was, in fact, a most unheroic moment in Russian history.

Despite this, or perhaps because of it, Belinsky's whole career was a restless hero-quest. The rapid succession in his own life of commitments—each more passionate than the preceding—to the ideas of Fichte, Schelling, Hegel, and, finally, of the left-Hegelians and the Saint-Simonians, illustrates his own sharply felt need for leadership from heroes of thought. In writing in 1841 of his abandonment of Hegel, against whom he now feels he has "special reason to harbour a grudge ... for I feel that I have been loyal to him ... in tolerating Russian reality,"[18] he acknowledges his own erraticism: "A year ago my views were diametrically opposite to what they are today, and, really, I cannot say whether it is a fortunate or unfortunate thing that for me to think and feel, to understand and suffer are one and the same thing."[19]

It is interesting that in the same letter to Botkin he sees this kind of shift from one view to its opposite as somehow tragic: "A man himself

[16] Belinsky, *Selected Philosophical Works*, p. 164.
[17] *Ibid.*, p. 152.   [18] *Ibid.*, p. 149.   [19] *Ibid.*, p. 150.

knows nothing—everything depends upon the spectacles which his disposition, the whim of his nature beyond the control of his will, places on his nose." He then goes on, in what is only apparently a change of subject, to give Botkin the correct text of a passage mutilated by the censor:

If we were to ask Lady Macbeth [he had written] why she had been created so awfully inhuman, she would no doubt answer that she knew as much about it as her questioner and if she followed her nature it was because she had no other.... These are questions that are solved only beyond the grave, this is the kingdom of fate, the realm of tragedy![20]

He adds a note on Richard II which is *not*, as we shall see in later chapters, part of the Belinsky legacy that is treasured in the Soviet Union:

The king, unworthy so long as he reigned, becomes great when he has lost his kingdom. He becomes conscious of the dignity of his majesty... of the legitimacy of his rights—and wise speeches, filled with lofty thought, rush in stormy torrents from his lips, while action reveals a great soul and royal dignity. Insignificant in good fortune, great in misfortune, he is a hero in your eyes. But in order to bring forth the powers of his spirit and become a hero he had to drain the cup of misery to the dregs and perish.... What a contradiction, and what a rich theme for tragedy, hence what an inexhaustible source of sublime enjoyment.[21]

Yet, in the same year, he had celebrated a very different kind of hero, one who "did not believe in the frailties of human nature,"[22] a destroyer who was also a builder, and one far more sympathetic to the later searchers for positive heroes—Peter the Great. "Who, throughout our history, can be nearer both to our heart and spirit?"[23]

Here, discussing Peter, he touches on the vital question of the aesthetic effect of contemplating virtuous men, which "rouses us from the drowsiness of humdrum life... attunes the heart to exalted feelings and noble thoughts [and] strengthens the will to acts of goodness."[24] Peter the Great or Richard the Second? Belinsky would have it both ways: he could comprehend both the view of the effective, successful hero whose example leads to positive moral instruction and that of the hero in defeat who arouses pity, and more than pity, awe. It remained for later radicals to recast the image of Peter the Great

[20] *Ibid.*, p. 152.   [21] *Ibid.*, p. 153.   [22] *Ibid.*, p. 142.
[23] *Ibid.*, p. 146.   [24] *Ibid.*

(stripped of his kingly rank, of course) as a permanent replacement for the tragic hero.

Toward the end of his career Belinsky dismissed the possibility that large-scale heroic images—whether tragic or not—might dominate the literature of his time. The downfall of Shakespeare's kings, whatever it revealed of the greatness of the human spirit, was to provide no part of Belinsky's guide to Russian writers, nor was "sublime enjoyment" in any sense the exclusive goal of literature. Heroes there had been, in life and in literature, and their influence had been enormous, but for his contemporaries Belinsky could offer no similar image. For the new writing had first of all to be "truthful." Heroes were not to be fabricated out of moral abstractions if they could not be found in Russian life. Belinsky had found it Pushkin's great merit "that he dis-established the vogue of monsters of vice and heroes of virtue, depicting instead just ordinary people."[25]

Belinsky also objected to the romantic hero of his own time. The division of the universe into contending factions was reflected in human nature, which was composed, he believed, of more or less equal parts of altruism and "egotism." In the romantic hero "egotism" had full sway. He simply could not be accepted at his own inflated estimate of himself. But when that estimate was deflated by a writer, Belinsky was more hospitable to the choice of such a person as subject. In fact, he wanted the hero's condition to be emphasized if that was "best and most natural."[26] Thus Onegin, stripped of his illusions and seen at a certain remove, inspires pity as a victim of unhealthy social attitudes. Byronism, seen wholly, loses its dangerous fascination. Belinsky took an astringent view of Aduev, the hero of Goncharov's novel *An Ordinary Story*, because he was handled too respectfully by his author. This early version of the superfluous man had a well-developed capacity for self-deception, it was pointed out, and would never be capable of genuine, reciprocal emotion or of effective moral behavior.

Belinsky, before Dobrolyubov, discovered the awful gap between intention and action:

They recognize the lofty and beautiful only in books, and that not always; in life and in reality they recognize neither the one nor the other, and because of this are quickly disillusioned (their pet expression!), grow chilly in the soul, grow old in the flower of their years, stop in mid-jour-

25 *Ibid.*, p. 212.   26 *Ibid.*, p. 469.

ney, and end . . . by becoming reconciled with reality. . . . That is, whatever they do they fall straight from the clouds into the mud; or they become mystics, misanthropes, lunatics, or sleepwalkers. Usually they are ludicrous or pitiful . . . but sometimes they are not at all pitiful but dreadful because of their reconciliation with reality.[27]

But if the full cycle of their careers is shown with all the consequences of their imperfect grasp of the world and their final state of degradation (their reconciliation with reality), they are valid subjects to write about. In the reader's pity, laughter, or indignation an educational function will be served; falsehood will be unmasked, and the dialectic of history will receive its forward thrust.

But the question *toward what?* remains unanswered. Here Belinsky has reached a way-station on the route to something else. The denunciation of false prophets will not forever remain the function of literature. Sooner or later, new prophets, whether destroyers or builders, are bound to announce their presence. Belinsky sensed the impermanence of the period of stagnation he lived in and felt called upon to justify the negative role of his "natural school" as somehow presaging a more positive phase:

The habit of faithfully rendering the negative aspects of life will enable the same men or their followers, when the time comes, faithfully to render the positive aspects of life without placing them on stilts, without exaggerating: in short, without rhetorically idealizing them.[28]

Belinsky felt that periods like his own were not uncommon in human history—periods of stagnation without discernible forward motion and without heroes. But appearances, he suggested, were deceptive: new forces were gathering under the surface and the oppressively motionless world of Nicholas I must inevitably give way to an era of growth, progress, and change:

Progress is not interrupted even during the epoch of decay and death of societies, for this decay is necessary as a means of preparing the soil for the blossoming of a new life, and death itself, in history as well as in nature, is merely the regeneration of a new life.[29]

From time to time Belinsky applied his standard of virtue to the world around him. The samplings were uneven: "A good man in Russia," Belinsky decided at one time, simply has no "terrain" to

[27] V. G. Belinsky, *Polnoe sobranie sochinenii* (Moscow, 1955), 6: 672.
[28] Belinsky, *Selected Philosophical Works*, p. 357.
[29] *Ibid.*, p. 312.

stand on; whatever virtue he possesses is a simple "gift of nature" retained somehow despite the poisonous social atmosphere he breathes. He will have no opportunity to display his virtue in concrete activity, and the chances are that he will be an imperfectly formed human being, that his moral impulses will be blocked by other flaws. On another occasion, the possibility of enlightened behavior seemed far more encouraging:

It is a fact beyond a shadow of doubt that the number of people who are endeavoring to realize their moral convictions in deeds to the detriment of their private interests and at the risk of their social position has been growing perceptibly with us.[30]

These contradictory observations register Belinsky's changing moods more than they do real shifts in the moral climate. In one sense we may dismiss Belinsky's attitude toward the question of heroes by saying simply that his longing for them was frustrated by their demonstrable absence from Russian life in the 1840s. By combining the qualities he believed the hero should *not* have, however, with a few hints as to the qualities he should possess and that Belinsky, himself, exemplified, it is possible to sketch an outline, at least, of the still undiscovered champion. Incomplete as it is, Belinsky's hero figure bears a strong resemblance to the archetype which the radical critics developed in the middle decades of the century and handed down to the Soviet cultural magistrates of the present day.

He will not be a sovereign, a lawgiver, or a conqueror, but a man much closer to his fellows in rank and abilities, distinguished from them only by the firmness of his convictions and the force of his character. He will not be the "brilliant exception," or the man touched by genius, or the man set apart by innate or supernatural qualities. He will be rather the "first among equals," a representative man. His exact social status is not specified, but he will certainly not be a member of the governing class, or, by all indications, a member of the popular masses. The value attached to the liberating, inspiriting effect of ideas suggests that he will be an educated man. And there is little doubt, finally, that he will be a man in revolt against established values and the social order they justify.

The ultimate sanction for attacking the status quo is the immense suffering caused by the Tsarist regime. The foremost victims, of

---

[30] *Ibid.*, p. 338.

course, are the peasants and it is in their name, finally, that he acts. What are his relations with the masses; in what sense is he their representative? Belinsky's use of the concept of *narodnost*,[31] the untranslatable term used by all political factions in the nineteenth century to anchor their theories in the aspirations of the peasant mass, gives a partial answer. He includes the peasant-serfs as integral parts of the nation, hence as participants in the forward movement toward national self-awareness. The educated man, then, who is in the forefront of this struggle, is the leader of a vast progressive upsurge toward enlightenment; he is, in the words of a Soviet commentator, the "crest of the wave."[32]

In the USSR today they welcome this identification of the active, moral personality with the masses as one of the most "progressive" discoveries made by Belinsky, and one that links him closely with the Marxist-Leninist tradition. Yovchuk, in his introduction to *Selected Philosophical Works*, says this of Belinsky:

He found a profound and, in general, correct solution for the problem of the role of the individual and of the masses of the people in history when he maintained that the masses of the people could and would become the decisive force in historical development. The masses could be raised to the level of such historical activity by the progressive, educated people in society, who must be guided by the requirements of society, by the spirit of the times, by the interests of the people.[33]

The link is organic, apparently, and the identification of interests is complete. It is not clear how the hero receives his appointment to the position of leadership, or by what process, exactly, he functions as the representative of the masses. It is difficult to avoid the impression that he is self-appointed, and that he represents them on the basis of his own estimate of their needs. His constituents are a source of energy and strength. Their plight documents his critique of the social order and their unarticulated needs are the basis of his program for the future. But neither the channel of communications between them nor the pattern of mutual responsibility is clearly set forth.

Soviet critics have tended to exaggerate Belinsky's contribution to

[31] Literally "peopleness" or "nationality"; by extension, the qualities of a people, and, by further extension, identification with the people's interests.
[32] A. Lavretsky, *Belinsky, Chernyshevsky, Dobrolyubov v borbe za realizm* (Moscow, 1941), p. 65.
[33] Belinsky, *Selected Philosophical Works*, p. xi. Belinsky discussed the subject in a review of Eugène Sue's *Les Mystères de Paris* in 1844. *Ibid.*, pp. 326–27.

the definition of the new hero. Makedonov maintains that Belinsky devoted his entire intellectual life to the search for "a democratic man-hero," as opposed to the semi-divine figures of neoclassic tragedy.[34] Lavretsky says the same thing in a vast and questionable generalization: "Essentially the struggle for realism is a struggle for an active human type, a new man."[35] "Essentially" here acknowledges the fact that Belinsky never knew that the "new man" was the goal of all his strenuous endeavors. In an unsigned editorial in 1936 the matter is put somewhat differently though in the same vein of exaggeration: "In his teaching about the new hero, Belinsky posed the question about the kind of man who is essentially an anticipation, a premonition of the socialist hero."[36] Again "essentially" marks a stretching of the truth, but it can be said that Belinsky "posed" questions that others were to answer, if it is also understood that consciously he taught almost nothing about the hero.

Far more interesting than the official adulation in Zhdanov's "Report," or routine declarations of doctrinal dependence, is the kind of testimony we find in Lebedev-Polyansky's study of Belinsky, at the point where it lapses into personal reminiscence. Belinsky's role as a hero for the early Bolsheviks, both as man and as thinker, is clearly expressed:

Our generation, born in the eighties of the last century, read the works of Belinsky with delight, as his contemporaries had done. And perhaps the great critic's ideas were clearer to us than they were to his contemporaries; in them we found that content—time had aided us—which was hidden from Belinsky's contemporaries: his passion, his moral force, his exceptional sincerity...his idea that literature, while continuing to be art, must serve the goals of social struggle, must contain precise ideas, must pass sentence on contemporary life, must be the foreteller of the future.

.   .   .

In the happy and unhappy accidents of life the youth often gave each other the works of Belinsky, knowing that in them one could find moral support and strength. The youth gave each other the works of Belinsky when, inspired by a great love for the people, by the idea of struggle, they went out, in Chekhov's words, "into the unknown distance."[37]

[34] A. Makedonov, "Problema geroya v estetike Belinskogo," *Literaturny kritik*, 6 (June 1936): 101.
[35] Lavretsky, *Belinsky, Chernyshevsky, Dobrolyubov*, p. 57.
[36] "Vissarion Grigorievich Belinsky," *Literaturny kritik*, 6 (June 1936): 22.
[37] P. I. Lebedev-Polyansky, *V. G. Belinsky, literaturno-kriticheskaya deyatelnost* (Moscow-Leningrad, 1945), pp. 300–301.

This type of sentimental veneration suggests the force of Belinsky's personal impact on a culture hungry for heroes. It is the inspiring image of Belinsky the fighter that was handed down from generation to generation of Russian radicals and intellectuals, as part of the Russian revolutionary ethos, and has finally been incorporated in the Soviet gallery of saints. Men of all persuasions have reacted to the force of his convictions, his purity, his integrity, and the furiously righteous style of his behavior. Isaiah Berlin, in his generous and discriminating appreciation of Belinsky,[38] has recovered this image as well, perhaps, as it can be done. He has made allowance for the extremism of Belinsky's judgments, for his drastic lapses in taste, and for the large gaps in his education, but he has not properly estimated those phases of his personality and of his critical practice that are hostile, in the final analysis, to the free intellect and imagination.

The ingredients of his moral personality actually are not so different from those of the Soviet hero-type. He hated dogma, it is true, and might well have suffocated in the Soviet intellectual atmosphere, but he was the author of his own dogmas, which he applied with ferocious assurance to the world around him. His celebrated sincerity might not survive in a moral climate of strategic maneuver and deception, but his fanatical attachment to a single system of ideas, and his intolerance of all others, the rudeness of his manner, the flat certainty, the right-or-wrong quality of his judgments, are familiar elements of Soviet behavior and intellectual practice. These are the qualities of revolutionaries, of wholly politicalized men. It is not absurd, perhaps, to suggest that these qualities have survived the metamorphosis of October which converted revolutionary nonconformists into vigilant defenders of the revolution's vested interests.

When this personality assumed the office of literary critic, it is hard to believe that the ultimate interests of literature were not endangered. Belinsky loved literature, but he threatened at times to smother it in his embrace. Berlin has said: "All serious questions to Belinsky were always, in the end, moral questions."[39] Without quarreling about the kind of morality, it is enough to recognize that a standard external to literature formed the basis of his literary judgments. The strong partisan certainty of these judgments, though it is not yet political or

---

[38] Isaiah Berlin, "A Marvellous Decade (III), Belinsky: Moralist and Prophet," *Encounter*, 5.6 (December 1955): 22–43.
[39] *Ibid.*, p. 26.

programmatic, not yet "party spirit" as either Matthew Arnold or Lenin meant it, is certainly menacing to a literature of paradox, or ambiguity. Belinsky believed in "a single knowable truth," as Berlin says, and "ideas were above all, true or false. If false, then like evil spirits to be exorcised."[40] It was the critic's job to bring them to light (to "unmask" them, Soviet Marxists were to say), and "all books embody ideas even when least appearing to do so."[41] The moral validity of the uncovered idea, then, forms the basis of the critic's judgment.

This kind of standard becomes possible because Belinsky did not honor certain important distinctions between life and art. The idea he sought (which also is an "attitude" or a revelation of preferences) "requires to be judged," Berlin says, "as it would be in life; in the first place for its degree of genuineness, its adequacy to its subject matter, its depth, its truthfulness, its ultimate motives."[42] This kind of *moral* judgment of art contains the seeds of all the brands of prescriptive criticism which accompanied the development of the Russian revolutionary movement. The work of art acts upon life and is judged in the end for the effect it has on the moral condition of its readers. The critic is the custodian of the meanings of "genuineness," "depth," and "ultimate motives," and the guardian of the truth of history as well. Thus a writer who fails is not only a poor craftsman, he is also a liar, or a hypocrite, or an obscurantist.

Unknown to himself, and despite his admirable devotion to truth, beauty, and justice, Belinsky is the author of an image of man (in his own person) steeped in hatred, which had only to be simplified, hardened, and shorn of sentimental scruple to become the revolutionary monolith of later generations. He is the author too of that strange Russian hybrid, the critic-revolutionary, who transformed the character traits of the political revolutionary into criteria of literary judgment. Belinsky was neither utilitarian nor totalitarian, Berlin insists, but he was the indispensable predecessor of both.

IV

Where Belinsky appears inadequate to Soviet critics the assumption is that he *would have* reached these conclusions if conditions had been different. Perhaps. But it is a fruitless speculation which rests on the questionable view that literary theory evolves in a single, determined line of development from lower to higher stages.

[40] *Ibid.*   [41] *Ibid.*   [42] *Ibid.*

Belinsky's real contribution is a set of ideas that has remained operative to the present day, even though it has been amended, embellished, upended, and given, with the ascendancy of Marxism, a new metaphysical foundation:

Optimism. Soviet commentators have welcomed every sign in Belinsky of the singularly cheerless optimism that has characterized the Russian revolutionary ethos. History unfolds in a necessary evolutionary order; the direction is forward and upward, toward the coming emancipation of men from the slavery of want and material contingency; and works of art created in awareness of the world in motion cannot fail to reflect the promise of the dialectic.

Under the influence of these assurances, literature will become less exclusively concerned with exploring the past and explaining the present. Conceived as dissent, and tied to the present and to life as it is, the new literature will go further and try to argue the likelihood and the desirability of moving from the imperfect present to a better future.[43] In the shift from present to future tense realistic literature will undergo basic changes in its traditional functions: from descriptive analysis to prophecy, from reminiscence to inspiration. It should be pointed out that the optimism of the dialectic is not based on glib promises or easy solutions. Allowance is made for the presence of pain, suffering, and partial or temporary defeats, but the total defeat of both the hero and the values he represents, in a downfall so complete that it counsels reconciliation or quietism, is impermissible in the new writing that is to grow from Belinsky's premises. In this emphasis, the crucial quarrel with tragedy and with the tragic view of life is prefigured in Belinsky's thought, although he himself never took a positive stand on the question of "the happy ending."

Service. Zhdanov said in his "Report":

From Belinsky onward, all the best representatives of the revolutionary democratic Russian intellectuals have denounced "pure art" and "art for art's sake" and have been the spokesmen of art for the people, demanding that art should have a worthy educational and social significance.[44]

[43] Compare Belinsky's remark that literature is the record "of treasured thoughts of the whole of society, of its ... still indiscernible aspiration" (*Selected Philosophical Works*, p. 426), with Timofeev's injunctions that "the artist sees today in the light of tomorrow" (L. I. Timofeev, *Teoriya literatury*, Moscow, 1938, p. 327), and that art must represent "the new, the growing, that which is not typical today but will surely be so tomorrow" (p. 302).

[44] A. A. Zhdanov, "Doklad o zhurnalakh *Zvezda* i *Leningrad*," *Literaturnaya gazeta*, 39 (September 21, 1946): 3.

In "A View of Russian Literature in 1847," Belinsky wrote of the new trends which replaced the former interest in "pure art":

Artistic interest ... could not but yield to other more important human interests and art nobly undertook to serve these interests as their spokesman. Art has not ceased thereby to be art, but has merely acquired a new character. To deny art the right of serving public interests means debasing it, not raising it, for that would mean depriving it of its most vital force, i.e., idea, making it an object of sybaritic pleasure, the plaything of lazy idlers.[45]

Soviet theorists have adapted this notion by interposing the intermediary of the Party and state through which the service to human welfare is rendered. In this tradition, art serves the people by educating them in principles that will lead to their own betterment. The issue is not merely a matter of reestablishing, as Zhdanov would have us believe, the principle that art must serve more than its own ends, but of harnessing it to increasingly detailed notions of what men should learn and of how and why their minds should be changed.

Typicality. The emphasis in the radical tradition on art's generalizing capacities really stems from the radicals' interest in controlling the content of the generalization. It is one thing to proclaim that art deals with the typical, quite another to prescribe what *is* typical, and what, therefore, is the legitimate concern of art at any given time. This prescriptive control over the choice of subject matter, which also operates as a principle for excluding undesirable (i.e., untypical) material, is central to the utilitarian approach.

The critic is free to challenge (and the editor to reject) the very conception of a novel, ignoring the writer's fulfillment of his intention, if the intention itself is "incorrect" or "harmful." The concepts of the "true," the "typical," and the "significant" are general descriptive terms about the nature of literature, until they are given exclusive, doctrinal definitions. Then they become tools for governing the very substance and significance of the work of art.

Belinsky's theory of realism offers with one hand what, in effect, it withholds with the other. The writer is *not* free after all to wander at will through Russian experience, nor will his decision about what is valid material for investigation be respected as the exercise of the

---

[45] Belinsky, *Selected Philosophical Works*, p. 431.

artist's inalienable prerogative. Belinsky stopped short of exercising the censorious potential implicit in his theory. It requires a fair measure of hindsight to isolate it in his writing and we cannot know how he would have felt about the subsequent use made of it. The increasingly political nature of literature in the years to come might have coincided with his own revolutionary aspirations, but it seems certain that he would not have accepted the conclusions his successors drew from his premises without a genuine sense of loss, a sense of the death of the "magic" of art, which he continued to value even as he undermined it.

Belinsky, in effect, issued a challenge to his successors: although he did not hope to find them in his own time, sooner or later heroes must exist: "society's tyranny demands heroes to combat it."[46] The radical critics of the fifties and sixties, armed with Belinsky's precepts and fired by his example, made the search for the new hero the focal point of their literary concerns and—behind this necessary disguise—of their urgent political concerns as well.

[46] *Ibid.*, p. 240.

CHAPTER 4

Dobrolyubov: Beyond the Superfluous Man

N. A. Dobrolyubov (1836–61) is the eternal, perhaps one should say the professional, youth of the Russian revolutionary movement. His brief career, brought to an end by consumption at the age of twenty-five, summarizes all the virtues and vices of the youthful radical. For his partisans, then and now, he expressed the energy, the optimism, the critical brilliance, and the refreshing anger against injustice that characterize the best of the radical ethos. To his enemies, his brilliance was arrogant precocity, his optimism callow, and his anger and energy were expressed in a blind urge to destroy. In all the senses that radicalism is youthful, Dobrolyubov comes down to us a classic example. In this role he was a compelling figure in his own time. He was a constant topic of discussion in public and in private and he was thought to be the model for a number of studies of the new man, including such "unfavorable" versions as Bazarov, the hero of Turgenev's *Fathers and Sons*. Turgenev denied it, but Bazarov's cocksureness, impatience, and scorn are certainly duplicated in the quality of Dobrolyubov's thought as expressed in his critical articles.[1]

There had been changes in the intellectual climate since Belinsky's death in 1848. Less than a decade later, the atmosphere of intellectual and moral stagnation which had compelled Belinsky to qualify his faith in progress had been dissipated by new and parallel currents of

---

[1] A thoughtful and thorough study of his public and private voices may be found in Alfred Kuhn, "The Literary Criticism of N. A. Dobroliubov" (unpublished dissertation, Columbia University, 1968). An excerpt appeared as an article, "Dobroliubov's Critique of *Oblomov*: Polemics and Psychology," *Slavic Review*, March 1971, pp. 93–109.

imaginative vitality and social protest. Turgenev, Goncharov, Ostrovsky, and the promising young writers Tolstoy and Dostoevsky had been heard from, and the new generation of radical critics, with whom some of the new writers were now in fruitful, if short-lived, alliance, had sharpened the radical challenge to the status quo after its momentary eclipse in the post-1848 repression. In this quickened climate Dobrolyubov led the attack on the social system in the pages of the influential journal *Sovremennik* (Contemporary), using the detour through literary criticism Belinsky had already charted.

Dobrolyubov's indebtedness to Belinsky is direct, heavy, and explicit. He felt a strong spiritual kinship with his predecessor, that "pride, glory and adornment" of Russian literature, and his intellectual dependence on Belinsky is evident in everything Dobrolyubov has to say about the nature of art and society. Frequently he gave sharp, dogmatic utterance to ideas which had been half-understood or unexplored premises for Belinsky. Dobrolyubov presents restatements of Belinsky's three key premises, optimism, typicality, and service, indicating that they are central in his own thought. We find him, for example, defining the problem of dialectical optimism with an assurance which Belinsky had lacked a decade before:

Recognizing the immutable laws of historical development, the men of the present generation do not place unreal hopes upon themselves, do not think they can alter history at their own will, do not think they are immune to the influence of circumstances.... But at the same time they do not in the least sink into apathy and indifference, for they are also aware of their own worth. They look upon themselves as one of the wheels of a machine, as one of the circumstances which govern the course of world events. As all world circumstances are interconnected and to some extent subordinated to each other, they, too, are subordinated to necessity, to the force of things; but beyond this subordination they do not bow to any idols whatsoever, they uphold the independence and sovereignty of all their actions against all casually arising claims.[2]

Dobrolyubov's formula for the individual's release from the power of circumstance resembles Engels's definition of "freedom" as the "recognition of necessity." The strong note of emotion on which it ends establishes a connection between true awareness of the world and the kind of independent, defiant, and self-contained personality which can operate most successfully in it. The ingredients of heroic behavior

[2] N. A. Dobrolyubov, *Polnoe sobranie sochinenii* (Moscow, 1937), 4: 62.

are, it is suggested here, implicit in the very nature of the historical process.

If Dobrolyubov sharpened some of Belinsky's ideas, he also reduced the range of his interests and eliminated the contradictions, always in favor of the prescriptive element, always to the detriment of literature's independence. There is no doubt that the narrow, systematized version of Belinsky used by Soviet critics had its beginnings here. That literature performs a kind of secondary service in the intellectual activities of the day is stated far more uncompromisingly by Dobrolyubov than by Belinsky:

Thus, speaking generally, literature is an auxiliary force (the importance of which lies in propaganda, and the merit of which is determined by what it propagates, and how it propagates it).[3]

The writer is given no leeway to distort or falsify; nor, though he works under the guidance of an idea, is he permitted to inject this idea as learned from a philosopher into his work. It must be verifiable against an objective norm, usually described simply as "real life."[4] Literature, then, is accountable to experience, but the principal reason for this restriction is that its propagandist function is impaired by falsification:

Thus we think that the principal function of literature is to explain the phenomena of life, and that is why we demand that it should possess a quality without which it can have no merit whatever. This quality is *truth*. The facts from which the author proceeds, and which he presents to us, must be presented truthfully. If he fails to do that, his literary production loses all significance; in fact, it becomes harmful, because it serves not to enlighten the human mind, but, on the contrary, still further to obscure it.[5]

Though the writer may end by agreeing with the philosopher, he must proceed to his conclusion by a different route. In comprehending social discontent, for example, the philosopher will analyze facts and then proceed to formulate general principles which will aid in the removal of the unrest. But "the author-poet . . . noticing the same dis-

---

[3] N. A. Dobrolyubov, *Selected Philosophical Essays*, ed. M. T. Yovchuk (Moscow, 1948), p. 565. Parentheses in the quotations indicate censored material throughout this chapter. There have been writers in the past, Shakespeare, for example, who have raised literature above this auxiliary function, who, "like great scientists and political leaders, have extended the broad frontiers of human awareness," but there are none among Dobrolyubov's contemporaries who have earned this exemption from service.

[4] *Ibid.*, p. 566.   [5] *Ibid.*

content, paints such a vivid picture of it that it attracts universal attention, and of itself suggests to people what it is they need."[6]

Both aspects of the truth have the same final purpose: the abolition
of the unacceptable present and its replacement by a better future.
Literature performs its "special services" by "awakening ... the consciousness of the masses to what the advanced leaders of mankind
have discovered," and by revealing to them "what, as yet, lives in them
vaguely and indefinitely."[7] It is clear that another part of the truth
contains a prediction about what will happen soon. The writer becomes a kind of prophet, and even when his expectations turn out to
be premature, they still are to be considered "true" at the moment
they are expressed. In their own time the radicals felt sure that history's promises had not been proved false, though they were sometimes forced to conclude that the estimated time of fruition had been
badly miscalculated.

Actually, description is a small part of the literary "truth." Literature is a technique for understanding experience in a very special
way and the writer must be quite clear about the standards he uses
to interpret and evaluate what he has seen. This is a far more calculated procedure than Belinsky's view that the writer worked under
the hypnotic influence of an idea he might not fully or rationally
comprehend. The writer consciously selects, sifts, evaluates, and pro-
nounces judgment on the material he incorporates in his work, and,
according to Dobrolyubov, must possess a trained clairvoyant sense
to enable him to detect major trends in their incipient phase.

A view of man more firmly in the grip of history's laws, yet freer
because he understands them better; a much narrower definition of
literature's obligation to serve social change; and a heightened emphasis on the tendentious uses the writer was to make of "the truth"—
these changes betray the drift within the premises of the radical theory.

There had, of course, been major changes in the intellectual climate
of Russia since 1848 which seemed to forecast even greater changes
in the social structure. Dobrolyubov was stimulated by widespread
restlessness and by the rising note of agitation which preceded the
Emancipation Act of 1861. He found evidence in life and in literature
to justify his optimism and to validate his philosophy of social action.
In addition to the belligerence among the leftist intellectuals, there

---

[6] *Ibid.*   [7] *Ibid.*, p. 565.

were strong "murmurings" from the people. And nothing seemed to offer a stronger guarantee that one era was about to give way to another than the discovery that a revolution was taking place in the personalities of Russia's men of conscience:

No matter where you look, everywhere you will find an awakening of personality (a claim for its legitimate rights), a protest against violence and tyranny (in most cases still timid, indefinite, ready to hide, but for all that) already making its existence felt.[8]

This new kind of person was a symptom of impending change as well as the agent who was to carry it out. Also, by all the tenets of Dobrolyubov's creed, he was an obvious candidate for the role of the literary hero. The quest for the hero gives a focus to all Dobrolyubov's moral, social, political, and literary concerns, and to his brief, hectic career as well.

II

Dobrolyubov's controversial manifesto, "What Is Oblomovism?" was intended to proclaim the ceremonial burial of the superfluous man. Looking back over thirty years of the new Russian realism, Dobrolyubov claimed to have made a striking discovery about Russian literary heroes. Using Goncharov's *Oblomov* as his point of departure, he generalized angrily about the unvarying pattern of weakness, egotism, and inactivity these heroes describe. A generalization which links Lermontov's Byronic bully, Pechorin, with Goncharov's amiable sloven, Oblomov, may seem too careless of distinctions to possess much meaning. But if we recall basic assumptions of the radical school the important likenesses shared by Onegin, Pechorin, and Turgenev's Rudin become clear. Literary event and literary character are seen and judged exclusively against the world they are taken from. These imagined figures are treated as *descriptions* of types in the real world and their common crime is their failure to act morally and effectively in the fictional semblance of the real world. Dobrolyubov is perfectly clear about this: Oblomovism is a moral and social disease widespread in Russian life itself. Literature has done its job well in exposing and diagnosing the illness. But life has moved on and literature must bestir itself to catch up.

Many reasons were advanced for the fatal self-absorption and the

[8] *Ibid.*, p. 575.

paralysis of will which afflicted these unhappy men. The crucial determinants, in Dobrolyubov's view, were the multiple pressures arising from the feudal environment. In the atmosphere of tyranny and
stagnation, a number of people, it is true, had been able to achieve a
certain independence from dominant values. But even when they had
reached the point of formulating their code of dissent, exhaustion or
cowardice or self-deception prevented them from acting. Their intentions often remained uncorrupted, but they were never tested by use.
Serfdom, however, was in its death agony, and the superfluous men,
who had filled a genuine need by questioning or standing aloof or
preaching, were now felt to be inadequate to the task of moving society forward to the new order. With the further decay of the social
order would come a lessening of its poisonous effects on moral character, a trend which would make it easier for men to liberate themselves and assert their "natural" virtue. Convictions held in idleness
could no longer be considered a praiseworthy achievement, or a sufficiently spirited response to the hateful milieu. "We need men of action and not of abstract ... argument,"[9] Dobrolyubov wrote in his
review of Turgenev's *On the Eve*, which bears the characteristically
impatient title, "When Will the Day Come?" Correct principles have
become common property, and now await the kind of men who will
put them into practice.

The successor to the superfluous man had a name and a set of characteristics before he had been reliably reported to exist: he was called
"the new man." As first conceived, he was in one sense a development
beyond his predecessors, and in another sense—notably in his thirst
for action—a direct antithesis to them. Writers were obliged to search
for the new active man in fulfillment of their public responsibilities.
The writer who continued to reproduce the images of alienated men
and the aura of defeatism that surrounded them made a bad work of
art because he had made an "incorrect" selection of subject matter.
Dobrolyubov is clear about the possibilities of error on this score:

If ... he [the writer] has tried to raise one of his personages to the level
of a universal type and the critic proves that the importance of the character is extremely limited and small, it will follow clearly that the author
has spoilt his production by his false views concerning the hero.[10]

9 *Ibid.*, p. 396.
10 *Ibid.* Here the critic appears as the custodian of the truth. Later, Dobrolyubov insisted that the new man must occupy a central position in literature because the public

But Dobrolyubov's tireless scrutiny of literature indicated that the image of the positive hero was disappointingly elusive. He suspected at times that the new type existed only in his own expectations. At other times, he indicated that he was very close to finding him, or that the hero had been discovered in some incomplete form, or that a careless author simply had not known a hero when he saw him. Then again, Dobrolyubov seemed ready to conclude that the circumstances of Russian life were still exercising their harsh sovereignty over the growth of the new moral personality, and, though the public expected him and the movement of history guaranteed that he would come, he had not yet reached maturity. But Dobrolyubov persisted in the certainty that the new moral type must ultimately come to exist.

III

According to Dobrolyubov's optimal expectations, the new man, freed of the curse of inertia when he became aware of his condition, would know his own strength, who his enemies were, and how to attack them. Factual knowledge of his environment, which had become widespread by this time, was not the only resource available to the man who thirsted to act. He was blessed with a generous endowment of "natural" goodness and strength, and a vivid emotional awareness of his "natural" rights. These resources, if they managed to survive the gauntlet of the Russian environment, including the adverse effects of a false educational system, would supply him with the energy and courage to put his principles into practice, and to make use of his knowledge.

These natural attributes of character which are the birthright of all men are described variously by Dobrolyubov at various points in his work, but they have one common denominator: they are the virtues that overcome inertia and lead to fearless, direct action. Dobrolyubov drew a sharp contrast between the moral characteristics of the people and of the gentry. The primary virtues retained by the people (and lost by the gentry) are not those the Slavophiles claim to find—passivity, endurance, resignation—nor are the common people without serious faults. But the burden of the destructive environment, contrary to belief, has weighed more heavily on the upper classes and caused

---

demanded it: "Russian life has at last reached the stage where virtuous and esteemed, but weak and spineless, individuals no longer satisfy the public conscience and are regarded as totally useless. An urgent need is felt for men who, if less beautiful in character, are more active and energetic." *Ibid.*, p. 594.

a much greater disfigurement of moral character than it has among the working people. The idleness and artificiality of the landowners' lives create a personality without purpose or resolution or the ability or inclination to act for moral ends:

General debility, morbidness, incapacity for concentrated and profound passions, characterize, if not all, then at all events the majority of our "civilized" brothers. That is why they are continuously darting hither and thither, themselves not knowing what they need and what it is they are sorry for. Their desire is so strong that they cannot live without gratifying it, and yet they do nothing to gratify it; their sufferings are so great that death is preferable—but they go on living just the same, except that they assume a melancholy air.[11]

Despite the effects of social inferiority and economic oppression, the people have kept intact much more of their inherited legacy of natural virtues: a natural acceptance of work, hatred of tyranny and exploitation, and a strong sense of the inviolable dignity of the human person. In the pursuit of a desired object, their behavior reflects these simple virtues:

Either he [the common man] ignores, pays no attention to an object, and certainly does not talk about his desires; or, if he becomes attached to anything, if he makes a decision, he does so vigorously, with concentration, and pursues his object relentlessly. His passion is deep and persevering and no obstacles daunt him when it is necessary to surmount them in order to achieve what he passionately desires and has deeply planned. If the object cannot be achieved, the common man will not stand by with folded arms; he will change his situation, his whole way of life; he will run away, join the army, enter a monastery; often he simply does not survive failure to achieve an object which has permeated his whole being and has become essential to his existence ... he does not hesitate to commit suicide. This, too, serves to prove to us that for the common, healthy man, once he has become conscious of his personality (and of its rights), the barren, useless life of an automaton (without principles and strivings) without meaning and truth ... becomes unbearable.[12]

Presumably, suicide registers in an ultimate way an individual's determination and capacity to act. It did not seem absurd, apparently, to the angry young revolutionary to consider suicide or martyrdom

[11] *Ibid.*, p. 511.
[12] *Ibid.*, p. 512. These contrasting evaluations are taken from the article "Features of the Russian Common People," in which Dobrolyubov develops his theory of human nature. The central problem is to harmonize personal with social interests, a synthesis denied the "civilized" man because "lack of self-confidence" has corroded his sense of his own rights and caused him to doubt the workings of his mind.

as "healthy" acts of rebellion. Although he never said it in so many words, he seems at times to be making the even more absurd proposal that suicide is a kind of program for social action. Dostoevsky may well have found his cue here when he created Kirillov, the brilliantly absurd philosopher of self-destruction in *The Possessed*, who hoped to liberate men from their fear of death and of God by his own exemplary suicide. Dobrolyubov had no such grandiose intentions but the gesture of angry defiance is the same in each case, and it seems plausible to read Kirillov as a grotesque extension of Dobrolyubov's light-minded views on self-destruction. As a plain tactical matter it would seem that Dobrolyubov's heroes are a little too ready to die to do the cause much good.

Suicide, in Dobrolyubov's uncomplicated understanding of it, signifies a simple kind of virtuous strength, which is found in abundance among the common people. Dobrolyubov is not suggesting that the new hero will be from the lower orders. He is saying, rather, that the new man in his search for moral strength should learn from the people in whose name he finds the ultimate justifications for his acts. It is the suffering of the common people that dignifies his efforts, it is their terrible anger that he must arouse, and their strength that he must direct. They may provide, too, in the example of their lives, the answer to the fatal breakdown of character which paralyzed the potential leaders of preceding generations.

With this blueprint in hand, Dobrolyubov set out in search of the hero of his time among current literary portraits. A number of examples are rejected out of hand. Any suggestion of the superfluous man's faint heart is unacceptable because history has rendered it obsolete. Also invalid are all efforts by writers to inject their own abstract notions of Russian valor into an imagined protagonist. The character must have genuine moral stature, must be capable of action, and must be presented in compelling and verifiable detail.

Anany, the peasant hero of Pisemsky's *A Bitter Fate*, is dismissed as absurd.[13] Driven to physical violence by the landowner's dalliance with his wife, he undermines the moral value of his position thereby, and exhibits in his behavior nothing more than brute strength. Goncharov's Stolz (in *Oblomov*), one of the most deliberate efforts to create a wholly positive, emblematically good man, is dismissed on two counts: the limited, mundane quality of his morality, and the ab-

---

[13] *Ibid.*, p. 595.

stractness of his literary portrait. The self-disciplined, practical businessman represents an advance, in some ways, over earlier types, but
the practicality of his concerns denies him participation in loftier
matters of social principle. Of this new bourgeois type, Dobrolyubov
says:

The best that we can hope for as regards these practical men is that they
should resemble Stolz, that is to say, be able to make a clean job of all
their affairs without sinking to roguery; they cannot, however, become
virile (public) leaders.[14]

"No greater hopes" can be placed in this individual than in the "man
of pathos" as "representatives of the public movement" that has come
alive in Russia.[15] This is enough to disqualify them as heroes in Russian life, hence, according to the view that recognizes no important
differences between life and art, in works of the imagination as well.
But Goncharov's failure to create Stolz with the wealth of detail that
he lavished on Oblomov is further justification for rejecting him. He
moves "in a mist," without effective motivation, without an inner
life that explains his self-confident behavior.

Turgenev's *On the Eve* was carefully scrutinized for traces of the
new Russian heroism. Insarov, the central male figure, is disqualified
on technical grounds—he is a Bulgarian, not a Russian! In addition,
he suffers from the blurred delineation that mars the image of Stolz.
"As a living image, as a real personality, Insarov is extremely remote
from us," Dobrolyubov said, and "is depicted for us only in pale and
general outline."[16] Because of his "indomitable loyalty to an idea," he
is a challenging figure, nevertheless, to find in a Russian novel. He
displays, in the unity of his private and public emotions, and in his
total dedication to the liberation of his country, an integration of mind,
body, conscience, and heart in the service of a cause that Dobrolyubov
was never to find realized in a Russian character. His abstract "outline," vague and unsatisfactory as it is, stands as a master design for
the dedicated revolutionary, as relevant in some ways to the Communist present as it was to the generation of the fifties and sixties. The
points of similarity are the total mobilization of personal resources in
the fulfillment of a single purpose, always a public one, the unquestioned rejection of the private pursuits of ordinary man, and a willingness to endure any sacrifice. He has no doubts: "The happiness of his

[14] *Ibid.*, p. 598.   [15] *Ibid.*, p. 599.   [16] *Ibid.*, p. 419.

whole life is vitally engaged in the single project; he has no personal ambitions at stake, and no disposition, for example, to quarrel over the leadership of his movement."[17] "Insarov's love for the freedom of his country lies not alone in his mind, or in his heart or in his imagination: it permeates his whole being, and whatever else penetrates his being is transformed by the power of this feeling, submits to it, and merges with it."[18] Dobrolyubov invokes his favorite measure to show the effects of frustration on Insarov if circumstances were to deny him the chance to perform his duty: "He would die."[19]

Eliminated from the Russian hero competition on a technicality, Insarov is nevertheless useful to Dobrolyubov as a yardstick against which to measure the Russians in the same novel. They are more brilliant and more complex than Insarov, and men of equally lofty moral aims. Yet they do not act. They still measure their private interests against the interests of society—a meaningless dichotomy for Insarov —and keep their highly developed sense of principle intact by never risking it in action. The Russians are not members of an inferior order of humanity. But they are deprived of a tangible enemy, and cannot play the relatively simple role of "hero-liberator" against a foreign occupier:

An external enemy, a privileged oppressor, can be attacked and vanquished far more easily than an internal enemy, whose forces are spread everywhere in a thousand different shapes, elusive and invulnerable, harassing us on all sides, poisoning our lives, giving us no rest. ... This internal enemy cannot be combated with ordinary weapons; we can liberate ourselves from him only by dispelling the raw, foggy atmosphere of our lives in which he was born, grew up and gained strength, and by surrounding ourselves with an atmosphere in which he will be unable to breathe.[20]

Dobrolyubov's conclusions are gloomy. There is no arena in Russia for Insarov's kind of heroism. In addition, the hostile environment has begun to disfigure the moral character of potential heroes from the earliest days of their education. Only a clear-cut, unambiguous cause could provide the scope for action which would release the latent energies of the men of good will. Dobrolyubov veers close to despair:

(How can you expect heroism here? And if a hero is born, where is he to obtain the light and wisdom to enable him to expend his strength in the

---

[17] *Ibid.*, p. 410.   [18] *Ibid.*
[19] *Ibid.*   [20] *Ibid.*, p. 437.

service of virtue and truth instead of wasting it? And even if he at last acquires this light and wisdom, how can he, weary and broken, display heroism? How can a toothless squirrel nibble nuts?)[21]

The individual's struggle to reach the threshold of heroic public service is itself a work of heroism, but he has so often suffered serious moral injury in this preliminary battle that the absence of a goal when he finally arrives causes him to succumb to his wounds or waste his remaining energies in trivial activities, "playing the Don Quixote."

IV

Is there any way to break out of the smothering environment without being destroyed in the effort? Are there any more trustworthy signs that the new personality, capable of rising above the world that created him, is likely to make an early appearance? There are, in fact, a number, and through a knowledge of them, sketchy and premonitory though they are, we shall arrive at Dobrolyubov's clearest definition of the nature of the new hero and of his arenas of action.

Not all the Russian characters in *On the Eve* are "toothless squirrels." There is one person who has moved beyond the stage of indoctrinated paralysis that afflicts the Russian men in the novel. This individual, together with two others, the creations of Goncharov and Ostrovsky, the dramatist, form, in composite, the most complete portrait of the new man Dobrolyubov was able to find. Curiously, it is a woman's face that emerges. Dobrolyubov arranges three literary heroines, typical of the impulsive, straightforward feminine figures in Russian literature since Pushkin's Tatyana, in an ascending order of virtue and effectiveness. Beginning with Olga in *Oblomov*, proceeding to Elena in Turgenev's *On the Eve*, and ending with Katerina in Ostrovsky's *Storm*, he thought he had discovered the basic trend toward stronger, more resilient characters. Though not yet fully developed, they were the first authentic images of the new type.

Olga is much preferred by Dobrolyubov to Stolz, the busy entrepreneur, more German than Russian, whose motivation is never made clear, whose goals lack public significance. It is true, the scope of her activity is scarcely of heroic dimensions. But in her hopeless effort to win Oblomov's love and reclaim him from sloth, she displays genuine moral strength; she is determined, ready to defy convention, and the

21 *Ibid.*, p. 433.

picture of a vital "natural" woman in love. Though the rehabilitation of a good-natured sluggard is ludicrous as a social project and is doomed, moreover, to failure, she has acted throughout with understanding and decision. She has, in addition, recognized one face of the ubiquitous internal enemy in the pitiable and "repulsive" figure of Oblomov and has fought strenuously against it. Finally, Dobrolyubov praises her because her defeat has not seriously discouraged her. A single hint in a conversation with Stolz that she is readier than he to fight against encroaching "troubles" is taken as final proof of her dignity and promise.[22]

Turgenev's Elena is the same kind of person, endowed in addition with the special radiance of all his feminine characters. Her sensitivity to the suffering of others and a habit of questioning dominant values have prepared her for purposeful activity. But, again, the arena of action open to her is severely restricted. She operates on a trivial scale, giving alms to the poor and rescuing stray kittens. Her one major act, however, her marriage to the Bulgarian activist, Insarov, is carried out with exemplary courage and directness, and in open defiance of social convention. Unfortunately for the novel's topical usefulness, her act removes her from Russia and serves only as a final preparation for a career of active service outside the framework of the novel. But the example of her virtuous behavior in these personal matters indicates the trend toward more and more effective people, specifically, toward a Russian Insarov.[23]

Ostrovsky's Katerina, the heroine of *Storm*, trapped in the suffocating tyranny of her husband's merchant family, is in a more desperate situation. She is bullied by her mother-in-law, is, in effect, deserted by her husband, and finally compromises herself in a hopeless effort to find love outside marriage. Consequently, she acts more drastically to free herself—by committing suicide. Dobrolyubov sees this as an act of defiance, not of despair, the only unblocked path to her liberation. Her refusal to submit to a way of life which smothers all her "natural" strivings is interpreted as the moral equivalent of an act of political rebellion. In the patriarchal household of one merchant family, Dobrolyubov found in microcosm the worst of Russia, "the kingdom of darkness." The rebel against it, then, represents in her single person vast legions in the outside world.

---

[22] *Ibid.*, p. 216.   [23] *Ibid.*, p. 436.

Katerina's character is analyzed at length to uncover the source of her strength. The central virtue she possesses is one which is lacking in the noblest and most brilliant of her superfluous predecessors. With a mind uncluttered by abstractions, she is motivated solely by the "instinctive consciousness of her inalienable right to life, happiness, and love."[24] Her awareness of her rights is so urgent that she meets and passes the supreme test of her courage, the willingness *to risk* death. Convinced that her death symbolizes an ultimate challenge to the existing order, Dobrolyubov insists that it is a "joyous" and "inspiring thing," serving notice to tyranny that "it is impossible to live any longer with its violent and deadening principles."[25] Contrasted with her husband, a "living corpse," who is afraid to die, Katerina's death reminds us of her life: ("What joyous, fresh life breathes to us from the healthy personality which finds the resolution to put an end to this decaying life at all costs.")[26] Her death is an inspiration.

V

The problem of the hero's need to break through the encircling environment comes into focus in recapitulation. Knowledge, both factual and theoretical, is a first requirement for the new man. But this need has long been met. First principles have been enunciated; facts to buttress them have been gathered and analyzed; and the hard-won legacy of Belinsky's generation is by now common property. Enough people have survived the Russian environment intact, and have reached an understanding of the need for radical change. Now the formula for social consciousness has been brought to the verge of completion as Dobrolyubov conceived it: from fact to idea to intention to longing and finally to action. The last was the most difficult step of all, the insuperable barrier for all the superfluous men. Since Dobrolyubov was sure that knowledge of the laws of history must lead to action, it is clear that an essential ingredient is still missing. It is, we are told, the inner moral strength of individuals which will finally set the mechanism of change in motion. "One must have," it is true, "the mind of a genius," but one must possess as well "the pure heart of an infant and a will of titanic power to dare to enter into a real and effective struggle against the environment."[27] Despite the relative triviality of their feats, and the modesty of their intellectual equip-

[24] *Ibid.*, p. 614.
[26] *Ibid.*
[25] *Ibid.*, p. 626.
[27] *Ibid.*, p. 287.

ment, Olga, Elena, and Katerina redress a most important imbalance. The superfluous ones had been men whose minds had been overdeveloped at the expense of their hearts. Now Russians had been shown vivid human images who incorporated a finished design for a harmonious relationship between intellect and emotion. This kind of harmony is the final desideratum in the prescription.

Action is generated in the individual's awareness of the discrepancy between the "natural strivings" of his heart and the repeated, senseless violations of human dignity in Russian life. The "natural" man, the vital, wholehearted person who has preserved his total human birthright, confronted with intolerable conditions, will simply refuse to submit to them. This new "strong Russian character," the prospective agent of social change, "is guided not by abstract principles but by practical considerations, and not by fleeting pathos but simply by its nature, by its whole being."[28] Dobrolyubov continues: "The integrity and harmony of this character constitute its strength." He is "concentrated and resolute, undeviatingly loyal to the sense of (natural) truth, imbued with faith (in new ideals) and is self-sacrificing (in the sense that he prefers death to life under a system which he detests)."[29]

The hero's moral personality contains the program and the means for action, as well as the guarantee of its success. The hero, in a sense, *is* the revolution. Discussion of doctrine and of action groups—parties, cells, circles, unions—was proscribed in the press. But the impatient Dobrolyubov suggests that as soon as the new hero has appeared in sufficient numbers, the process of change will be launched without the need for further preparations. This man, in whom such extravagant hopes were invested, would not be alone—any number could join his ranks; the virtues and the ideas that would motivate him were available to all, even the illiterate; and he would have willing followers among all oppressed sections of the population.

From his criticism of Goncharov, Turgenev, Saltykov, Pleshcheev, and others, it seems clear that if a literary protagonist acted with moral courage in virtually any personal relationship—a love affair or a family situation, for example—Dobrolyubov was ready to accept his conduct as proof of his capacity to act positively and humanely in other arenas. It was a commonplace of Russian criticism to view a novel's intimate

[28] *Ibid.*, p. 597.   [29] *Ibid.*

personal settings—Turgenev's drawing rooms and rose arbors, for example—as testing grounds of behavior in more dangerous, frequently unmentionable, arenas of action. With this reduction of scale, it is easier to identify the enemy. Since the crushing of human personality by any means is the ultimate measure of society's evil, artificial conventions, or tyrannical parents, or the compound injustices of woman's status are seen as *causes* of human suffering and acceptable targets for those not yet able to attack the social system *in toto*. A strong, active, flexible person will meet these hostile forces head-on by acting morally as father, husband, lover, employer, or friend.

The enemy, once the "raw, foggy atmosphere" has been dispelled, can be found, and every blow struck against him is valuable. These are only preliminary engagements, it is true, but they lead directly into the final, decisive conflict. Dobrolyubov's essays are full of cryptic references to the approaching moment of explosion.[30] This note, which sounds just below the surface of his writings, promises a no-quarter, physical struggle instead of the contest waged solely in the indirect discourse of literary criticism. In one of the analogies favored by these critics, as necessary circumlocution, Dobrolyubov compares progress to a road reaching into the future. The road is blocked by an "obstacle" which has thwarted the effort of previous generations, forcing them on hopeless searches for detours, or destroying their characters by its immovability. Dobrolyubov's prescription was simple, and of course unprintable—("blow it up!").[31] Literature stands fully revealed now as a camouflage for more urgent purposes. We may conclude that when Dobrolyubov's hero reaches the height of his moral and intellectual power he will be a disciplined, dedicated, one-man revolutionary movement, incapable of compromise and indifferent to personal defeat. And his literary representation will have been no more than a means to bring him into being.

Dobrolyubov's theory of human nature and his view of the sources of social consciousness have been criticized by some Soviet commentators who felt that he was too inclined to fix the locus of the conflict between old and new in the realm of ideas, in the mind, and within the individual's power to arbitrate. But the profound shift of emphasis since 1930 in the Soviet theory of human behavior has brought Soviet

---

[30] Their dangerous import is confirmed by the censor's deletions.
[31] Dobrolyubov, *Selected Philosophical Essays*, p. 452.

critics to a more sympathetic consideration of Dobrolyubov's view of freedom.[32] His hero and the new Soviet man are conscious, disciplined, morally responsible individuals, made free by their knowledge, yet entirely dominated by their sense of responsibility to history and to the public welfare. All their choices are preceded by an act of basic commitment to the cause, which may be likened to a one-party election, that is to say, it is a one-choice decision. But the theorists of both views place heavy emphasis on will, initiative, and consciousness within the limits of the code of loyalty.

It is well to remember that Dobrolyubov frankly disqualifies himself from the traditional offices of literary criticism. "The main task of the literary critic," he wrote, "is to explain the phenomenon of reality which called a given artistic production into being."[33] This explains the fact that he ignored the problem of incorporating the new affirmative hero in conventional literary forms. He assumed, apparently, that the new hero would succeed the tragic-pathetic figures of the superfluous era without difficulty on the formal level. The new literature would be better simply because it reflected a more advanced social morality. The writer, expected to produce a condensed record of Russian life, had only to worry about the accuracy of his eye and the soundness of his judgment in discerning the true, the typical, and the significant. Dobrolyubov never dwelt at length on problems of conflict or suspense, or of dramatic resolution, whether tragic, comic, affirmative, or inspirational. The degree of his indifference is made clear in his misreading of Ostrovsky's *Storm*. He simply overlooks the fact that Katerina kills herself in a mood of despair, not of defiance. By this ingenious misinterpretation, in which he is encouraged by his peculiar view of suicide, he reads his own topical concerns into the play and converts it from a conventional tragic drama into an inspirational document with a kind of happy ending. Dobrolyubov simply felt that an heroic death moved people to admiration. In one of his first prescriptions for the new man he pointed out that he must be unafraid of death, but that if he does die (whether or not by his own hand) the example of his defiant courage, as recorded in some sort of literary communiqué, will surely summon others to fill the gap he has left.

[32] This is confirmed, for example, in V. S. Kruzhkov, *Mirovozzrenie N. A. Dobrolyubova* (Moscow, 1952).

[33] Dobrolyubov, *Selected Philosophical Essays*, p. 391. Elsewhere he describes his work as "factual criticism."

CHAPTER 5

Chernyshevsky: "The Salt of the Salt of the Earth"

Nikolai Chernyshevsky (1828–89) was the encyclopedist of the radical democratic movement. He worked in many disciplines—philosophy, political economy, history, philology, and literary criticism—to provide an intellectual foundation for the movement of political protest he headed. Among many accomplishments, he gave consistency and unity to the doctrine of the literature of social service. In his important dissertation, *The Aesthetic Relations of Art to Reality*, he formulated the critical ideas of his school in the terms of formal philosophical discourse. When no one else could meet his literary standards he wrote a novel, the celebrated *What Is to Be Done?* By his work at these opposite ends of literature, and by the sheer weight of his influence, he established himself as the central figure in the radical literary tradition. He performed the principal work of interpreting (and reducing) Belinsky; he supplied Dobrolyubov with the philosophical assumptions of his journalistic criticism; and his novel is the chief literary souvenir of this phase of the utilitarian movement. The full extent of his influence on Soviet thinking is yet to be assessed. It has become apparent, for example, that he was an enormously important figure in Lenin's life,[1] and must be considered one of the principal authors of the native strain in Soviet Marxian ideology.

In his dissertation Chernyshevsky attempted to fix his view of literature with respect to some of the permanent problems of art—the nature of the beautiful and of artistic invention, and the quality of

[1] See below, p. 82.

art's relations with nature and society. His enforced adherence to canons of academic respectability and to the idiom of abstract argument kept his topical concerns in the background, though there is evidence that they were obscure to no one: his followers welcomed the dissertation as a powerful new weapon in their armory; Turgenev reacted as though stung; and the academicians expressed their doubts about its disinterestedness by piously delaying their approval.[2] No doubt, his ultimate point of reference in this essay, as in all else he wrote or did, was the unhealthy condition of Russian society. He wrote a number of popular articles—one an unsigned "self-review" of his published dissertation—to give his ideas a cutting edge for use in the literary battles of the time. With the help of this comment and interpretation by the author we are able to move from a level of abstraction, to the level of polemical comment inhabited by Dobrolyubov, and, finally, to the act of literary creation itself. The novel *What Is to Be Done?*, with its gallery of radiantly virtuous new men, appears as the logical end product of the theory, a kind of pilot-model, designed to illustrate his new aesthetic principles. As a result of this link between theory and practice, Chernyshevsky's work transcends its local origins in Russian intellectual history and presents the essence of the radical utilitarian literary position.

The tenor of Chernyshevsky's approach is suggested by his approval of Plato's scornful estimate of art's value to a well-ordered society. The Russian critic felt that Plato's "sarcasms" were perhaps too cruel and "one-sided" for modern times.[3] But his sympathy with the underlying trend of Plato's thought is evident, and there is an ironic forecast, too, of the relations between poet and magistrate—and of the arguments used to justify them—in the Soviet Union:

First of all Plato thought that man must be the citizen of a state, must not dream about things not needed by the state, and must live nobly and actively, promoting the material and moral welfare of his fellow citizens.... He looked on science and art, as he looked on everything, not from the scholarly or artistic but from the social and moral point of view. Man does not live to be a scholar or an artist (as many great philosophers have thought, among them Aristotle) but science and art must serve man's welfare.[4]

[2] N. G. Chernyshevsky, *Estetika*, ed. N. G. Bogoslovsky (Moscow-Leningrad, 1939). See Bogoslovsky's introductory article for a summary of these reactions.
[3] See Chernyshevsky's review of a contemporary translation of Aristotle's *Poetics*, "O Poezii, sochinenie Aristotelya," in *Estetika*, pp. 224–28.
[4] *Ibid.*, p. 226. Chernyshevsky's views differ considerably from Soviet attitudes

Chernyshevsky was not concerned, of course, with protecting the stability of a future social order from art's subversion. In his view a frivolous, irresponsible, or self-serving art was simply a pernicious waste of time. Therefore, though he agreed with Plato in demeaning all views of art as "play," or as an object of pleasure, his attitude was one of suspicious impatience with art, rather than of fear of its effects. His tone is drastic, nevertheless, and his denunciations are sweeping.

Chernyshevsky begins with one basic proposition: that art is in all ways subordinate to life, that it is dependent on the external world for its substance, its form, its energy, its relevance to human affairs— and for its appeal to man's sense of beauty, to the extent that beauty is a concern of art at all.[5]

The severity of his attack on all inflated estimates of art's mission is prompted in part by the extreme position of his hand-picked opponent, the German idealist Vischer.[6] But in his denunciation of Vischer he challenged positions much closer to home, notably Turgenev's. He quarrels with all views which assert that art improves on reality, or completes or gives permanence to it, or has the right to impose on it a design of its own. Art dare pretend to no such preeminence over the world it depends on and rather imperfectly reflects. And when Vischer maintained that art was a search for absolute truth, above the imperfections and the impermanence of natural phenomena, and that fantasy, which departs entirely from reality and bases its perceptions on dreams, was the highest form of art, Chernyshevsky felt that an ultimate absurdity had been reached. In rebuttal, he asserted flatly that the material of art is always and unavoidably drawn from life, and that art may record experience well or badly, but it may never claim to transcend its model, which is the source of all significance and beauty. Art is essentially a medium for discovering the meaningful facts in the real world, and for transmitting this information directly to the reader. Its value depends on the accuracy with which this relatively humble act of reporting is carried out; and any effort by the

---

toward Plato and Aristotle. Despite resemblances between the authoritarian elements in Plato's prescription for the model society and certain aspects of Soviet reality, his overall position is rejected as "idealist" and reactionary. Aristotle, on the other hand, is celebrated as the first materialist aesthetician, the first "predecessor," therefore, of the Marxist aesthetic. See L. I. Timofeev, *Teoriya literatury* (Moscow, 1938), p. 42. Aristotle is a figure of special importance in this study because his theory of tragedy is the most enduring obstacle in the way of the literature of positive heroes.

[5] *Estetika*, pp. 12–13, 50–55.

[6] Friedrich Theodor Vischer, whose six-volume *Aesthetik oder Wissenschaft des Schoenen* (Leipzig, 1846–58) is the single source he cites in his dissertation.

artist to interfere in this process by embellishing the original, or by imposing "artificial" formal patterns on it, can only result in falsification.

The imaginative faculty itself comes under attack in this connection. It is first of all weak:

The power of our imagination is extremely limited and its creations are
very pale and feeble compared with reality. The most vivid imagination is
overwhelmed by the thought of the millions of miles that separate the earth
from the sun.[7]

Careful observation of everyday life indicates that the most intensely
imagined hero or villain can always be eclipsed by instances from life,
and that art deals only with "copies of what is provided by the phenomenon of reality."[8] Elsewhere he suggests that the imagination is
associated with self-serving daydreams and the fantasies of self-indulgence. Here he collides head-on with Turgenev and others who
felt that the artist's vocation was a kind of priestcraft, that the truth of
art was a special kind of personal vision, and that the imaginative
ordering of experience was the indispensable means to its unique discoveries.

Chernyshevsky's definition of what art is not and cannot do rests
on his view of the aesthetic process itself. The beautiful, as we have
seen, is a property of nature and is not "created" by the artist. Even
in its original state the beautiful is a by-product of natural processes,
incidental to their purposes, and irrelevant for the most part to human
life. The enjoyment of beauty is a secondary aspect of the emotion
communicated by art, but is one of the many services, nevertheless,
that art provides. To maintain that pleasure in the beautiful is the
end of art is to debase it, Chernyshevsky insisted, to reduce it to the
level of a good dinner or a comfortable apartment.[9]

Art's purposes are far more solemn and more profoundly concerned
with vital problems of human existence: "The source and aims of art
are the needs of man," Chernyshevsky wrote in his "self-review,"[10]
and the legitimate province of art, as a consequence, is simply "everything that interests man."[11] Freed from arbitrary limitations on its
subject matter and endowed with a purpose much greater than plea-

[7] From the seventh of the "Essays on the Gogol Period of Russian Literature," in
N. G. Chernyshevsky, *Selected Philosophical Essays* (Moscow, 1953), p. 489.
[8] *Ibid.*   [9] See *Estetika*, pp. 229–30.
[10] *Ibid.*, p. 206.   [11] *Ibid.*, p. 88.

surable gratification, art is prepared for the career of service which alone entitles it to man's highest respect.

Having arrived at Belinsky's definition of literature's basic moral purposes, though by a different route, Chernyshevsky twice (and rather casually) connects the idea of the beautiful with these purposes. The search for beauty must not become the artist's primary activity, but, since it is a legitimate end, let the artist know where to look for it. Beauty is found in life and in nature but there are differences of degree in its intensity. No landscape painting or nature lyric can bear comparison with the representation of man, himself, in art. Since man is nature's "highest" product he is, therefore, its most beautiful object:

In the entire sensuous world man is the highest being; therefore, the human personality is the highest being in the world which is accessible to our feelings, and all other aspects of existence partake of the beautiful only to the degree that they allude to or remind us of man. . . . The highest sphere of the beautiful is human society.[12]

Since a moral and social ideal of man is at the very heart of the concept of the beautiful, the artist who represents virtuous men in their social role is assured that he is at the same time "copying" nature and conveying beauty to his readers.

In another connection Chernyshevsky identifies the beautiful with the morally and socially desirable. Summoning Aristotle to his support, Chernyshevsky includes both elements of the famous distinction between life "as it is" and life "as it should be" as essential ingredients of his realism. In his dissertation he offers this definition: "The beautiful is the essence in which we see life as it should be according to our concepts."[13] There can be no doubt that however "should be" is defined—as the necessary, the probable, the desirable, or the hoped for—it introduces an alien element which may challenge realism's canon of verisimilitude. Elsewhere he puts it this way: "The beautiful is that in which we see life as we understand it and wish it."[14] Chernyshevsky did not insist too much on this point—it is even possible that he did not sense the difficulty—but, as we shall see, by injecting his expectations into the fabric of his own novel, without distinguishing them from "actual" events, he damaged his novel so badly that he subverted his own purposes.

[12] Quoted in Timofeev, *Teoriya literatury*, pp. 45–46.
[13] Chernyshevsky, *Estetika*, p. 8.   [14] *Ibid.*, p. 20.

On this abstract level Chernyshevsky's thought pursues a course already observed in Belinsky: from a broad attack on conventional restrictions, he goes on to impose a new pattern of limitations on the artist. In this pattern we discover the actual conditions of art's subordination to "life," to "nature," and to "human needs." Art occupies a secondary position, for example, with respect to the social and natural sciences:

Poetry distributes an enormous amount of information among the mass of readers, and, what is more important, a familiarity with concepts developed by science—this is poetry's great significance for life.[15]

Art will convey these data in its own idiom but its value to mankind will depend on the performance of this task, not the grace or skill with which it is done. The transmission of this kind of data is a logical consequence of literature's obligation to serve human needs and to deal with whatever "interests men." When we realize what "interested" Chernyshevsky and what he assumed "interested" the reading public, it becomes clear that under the pretense of broadening literature's horizons he has only shifted its focus to material as marginal to the concerns of realism as the "fantasies" of Vischer. By converting art into an educational medium, or a means of publicizing the findings of other disciplines, he renders more explicit his desire to make art's local utility the first standard for judging it. The desire to communicate data and ideas about social and economic problems—the status of women, the advantages of producer cooperatives, his ethic of social service—was Chernyshevsky's primary motive in writing his own novel.

His general insistence that art subordinate itself to "life" or even to human needs need not, in itself, have offended leading writers. The view that art existed for its own or for the artist's sake had no great currency during the fruitful years of the classical tradition. But Chernyshevsky's further restrictive definition of these terms betrays the real narrowness of intention, which was decisive in alienating the great writers from his views. Turgenev reacted violently to Chernyshevsky's celebrated description of art as life's "surrogate,"[16] or "textbook," and raised important objections to the whole radical aesthetic:

Concerning Chernyshevsky's book—here is my chief objection to it: in his eyes, art, as he himself expresses it, is only the surrogate for reality, for

[15] *Ibid.*, p. 231.   [16] *Ibid.*, p. 83.

life—and in essence is suited only for immature people. Whichever way he turns, this idea of his lies at the basis of everything. And this in my opinion is nonsense. In the real world there is no Shakespearean Hamlet—or perhaps he exists—but Shakespeare discovered him and made him public property. Chernyshevsky takes a great deal on himself if he imagines he can always go to the heart of life.... No, brother, his book is false and harmful.[17]

Art is only a substitute for firsthand experience, or, as Chernyshevsky sometimes puts it, it "reminds" (the word suggests vacation snapshots or family portraits on the wall) the reader of what he has already experienced. He could, of course, simply assert that this was so. But to establish his point he had finally to come to terms with literature's traditional modes of expression: the comic, the sublime, and—a major obstacle for the advocate of an optimistic literature—the tragic.

The persistence of tragic forms through history, and their repeated success in organizing experience into illuminating moral patterns, presented Chernyshevsky with a primary challenge. His response was to discredit the entire tragic mechanism by demonstrating its rigidity and falsity when set against the variety, the accidents, and the consequent unpredictability of experience. The source of tragedy's inflexibility he traced back to Aristotle, who taught, he said, "the writing of tragedy ... according to recipe":

From this it is evident that Aristotle as an aesthetician belongs to the times of the decline of art: instead of a living spirit there is the teaching of rules, a cold formalism.[18]

The tragic "rules" are harmful because they offer only a single mold into which a countless number of human situations must be forced, and they offer only one kind of response for the spectator, catharsis through pity and terror. The tyranny of this single pattern rests on the unchallenged supremacy of formal devices and the uncritical acceptance of primitive superstitions. The concept of fate, for example, is an outworn legacy from the primitive Greeks without basis in

[17] Letter to V. P. Botkin (July 25, 1885), *Sobranie sochinenii*, 11 (Moscow, 1949): 130. We simply note here the vehemence of his feelings and the quality of his objections. In the flurry of letters he wrote after he read the dissertation his language is sometimes stronger—words like "filth," "vermin," "outrage" are close to the limits of the well-mannered Turgenev's vocabulary.
[18] Chernyshevsky, "O Poezii, sochinenie Aristotelya," in *Estetika*, p. 228. The attack on tragedy is developed at much greater length in the dissertation itself.

scientific fact. Nature is not the capricious, vengeful force the Greeks called fate, but is, as modern science has shown, supremely indifferent to the just or unjust punishment of individual men. A formula which rendered the tragedies of accident bearable for a primitive people has no relevance for modern man. And with fate must be discarded the ancient notion of tragic guilt blindly incurred and inexorably punished. Even in the higher tragic forms of modern times, in which the conflict is between two individuals, or between the conflicting desires of a single individual, the effort to resolve the dramatic situation through the intervention of moral law merely repeats the error of the Greeks in a new form. A glance at history is enough to demonstrate that the evil deeds of great public men are more often than not exempt from external correction by moral law or by the public conscience. Test the artificial symmetry of Macbeth's rise and fall against the life of Gustavus Adolphus, who died by accident at the height of his conquests, whose death, therefore, can in no way be construed as a punishment for his crimes. The history of the Swedish king is closer to the rule than the exception and we must, therefore, regard the enforced tragic destiny of literary heroes simply as adherence to a literary convention, not as a description of experience itself.[19] This is not to say, of course, that human experience is not at times tragic. But art's treatment of suffering should correspond to its occurrence in life both as to incidence and as to cause. Thus viewed, the tragic takes its place with many other kinds of experiences as simply "the terrible" in human life. Tragedy is not banished from art, but its monopoly must be ended.

The tight pattern of inevitability in tragic dramas in which denouement flows inescapably from the previous action is also brought into question by Chernyshevsky, and again the diversity of experience is invoked to lift its restrictions from the artist. The kingpin of *tragic* inevitability is the concept of fate. But once it is removed the result is not necessarily the reign of accident in art. Rather the true design and coherence of the necessary in actual experience takes its place.[20] Thus a genuine inevitability supplied by life replaces the false in-

[19] The question of fate and accident is discussed at greatest length in the dissertation itself. See *Estetika*, pp. 21–30.

[20] Chernyshevsky's extreme position is not shared by many members of his school. Timofeev favors a tight dramatic structure for all prose narrative. In his prescription he actually uses the Aristotelian concepts of "tying" and "untying" (Russian *zavyazka* and *razvyazka*) as the basic moments in the organization of the action.

evitability of form which shapes life to its own monotonous ends. Chernyshevsky enjoins the artist to

choose the coherent and lifelike event and tell it as it was in actuality: if your choice is not bad (and this is so easy!) then your story, not recast from reality, will be better than any story remade according to the "demands of art," that is, according to the requirements of literary display.[21]

Here Chernyshevsky denies the writer the right to manipulate experience at all. He attempts to anticipate objections: "But what then will manifest creativity? In that you [the artist] will know how to separate the necessary from the unnecessary, what belongs to the essence of the event from the extraneous."[22] For the artist as Turgenev conceived him, this completely denies his creative function, placing the emphasis exclusively on acuteness of observation.

Chernyshevsky turns at last to the conventional tragic hero. His challenge to this traditional literary type is issued casually and is directed only against falsified historical novels, but it brings us close, we may feel sure, to the heart of his intention:

What purpose is served by these invented heroes who stand in the way of real heroes, who are introduced only to "provide," with their fabricated adventures, "a poetic unity" to the representation of the epoch, as if it were impossible to find truly poetic events in the life of our current heroes.[23]

With the apparatus of tragedy lying in ruins at his feet—fate, guilt, inevitability all destroyed by exposure to "real life"—the way is cleared for the entrance into literature of other kinds of heroes to whom an infinite variety of destinies will be permitted. One of these, of course, will be the courageous, virtuous man who instructs by his example and whose victory over hostile circumstance is expected to stimulate others to imitate him. This remains implicit in Chernyshevsky's formal writings on aesthetics, but it is made perfectly clear in his critical articles. He issued the first call for new heroes in 1856, in a review of Ogarev's poetry, which noted the passing of the superfluous men, in terms already made familiar to us by Dobrolyubov, and went on to describe the type that would replace them, and, presumably, the long line of tragic heroes extending back to the Greeks:

We are still waiting for this successor, who, having accustomed himself to the truth from childhood, regards it not with tremendous ecstasy but with joyous love; we are awaiting such a man and his speech, a very cheer-

---

[21] *Estetika*, p. 240.   [22] *Ibid.*, p. 241.   [23] *Ibid.*

ful ... calm ... decisive speech, in which would sound not theory's timid-
ity before life, but proof that reason can achieve mastery over life and that
man can harmonize his life with his convictions.[24]

Here certainly is a design for a literary hero who, granted lasting
"mastery over life," is as antithetical to Oedipus and Hamlet as he is
to Oblomov and Rudin. It is clear from this and from other sources
that the Russian advocates of a "civic" literature hoped, by reversing a
local trend, to effect a major change in the direction of world literature. The extent of their expectations is suggested by Chernyshevsky's
testy dismissal of Shakespeare as a model for modern writers: "Now
... when the reasons for objecting to the too passionate imitation of
French writers have passed, it would perhaps be as unnatural to give
Shakespeare uncontrolled dominion over our aesthetic convictions ...
to introduce his tragedies as examples of everything that is beauti·
ful."[25]

It is not surprising that a spokesman for radical social change would
distrust those aspects of tragedy which counseled reconciliation with
the status quo, and would dismiss the intervention of restraining
forces, in whatever guise, as manifestations of the vested interests of
inertia. But his willingness to invade the inner frontiers of the literary
craft—in what doubtless appeared to him as a gesture of liberation—
promised such wholesale destruction that it seemed to invite formal
anarchy. Under the pretext of removing one ancient formula, he seems
to have deprived art of the right and the means to organize experience
at all. His repeated references to the role of chance in life threaten to
reduce literature to a purposeless description of the accidental. We
may justly ask what traditional prerogatives of the artist he proposes
to keep, what he proposes to substitute for the aspects he discards, and
how, if at all, the artist's functions will differ from those of the mere
copyist or the moralizer?

As we have seen, the essence of creativity lies in the writer's ability
to separate the necessary from the extraneous. The artist must be a
superb observer. But he is also an observer with *a priori* notions that
direct his eye and help him to discern the necessary, the general, the
probable, and the significant in the chaos of experience. The principle

[24] N. G. Chernyshevsky, *Estetika i literaturnaya kritika,* ed. B. I. Bursov (Moscow-
Leningrad, 1951), p. 409. The article in question, "The Poetry of Ogarev," appeared
three years before "What Is Oblomovism?"
[25] *Estetika* (1939), p. 243.

of selectivity, first invoked by Belinsky, is the only substitute Cherny-shevsky offers for invention, manipulation, and all formal organizing techniques, which are suspect in his eyes because they embellish, ri-gidify, or otherwise falsify life. An art based on selectivity alone must find its design in life and must therefore seem at first glance to be totally dependent on observation. But the second aspect of selection, the principles that lie behind the observing eye, introduces value judg-ments to an almost unlimited extent, and tends to reverse the order of priorities in the creative process. Whereas formal structure at first seemed to be conferred by life, the reverse often turns out to be the case: design is stamped upon the work by the defining principles, life becomes a source of documentation for them, and the artist finds him-self merely an illustrator of principles derived from extraliterary sources. By demeaning formal discipline, Chernyshevsky has opened literature to alien material, and at the same time diminished litera-ture's ability to digest it.

In his bout with the tragic, Chernyshevsky has failed to replace other elements he can ill afford to ignore. Nothing is said of the psycho-logical process by which aesthetic emotion is transmitted. Tragedy weakens the will of the spectator by summoning superhuman antago-nists to crush the hero with whom he is identified. Viewed thus, with-out allowance for the disengagement permitted the spectator through catharsis, or for the possibility of affirmation achieved despite defeat, tragic literature is simply "pessimistic." Chernyshevsky is obliged, one would think, to replace the traditional effects of "pity and terror" with an equivalent combination—"respect and inspiration," for example— more suitable to his "optimistic" purposes. But no such effort is made. The nature of the aesthetic transaction is largely ignored by him, as it is, for the most part, by his successors. Though it is never made ex-plicit, a notion of direct identification between the reader and the hero, with emulation in thought and *in action* as the end, underlies the whole of his theory.

When we add the obligation to choose (and, of course, to exclude) material to all the other roles that are assigned to literature—the con-veying of "scientific" ideas, the representation of beauty as aspiration, the stimulation to action as an aesthetic aim, the portraiture of men who have gained "mastery over life"—it becomes evident that the artist operates with a set of blinders at least as restrictive of his freedom as the formal demands of tragedy, and far less congenial to the possibilities of his medium. When we consider, further, that each of the charges laid on literature is subject to specific interpretation—the ideas to be propagated, the aspirations to be fostered, the action to be encouraged, and the masterful type to be shown—we comprehend the distance Chernyshevsky has traveled from his initial insistence on art's subordination to life to his final assertion that art rises above life not only "to explain it" but "to pass judgment" on it. He has reassigned the artist to the position of superior vantage from which great works of art issue, but under such a burden of injunctions and inhibitions that we may predict the kind of directed verdict the artist must render under such conditions.

II

One of the critics' aims was to validate their credentials as guardians and supervisors of the literary product. It was the intemperate pressing of this claim that alienated so many of the important writers, and drove them into opposition. In the case of Chernyshevsky's *What Is to Be Done?*[26] the friction between critic and writer is happily eliminated since the critic himself has turned novelist and undertaken to fulfill his own importunate demands. For this reason we may consider this work with the certainty that it stands as a perfect point-by-point illustration of the radical democrats' blueprint for fiction.

Allowance has to be made for Chernyshevsky's inexperience with the craft, and the inhibiting conditions under which it was written: he was a prisoner in the Peter and Paul Fortress en route to years of exile. These circumstances may be advanced to forgive flaws in the execution but they do not excuse the eccentricities of its conception. In point of fact, the imperfections on the novel's surface point to faults in the novel's design, and to the principal difficulties inherent in this kind of writing.[27]

In the tension already noted in Chernyshevsky's thought between description and aspiration, between "is" and "should be," he has yielded in practice almost entirely to the second. The desired and the hoped-for dominate not only the selection of characters—the novel's

[26] The novel first appeared in the March, April, and May issues of *Sovremennik* in 1863. It was an immediate success with the revolutionary youth because of its partisan views, and failed for the same reason with other factions.

[27] My unfavorable judgments on Chernyshevsky's novel coincide with most others made by Westerners. For a review of these opinions, and for a sympathetic, non-Soviet reading of this work which specifically challenges my own, see Francis B. Randall, *N. G. Chernyshevskii* (New York, 1967).

subtitle, "From Stories about the New Men," tells us that we have at last caught up with Dobrolyubov's quarry—but determine their every action and utterance. With the initial decision to write a *roman à thèse*, picturing the future, and personifying worthy moral qualities, Chernyshevsky might have made the clean break with reality that distinguishes certain kinds of Utopian fiction. Though the "is" in his novel is hidden under a heavy gloss of "should be," he nevertheless insists on grounding his novel in the illusion of the contemporary and the everyday. The only deliberate use of literary artifice is an attempt to create suspense through the melodrama of a faked suicide. On this flimsy device is heaped the heavy load of instruction—by example, by exposition, and by exhortation—that forms the substance of the novel. Every motive of the characters is contained in a creed. An ethical theory underlies the entire work and guides the behavior of the principals at every step in the story of a model marriage between two representatives of the new men, a subsequent triangle involving a third new man, and a miraculously rational resolution.[28] The novel illustrates Chernyshevsky's formula for marital relations, with its ludicrously elaborate code for assuring the rights of each partner, which is, at the same time, a manifesto calling for the liberation of women. The characters' control over their emotions rests on the moral formula, "enlightened self-interest," borrowed without alteration from the British Utilitarians, which is commended to the reader's attention for his instruction. These marriages are made complete—in this arid atmosphere we might almost say consummated—by a program of shared activity in the service of others, as scientists, doctors, educators, and directors of cooperatives. At the basis of these doctrinal tags which direct their lives and which their lives, in turn, illustrate stands the public emotion "Love of Mankind." No action of the characters occurs—or can conceivably occur without forfeiting their standing as "new men"—which violates this all-embracing commitment.

[28] The resolution is connected with the "suicide," which is arranged to ease Vera's transfer of affections from Lopukhov to Kirsanov and is explained to her when she has completed the switch, bringing the story to a happy conclusion. Lopukhov by this time has found himself another "new person" and they all settle down in a very proper *ménage à quatre*. The poverty of invention reflects Chernyshevsky's indifference to formal problems. His own plan for the novel is instructive: he conceived it as a kind of illustrated manual for his *Encyclopedia of Knowledge and Life*. He wrote to his wife from prison: "I am reworking this book in the lightest, most popular spirit, almost in the form of a novel, with anecdotes, scenes ... so that it will be read by people who read almost nothing but novels." Quoted by N. Vodovozov in a postscript to a Soviet edition of the novel: N. G. Chernyshevsky, *Chto Delat?* (Moscow, 1947), p. 465.

One character stands apart from all the others, a truly "uncommon man" among uncommon men. Though he plays a minor role in the central intrigue—intervening at one crucial point to set everything right with his superior wisdom—the entire novel, in a sense, is his vehicle. He is Rakhmetov, the "rigorist," and, though Chernyshevsky can never say so, a dedicated professional revolutionary. Having chosen his career consciously and deliberately, he embarks on a fantastic training program designed to broaden his mind, toughen his body, and harden his will. His regime of gymnastics, hard physical labor, raw beefsteak diet, voracious though selective reading, and sexual continence reaches an absurd climax when he arises one morning soaked in blood from head to foot after a night spent on a bed of nails. Once trained, every capacity of his heart and mind is submitted to a self-defined concept of duty. He is impersonal, abrupt, and businesslike in all his relations with others.[29] Though he is once tempted by a beautiful young widow, he is "not free" to love or to marry. In all his character traits he is a nearly perfect early model of the Bolshevik. He does not have the apparatus of the Party to discipline and direct his energies and Chernyshevsky cannot tell us much about his specific political activity, but in his mystique of dedication and, above all, in his reliance on a will of steel, Rakhmetov prefigures the personal moral code of the "leather men in leather jackets." He is, like them, a member of a tiny elite which aspires to change the world. "They are few in number," Chernyshevsky wrote, "but through them the life of all mankind expands." He is "marked" for leadership, but not by birth or intrinsically superior qualities. He is a self-made superman who has shaped himself into a revolutionary instrument out of the natural resources that are given to all men. Men like him are, at the height of their powers, "the flower of the best people, the movers of movers, they are the salt of the salt of the earth."[30]

It is the mood of superlatives, of course, that robs him of literary credibility, and it is the power of his will, the most important ingredient of his character, that makes him aesthetically impossible. (It is clear that the political saint is no easier to present in a novel than any other kind.) A great deal of the difficulty has to do with the fact that the characters' primary motivations are doctrinal. Yet this is an indispensable attribute of political men—only by subordinating them-

[29] For Rakhmetov's biography, see *Chto Delat?* pp. 258–78.
[30] *Ibid.*, p. 278.

selves to these guiding concepts did the new men achieve the mastery over events and over themselves that gave them the freedom and the courage to act. The new man enters this state of grace not by study alone (Dobrolyubov has already suggested that too much intellection might blur the need to act), or by responding consciously or unconsciously to one's experience as a member of an economic class. The awareness comes through a simple revelation, by opening one's eyes and stepping from the "cellars" of prejudice and regressive values into the sunlight of natural truth.[31] The discovery of "natural truth," which is most often achieved with the help of an earlier convert, is then followed by a deliberate decision to act forever after in the light of its dictates:

Consciously and firmly he decided to renounce all the advantages and honors which he might have demanded of life in order to work for the benefit of others, finding his own greatest interest in the pleasure from that kind of work.[32]

The life that follows is rigorous, dedicated, and self-disciplined, we are told, but quite lacking in hesitation, anguish, or doubt. When the new man has reached his full stature, he is a model of modest, virtuous behavior. He has overcome "inertia," "ennui," "exaltation," "romanticism," "whimsicality," all the vices of his superfluous predecessors, and has learned "tact, coolness, activity . . . the realization of common sense in action." He is "bold," "resolute," and of "irreproachable honesty."[33] His private moral behavior is inseparable from his public activity, since the publicizing of every phase of his existence is one of the *social* functions of the novel. He emerges finally as the monolithic personality Dobrolyubov sought in his criticism, with hardly an identifying mark of his humanity, or a single flaw to involve him in interesting, tension-producing situations. He makes difficult decisions, but the process itself is so calmly rational, and the outcome so foregone, that no sense of loss or sacrifice is communicated. Every source of the novel's unreality can be traced back finally to the qualities of the new men—their total self-assurance (as smug as it is arrogant), their absolute incorruptibility, their unquestioned expectations, and their apparent inability to hesitate, stumble, or fail.[34]

[31] *Ibid.*, p. 102.   [32] *Ibid.*, p. 92.   [33] *Ibid.*, p. 190.

[34] Chernyshevsky anticipated this problem: "Kirsanov and Lopukhov appeared to the majority of the public as heroes, as people of the loftiest kind, perhaps even as idealized figures, perhaps even as people who could not exist in reality because of this too lofty nobility. No, my friends, they do not stand too high, you stand too low." *Chto*

The falseness of the hero guarantees the failure of the work of art in this kind of writing. Much may be attributed to Chernyshevsky's inexperience as a writer or to his indifference to the canons of the developing literary tradition that surrounded him. But the novel's sins are more significant as errors of commission than of omission, errors which arise from the deepest operating assumptions of the radical literary doctrine as formulated then and still practiced today.

This kind of novel begins, as we have already suggested, from a tiny patch of reality which is subjected to specific ideological tests to determine its significance, its typicality, and its potentialities for development.[35] Then, through all the openings Chernyshevsky permitted himself, the certified area is saturated with the writer's interpretations and expectations, and it is at this point that the question of "isness" and "oughtness" (as Harold Laski put it) comes to the fore.

The Russian radicals misused the idea as it was conceived by Aristotle and other formulators of the tragic discipline. In tragedy, "life as it should be" exists largely as a negative inference to be drawn from the drama's presentation of life as it *is* and should *not* be. The Russian radicals on the other hand incorporated their vision of life as it should be into the literary work itself and presented it as the inevitable and desirable extension of life as it is. This involves a second, related distinction. Tragedy rests in part on the premise of an unchanging universe. Faced with the same set of conditions that confront the hero of tragedy, let the reader not be tempted to emulate him. The didactic aim, in broad terms, is stasis, reconciliation, and harmony. But in the dialectical view of the universe, not only are the same set of conditions never repeated, but change toward the better is in the nature of things and is to be sought and encouraged. A strong quotient of "shall be," therefore, is added to "should be," and it is not difficult to anticipate the moment when "should be" is translated into the "must be" of the five-year plan and other policies of the Soviet government. The writer, in other words, invites the reader to view the future through the prism of an ethical imperative that is soon to be enacted. The juxtaposition

---

Delat? p. 302. This hardly solves the problem: the *relative* moral positions of the literary heroes and the readers are unchanged.

[35] No one can say, of course, that the new men did not exist in the Russia of the sixties. Though he pointedly denied it, Chernyshevsky might well have been writing about himself or his friends. If he had been immodest enough to make himself the hero of a novel, the long, bitter struggle between the forces of tsarism and his own revolutionary toughness would certainly have produced a better story than the easy victories of the moralizing do-gooders he chose to represent.

of "is" and "should be" gives rise, in this case, not to reconciliation but to discontent, which is balanced with the assurance that the better future is within man's grasp, provided he accepts the obligation to bring it into being. Thus, tragedy, in any form, is challenged at its very foundation by the optimism of the dialectic.

Entanglement with the future involves the writer in a number of difficulties. It confronts him first of all with the general problem, perhaps insoluble in the nature of things for the realist, of "describing" what has not yet taken place. He runs the serious risk of setting forth his optimistic prediction of the course of events, reflecting his own aspirations, while the world, containing a far more complex and much less hopeful "emergent reality," stands by, as it were, to correct his predictions. Hindsight suggests the hollowness of Chernyshevsky's optimism: the belief that Russia's future well-being lay in the spread of a new sexual morality, in the steady multiplication of the number of morally motivated people (the new men), in the gradual spread of Fourierist producer cooperatives—all this now seems like the "fantasy" which Chernyshevsky himself attacked so strenuously in his dissertation.

In the shorter view the risk is even graver. The novel's immediate function, as Chernyshevsky saw it, was to hasten progressive social forces by giving them attractive publicity, and by enlisting the efforts of larger and larger numbers of men in their service. The new man, Chernyshevsky said, represented one man in ten in Russian life at the time the novel was written.[36] The number was growing irresistibly, would soon constitute a majority, and, by this simple arithmetic progression, Russia might in a very short time enter a new era.[37] *What Is to Be Done?* is a primary document in the recruiting campaign, and exerts in this way its own pressure toward social change. In this short-run view the writer's commitment to the future is concerned with that hairline between the present and the immediate sequence of moments that follow it. He stirs men's emotions, in the hope of pushing them over the borderline between conviction and action, and assures them that their concerted actions will bring what all virtuous

[36] Apparently there are two categories of new men, the leaders and the rank-and-filers. The first group remains small and select, while the second group is capable of infinite numerical expansion. There is a contradiction between the kinds of political action each is to engage in. It is possible they represent alternative paths to social change: the rank-and-filers proceed there by peaceful, evolutionary means; the leaders are to direct this movement, or, if it becomes necessary, to undertake acts of violence.

[37] See *Chto Delat?* pp. 12, 55–56, and 191.

men want, and relatively painlessly at that. The serenity and assurance of his heroes, then, involve him in the deceptive promises of the propagandist, and their portrait is as false, for what it omits, as recruiting posters in the post office.

The picture of the whole truth, we must conclude, would have endangered the novel's extraliterary purposes. The writer who predicted the mangling or destruction of such a person in his unequal struggle with Russian reality, or showed him wearied by the passage of time and the endless series of obstacles stretching into the future, or discovered a dangerous flaw in his character or in his view of the world —who, in short, suggested the bitter conflict or the frustrations or the suffering he faced—would have contributed, however unwittingly, to the mood of futility which arose from the literature of alienation. This, at least, is the radical position and, stated thus, it serves to illustrate the central dilemma of their tradition. We need not wonder at the uproar on the left that greeted Turgenev's portrait of the new man in *Fathers and Sons*. Bazarov is not simply a revolutionary who is defeated through his own fallibility; what was more offensive to the practicing revolutionaries of the time, his downfall is brought about through a fatal split along the crucial and vulnerable line where personal emotions are fused, according to the radical critics, with social convictions. On this point and on many others, Turgenev's novel, within its small compass, demonstrates remarkable prescience about the destinies of the coming generation of Russian revolutionary youth, particularly the nihilists and terrorists, both anarchist-tinged and both inclined, therefore, to put a huge value on their acts as personal statements. Both as description and as forecast, we may say in the idiom of the radicals that *Fathers and Sons* is truer "to real life" than *What Is to Be Done?*

Chernyshevsky's work, which exposes so many of its deeper inadequacies through its surface ineptitudes, is of course only the first crude effort in a prolific tradition. More skillful writers were to ring ingenious variations on the basic theory he set forth. But his failures have served to outline sharply the most troubling creative problem in this tradition: the matter of assimilating the ideological dosage with the fictional illusion of life, or more precisely of rendering plausible—in effect of disguising—the point where the leap is made from the present to the future, or from the actual to the desired.

One other quality of the novel has been evident from the beginning of this inquiry: that it is a thorough exercise in reducing important areas of human experience to political terms. Thus Chernyshevsky's "mastery" over life is in reality a mastery of the political means to change the social order; the fusion of personal life with convictions is actually a subordination of private emotion to the dictates of public attitudes. Finally, it is clear that Chernyshevsky's attempt to discredit "the demands of art" as false and unreal, together with his repeated invocation of the variety and disorder of "real life" to accomplish this end, is then followed by the substitution, under various guises, of the "demands" of revolutionary politics as the organizing principles for the successful work of art. We may not doubt that the politicalizing of the literary process is the final destination of his zigzag journey.

It is in these terms that the novel was received by later representatives of this trend. Plekhanov seems to have discovered a universal value in Chernyshevsky's evocation of the moral code of revolutionaries and of the generalized human striving for a better world:

Who has not read and reread this famous work? Who has not been charmed by it, who has not become cleaner, better, braver, and bolder under its philanthropic influence? Who has not imitated the purity of the principal characters? Who, after reading this novel, has not reflected on his personal life, has not subjected his personal striving and tendencies to a severe examination? We all draw from it moral strength and faith in a better future.[38]

In a similar vein, Georgi Dimitrov, the Bulgarian Communist leader, suggests that, for a believer, the novel had exactly the "aesthetic" effect that Chernyshevsky intended it to have. Dimitrov singles out Rakhmetov as a basic influence on the formation of his own character:

I must say that...there was no literary work which influenced me so strongly in my revolutionary education as Chernyshevsky's novel. For months I literally lived with Chernyshevsky's heroes. Rakhmetov was my particular favorite. I set myself the goal of being as firm, as self-possessed, to temper my will and character in my struggle with difficulties and deprivations, to subordinate my personal life to the interests of the great cause of the working class—in a word, to be like this irreproachable hero of Chernyshevsky.[39]

[38] Quoted by Vodovozov in the postscript to *Chto Delat?* (p. 464). This, despite Plekhanov's many quarrels with Chernyshevsky as a thinker.
[39] Quoted by Vodovozov in his editor's postscript to *Chto Delat?* (p. 470), from Dimitrov's foreword to an unavailable 1935 edition of the novel. Dimitrov himself is proposed for the hero roster by the British Marxist Ralph Fox, in an appeal to Western writers in the 1930s to make Dimitrov, whose self-defense at the Reichstag fire trial he

Lenin's feeling of identification with the novel is striking. Valentinov has recorded his passionate reply over a Swiss café table to a colleague who had dismissed it as "primitive":

> Will you be careful what you say? ... How can the monstrous, absurd idea enter your head of calling the work of Chernyshevsky, the greatest and most talented representative of socialism before Marx, primitive and ungifted. ... I declare it's inadmissable. ... Under his influence hundreds of people became revolutionaries. ... For example, he fascinated my brother and he fascinated me. He ploughed me up more profoundly than anyone else. When did you read *What Is to Be Done?* It's useless to read it if the milk hasn't dried on your lips. Chernyshevsky's novel is too complicated ... to understand and evaluate at an early age. I myself tried to read it when I was about fourteen. It was no use, a superficial reading. And then, after my brother's execution, knowing that Chernyshevsky's novel was one of his favorite books, I really undertook to read it, and I sat over it not for several days but for several weeks. Only then did I understand its depth. ... It's a thing which supplies energy for a whole lifetime. An ungifted work could not have that kind of influence.[40]

Lenin's invocation of Marx and of his own brother, as well as the excited terms of his praise, testify to the depth of its influence. It was clearly instrumental in his conversion to the revolutionary way of life after his brother's death. Valentinov notes elsewhere that before this climactic moment Turgenev was Lenin's favorite writer, and speculates on the reasons for it. Perhaps Lenin loved the life in nature of the nobleman's estate, which we now know was very familiar to him in his youth.[41] But, Valentinov points out, he also must have accepted Turgenev's unfavorable portraits of revolutionaries without distaste.[42] It is remarkably symbolic to find Lenin taking sides in that debate of the sixties when certain fateful choices Russia has felt compelled to make were dramatized more vividly than has ever happened since.

These testimonials from distinguished revolutionaries provide a good sense of the terms of the novel's acceptance by Soviet critics. One authoritative statement connects the novel with Soviet literature's most solemn purposes:

---

calls an "example of moral grandeur and courage worthy to stand beside the greatest in our human history," the hero of a new kind of novel for our time. See Ralph Fox, *The Novel and the People* (New York, 1945), pp. 100–107.

[40] N. Valentinov, "Chernyshevsky i Lenin," *Novy zhurnal*, 27 (1951): 193–94.

[41] N. Valentinov, "Rannie gody Lenina. Lenin v Kokushkine," *Novy zhurnal*, 36 (1954): 231–35.

[42] N. Valentinov, "Vydumki o rannei revolyutsionnosti Lenina," *Novy zhurnal*, 39 (1954): 222–29.

The enormous educational significance which Chernyshevsky's novel, *What Is to Be Done?*, had for contemporary revolutionary youth is well known, forming in the persons of Rakhmetov, Kirsanov, Lopukhov, Vera Pavlovna a well-defined system of social conduct. Thus Soviet literature, exposing the survivals of capitalism and at the same time depicting the positive hero of socialist construction, carries out an enormous educational work. This cognitive-educational significance of literature is disclosed with special sharpness by Comrade Stalin who defined writers as the "engineers of souls." In this way, through the specificity of its content, through its form, and through its function, all indissolubly linked, literature appears before us as a specific ideology.[43]

Given the Soviet Marxian premise that *literature is ideology*, then Chernyshevsky had found the way, before anyone else, to write a novel that propagated a "specific," healthy, progressive brand of it.

An elementary respect for their own national heritage prevents Soviet critics from including *What Is to Be Done?* among the classics of the nineteenth century. By the curious double standard which regards the great writers of the past with reverent awe, yet supports a creed for its own literature which opposes them, Chernyshevsky's novel stands as a pioneering work in the second tradition, which was to reach fruition in socialist realism, a significant forecast of that "higher" order of literature to come.

[43] *Literaturnaya entsiklopediya*, 8: 190–91.

CHAPTER 6

Rebuttal I: The Theory

❧❧❧

The political excludes the artistic because, in order to
prove, it must be one-sided. TOLSTOY

On the situation of literature in periods of social stress, Lionel Trilling writes: "Any large, intense movement of moral-political action is likely to be jealous of art and to feel that it is in competition with the full awareness of human suffering."[1] Save that the spokesmen for the "large, intense movement" and the writers themselves believed that they had a common cause on many matters, and that there was, as we have seen, in nineteenth-century Russia a unique responsiveness each to the other's vision, Mr. Trilling's insight is a particularly fruitful one for approaching the historic split of the 1860s.

Though the writers felt themselves in competition with the radicals, they were not indifferent to politics, and felt more or less compelled to choose the most hospitable among three major currents of political protest: the revolutionary socialist, the insurrectionary anarchist, and the evolutionary libertarian. In a sense, they represented a fourth group, a kind of writers' party, but they were completely unorganized, and generally worked in closest association with the libertarian group. Even Dostoevsky, who disagreed strongly with the social views of this group, or Tolstoy, who held aloof from all groups, may be said to have enjoyed the climate of tolerance it engendered.

Considering for a moment the ideological aspects of the controversy, we see why the radicals might look to literature for an energizing influence on the confused men of good will, and why, by the same token,

[1] Lionel Trilling, "Introduction," in Henry James, *The Princess Casamassima* (New York, 1948), 1: xx.

the hesitations, qualifications, and tragic insights of the liberal writers would have local aspects of "defeatism." But we cannot draw much advantage, for example, from the uproar that greeted Turgenev's *Fathers and Sons*. Was the novel a "slander" on the younger generation? Did it harm the progressive movement, benefit the status quo? Was Bazarov a veiled portrait of Dobrolyubov; was he copied from another model; or was he entirely imaginary? Turgenev himself, in his defense of that novel, made many contradictory statements on most of these questions, and we are not equipped to answer them. It may be said, however, that his defense was based on the concept that the author is—and indeed must be—responsive to burning social questions, but must at the same time be free to deal with them as his discipline permitted.[2]

We should fare better in seeking out the assumptions about art from which these charges arise. The public statement of the liberal position was sporadic and unsystematic. Often we shall find its most effective defense in letters, diaries, and reminiscences. A consistent theory, which meets the radical position at every essential point, does emerge, however, to help us in detaching the central issue from its local origins and from the terms of the contemporary debate.

The issue was joined on three main points: the situation of the artist and his relation to the truth of his work; the aesthetic function of literature; and the attitude toward universal values in art. Closely involved in these three questions are the definitions of the hero as they relate to theories of human nature and to possibilities for exploitation by the writer.

II

The competition between the two groups involved their professional vested interests: the liberals were writers, the radicals—"the literary

[2] Turgenev was to abandon this position in one important particular in a letter to Saltykov in 1876: "I am ready to confess that . . . I had no right to give our reactionary riffraff the opportunity to seize upon a sobriquet ["nihilist"] . . . ; the writer in me should have made this sacrifice to the citizen—and therefore I acknowledge as justified both my alienation from the youth and all kinds of reproaches. . . . The question that arose was more important than artistic truth—and I should have known this in advance." I. S. Turgenev, *Sobranie sochinenii* (Moscow, 1949), 11: 305. This attitude of capitulation was expressed earlier in his *Literary Reminiscences*, though in more modified form. A. Yarmolinsky, his biographer, notes Turgenev's tendency to cater to the ideas of his correspondents. This surrender of a key position in his letter to Saltykov may be accounted for by the expectations of his stern correspondent, the unreconstructed radical satirist.

Robespierres" in Turgenev's phrase—were critics, for the most part. The latter expressed more than the usual resentment at occupying a secondary, mediator's role in the literary process. As self-appointed guardians of a new civic virtue, they exerted enormous pressure on the writers with the aim, finally, of controlling the moral substance of the creative output. In this contest, the two groups invaded each other's disciplines from time to time: Turgenev discussed literature publicly and at length, notably in articles like "Hamlet and Don Quixote" and in his *Reminiscences*; Tolstoy, Dostoevsky, and, later, Chekhov did so too, though less formally; and the radicals, as we have seen, at least once tried to show the writers how it "must be done." But in the course of these incursions, each remained true to his professional interests: the writers entered criticism to defend and clarify their view of the writer's function; the critics wrote novels to illustrate their own critical prescriptions. The conflict between them remained unresolved on this level until decisions by the Communist Party during the early five-year plans vested ultimate control over literature elsewhere than in the creative faculty of the writer himself.

In their defense against the jurisdictional claims of the critics, and in their rejection of all forms of subservience—to politics, to science, to ethical systems, or to predetermined aesthetic effects—the writers invoked an informal ideology of literature's independence from any prescription which threatened to reduce it to the terms of other disciplines. In some alarm, and with characteristic vehemence, Tolstoy wrote on January 4, 1858, to V. P. Botkin:

What would you say if now, when the filthy stream of politics is trying to swallow everything, and to soil if not to do away with art—what would you say about the people who believe in art's independence and its immortality coming together and demonstrating this truth both by deed (the practice of art) and word (criticism), and trying to save what is eternal and independent from the accidental, one-sided, and all-pervasive political influence.[3]

Tolstoy went on in the same letter to propose the formation of a journal, together with Turgenev, Fet, and others, devoted to "artistic enjoyment" and to "taste," indifferent to any "tendency" and to the "demands of the public." His central insistence on art's (and, of course the artist's) independence sustained him in his own work, until the

---

[3] L. N. Tolstoy, *Polnoe sobranie sochinenii* (Moscow, 1935), 5: 536–37.

great personal "crisis" before 1880 led him formally to abandon this stand.

The crux of the dispute is in the effort to locate the center of the creative process. For the liberals it is unquestionably fixed in the sovereign moral intelligence of the artist. For the radical it is elsewhere—in life which can always be invoked to challenge a novel's formal design, in ethical obligations which arise from the needs and suffering of the masses, or in a doctrinal truth which alone directs the writer to "the significant" in experience.

In asserting their independence from the views and aspirations of other men—above all from the tactical needs of an underground political movement—the artists were merely insisting on minimal conditions for the performance of their work, which they conceived as the discovery of the whole truth about human experience. "Truth," unadorned and without qualification, became a battle cry of the group. "My hero is truth," Tolstoy shouted at Sevastopol, refusing to falsify for patriotic purposes any of the human beings he observed there. Art's truth, Turgenev felt, was a special personal vision of experience to which the artist dedicated himself as to a holy mission. The critics simply did not understand the creative process:

They do not imagine that enjoyment ... which consists of punishing oneself for the shortcomings ... in the people one invents; they are fully convinced that an author unfailingly creates only that which conducts his ideas; they do not want to believe that to reproduce powerfully and accurately the truth, the realness of life, is the greatest happiness for a writer even if this truth does not coincide with his own sympathies.[4]

Formal discipline is no end in itself—art is not a game—but a means to this greater end. Political truth is not false but "one-sided," simply one aspect of the totality of man's experience. The goal is the rendering, compactly but completely, of the whole of the human condition as one's characters share it. The writer does not address himself to the "significant" truth or to the useful truth or to the probable truth, but to the whole of its gnarled and knotty substance. Chekhov, the last and often the most perceptive spokesman for the writers, makes it clear that no limitation within the writer's awareness must be allowed to infringe on the fidelity of his image. Since it is in the artist's mind that order and meaning are discovered in experience, he must

[4] From Chapter 5, "À propos de *Fathers and Sons*," in his *Literary Reminiscences*, dated 1868–90. *Polnoe sobranie sochinenii* (St. Petersburg, 1913), 10: 104.

clearly be independent (though not necessarily unaware) of the imperatives derived from other disciplines, if he is to meet this challenging and exhausting standard of "absolute and honest truth."

In a sense the writers' claim to autonomy is based on the notion than the act of creation is in itself an act of discovery. Art maintains its own outposts on the frontiers of experience, conducts its own explorations according to its own rules, and presents its findings to the public without referral to any authority outside the writer's conscience. Art bears comparison in this connection with a scientific experiment. Lionel Trilling has compared the fabricated world of the work of art—Marianne Moore's "imaginary garden"—with the artificial situation of the experiment, "which is devised to force or foster a fact into being."[5] Both wings of Russian realism accepted some such view of the creative process. But there is a significant difference between them on this point. It is not that either group really rigged the experiment or allowed the unrestricted play of the experimenter's subjectivity. The distinction is rather to be found in differing standards of selectivity regulating the amount and kinds of data to be taken under consideration. The liberal in spite of his prejudices and predispositions seemed always inclined to permit more data—in terms of variety of character and situation—as raw material to be tested in his experiment. The radical favored smaller amounts with a larger share pretested by other disciplines. To the extent that this was so, the outcome always tended to be predetermined in this kind of fiction, as Chernyshevsky's novel clearly indicated.

The writers' effort to remain true to the logic of the data, and to organize them without damage or distortion, gave rise more than once to the peculiar situation in which the writer struggled desperately, and sometimes unsuccessfully, to control the outcome of his story, and asked in bewilderment what had gone wrong when he failed. Gogol's Chichikov (*Dead Souls*), Tolstoy's Levin (*Anna Karenina*), Dostoevsky's Myshkin (*The Idiot*)—all represent intentions unfulfilled. It may be argued that Raskolnikov's questionable conversion violates the logic of the data, and the writer's better judgment, too, as it is revealed in his working notes for the novel's conclusion: "Raskolnikov goes to shoot himself."[6] Ivan Karamazov's

---

[5] Lionel Trilling, "Introduction," in James, *The Princess Casamassima*, 1: xiv.
[6] F. M. Dostoevsky, *Iz arkhiva F. M. Dostoevskogo. Prestuplenie i nakazanie: neizdannye materialy*, ed. I. I. Glivenko (Moscow-Leningrad, 1931), p. 216.

state of suspension, far from fulfillment but as far from defeat, does not express the author's explicit beliefs as we know them to be. In all these cases the writer has created someone as strong and assertive as himself, with an independent identity and destiny. Turgenev is painfully honest and frankly at sea about his relation to Bazarov. True to his precept: to present "the whole of the living human face," he found himself unable to say, after he had done so, that Bazarov was the creature of his hopes, or even whether "I love him or hate him."[7] Working out of this ambivalence, Turgenev endowed Bazarov with a striking combination of good and bad qualities: he has in his make-up "coarseness," "heartlessness," "ruthless dryness and sharpness," yet he is "strong," "honorable, just, and a democrat to the tip of his toes."[8] These, at least, are some of the qualities Turgenev discovered in him after the fact. But they were not the result of a calculated balancing of vices and virtues during the act of creation itself. At that moment his governing intention was to exclude arbitrary manipulation and to submit to the logic of his invention. He has described his curious feeling of helplessness before his creation:

It seems that an author himself does not know what he is creating; my feelings for Bazarov—my personal feelings—were of a confused nature (whether I loved him or hated him, the Lord knows!), nevertheless the image came out so defined that he immediately stepped into life and started to act in his own particular way. In the end what does it matter what a writer thinks of his work. It is a thing in itself and he is a thing in himself.[9]

Turgenev would have been a happier man if he had really believed in the separate existences of author and hero. He was never able to disclaim responsibility for Bazarov entirely, but he achieved a degree of detachment that enabled him to penetrate to the real reasons for the clamorous and discordant reception of "his favorite child." The danger lay in his own ambiguity:

If the writer's attitude toward his characters is not defined ... if the author himself doesn't know whether he loves the character he has set forth ... then it is thoroughly bad. The reader is prepared to attach to the author imaginary sympathies or imaginary antipathies, if only to escape from the unpleasant "uncertainty."[10]

[7] Letter to A. A. Fet, dated April 6/18, 1862, *Sobranie sochinenii*, 11: 212.
[8] *Ibid.*, pp. 212–16.
[9] Letter to I. P. Borisov, January 5, 1870, *ibid.*, p. 259.
[10] From the *Literary Reminiscences* in *Polnoe sobranie sochinenii*, 10: 106.

Fathers and Sons fell, as Turgenev put it, "like oil on the fire."[11] In this superheated time readers "read through" the novel and groped for direct, immediate identification with the life around them. There was neither the leisure nor the tolerance to honor his real purpose as he explained it to Dostoevsky: "Nobody, it seems, suspects that I tried to present...a tragic figure—and everybody comments: why is he so sinister? or why is he so good?"[12]

Turgenev was a victim of the partisan view of truth held by the political extremists on both sides, a view impatient of paradox or ambiguity, hence unwilling to accept the complexity or the contradictions of tragedy. In the radicals' universe allowance was made for obstacles and setbacks but not for doubt or bewilderment. They felt that much larger sectors of the available truth were known than the liberal writers believed. And, in any case, important new discoveries would not, in all likelihood, be made by freely ranging writer-explorers. The writer, in the radical prescription, was expected to deal far more with the given—to illustrate the known, not to seek the unknown. Behind the words "typical," "healthy," "progressive," and "necessary" lay the certainty that such words had fixed and exclusive definitions, and, still further in the background, the implication that these definitions, constituting the essential truth, must be accepted by —or even imposed on—writers.

In deciding what truth is for the writer, certain judgments must be made about what aspects of the truth of human life or what moments in man's life cycle are of greatest fictional interest. For the great Russian novelists ideas and doctrine were not excluded, but were contained in character, and made a function of the whole man. The truth of fiction for them embraced all varieties of love, friendship, and hatred, had as its permanent backdrop the perspective of growth, decay, and death, and, because of the artist's elevation above, and independence from, his characters, included the human facts of fallibility, error, and failure. The radicals, on the other hand, were interested in ideological man. In their view of literary truth—and undoubtedly in their own private moral code—character was a function of doctrine, and men generally were most "interesting" when seen in active response to their social situation. Against the liberal creed of knowledge of life for its own sake whatever the consequences, the

---

[11] Letter to P. V. Annenkov, June 8, 1862, *Sobranie sochinenii*, 11: 217.
[12] Letter to F. M. Dostoevsky, April 22, 1862, *ibid.*, p. 216.

radicals opposed an ideology, a body of organized knowledge designed to affect men's future social behavior in a specific way. Since the doctrine was known to be valid, its spokesmen in art could not be permitted to fail, or if they did, for personal reasons, they became simply uninteresting or untypical in the radicals' special use of those words. For the liberal with his eye focused on the individual in all his observable relations with life, this doctrinal view of man was, as Tolstoy put it, "one-sided." Turgenev was undoubtedly reacting against this view when he enjoined young writers to steer clear of any and all "dogma." Also, since an ideological view of the world involved a calculation about the future, literary truth for the radicals must contain that diagram of what is to come, as they discerned it in present events. According to the canons of realism, the future, seen either as the inevitable or as the desirable, must remain an unknown. Possibilities might be stated, but any effort to force character into one of these possibilities had unhappy results, as we have seen in the case of Chichikov, Raskolnikov, Levin, and others.

III

The two views of art contain sharply contrasting assumptions about the aesthetic effect a novel should have on the reader. Radical criticism displayed a parental concern for the *immediate* effect of a literary work upon the reader's conduct and morale. In this setting art becomes a discourse not between equals but between teacher and students, or for that matter, between fathers and children. Turgenev's remark that Chernyshevsky's dissertation set forth a view of art for "immature" people is very shrewd, for these matters are the proper concern of writers of juvenile literature. There is no question here of the author's posing his informed judgment against the reader's own. Rather, a number of fundamental decisions have been taken by self-appointed guardians of morals, and the reader is invited to share them but is not expected to find his own way among them or to reject them. This situation has obtained, of course, to a greater or lesser degree since 1929 in the Soviet Union. Zhdanov poses the issue with devastating clarity in his "Report on the Journals *Zvezda* and *Leningrad*." After belaboring Zoshchenko and Akhmatova for corrupting the ideals of youth, he attacks them further for daring to suppose that "if a man has done a good, artistic, fine piece of writing, his work should be published even though it contains vicious elements liable to confuse and poison the minds of our young people."[13] This at least is frank.

At bottom this attitude rests on the radicals' premise that art's proper aim is the stimulation and direction of action. Chernyshevsky disagreed with Aristotle's view that art "imitates" life and that its instructive value is contained therein: "We imitate in order to act, not in order to know something."[14] In distinguishing between the two schools on this point, it is safer to rely on this remark by Chernyshevsky than to accept his more formal distinction between an art concerned with practical human strivings and an art directed toward "enjoyment," with its connotations of frivolity and indulgence. We are confronted then with an opposition between action to change life, on the one hand, and a general knowledge about life, on the other, as the ultimate aim of art, between, that is, a manipulative and a contemplative aesthetic.

In formulating this view of art the Russian literary radicals came close to paraphrasing Marx's celebrated prescription for philosophy: "The philosophers have only *interpreted* the world in various ways; the point, however, is to *change* it."[15] In this view, knowledge is measured by its persuasive value. The liberal would doubtless agree with the radical that art was indeed a kind of instruction in life. But he would certainly demur at the further step that converts education into agitation. He might agree that satire led most directly and most validly to action by arousing disgust with a given state of things, but he would add that successful satire does not break its mood of mockery by including a set of instructions for removing the evils under attack. As in the case of tragedy, the instruction is primarily an inference to be drawn by the reader, and any action on his part will proceed from his own conclusions. The radicals hoped to control the reader's response by drawing the conclusions within the work of art, and by showing the action they hoped he would take.

Chekhov defended himself against the same kind of pressures, and may be quoted as a final rebuttal speaker for all the writers. He is quite explicit in a letter to A. S. Suvorin:

13 A. A. Zhdanov, "Doklad o zhurnalakh *Zvezda* i *Leningrad*," *Literaturnaya gazeta*, 39 (September 21, 1946): 4. This raises the question of a *youth-centered* literature, in effect of a national literature of juvenilia.

14 N. G. Chernyshevsky, *Estetika*, ed. N. G. Bogoslovsky (Moscow-Leningrad, 1939), p. 234.

15 The Eleventh Thesis on Feuerbach, in Karl Marx and Friedrich Engels, *Selected Works* (Moscow, 1951), 2: 367.

You are right to require a conscious attitude from the artist toward his work, but you mix up two ideas: *the solution of the problem and a correct presentation of the problem*. Only the latter is obligatory for the artist. In *Anna Karenina* and *Onegin* not a single problem is solved, but they satisfy you completely just because all their problems are correctly presented. The court is obliged to submit the case fairly, but let the jury do the deciding, each according to its own judgment.[16]

Thus Chekhov frees the artist from responsibilities which are, properly, not his at all, and at the same time protects him in his role as observer and organizer of experience. In the final libertarian image he surrenders any claim to legislative, parental controls over the reader's response: it is not for the artist to worry about what the work of art causes people to do. His maximum offering to the reader is a precious, hard-won illumination. The adult reader may come away depressed or elated, with his sense of life clarified or confounded. He may act more resolutely, less so, or not at all. That is the reader's business. Tragedy may numb his will or blight his expectations, but as a sure road to the truth it cannot be by-passed.

We return, finally, to the incompatibility already noted between realism and the projection, in whatever form, of future events. The writers' reluctance—and their inability when they tried—to cross the line between *is* and *should be* did not mean that they were indifferent toward what was to come. Any knowledge of life—particularly the kind of moral investigations in Russia's great writing—should be of use to the prophets and activists who would *change* life. But it was not, largely because the kind of human truth that literature dealt with was too complex, too ambiguous, and too imprecise to sustain predictions or to promise solutions. The writers felt that it was their responsibility only to show man as he was, and he would change himself.

It was Turgenev who made the most telling comment on the radical orientation toward the future. Bazarov, his own version of the radical personality, was a tragic figure precisely because of his involvement in what was to come. "I dreamt of a dark, wild, large figure," he wrote, "half growing out of the soil, strong, malicious, honorable—and doomed all the same to perish because ... he stands on the threshold of the future."[17] The source of the radicals' optimism

---

[16] Letter to A. S. Suvorin, dated December 23, 1888, in Anton Chekhov, *The Selected Letters of Anton Chekhov*, ed. Lillian Hellman (New York, 1955), p. 57.
[17] Letter to K. K. Sluchevskii, April 14, 1862, *Sobranie sochinenii*, 11: 215.

became for Turgenev, since he did not share their faith in the rapid, upward evolution of things, the very source of Bazarov's undoing. The doctrinal motives which constitute Bazarov's commitment to the future become devalued and evaporate in the face of his present personal needs. Thus stripped of his ideals he is confronted with the last responsibility of all large men, of "dying with dignity."[18]

Turgenev's implication that man always looms larger than the doctrine he professes brings up the problem of general truths in art. Radical art is virtually indifferent to universal statement. It operates so fixedly in the glare of the immediate political present and future, and its limited, topical, agitational view of truth is so concerned with the contemporary and the concrete, that there is no opportunity for the artist to concern himself with the timeless. Because of the radicals' materialist distrust of absolutes and permanent categories, their kinds of social generalization do not readily extend themselves through time, since society changes, and its labels are constantly rewritten. Value is conferred on art from without, by the service it performs at any given moment, and, by all accounts, the modern Soviet reader is still expected to value *Dead Souls* for its exposé of social conditions and to derive a kind of *ex post facto* indignation from it. Even the radical hero-type, whom Lenin, Plekhanov, and Dimitrov found a source of strength many years later, exerted a sectarian appeal, aimed mainly at believers. The one value he expressed, which transcended the specific articles of his faith, was that virtue is found in complete personal subordination to a doctrine of revolutionary social change. The one universal tenet of the radical view of literature would seem to be that it concern itself eternally with the momentarily relevant. Should the artist achieve a level of universal interest, it must be regarded as an unimportant by-product of his solemn attention to the present and to the immediate future.

It must not be supposed that in contrast to the radicals' myopia, the writers deliberately set out to explore the timeless or to search for philosophical absolutes in the manner of Chernyshevsky's whipping-boy, Vischer. Turgenev was as topical as a gossip columnist, and Dostoevsky's source books were as often as not the crime stories in the daily newspaper. The essential difference between the two approaches shows up most clearly in their view of character: in the radical prescription character was a function of ideology; in the writers' practice

18 Letter to A. A. Fet, September 4, 1862, *ibid.*, p. 219.

ideology was a function of, or was contained in, character. Grounding their conception in the wholly recreated human being, the writers proceeded outward from that and were free to explore him in all his relations to the world, to sex, to society, to belief, or to death. When the radicals and the liberals looked at the same type they saw him differently: one saw him governed through his reason by "convictions" or doctrine and powered by the disciplined emotions that flowed from this combination; the other comprehended the entire human vessel in which reason and conviction were contained. The writers anchored their concept of character in the timeless biological cycle of human life and the permanent emotional and psychological needs implicit in this cycle. As Chekhov said: "It seems to me that it is not up to writers to solve such questions as God, pessimism. . . . The job of the writer is to depict only who, how and under what circumstances people have spoken or thought about God and pessimism."[19] Focused thus on the man and not the idea, we see that the balance of good and bad qualities in Bazarov which may well have been "ideologically harmful" to the revolutionary cause in 1862 is the precise source of his universal appeal.

Though it was not their primary concern, the writers felt that the expression of permanent truths was, nevertheless, a legitimate aim. Tolstoy, addressing the Society of Lovers of Russian Literature in 1858, not long before the height of the controversy, divided Russian literature into "two separate kinds," and summarized some essential differences between the two aesthetics:

In the past two years it has seemed that political, and particularly denun-
ciatory, literature, which borrowed the media of art for its purposes and
found remarkably intelligent, honorable and talented representatives who
responded warmly and decisively to every question of the moment, to society's every temporary wound, would completely absorb the public's attention, and would deprive literature of all its significance. The majority of
the public began to think that the problem of all literature consisted only
in the denunciation of evil, in discussing it, and correcting it. In the past
two years I have heard and read opinions to the effect that the days of the
story and of verse have gone forever, that the time is coming when Pushkin . . . will no longer be read, that pure art is impossible, that literature is
only a weapon for the civic development of society, and so forth. One could
hear, it is true, during that time the voices of Fet, Turgenev, Ostrovsky,
muffled by the political uproar . . . but society knew what it was doing, con-

19 Letter to A. S. Suvorin, dated May 30, 1888, in Chekhov, *The Selected Letters*,
p. 54.

tinued to sympathize with political literature alone, and to consider it alone as literature. This enthusiasm was noble, necessary, even just. In order to have the strength to make those enormous strides forward which our society has made in recent times, it had to be one-sided, it had to become enthusiastic about further goals in order to reach them, it had to see that single goal ahead. And actually can one think about poetry when for the first time a picture of the evil that surrounds us is unveiled before one's eyes, and when the possibility of putting an end to it is presented to us? How could we think about the beautiful as we fell ill? It is not for us who make use of the fruits of this enthusiasm to reproach it. . . . But however high-minded and wholesome this one-sided enthusiasm has been, like any enthusiasm it could not endure. The literature of a people is its full, many-sided consciousness, in which must be reflected equally the national love for goodness and truth and the national contemplation of beauty in a given epoch of development.[20]

Tolstoy was convinced that public taste was swinging away from "civic" problems toward a more balanced appreciation of the uses of literature:

Society now understood, not from critical articles alone, but discovered through experience . . . that seemingly simple truth that, however great the significance of a political literature which reflects the temporary interests of society, however necessary it is for national development, there is another literature which reflects eternal, universally human interests, the most precious, heartfelt consciousness of a people, a literature accessible to men of every nation and every epoch, a literature without which no people possessing strength and richness has ever developed.[21]

Tolstoy concluded that, in spite of his personal preference for the second kind of literature, the two kinds could and should coexist, and together would constitute a total "consciousness" "responsive to the many-sided needs of its society."[22] But there are times of great social stress apparently when literature cannot be exempted from the vital public concerns of its day. This is the escape clause Tolstoy was to invoke for his own retreat into a fiercely limited and tendentious definition of its function; and it is the clause that has become a permanent statute of the Soviet literary code since the First Five-Year Plan.

[20] Tolstoy, *Polnoe sobranie sochinenii*, 5: 271–72.
[21] *Ibid.*, p. 272.   [22] *Ibid.*

CHAPTER 7

Rebuttal II: Hamlet and Don Quixote

Two kinds of heroes represented the two kinds of literature. In a sense, the crux of the entire argument may be found in the distance that separates Bazarov and Rakhmetov, seen as two views of the same social type, but the full range of the argument involves us finally in *two* opposing views of *two* distinct social types, members of successive generations, which were loosely identified as the "men of the forties" and the "men of the sixties." For this reason, their dispute often had the aspect of a family squabble (between "fathers" and "sons") with all the bitterness born of familiarity. But they differed too in birth, in education, and in the quality of their sensibilities. The earlier generation were, as a rule, disaffected and conscience-stricken members of the serf-owning gentry. They were highly educated at home and abroad, and their basic intellectual endowment was composed of roughly equal parts of French political rationalism and German philosophical idealism. They attached great weight to the schematic principles of the first and the inflated, capitalized abstractions of the second. The end product of their training was most often the erection of a system of "convictions" which they defended in print when they found an opening, or discussed in study circles. They solemnly proclaimed their reverence for art and philosophy as the "loftiest" manifestations of the human spirit. What diffuse political pressure they were able to exert was toward a high-minded reformism. They were talkers and definers, not doers, and, as such, offered a much better recruiting ground for artists than for revolutionaries. Their times, the "leaden" reaction of Nicholas I, contributed more, whether directly or indirectly, to the blunting of their social aspirations than any cowardly evasion of their responsibilities. Even their detractors gave them credit, by and large, for keeping their moral identity intact, even if little or nothing of public benefit issued from it, and, in honoring the purity of their intentions, would accept their defenders' contention that essentially they were men of sensitivity and honor.

Their successors were generally identified with a quite distinct social group: the *raznochintsy*, the classless intelligentsia which was open to anyone who could find his way to an education. They were free of the cultural prejudices of the cultivated nobility, and resentful of its pretensions and apartness. But in spite of their relatively "democratic" origins they were as cut off by their education from the masses they would help as their rivals were by the circumstance of birth. In the major articles of their intellectual creed they were advocates of a doctrine by no means hostile in all respects to what had gone before. Their ideas represented an evolutionary step beyond their predecessors' and often rested on the same intellectual foundations. Thus their commitment to the French rationalists remained intense even as it changed from a well-mannered respect for human rights in the abstract to the belligerent advocacy of Jacobin leveling tendencies. On the philosophical level, though they stopped short of Marx, they followed closely the epochal transition within Hegelianism from idealism to materialism, acknowledging their debt to Feuerbach and others of the left-Hegelians. In their thinking about society they accepted the possibility of violent change. Indebted though they were to the French Utopians, Fourier, Blanc, and Saint-Simon, they found native sources for a socialist economic order which implied a drastic alteration of existing property relations. Science—both natural and social—replaced art as the most trustworthy source of truth, though art, as we have seen, was given a subsidiary role as a publicist of its findings. The men of the new generation portrayed themselves as blunter, less speculative, and more concerned with concrete achievement than with the formal symmetry of their beliefs or the nicety of their expression. Direct, unsentimental, and practical, they were likely to find more meaning in an autopsy report or an economic monograph than in the ambiguities of art.

As they appeared to their partisans, the men of the forties were praised for their intentions, excused for their failures, and viewed generally in a compassionate light. According to their most prominent defender, Alexander Herzen, they were honorable and pitiable victims of an implacably hostile environment. But to their radical opponents nearly every virtue that was claimed for them displayed its unattractive underside. Their vaunted sensitivity was an aristocratic finickiness; their pride in their convictions was simply another aspect of their enormous vanity; and their estrangement from work and activity was not tragic, nor was it even an enforced idleness, but the result of an atrophy of the will and of the emotions that was a natural result of their parasitic economic existence. From this vantage point they were credited with honorable intentions during the darkness of the thirties and forties, when their convictions kept the tradition of dissent from extinction, but were regarded as contemptible for their nonperformance in a period of rapidly widening arenas for action.

The men of the sixties felt that their own champion had inherited the best properties of his fainthearted predecessor, and had developed correctives for his every fault. The new man, they said, was abrupt, direct, fearless, practical, unsentimental, and selfless. But, as might be expected, each of these qualities had its evil counterpart in the eyes of the older men. The young revolutionary, according to them, was arid, insensitive, crude, and, because of all the virtues he claimed for himself, conceited to the point of arrogance. Indeed, his "rudeness" was one of the points at issue most fruitful for its relevance to the new man's literary possibilities.[1]

All the men of the forties, by the admission of their own defenders, share one important condition: they are alienated men, cut off by a combination of inner failing and outer prohibition from personal fulfillment on any level of private or public endeavor. This condition is intricately—even mysteriously—brought about, as the literature tells us so often, but it unites them all, despite the variety of individual types, in a tragic brotherhood. The younger generation claimed that it had found the way to avoid this unhappy condition. Their elders, of course, were willing to grant them no such exemption and it was their effort to include the young radicals among the alienated that touched off the controversy. Three related arguments may be dis-

---

[1] Isaiah Berlin traces this rudeness to Belinsky's God-given bad manners and vehemence of expression. Later generations of radicals, he says, cultivated rudeness as a style of behavior, designed to express their disgust with the old ways. See Mr. Berlin's article, "A Marvellous Decade (III). Belinsky: Moralist and Prophet," *Encounter*, 5.6 (December 1956): 39.

tinguished, all of which concern the very points at which the radicals undertook to protect themselves against alienation. These took the form, first, of a breathtaking assertion of freedom from the values and institutions of the status quo; second, of an unshakable faith in human reason and the principles it made known to them; and, finally, of a powerful belief in themselves, as the personal instruments of the historical process. Thus armed they proposed to complete the hazardous journey on which the liberals had become lost midway: from integration with the intolerable status quo, thence to a state of estrangement from it through the action of education and of the moral sensibility, and, finally, to a renewed state of integration, through their philosophy of action, with a rational future world of which they were the first heralds. They had found the way to a state of personal engagement, they were convinced, that would sustain them in their struggle with the Tsarist system, because they believed in the justice of their attack and in the inevitability of its outcome.

The radical state of mind with its special defenses against alienation was subjected, however, to a merciless critique, designed to show that it too was vulnerable and precisely at those points where its spokesmen considered it strongest. The radicals' belief in the power of reason, for example, represented a fatal error of judgment, and made them extremely vulnerable to the germs of alienation. Bazarov's convictions did not square with his emotional needs, or, as some felt, were merely a manifestation of his personality unbalance, and he disintegrated as a result of the tension between them. Dostoevsky directed his attack on the new men in *Notes from Underground* at precisely this point. Reason constituted perhaps "one-twentieth" of the human make-up, and served only as a presumptuous excuse for the expression of the capricious, criminal impulses which aspire continually to dominion over man's nature. In the contest between good and evil instincts, reason is but the tool of the animal in man, of the "weak," "rebellious," malicious, destructive side of man's nature.

A good part of Tolstoy's polemic against historians in *War and Peace* is directed against an inflated estimate of the power of the mind. In his blindly determinist view of history, no man is granted the privilege of directing the course of events, or of predicting the course they will take. History is the unforeseeable resultant of the minds, will, and hearts of all who take part in it. Any tendency to overemphasize the rational faculty is mistaken and dangerous: "If we admit that human life can be ruled by reason, the possibility of life is destroyed."[2]

In the radicals' defense it should be noted that their concept of reason lacked the arid quality of the French *philosophes*, and that its election to the governing position in their lives was not an easy or automatic matter. On the contrary, it was an expensive and difficult, though unavoidable, choice. Chernyshevsky wrote in a letter to Nekrasov:

I myself know by experience that convictions do not constitute everything in life—the demands of the heart exist, and in the life of the heart there is genuine joy and genuine sorrow for all of us. This I know by experience, I know it better than others. Convictions occupy our mind only when the heart rests from its joy or sorrow. I will even say that for me, personally, my private affairs are more significant than any world problem—men do not drown themselves, or shoot themselves, or become drunkards because of world problems—I have experienced this and I know that the poetry of the heart has the same rights as the poetry of thought—for me, personally, the first is more attractive than the second. . . . I have allowed myself this frankness not only to tell you that I look on poetry by no means exclusively from the political point of view. On the contrary, only by force does politics dig its way into my heart, which does not by any means live by it, or, at least, would not like to live by it.[3]

The last wistful qualification suggests the final outcome of the tension between heart and mind in his own case.

However reluctantly the decision is made, and however slight is the margin of the heart's subjugation, certain drastic consequences flow from this choice, according to the liberals' critique. Reason is the principal justification for the radicals' sweeping—and to many, terrifying—claim to freedom from all the taboos and restraints of the culture they despised. By their apparent willingness to take human life, to commit "the necessary murder," they had, according to Dostoevsky, discarded timeless moral principles. In their scorn for a particular social order they seemed to others to threaten many of the permanent achievements of human civilization. The freedom to which

[2] L. N. Tolstoy, *War and Peace*, trans. Louise and Aylmer Maude (New York, 1942), p. 1256.
[3] N. G. Chernyshevsky, *Polnoe sobranie sochinenii* (Moscow, 1949), 14: 320. Compare this quotation with Lenin's famous remark to Gorky after listening to the *Appassionata*: "It affects your nerves, makes you want to say stupid, nice things and stroke the heads of people who could create such beauty while living in this vile hell. And you mustn't stroke anyone's head—you might get your hand bitten off. You have to hit them on the head, without any mercy, although our ideal is not to use force against anyone. . . . our duty is infernally hard." Maxim Gorky, *Days with Lenin* (New York, 1932), p. 52.

"all is permitted" could lead only to license, destruction, and anarchy.

But for the radical, deliverance from every oppressive institution and every inhibiting code of the environment was an indispensable precondition for action—the more absolute his opposition, the more drastic his program for change, and the more thorough his rejection of contemporary values. Yet the aim of this break, as he saw it, was never self-indulgence. Reintegrated, as the radicals thought they were, by a combination of personal indignation, social analysis, programmatic doctrine, and "scientific" expectations, their freedom existed within sharply defined limits, and with a narrowly prescribed outlet, similar to a gun barrel, through which it could be discharged. It was a freedom only to be effective or useful, and entirely lacking in easy rewards. Yet within its compass the radical felt himself protected from all the compromises, the contradictory loyalties, and the wracking doubts that led to alienation.

But the nonradicals replied that this sort of freedom ended in an even more drastic kind of alienation. By casting off so many moral and social restraints, by rejecting such a broad cross section of human achievement, by asserting their superiority over so many disciplines of the mind, and by denying their own human needs, the radicals, they felt, paid a fatally high price. Raskolnikov cut himself off from love, from God, from Russia, and from mankind when he dared to act. His awful isolation resulted in a crippling distortion of values. With their eye always on the whole man, the writers believed they had discovered here a point of primary vulnerability.

To the extent that the radicals' defenses were based on doctrine and on expectations, the writers were unimpressed since they shared neither. To the extent that they were made of raw personal courage, the writers were, on the other hand, thoroughly respectful. But to the extent that they involved a monumental and disfiguring self-assurance, the writers were extremely interested, because here again they detected a flaw, that led as surely—and for the same reasons—to alienation as Pechorin's thirst for self-immolation or Rudin's self-delusions. Whether the radicals' defenses were regarded as a general character trait, or as an emotional orientation toward the world, and quite apart from ideological labels, the writers felt they had discovered a new variation of a familiar pattern.

This is the celebrated "rudeness" of the radicals, a term which refers to the quality of their sensibilities, more than it does to their table manners, though these too, we are assured by the gently bred liberals, were deplorable. The arrogance of their posture toward the world, whether viewed as cause or symptom of their maladjustment, was for the outside observer the outstanding feature of their personalities. This is the burden of Herzen's harsh personal attack on the radical youth. Himself one of the least "superfluous" representatives of the men of the forties and a political revolutionary to boot, he nevertheless felt himself separated from the men of the sixties by birth, training, and outlook. His most famous article on the subject, "The Superfluous Men and the Men with a Grudge," which appeared in his journal, *The Bell*, in October 15, 1860, is one of the landmarks in the quarrel between the generations.[4] He was principally concerned with defending the older men against unjustified attacks from their overbearing young successors. It is a sentimental defense of the liberal group, by one of its members. They were, he insisted, the honorable, well-intentioned, and far from inactive victims of the savage repressions of the Nicholas era. Their idleness was enforced by circumstances, and their lethargy concealed sharp suffering. They had become, he confessed, pathological types toward the end of their ordeal, prematurely burnt out, disillusioned, and "sick in body and soul."[5] But for all their sins and shortcomings they were guiltless of the insulting charges directed at them by the "sullen" new men, who were, if anything, sicker than their forebears. Herzen characterized the new types in vividly uncomplimentary terms. They were, he said, gravely deficient in sensibility. They were able, for example, to surmount the defeat of the revolution of 1848 without pausing to weep a single tear for its fallen heroes. There was a sinister "lightness" to all their emotional responses which, combined with the immoral pleasure they found in negation, and the "terrible ruthlessness" of their personal code, made for a most unappetizing kind of person. They displayed a monk's hatred for human frailty; they had the speech, the manners, and the sudden, explosive rages of bureaucrats; and they were, Herzen insisted, hypochondriacs to a man. At bottom he detected the starved

---

[4] A. I. Herzen, *Polnoe sobranie sochinenii i pisem*, ed. M. K. Lemke (Petrograd, 1919), 10: 413–23. The article is believed to be a response to Dobrolyubov's review of Turgenev's *On the Eve*. The model for the radical type whom he compares with a narrow-minded, joyless Russian preacher of the Middle Ages named Daniel Zatochnik is probably Dobrolyubov himself. It was written not long after Chernyshevsky's clandestine trip to London, in the course of which he tried without success to effect a rapprochement with Herzen.

[5] *Ibid.*, p. 417.

egos of ambitious and unsuccessful mediocrities. On their faces were the marks of a "gnawing, short-tempered, and curdled self-love."[6] In spite of the polemical ferocity of his tone, which damages his case at times, Herzen has diagnosed their trouble in a way that was echoed by most nonradical commentators. Although they too were victims of traditionless, Russian barbarism, and their intentions were no less exalted than their predecessors', their ingrained arrogance made it impossible to admire them, or to share their convictions or their hopes. They were inadequate as people, hence unworthy of the purposes they professed to stand for.

Turgenev, whose indictment of the radical is far gentler than his friend Herzen's, had, nevertheless, to acknowledge the presence of a towering arrogance in the radical type.[7] In Bazarov this quality provides the outlet for his admirable courage and energy and is, at the same time, a crippling malformation of his character. When his doctrinal supports have been worn away and shown to be inadequate, Bazarov lapses fleetingly into a Nietzschean image of himself as a kind of superman, before he collapses under the weight of his swollen ego.[8] When charged with falsification and slander on this point, Turgenev looked beyond Herzen's concrete explanations and sought to explain it in general, psychological terms:

What kind of artist would I be (I don't say man) if I did not understand that self-confidence, exaggeration of expression ... and posing, even a certain cynicism, constitute inevitable attributes of youth.[9]

Turgenev was not always able to remain on this level of universal comment, oscillating as he did between it and the specific terms of reference forced on him by his enemies. But he was firmly established in this mood when he wrote his subtle and comprehensive essay on literary heroism, "Hamlet and Don Quixote."[10] It is the final docu-

[6] *Ibid.*, pp. 418–19.
[7] Even Chernyshevsky acknowledges this. But with Rakhmetov, his self-assurance and his abruptness in personal relations are seen as a refreshingly direct and time-saving manner which all his friends understand and appreciate.
[8] Turgenev makes it clear in a letter to K. K. Sluchevskii that the slip of a knife that kills Bazarov is not an accident but part of a coherent tragic design. *Sobranie sochinenii* (Moscow, 1949), 11: 214–15.
[9] Letter to A. P. Filosofovaya, August 18/30, 1874, *ibid.*, p. 288.
[10] First delivered as a speech on January 10, 1860, at a public meeting for the benefit of the Society for the Assistance of Needy Writers and Scholars, it was then published in the radical *Sovremennik* (No. 1, 1860), though it received an entirely hostile reception from the magazine's policy-makers. Its appearance is often used to mark the decisive moment in the break between liberals and radicals. I have used the text of the public lecture as found in I. S. Turgenev, *Sobranie sochinenii*, 11: 5–20.

ment of the writers' rebuttal and is the nearest thing there is to a public manifesto of their position. In it Turgenev clearly takes his departure from the specific issues of his day, but he arranges them in new ways, draws refreshingly different distinctions, and proceeds to a level of universal statement. The essay purports to be a study of human nature and of the two polar types that make it up. But it is unmistakably a writer's view of human nature, and we are aware at every moment that his classification and analysis are rooted in the literary possibilities these types present to the working novelist. Although his versions of Hamlet and of Don Quixote are plainly intended to comment on the quarrel then going on about character types, his insight raises the entire question of the literary hero to a plane of general aesthetic discussion, which touches on some of the outer limits of the possibilities of fiction. To be sure, the essay was generated out of an intense concern with contemporary problems. To view it *only* as a narrow "superstructural" reflection of local conditions, however, is to deny its continuing relevance to creative problems.

Turgenev has cast the whole of his elaborate distinction in typically ambivalent terms. There is no favoritism or invidiousness in his judgments: each type has his virtues; each type has his faults; and both are held within the orbit of his sympathy. He first distinguished between them by noting the relation each man had to his moral code: "The ideal, this basis and goal of their existence is either outside them or within them; in other words, for each of us, either the private 'I' stands in first place or something else which is acknowledged as more exalted."[11] Between egoism and altruism, the apparent advantage lies entirely with Don Quixote because he has faith:

Faith, above all, faith in something eternal, immovable, in truth, in a truth which is outside the individual man, to which it is not easy to give oneself, which demands sacrifices and services.... Don Quixote is imbued with devotion to the ideal, for which he is prepared to subject himself to every possible deprivation, to sacrifice his life; he values his life only to the extent that it will serve as a means for the realization of the ideal, for the establishment of truth and justice on earth.[12]

But in the very assertion of his moral nature Don Quixote's great failing is made evident, although it is not enough to devalue the purity of his purpose:

[11] *Ibid.*, p. 6.   [12] *Ibid.*, p. 7.

A constant striving toward one and the same goal lends a certain monotony to his ideas, a one-sidedness to his mind; he knows little, but he need not know much: he knows what his cause is, why he lives on earth, and this is the principal knowledge. At one moment Don Quixote can seem a complete maniac, because the most indubitable materiality disappears before his eyes, melts like wax in the flame of his enthusiasm (he really sees live Moors in wooden dolls, knights in sheep)—at another moment, limited because he does not know how to sympathize easily, or to enjoy himself; but, like an ancient tree, he has struck his roots deep in the soil and cannot change his convictions, or be shifted from one subject to another; the strength of his moral substance (note that this madman, this wandering knight, is the most moral being on earth) gives special force and grandeur to all his judgments and speeches, to his whole figure, in spite of the comic and the ridiculous into which he perpetually falls.[13]

Don Quixote's strength, then, *is* his weakness. His singleness of purpose requires that he be both deficient in understanding and limited in sensibility, to the degree that he has a well-developed capacity for self-delusion.[14]

Thus far, Turgenev has dealt with the revolutionary as he was. With the introduction of the idea of the comic, however, we become concerned with the observer's response to his image. And not far in the background we sense the preoccupations of the novelist, who is concerned with the face the revolutionary presented to him to write about, and with the problem of rendering his moral purity bearable for the reader by "reducing" it to acceptable terms through the devices of art. The source of the comic is first of all the blindness that characterizes the revolutionary's dedication to the cause. In a related sense comedy arises from his commitment to the future: only "the fates" will decide whether the apparent chamber pot on Don Quixote's head will turn out later to be what he had known it to be all along, a helmet of shining armor. Turgenev, here, in taking two of the most antagonizing features of the radical ethos, and making them acceptable through the agency of comedy, assures the reader that the radical is as fallible and as foolish as he. Turgenev says: "A certain allotment of the ridiculous must inevitably be added to the actions, to the character of the people dedicated to a great new cause, as a tax...as a

---

[13] *Ibid.*, pp. 7–8.

[14] This searching yet belittling insight could not be expected to endear itself to the radicals for all the gentleness with which it is expressed. At a time when their lives, and more important, their cause, were at stake, they were not disposed to welcome such a condescending evaluation of themselves.

calming sacrifice to the jealous gods."[15] We are entitled to interpret "the jealous gods" as both the rules of art and the expectations of the average, nonbelieving reader. The ultimate purpose of the "comic envelope" is to release "a reconciling and cleansing force" through laughter. And, Turgenev adds: "Whom you laugh at you forgive and are ready to love."[16] Turgenev has mediated between the image and the reader, and has brought this encounter to a typically literary resolution. The love toward which Turgenev would lead the reader is composed of equal parts of respect (for the purity of Don Quixote's purpose), of affection, and of pity. Pity, in a sense, is Turgenev's final destination. Through it, the sting of the radical's arrogance is removed. At the same time the reader is detached from that direct identification with the literary figure which the radical aesthetic posited, and is elevated to the writer's superior point of sympathetic (and condescending) vantage. In showing how this type can be assimilated into a work of art, Turgenev has extended the definition of alienation to embrace the revolutionary as well. For he is cut off from awareness, from a rich emotional life, and from a genuine knowledge of evil as surely as Hamlet is cut off from action and from love by his egotism and by his perceptive, skeptical, and hungry intellect.

Hamlet is easier to write about than Don Quixote because he possesses so many of the conventional attributes of the tragic hero. But the literary problem, as Turgenev sees it, is substantially the same: to reduce him to a condition in which he arouses the reader's pity. In the case of the dry, withdrawn Hamlet, who is incapable of love, hence of being loved, who is barred from action because of the range of his awareness, the principal obstacles to his acceptance by the reader are his scornful pride and his apparent lack of moral commitment. Don Quixote's condition of moral purity and the consequent foolishness of his mien is exactly reversed in Hamlet's case: it is inconceivable that the latter be laughed at, and in his anxious, twisting flight from commitment (until it is too late), he seems to abandon the possibility of asserting any moral position. Yet as he approaches death it becomes clear that scorn is his kind of moral utterance, and that the target of his negation is evil. As he becomes more deeply entangled in hostile circumstance, his pride is shown to be a mask for personal courage and dignity, which dissolves on the point of death

---

[15] Turgenev, *Sobranie sochinenii*, II: 18.
[16] *Ibid.*, p. 9.

into a quiet humility. By this route he reaches his final destination beside Don Quixote in the pity and understanding of the observer.[17]

Art, Turgenev seemed to insist, must be granted the privilege of rendering the activist and the intellectual equal in the face of death, through the universal solvent of pity. Certainly the artist may accept neither type at his own evaluation of himself. The injunction to pity the revolutionary was anathema to the radicals, of course, who could not see themselves in the whole context of their deprivation, sacrifice, and self-delusion. Yet it is Chernyshevsky's refusal or inability to account for, or to contain, or to rise above their sense of superiority that makes his heroes unacceptable to the reader who does not share their creed. The human faults Turgenev perceived are there, but because the author has failed to explore them fully or to show them as sources of vulnerability, as well as of strength, the novel fails to supply that kind of total illumination that is art's function. Dealing with his heroes, the writer must insist on his claim to occupy an eminence above and independent of the ideas and values that sustain them. He must reject the assumption that any man's social reality is entirely congruent with his human reality and must see him in all his dimensions. Finally, he is obliged to detach the reader's emotion from the character's assertion of his own views. The hero in Turgenev's formula ends as an object of contemplation, not of emulation, more to be pitied than imitated. There is instruction in his fate but it is not the same lesson the hero, himself, would have the reader learn.

The revolutionary, no less than any other type, can best be explained in art's terms through defeat. His fallibility and his suffering are the surest means of access to understanding his total condition, whether he is proud, isolated, and tragic, or single-minded, deluded, and comic. Here, Turgenev has transcended the political categories with which he began his analysis and has suggested a scale for the reclassification of Russian hero-types. The proud, self-centered, and conventionally heroic figure who dares to act in defiance of his surroundings appears

---

[17] Arthur P. Mendel has called attention to one of the most poignant moments in thaw literature in his review of the extensive attention paid to Shakespeare's *Hamlet*. In obvious reference to their own time, several Soviet critics and filmmakers have celebrated Hamlet as the embodiment of the active individual conscience, and of the probing moral intelligence which understands, among many other things, that direct action may solve nothing. This concern with "Hamletism" suggests how badly Soviet artists feel the need of the tragic mode to confront and account for their own experience. Arthur P. Mendel, "Hamlet and Soviet Humanism," *Slavic Review*, December 1971, pp. 733–46.

both within and without the movement of extreme political dissidence. Thus the Pechorins and Bazarovs, as well as the Stavrogins
and Prince Andreis yet to come, are brothers beneath their ideological
labels, and are, in turn, joined by the bond of suffering with the mock-
heroic Onegins, Rudins, even with the quixotic Myshkin, and, conceivably, at the far end of the scale of heroism, with the monstrous
antihero of *Notes from Underground*.

The writer's job is done, Turgenev suggests, when he has explored,
clarified, and generalized human suffering. But the radical responds to
suffering with the blunt and urgent question which is echoed so often
by Russian intellectuals: what is to be done about it? It is not misreading Turgenev's essay, perhaps, to propose, in a final look at it,
that the Hamlet and Don Quixote figures also stand for the artist and
the revolutionary respectively, the first dedicated to awareness at all
costs, the second to action at all costs, and that both share a common
painful destiny. Turgenev's proposal, if such it may be considered,
could not be accepted by the radicals. They saw their own suffering as
a tiny sacrifice when set against the misery of the mass, and, if it contributed to the alleviation of the general misery, it was irrelevant, even
shameful, to dwell on it. If the writer replied that the revolutionary
nevertheless suffers as all men do, and that by the drastic, though high-
minded, decisions on which he bases his life he invites a new and
more awful kind of suffering, the agony, say, of an Ivan Karamazov,
which art cannot fail to record, the radical might respond that Ivan's
private hell is not typical or useful, or even, in his sense, truthful, and
that it fades into triviality when set against the consuming agony
of a nation.

II

The great controversy of the decade between 1855 and 1865, which
illuminated so many crucial questions in the history of the Russian
intellect and imagination, did not have a conclusive outcome on all
its many levels. The events of 1917 came closest to deciding the fundamental political questions at issue. The First All-Union Congress of
Soviet Writers in 1934, though it too appeared to make an irrevocable
choice between a free and a proprietary approach to literature, lacked
the finality of the Bolshevik seizure of political power. The creed of
Russian classical realism continued to show itself after 1934, as it had
between 1917 and 1934, sometimes with the apparent indulgence of

the political magistrates, at other times to their surprise and discomfort. The images of the hero continued to reflect the tension between the two approaches to literature.

In the intervening years between 1865 and 1917 the literary competition continued in new forms, corresponding to new conditions, but unchanged in its essentials. The new man went through a number of metamorphoses after the decline of the radical democrats, making his major reappearances first in the Narodniks' "little band of heroes," then as the early Bolshevik who, in turn, became the "new Soviet man." In the nineteenth century the radical continued to be viewed by many writers with detachment or outspoken hostility. Dostoevsky's *Possessed* and Chekhov's *Ivanov* are among the better-known works that contain unflattering portraits of the activist or the man of "progressive convictions." The literary portraiture of the alienated man, on the other hand, was to reach new heights of complexity and richness in the years that followed the decade of controversy: *War and Peace, Anna Karenina, The Death of Ivan Ilyich, The Idiot, The Raw Youth,* and *The Brothers Karamazov* were yet to be written.

Chekhov carried the alienated man, in his mock-heroic aspect, to a kind of apotheosis, in response, perhaps, to the general antiheroic trend in modern European realism. If this attitude had been as prevalent in Russia in the mid-century as it was in Western Europe, there might not have been the persistence of the large, taciturn, self-enclosed figures, whether rebels or revolutionaries or madmen, whom Turgenev epitomized in his image of Hamlet. Certainly Tolstoy was expressing this antiheroic current when he wrote in *War and Peace*:

For an historian considering the achievement of a certain aim, there are heroes; for the artist treating of man's relations to all sides of life, there cannot and should not be heroes, but there should be men.[18]

His only hero, as he had said earlier, was truth; and when he repeated the same thought to Gorky years later in more general terms—"Heroes—that's a lie and invention; there are simply people, people, and nothing else"[19]—he was taking a positive stand against the new heroic romanticism Gorky was advocating.

In the decades after 1865, the contest between the two schools had no decisive outcome: political extremists did not gain control of the

18 Tolstoy, *War and Peace*, p. 1356.
19 Maxim Gorky, *Reminiscences* (New York, 1946), p. 54.

great instrument of Russian realism; the writers kept the realist creed alive and in active service, through the death of Chekhov and beyond. But there were notable defections from their position. Turgenev, who was distressed by the clamor he touched off through his interventions in the controversy, lapsed into a state of confusion. A great loss to literature was registered when it became apparent that he had been jarred loose from the delicate balance of ambiguities that had sustained *Fathers and Sons* as well as "Hamlet and Don Quixote." His petulant satires against the new generation of radicals made it clear that he had surrendered important positions to the radical view of art, even as he opposed radical political ideas. A polemical, topical view of the truth had replaced the Olympian claims he had earlier asserted for the artist's kind of truth. And when he labored and brought forth his own "positive hero," the sluggish Solomin of *Smoke* (1867), so well armed against failure because he ventured so little, a "helper" not a "leader," he had permanently impaired his vision by making his art the servant of his inconsequential political views. Tolstoy was the most dramatic "turncoat," of course, and his repudiation of art was, characteristically, more deliberate, more drastic, and more flamboyant. "Art is a lie,"[20] he told Gorky. Earlier he had written *What Is Art?* (1897) to set the narrow boundaries within which art could be trusted to deal with essential moral truths. Turgenev's retreat and Tolstoy's desertion testify to the urgency with which the social question forced itself on all men of conscience in prerevolutionary Russia. There was a point of fundamental choice, apparently recognized by all, between the concerns of artist and revolutionary. To decide that in the face of suffering of a certain quality, quantity, and intensity, art became expendable, was a tragic but not always an impossible choice for Russian men of letters.

The radical critics worked on the margins of the great creative currents of the age, exerting a steady pressure of conscience, often posing the questions the writers undertook to explore. It was when the alliance between them broke down, when the tactical requirements of political action asserted themselves too urgently, that the artist and the revolutionary were thrown into direct competition for "the awareness of human suffering." Each was forced to default on one premise of his alliance: the revolutionary had to compromise with the expedient choices that the social crisis offered him, the writer to fall back

[20] *Ibid.*

on that necessary "compromise" with his civilization without which he could not function. The rupture in the 1860s was costly, resulting in disillusion and bitterness. More robust spirits like Tolstoy and Dostoevsky maintained themselves intact as artists against the ferocious pressures of the next two decades, until Tolstoy, independently, felt himself driven to make that ultimate choice between art and action which he had acknowledged twenty years before. When he did, he found himself involved in the creation of a positive, emblematic hero— in this case, himself. For the power of his doctrine flowed from the example of his own moral life, which was to radiate outward until it was accepted by enough men to bring about the nonviolent, but nonetheless total, overthrow of the social order. Tolstoy was reflecting the belief, so deeply ingrained in the Russian consciousness since the time of the *bogatyr*, that the surest promise of their release from intolerable suffering was the appearance of a new kind of moral personality, not a Messianic leader, but a more general type, susceptible of imitation, whose personal qualities would contain and express the means to that liberation.

PART TWO

The Marxian Increment

CHAPTER 8

Marxism, Realism, and the Hero

﷽

Among the qualities inherent in matter, motion is the
first and foremost, not only in the form of mechanical and
mathematical motion, but chiefly in the form of an impulse,
a vital spirit, a tension. KARL MARX, The Holy Family

Marxism, John Strachey has said, is not merely a body of ideas, but a separate "country" of the intellect. One visits it in pursuit of the answers to a single, delimited question—in this case the connections between Marxian ideas and the properties of realism—at the risk of returning with incomplete findings, rendered useless by loss of context. In any case, one is automatically exposed to the charge of "distortion," both from the nationals of that country, and from outsiders who have never crossed its borders. Yet the matter cannot be sidestepped. Marxism makes up the bulk of the Soviet intellectual inheritance according to all official comment on the matter; the Soviet habit of scholastic dependence on past intellectual authorities makes it imperative to inquire into the literary consequences of Marxism. The little Marx and Engels had to say about literature itself has been piously, exhaustively, and repeatedly explored by Soviet critics in search of a viable "literary policy."

I

A fundamental polarity in the Marxian concept of human behavior is defined in two of Marx's most familiar notions. The first summarizes his view of man as a determined creature:

The mode of production of material life conditions the social, political and intellectual life process in general. It is not the consciousness of men that determines their being, but on the contrary, their social being that determines their consciousness.[1]

The second emphasizes man's role as a free, conscious, and responsible agent, as the "maker of his own history." A great distance separates these two ideas and very different consequences have flowed from the varying emphases Marxists have put upon them. But for Marx and Engels there was apparently no formal contradiction between them. They are found side by side in the same sentence in a state of harmony which certainly is intended to express more than a verbal resolution of the tension between them. In the Third Thesis on Feuerbach, Marx wrote:

The materialist doctrine that men are products of circumstances and upbringing, forgets that it is men that change circumstances and that the educator himself needs educating.[2]

The unity that contains these contradictory propositions can be described briefly: man's capacity to acquire true objective knowledge of his history, of his social milieu, and of all his real relations with his environment leads to a state of awareness that permits—indeed, requires—action. "Freedom," Engels said, "... consists in the control over ourselves and over external nature which is founded on knowledge of natural necessity."[3] Man becomes the hastener of history, struggles to master it, and, when he achieves that mastery, gains control over his destiny. As Vernon Venable, writing on the central "dilemma of inevitability," has pointed out, man, himself, "the needing organism, purposive human activity ... is a nuclear causal factor"[4] in *determining* history's course.

Soviet experience has shown that the search for a "correct" solution to this perpetual problem has affected every area of thought and action at one time or another—political strategy, philosophy, education, psychology, literature, art, and economic theory, to name some of the important ones. The opposition between Bolshevist and Menshevist

[1] Karl Marx and Friedrich Engels, *Selected Works* (Moscow, 1951), 1: 329. Solzhenitsyn indicates in his fiction that this idea is, in a sense, the doctrinal foundation of the prison society. See below, pp. 302–5, for my discussion of this matter. A fuller version of this passage from Marx may be found in footnote 17, p. 302.

[2] *Ibid.*, pp. 365–66.

[3] Friedrich Engels, *Herr Eugen Dühring's Revolution in Science* (New York, 1939), p. 125.

[4] Vernon Venable, *Human Nature: The Marxian View* (New York, 1946), p. 190. I should pause here to acknowledge my debt to this excellent work, particularly for its elucidation of the ethical question in Marxian theory.

tactics before the revolution, the historic debate of the philosophers in 1929 between the "mechanists" and the "dialecticians,"[5] and the drastic reversals in psychological theory after 1929[6] reflect conflicts between Marxian sects according to the construction each has put upon this troublesome unity of conceptual opposites. In standard Soviet terminology the principal schism has been described as between "Leninism" and "Plekhanovism." One of Lenin's major contributions to Soviet Marxian theory is now said to be his redefinition of man as the conscious, responsible, and disciplined maker of his own history, as opposed to Plekhanov's emphasis on man as the creature and passive beneficiary of the historical process. It was Stalin who extended Lenin's notion of conscious political partisanship to every field of intellectual endeavor, including literature and art, and such self-contained activities of the human intellect as astronomy and musical composition.

Applied to the scholarly and creative disciplines, the dilemma is expressed in another kind of antithesis: as the opposition between a science of history and of society, on the one hand, and a summons to revolutionary struggle, on the other. Marx made his famous distinction between the function of the philosopher as *interpreter* or *changer* of the world, insisting that the second had become his true vocation.[7] Yet if we apply this distinction to Marx's and Engels's own careers, it is clear that though they played both parts, the best years of their lives were spent investigating social phenomena, not in devising revolutionary strategies. Hecker distinguishes two peaks of the activist phase within the history of Marxism—1848 and 1917.[8] Marx's most productive years, between 1850 and his death in 1883, were largely spent in the British Museum, not on the barricades. According to Marx's example, each adherent of his system had to make a decision about the importance he would assign to knowledge as against action. Thus the Marxist chooses between two approaches to experience, two kinds of truth: one objective, analytical, and descriptive, the other selective, tendentious, and agitational. Obviously the first is more congenial to scholarly investigation and is, at the

[5] See Julius F. Hecker's summary of the debate in *Moscow Dialogues* (London, 1934), Dialogue XIV, pp. 157–73.

[6] Cf. Raymond Bauer's *The New Man in Soviet Psychology* (Cambridge, Mass., 1952), particularly Chapter 2, "Two Kinds of Marxism," and Chapter 6, "Consciousness Comes to Man."

[7] Eleventh Thesis on Feuerbach, in Marx and Engels, *Selected Works*, 2: 367.

[8] Cf. Hecker, *Moscow Dialogues*, pp. 134–35.

same time, closer to the determinist pole in the Marxian dichotomy. The investigator of a given historical event will explore all lines of causal development, including the role of human consciousness, because all events in the Marxian materialist view of the universe are assumed to be determined when seen in the past. Even the Marxian "accident," an intersection of two or more lines of causal development, which could not have been foreseen by the historical actors at the time, becomes a determined event as soon as it is completed. The pragmatic agitator is less interested in the past, though he knows that he is history's instrument and has its momentum behind him.

It is more than a question of the uses the Marxist shall make of his time or of the *kinds* of information that will serve his purposes. In theory, all information must be accessible to the revolutionary movement at some level in its hierarchy of command, as it was to Marx in the British Museum, but it is not necessarily to be shared with the entire rank and file in undigested form. Before he passes it on he sifts it to discover what it tells of coming events, and "interprets" it to square with certain basic attitudes of the rank-and-filers and to stiffen their wills and arouse their emotions. The scholar-determinist might venture to extend his findings into the future in the form of a "scientific" prediction, but the moment he looks up from the data he is expected by his alter ego, the agitator, to exert all the influence he can on the most controllable causal agency in the historical process—the human mind. Would this not result in an abrupt and bewildering change of key in any single work? Actually, in the Marxian classics the two kinds of truth are always present in some kind of synthesis. Marx and Engels did not often face problems of revolutionary strategy, or permit themselves to predict the immediate how and when of social change, but their great analytical works are charged with emotion and constitute in their totality a generalized call to arms.

Lenin, the activist and strategist, drastically altered the emphasis by insisting on the indissoluble unity and interdependence of "theory and practice."[9] Practice poses the questions and tests the answers

9 See V. I. Lenin, *Materialism and Empirio-Criticism* (Moscow, 1952), pp. 190–96, for a typical discussion of this matter. Raymond Bauer has very acutely traced the consequences of Lenin's epistemology in its Soviet application. For his account of the successive steps by which the Marxian notion that knowledge must be tested by use (Marx's Second Thesis on Feuerbach) became the doctrine that usefulness to the Party is the final determinant of all truth, see Bauer, *The New Man in Soviet Psychology*, pp. 103–6.

that theory returns in a close, continuous interchange. Bound by a rigid standard of practical application, theory is not granted the right to explore freely, or to wander any great distance from immediate political tasks. Lenin is concerned, of course, with *political* theory and practice, but this approach to knowledge has been extended at times to many intellectual spheres in the USSR through the limitless definition of what is political, that is, of what affects the power or security of Party and state.[10] Here theory turns into ideology.

How does the Marxian polarity manifest itself in those writings of Marx and Engels which bear on problems of the literary imagination? It is already clear that the "agitational" truth of Marxism, with its emphasis on stimulus and persuasion, resembles the views of the Russian radical critics at several points: the attitude toward the future, the doctrinal view of truth, and the consequent posting of a rigid standard of selectivity. It is also evident, I think, that the opposition between investigation and agitation corresponds closely to the tension we have already noted in literature between "is" and "should be." Shall literature, then, be primarily concerned with interpreting or changing the world? And, in this connection, is there any formula for the literary hero? The central division in Marx's thinking, we may note here, manifests itself in a suggestive way on this very question. When asked by his daughter in a parlor game to name his favorite heroes, he responded with two: a hero of action—Spartacus, and a hero of thought—Kepler.[11] Should the literary hero be Spartacus or Kepler, or both, or neither, or no one? In any case, how free should the artist be to explore his universe?

II

The scattered observations Marx and Engels made on literature are impressive for their range. Their cultivated tastes bear the imprint of

[10] It is on the levels below the one where policy is made that writers, scholars, commentators, and other "toilers of the brain" are exposed to the dangers of over-emphasizing one or the other aspect of Marxian truth. Thus, a history of philosophy may be charged by *Pravda* with "objectivism," or "the passive reflection of events," and its author subjected to a torrent of abuse on that account. On the other hand, when a linguist, say, or a geneticist says he has found a superior "Marxian" or "Soviet socialist" approach to his discipline, the passage of time may reveal that in his agitational zeal he has paid inadequate attention to the objective data, or to the special requirements of his field, and that his leadership has brought the Soviet section of his branch of science to intellectual bankruptcy.

[11] A. V. Lunacharsky, ed., *Marks i Engels ob iskusstve* (Moscow, 1933), p. 208.

a solid nineteenth-century humanist education, and the general tone of their approach differs markedly from that of the Russian radicals in its lack of suspicion or hostility toward the literary imagination. The question to determine is whether or not their random remarks on the subject fit together in any kind of scheme, and where, if at all, the scheme connects with deeper currents of Marxian thought. In this connection the issues brought to light in the Russian literary debate offer a useful set of testing devices. Marx and Engels may not belong under either heading, but a tendency in either direction is important because of the close attention Soviet intellectuals affect to pay to the founders of their tradition.[12]

Marx and Engels insisted, of course, that literature, together with all other products of the human intellect, has its being within an ideological superstructure, the content of which is ultimately determined by the economic and political structure of society. But, once they had established the *primacy* of the economic factor, they felt constrained in several subsequent utterances to correct the tendency of their interpreters to make the socioeconomic situation not the *ultimate* but the *sole* determinant of the shape and substance of "intellectual products." Engels, on two occasions, attempted to set general limits to the efficacy of the economic factor as the governor of man's spiritual life. In a letter to Conrad Schmidt in 1890 he discussed the philosophy and art of the Enlightenment in these terms:

I consider the ultimate supremacy of economic development established in these spheres too, but it comes to pass within conditions imposed by the particular sphere itself: in philosophy, for instance, through the operation of economic influences . . . upon the existing philosophic material handed down by predecessors. Here [the] economy creates nothing absolutely new, but it determines the way in which the existing material of thought is altered and further developed, and that too for the most part indirectly, for

12 Peter Demetz discovers in Marx and Engels, through "the distinct inclinations of their respective tastes," what he calls "a basic structure of doctrine that is grounded in a social derivation of literary phenomena." *Marx, Engels and the Poets: Origins of Marxist Literary Criticism* (Chicago, 1967), pp. 232–33. I would not quarrel with this conclusion, but would maintain that if Soviet exegetes ever came upon this doctrine in their early work, they had rejected it by 1932, as unsuited to their needs.

In my treatment I have not distinguished between the ideas of the "young" Marx and the older or "Marxist" Marx, or between the ideas of Marx and Engels as separate thinkers. I regard all they have said on art as a single legacy Soviet commentators might have been expected to consult as a whole, or selectively, according to their practice of scriptural referral—but not to reject, as they eventually did.

it is the political, legal and moral reflexes which exercise the greatest direct influence upon philosophy.[13]

Engels is arguing here against a too simple view of the relations between economics and culture. The inference may be drawn from the phrase "existing material of thought" that every discipline of the mind has a history of its own, laws of its own development, concerns which are unique to it, and the power to exert its own causal influence on men and events. On the last point Engels is quite explicit:

Political, juridical, philosophical, religious, literary, artistic, etc., development is based on economic development. But all these react upon one another and also upon the economic base. It is not that the economic position is the *cause and alone* active, while everything else has only a passive effect. There is, rather, interaction on the basis of the economic necessity, which *ultimately* always asserts itself.[14]

Confronted with the achievements of the Greeks, Marx went further:

It is well known that certain periods of the highest development of art stand in no direct connection with the general development of society, nor with the material basis and the skeleton structure of its organization. Witness the Greeks as compared with modern nations or even Shakespeare.[15]

Soviet Marxists, in general, have ignored these qualifications and have assumed an extremely direct and restricted relation between base and superstructure. The permanent, all-determining war between the classes is inevitably present in all works of the mind and imagination, whether or not the human agent is aware of it, and is the key to their meanings as well as the touchstone of value-judgments about them. Every work of art presents itself to the critic as an expression, in rationalized or direct form, of class interest. The Soviet Marxist does not say that literature partakes of ideology or has a relationship to it, or is influenced by it. Literature to him *is* ideology or, even more narrowly, every literary work is a form of class consciousness. I. Nusinov leaves little room for qualification in a typical definition of the Soviet attitude on this matter:

In class society where all human consciousness and behavior is defined by class being and conditions of class struggle, all human social activity, in-

[13] Karl Marx and Friedrich Engels, *Selected Correspondence, 1846–1895* (New York, 1942), pp. 483–84.

[14] Letter to H. Starkenburg, January 25, 1894, *ibid.*, p. 517.

[15] Karl Marx and Friedrich Engels, *Literature and Art* (New York, 1947), p. 18.

cluding all conscious activity, serves the tasks of class struggle. Literature, like any other ideology, takes the form of class consciousness serving class self-definition. In this is to be found the common ground of social genesis and social function which literature shares with other ideologies.[16]

Before 1929, the work of art, seen as a reflection of its social milieu and of the class attitudes of its author, was analyzed by Plekhanovist criticism to reveal—or "to unmask"—its ideological essence and its relation to progressive and regressive social forces at the time it was written. This was the critic's primary function—the "sociological moment" of the act of criticism. The critic then moved on to the second, or "aesthetic moment," the critical estimate of the work's formal properties. At its most absurd this approach turned into a search for the writer's birth certificate. And, though much of the nonsense in this attitude was swept away by the attack on "vulgar sociologism" in the late twenties, the close, uncomplicated connection between art and society went unchallenged.

With the shift of emphasis to conscious, willed behavior after 1929, the base-superstructure framework was simply stood on its head. It was assumed, apparently, that the largely unconscious process of reflection which had been brought to light by Marxist analysis had only to be reversed, and made conscious, so that the artist not only reflected the base but deliberately worked to influence those who were changing it. Literature was no longer a form of passive ideological reflection, but an active, "healthy," controlled ideological instrument, not a mirror any more but a weapon. Stalin's massively simple definition of the relation between base and superstructure emphasizes the instrumental character of disciplined consciousness, and doubtless has served to justify every restriction on Soviet intellectual life. In his article on the linguistics controversy of 1950, he wrote:

The superstructure is generated by the base but this by no means signifies that it merely reflects the base, that it is passive, neutral and indifferent to the fate of its base, to the fate of classes, to the character of the system. On

16 I. Nusinov, "Literatura," *Sovetskaya entsiklopediya*, VI, 404. Nusinov defines characteristics which distinguish literature from other forms of "thought." The main distinction he makes between poetry and science is Belinsky's, not Marx's, namely, that the artist thinks in "images," the scientist in propositions. Lukács considers it one of the greatest achievements of "Russian democratic-revolutionary criticism" that it "advanced to a point where the social genesis and the aesthetic value of a literary work were linked up with each other." Georg Lukács, *Studies in European Realism* (London, 1950), p. 116. This forced marriage of incompatibles is precisely what neither Lukács nor the Russians were able to accomplish. Marx and Engels never really tried.

the contrary, having put in an appearance, it then becomes a most active force which contributes vigorously to the formation and consolidation of its base, takes all steps to assist the new order to drive former classes into the dust and liquidate them.

It could not be otherwise. The superstructure is created by the base to serve it, to help it actively in taking shape and growing strong.[17]

In this view of the proper goals of human spiritual activity, there is no reason to doubt that the work of art will be valued above all for its ideological leverage. From the absolute preeminence of the social task —the remaking of the base—is derived the society's entire system of rewards and punishments, of restriction and permission. No one is exempt, including the writer. Marx and Engels never faced the problem of building the new order. All they had to say about art is subject to this qualification, but there is a dramatic contrast, nevertheless, between modern Soviet attitudes and Marx's remarks in 1842 on the writer's freedom:

The writer, of course, must make a living in order to have the opportunity to exist and to write, but he must in no way exist and write in order to earn a living. . . . The writer, in no way, regards his work as a means. It is an end in itself; it is so little a means either for him or for others, that when necessary the writer makes sacrifices to its existence, when necessary, his own existence, and, like the preacher . . . he takes as his principle: "Obey God more than men," men among whom he includes himself with his human needs and desires. . . . The first freedom of the press consists in its not being a trade.[18]

This passage has greatly troubled Soviet commentators. M. Lifshitz, one of the principal curators of the Marxian inheritance, has devoted a good deal of time and ingenuity to interpret it so that it loses all validity as a general statement about the situation of the writer. His qualifications are designed to prove that all its meaning is derived from Marx's personal situation and from the tactical political needs of the movement.[19] Its lasting significance, he insists, is to be found in

---

[17] J. Stalin, "On Marxism in Linguistics," in *The Soviet Linguistic Controversy* (New York, 1951), p. 70. The primacy of social issues, a sense of disciplined struggle, service, and partisanship are all suggested here. In *First Circle*, Solzhenitsyn imagines the scene in Stalin's study when this article was written. See below, pp. 301-2. Sinyavsky cites it in his essay on socialist realism. See below, footnote 16, p. 302.

[18] He was defending his own newspaper from political censorship in Germany when he was editor of the Jacobin *Rhenish Gazette*. The quoted passage is taken from Karl Marx and Friedrich Engels, *Literaturnoe nasledstvo*, ed. Franz Mehring (Moscow, 1907), p. 225.

[19] See his article "Marx," in *Literaturnaya entsiklopediya* (1932), 6: 886-87.

the remark about literature as a "trade," which finds a logical extension in Lenin's famous article in 1905, "Party Organization and Party
Literature," a violent attack on the bourgeois writer as a hireling of
reactionary political forces who makes a business out of literature.
Lifshitz's interpretation, with its suggestion that Lenin is merely
completing Marx's thought, overlooks the fact that Lenin not only
ignored Marx's view of the artist's autonomy but, at important junc-
tures, completely reversed it.[20]

This questionable interpretation could be validated only if Lifshitz
were able to show that Marx ever said that art should subordinate itself to political, or other alien, interests. There is no such reversal of
attitude in Marx's later remarks, and their humanist temper suggests
that he always honored the differences between the concerns of the
artist and the political activist. Not that the autonomy of art ever
meant irresponsibility. The great writers of the past were never free
of the pressures, or blind to the issues, of their time. But there is no
tendency in Marx to proclaim that the "correctness" of a work is the
source of its value, or that progressive political commitment is any
primary obligation of the writer. The literary achievement *per se* of
Shakespeare, Aeschylus, Cervantes, or Dante—to name his favorites—
is the mark of their greatness and the source of their value. The great
writers of the past are giants among men, who bear impressive witness
in their persons and in their work to the wonder of the human potential. And, though their work may reflect the general excitement
and vitality of an age, Marx and Engels never try to connect them
more intimately with the contending factions in their society.[21] In
discussing contemporary writers, with whom they had sharp, doctrinal
quarrels, or whose relationship to class alignments was the opposite
of their own, Marx and Engels were strongly inclined to respect the
man as an artist. Political considerations were deliberately set aside.
Goethe, who, Engels felt, displayed a distressing ability at times to

---

[20] See Chapter 10 for a full discussion of Lenin's article.

[21] Engels's remarks on Dante are in point here: "The close of the feudal Middle
Ages, the threshold of the modern capitalist era, was marked by a gigantic, colossal
figure. It was an Italian, Dante, who was both the last poet of the Middle Ages and the
first poet of modern times. Today, a new historical era is unfolding. Will Italy give us
the new Dante, who will mark the hour of birth of this new proletarian era?" *Literature
and Art*, pp. 76–77. Comment on other great moments in the history of culture exposes
the same general assumption: that the excitement of an era of change is the best soil
for great art. Ancient Greece is an exception, in that its art rests on the perfect fusion
of social values with patterns of mythological belief.

accommodate to the worst values in his society, was, nevertheless, at other moments in his career "a defiant, ironical, world-scorning genius."[22] Heine, whom he knew and disagreed with, was always spared Marx's terrible wrath.[23] In the case of Balzac, Engels again demonstrated his belief that art and politics are separate domains, simply by disconnecting the writer's political intentions from his literary achievement.[24] Balzac told the truth, Engels felt, despite his royalist aspirations, because he reflected the major currents of social change in France exactly as Marx and Engels had, by other means, discovered them to be. Indeed, this is the usual interpretation given to this passage by Soviet commentators: art may tell the Marxist truth despite the social preferences of the writer. But Engels's point has a number of other implications that must be unsettling to any advocate of prescriptive control over literature. Engels makes it clear that the value of a work of art is not a necessary function of its social genesis or of its political intentions, and, further, that if it is a well-made work of art without notable historical falsity, it is *ipso facto* valuable and true. Balzac disclosed what he did because he was a great artist, not an indoctrinated socialist, or a confused royalist, and, in his devotion to his calling, he betrayed or set aside his lesser allegiances. Finally it would seem reasonable to infer that, if great works of art proceed from bad political intentions, then bad works of art may issue from the best of intentions, and that in the end, talent and integrity—"the courage of the true artist"[25]—are all.

The celebrated discussion of realism and tendentiousness confirms this view of Marx's and Engels's true feelings about art. As materialists they were disposed to favor realism, and as social scientists they adhered to a rigorous canon of verisimilitude in their judgments on the recreated world of fiction. In addition, the realist writer must gen-

---

22 See *Literature and Art*, pp. 81–83, for the whole of his opinion. Engels carefully qualifies the negative aspects of his judgment. Goethe is "too universal," "too active," "too fleshly," "too sharp-sighted," to stand accused of cowardly flight from his dilemma. His final weariness is the result of a defeat inflicted on him by the environment he despised but required in order to fulfill himself. Engels is careful to point out that his judgment proceeds "neither from moral nor from partisan . . . but chiefly from aesthetic and historical standpoints." The artist shall be judged by his work, apparently, and shall be granted immunity on that basis from the furious political abuse reserved for lesser men.

23 Marx said in a letter to Engels, that like Horace, Heine was "at bottom a cur in a political sense." "Yet in other respects," he added, "the old wretch is very lovable." *Ibid.*, p. 107.

24 See Engels's letter to Margaret Harkness, written in April. *Ibid.*, pp. 41–43.

25 *Ibid.*, p. 41. From the same letter to Margaret Harkness.

eralize, and in his generalization cannot fail to comment on the world he lives in:

Realism, to my mind, implies besides truth of detail, the truthful reproduction of typical characters under typical circumstances.[26]

There is no doubt, too, that the "typical" in a novel must coincide at some point with their own analysis of society. To this extent their ideas parallel those of the Russian radical democrats. Engels was even willing to criticize lesser works that were submitted to him for comment on the ground that they did not square with his own analysis of a specific social milieu.[27] But when the question of conscious tendency in the novel was put directly to Engels, his acceptance of the idea was so qualified that it offered little encouragement to the untalented petitioners who sought his support. He stated his position not as an advocate, but negatively, as one who was "not at all an opponent of tendentious poetry as such."[28] To illustrate his position, he named his models:

The father of tragedy, Aeschylus, and the father of comedy, Aristophanes, were both decidedly tendentious poets, just as were Dante and Cervantes; and the main merit of Schiller's *Craft and Loves* is that it is the first German political propaganda drama. The modern Russians and Norwegians, who are writing splendid novels, are all tendentious.[29]

Protected by the breadth of his definition and by the great figures he invoked in its support, he was willing to grant, not that all great works of art are tendentious, or that all works of art should be tendentious, but that some great works of art have not ceased to be great because they have been tendentious. The order of values implicit in this statement seems unmistakable: works of art may be both great and tendentious, but the artist who imitates them might attempt the second only if he achieved the first. The propagation of "healthy," "correct," "progressive" ideas is nowhere declared to be the writer's preeminent obligation. If his work is "to serve," the implication is clear, it will do so by being true to its own nature, by performing its persuasive function unobtrusively, through the fictional material itself. Engels

[26] *Ibid.*
[27] See his letter to Margaret Harkness in this connection. *Ibid.*, p. 42.
[28] *Ibid.*, p. 45. From a letter written to Minna Kautsky in 1885.
[29] *Ibid.*

is clear on this point: "The more the author's views are concealed the better for the work of art,"[30] because "the tendency should flow by itself from the situation and action without being explicitly formulated."[31] He was prepared to admit tendency into the work of art under certain conditions, but he was unwilling to say what *kind* of tendency, or even that it was essential.

Engels's most explicit statement about art's potential value to the socialist movement stopped far short of the prescriptive strictures of the Russian radical democrats. His qualifications tend to associate him much more closely with their opponents' position in the controversy of the sixties, particularly in their unwillingness to impose an explicit educational or inspirational function on art:

A socialist-biased novel fully achieves its purpose, in my view, if, by conscientiously describing real mutual relations, breaking down conventional illusions about them, it shatters the optimism of the bourgeois, instils doubt as to the eternal character of the existing order, although the author does not offer any definite solution or does not even line up openly on any particular side.[32]

Apparently any gifted and honest writer could penetrate the fog of bourgeois rationalizations and come upon the Marxian truth about the real relations that bound men together. But this was service enough for art to perform. The artist was a welcome ally but he was free of any obligation to subordinate his work to agitational considerations. Engels not only granted the artist this exemption, he insisted on it. It seems clear, too, that Marx and Engels tend to associate literature with the objective, analytical, not with the agitational, world-changing, phase of their own theory. Even when art makes use of their analytical concepts it must conceal them, and must state its "case" in the terms traditionally proper to its medium.

The realism they favored had, by its nature, to deal with the past. It was perfectly proper, Engels told Margaret Harkness, to write of the working class's "convulsive attempts ... to attain their rights as human beings," because these efforts "belong to history and may therefore lay claim to a place in the domain of realism."[33] But Engels declared himself opposed to any entanglement in the future: "The writer is not obliged to obtrude on the reader the future historical solutions

[30] *Ibid.*, p. 42.   [31] *Ibid.*, p. 45.
[32] *Ibid.*   [33] *Ibid.*

of the social conflicts pictured."[34] His obligation toward history's dialectic was not to concentrate on its emergent phase, but only to record its history up to the present. On this crucial point, the advocates of an agitational realism can find no sanction for the inclusion of prediction and promise which is central to their aesthetic.

The response of Marx and Engels to a number of politically emblematic heroes was entirely consistent with the standards and attitudes explained above. In Engels's criticism of Minna Kautsky's novel, *Old and New*, which he praised for its precision and "naturalness," he found the hero absolutely unacceptable:

In truth he is too faultless, and if at last he perishes by falling from a mountain, this can be reconciled with poetic justice only in that he was too good for this world. It is always bad for an author to be infatuated with his hero, and it seems to me that in this case you have given way somewhat to this weakness. Elsa still has traces of personality although she is also somewhat idealized, but in Arnold personality is entirely dissolved in principle.[35]

The author has violated the integrity of her story because, as Engels told her, "you felt the need of publicly declaring your convictions, of bearing witness to them before the whole world."[36] The declamation of principles was no substitute for the creative and lifelike handling of character. By making her protagonist a flawless representative of her own aspirations, she had lost control of him by surrendering "that fine irony which demonstrates the power of the writer over his creation."[37]

Marx, too, considered political heroism in literature, and found similar grounds for rejecting the two examples that came to his attention. Revolutionaries, he felt, were valid subjects for the artist. But, he also seems to suggest, if they are done badly they need not be done at all. Marx's comment on two obscure French novels in no way im-

[34] *Ibid*. On this point, Soviet critics rely on other evidence to support their view of the future. Paul Lafargue reported: "Marx looked upon Balzac, not merely as the historian of the social life of his time, but as a prophetic creator of character types which still existed only in embryo during the reign of Louis Philippe, and which only reached full development under Napoleon III, after Balzac's death." Quoted in *ibid*., p. 139. This second-hand report does resemble the ideas of the Russian radicals and the socialist realists. But it should be pointed out that Balzac's prescience is seen as an additional attribute of his genius, and is nowhere advocated by either Marx or Engels as a quality to be deliberately cultivated.
[35] *Ibid*., p. 45.   [36] *Ibid*.
[37] *Ibid*., pp. 45–46. It is this "ironic" control that the modern Soviet writer has lost, too.

plies that a shabby piece of work might gain his approval on political grounds alone. He wrote:

Nothing is more desirable than that the people who stood at the head of the revolutionary party, either before the Revolution, in secret societies or in the press, or later in official positions, be finally depicted in strong Rembrandtian colors, in all their living qualities. Hitherto these people have never been pictured in their real form; they have been presented as official personalities, wearing buskins and with aureoles around their heads. In these apotheoses of Raphaelite beauty all pictorial truth is lost. The two books under review do get rid of the buskin and aureole. . . . They go into the private lives of these people, showing them in carpet slippers, together with their whole entourage of satellites of various kinds. But that does not mean that they are any nearer a true and honest presentation of persons and events.[38]

Marx's reasons for dissatisfaction are suggested in the word "Rembrandtian." As elsewhere in his and Engels's remarks about art, an unqualified classical standard of excellence formed the basis of their judgments. Its ingredients are depth, color, richness, vitality, and energy; and when these qualities are present the result is a unique kind of "pictorial truth." No lapse from this standard was to be condoned for the local gains which might be derived from the *merely* favorable portraiture of revolutionary heroes. There is certainly nothing in what they say to suggest that political virtue is, in itself, a source of artistic excellence. It was a legitimate—even "a desirable"— subject for art, but it must always be measured against a Shakespearean or a Dantean or a Rembrandtian standard.

There was no departure from this approach—and no support, therefore, for Soviet attitudes on these matters—on the two other occasions on which Marx and Engels discussed the literary hero. Both men wrote long letters to their colleague, Ferdinand Lassalle, about his play *Franz von Sickingen*, a tragic drama of the civil wars in sixteenth-century Germany. In their severely qualified praise of the play three points deserve mention: their acceptance of the tragic mode, their suggestive formula for adapting it to the Marxian view of history, and the further exposure of their Shakespearean standards of judgment.

On the first point Marx was perfectly explicit: "I can therefore only express my full approval of making this the central theme of a modern

[38] *Ibid.*, p. 40.

tragedy."[39] The trouble came in working out the theme, the tragedy
of an inopportune revolutionary, of a man of conviction and energy,
who saw the need to act but was doomed to defeat because of the discrepancy between his personal aspirations and his situation in history.[40] Engels described the central conflict in abstract terms as "the
tragic collision between the historically necessary postulate and the
practical impossibility of its realization."[41] Sickingen died, Marx said,
because as a knight he was the "representative of a perishing class"
and could not, therefore, make an alliance with the peasantry which
would have fulfilled his morally praiseworthy but historically unrealizable purposes.

In their criticism of Lassalle's treatment of his theme, Marx and
Engels again invoked a standard of Shakespearean complexity and
vitality. The historical data were correct and the principal characters
were correctly identified with social forces, but thinness of characterization meant the absence of that indispensable union of the general
and the particular through which ideas are expressed in literature.
Sickingen, Marx said, "is drawn too abstractly," and failed, therefore,
to participate in the drama as an active moral personality. He was,
rather, the unhappy "victim of a collision independent of all his personal calculations."[42] In their critique of the play, Marx and Engels
returned repeatedly to the idea that sterility of characterization robbed
the play of dramatic interest and intellectual significance. Dialogue
sounded like "lawyers' speeches"; the character Mina was turned into
"a doctrine of rights"; individuals were made into "the mere mouth-
pieces of the spirit of the times"; "argumentative debate" should be
replaced by "motives more lively, active, spontaneously occupying the
foreground ... through the course of the action itself."[43]

[39] *Ibid.*, p. 46.   [40] Ibid., p. 55.

[41] *Ibid.* This formulation of the tragic possibility in a determined universe has had
little attention from Soviet Marxists. The thought that the revolutionary is always,
in some sense, *inopportune*, that he lives in a state of dangerous tension between his
expectations and the historical process, has been very little used by Soviet writers.
Leonid Leonov is the only one who has sensed Marx's idea here and exploited it with
any success. (See Chapter 13.)

[42] *Ibid.*, p. 48.

[43] These judgments are taken from the letters written by both men in 1859 to
Lassalle. *Ibid.*, pp. 46–56. The ideas expressed in these letters are so similar as to be
uncanny, unless, of course, they had discussed the play together and agreed on the line
to be taken. Engels is politer and more detailed, but both men interlard their criticism
with extravagant praise, perhaps to flatter an important colleague, or perhaps because,
as Engels pointed out unctuously, the Socialist movement would gain from the play's

Marx summed up his objections to the play's lifelessness in the epithet "Schillerism." As an antidote, he proposed to Lassalle simply that he "Shakespearize more."[44] Engels echoed this thought more politely: "You could without harm have paid more attention to the significance of Shakespeare in the history of the development of the drama." He went on to predict a future synthesis of the "great intellectual depth and conscious historical content" of German drama with "Shakespearean vivacity and wealth of action."[45] But until this was achieved, we may conclude, the absence of "Shakespearean vivacity" would always invalidate the German intellectual contribution. Marx's and Engels's uncompromisingly high standards did not discourage their sympathizers from attempting to forward history's course by the calculated use of imaginative fiction. In resisting their disciples' efforts in this direction, it is clear that Marx and Engels were not merely expressing a cranky personal preference. Marx's remarks on the lasting value of Greek art indicate that he spoke out of a broad view of the separate histories of art and society. The question at issue was the general one posed by Marxian evolutionism: does a higher stage of social development guarantee higher forms of art? All the aesthetic evidence, Marx felt, pointed to a negative conclusion.[46] But this, in turn, raised another important question: wherein is the permanent appeal of Greek works of art? The answer, Marx said, "lies in understanding why they still constitute with us a source of aesthetic enjoyment and, in certain respects, prevail as the standard and model

---

success, and "we are all very pleased at every new proof that whatever field the party enters it always shows its superiority." *Ibid.*, p. 56. The severity of their criticism, nevertheless, indicates that neither Lassalle nor "the party" would profit anything until extensive revisions had been made.

[44] *Ibid.*, p. 52.   [45] *Ibid.*

[46] Marx and Engels touched a number of times on the question of the *kind* of social situation (as distinct from the *stage* of social evolution) that was most favorable for art. The great intellectual currents that swept through Europe with the disintegration of the Middle Ages Marx associated generally with the beginnings of the capitalist era. At the same time he was aware of national differences: Dante, da Vinci, Shakespeare, Luther, Cervantes, for example, bore the stamp of their milieux. Yet he never attempted to establish close connections between these men and the rising middle class. The ferment attendant upon a colossal shift in economic power seemed, in the case of the Renaissance at least, to furnish favorable conditions for great art. In the eighteenth century, and to a certain degree in the nineteenth, the artist seemed to succeed best in a stance of protest against the moral falseness of his society. Neither of these conditions was present in Greek society where the serenity and security of shared values and beliefs—the real source of Greek art was mythology, Marx said—furnished a different set of conditions for the artist. It is a pity Marx never brought his powers of generalization to bear on these problems of cultural history.

beyond attainment."[47] Marx avoided a direct answer to this question by invoking one of the overworked clichés of his century. Greek civilization was not the "adolescence" of mankind, as Hegel asserted, but its "natural" childhood, the spontaneity, innocence, and vitality of which were as ephemeral in history as they were in man's life. Evasive as his answer was, it permits several inferences which challenge both the Russian radicals and their Soviet legatees at several important points. In the first place, by disconnecting the value of works of art from their relative place in the evolution of history, Marx completely undermines Timofeev's grotesque assertion that Soviet art is more valuable than prerevolutionary art because it expresses a "higher" form of social development.[48] Second, Marx did not suggest that art's value depends on the "progressive" or "reactionary" attitude it assumed toward contemporary social struggles, which is the only explanation the modern Soviet aesthetic gives for the permanent appeal of classical works of art. On this problem, Marx and Engels are much closer to Tolstoy's remarks in 1858 that great art is accessible to all peoples in all times,[49] and seem to insist that all art be measured against the greatest men have made. Finally, Marx's use of the analogy of childhood to explain Greece's greatness directs our attention to his and Engels's sense of the underlying human unity of history, subsuming all the stages society passes through, and suggests that art's permanent anchorage is in the indestructible wealth of the human being, which it expresses and celebrates.

It has already been pointed out that Marx and Engels associate imaginative literature with interpretation, not with change. The prose realism they favored in their own time dealt most properly and most successfully with events in the past and touched on the future— whether as prediction or inspiration—only at grave risk to itself. For these and other reasons it is clear that Marx and Engels were not disposed to connect literature with the activist phase of their theory. Perhaps the wonder is that they never did. Literature was of great personal concern to both men, but it was less than a secondary interest

[47] *Literature and Art*, p. 19. Lifshitz's treatment of these two questions is interesting. In answer to the first he refers to Hegel. At different moments in history, he says, the ratio between alienation and integration in a given society varies quite independently of that society's position on the ladder of social evolution. Thus a healthy Greece is perfectly capable of producing a greater art than, say, a disintegrating capitalism. The second question, the matter of universal value in art, Lifshitz ignores. See his article "Marx," in *Literaturnaya entsiklopediya*, 6: 888–90.

[48] See above, p. 23.   [49] See above, pp. 95–96.

in their intellectual lifework, a source sometimes of the apt example or the trenchant quotation. Beyond that it was largely a private matter, discussed in correspondence or in conversations with friends. It is a tribute, perhaps, to the soundness of their education that they resisted the temptation to make literature an instrument of their mission. They were no less embattled at times with the world than the Russian radical democrats, who showed no such scruples. Their reluctance to make use of literature tends strongly to align them with the position of the realists, not with their radical opponents, in the mid-century debate in Russia.

Engels's hope that the literature of the future would contain "great intellectual depth" and "conscious historical content" represents their maximum claim that literature possess social utility. The presence or absence of these elements would give the Marxist critic grounds for a kind of ideological judgment. But an adequate emphasis on the third and balancing ingredient—"Shakespearean vivacity"—would, presumably, keep literature free from any crippling subordination to doctrine. Marx and Engels surrendered all major claims to political dominion over it, by indicating that the presence of ideology would never be permitted to compensate for the absence of artistry. Their prescription, if such it can be called, was mild and general: any morally honest exploration of the capitalist world would bring to light the disturbing truth about it. This knowledge might arouse indignation, hope, or disgust, but apparently the reader's response was not to be directed beyond these generalized emotions. At no time did they cross the line into the realm of political uplift favored by Chernyshevsky, Dobrolyubov, Lenin and Zhdanov.

It is not possible here to survey the monumental labors that have attended the Soviet exegesis of Marx and Engels on the arts. But a general trend is evident: the gradual replacement of Marx and Engels by the Russian radicals as guides to "literary policy." Soviet disenchantment with their original Marxian literary bequest has made itself increasingly evident since 1934. The "pre-Marxist materialists," as the Russian radicals were often called, were found to have greater and greater relevance to the Soviet scene. Lenin's central notion of art's "partisanship" in the social struggle, whether he knew it or not, reflected a position much closer to Chernyshevsky's than to Marx's. Zhdanov's failure to mention Marx and Engels once in his 1946 review of the Soviet literary scene is a conclusive sign of their eclipse as

commentators on cultural matters. In a later article, "Lenin and Soviet Art," G. Nedoshivin suggests the thinking that lay behind
Zhdanov's omission:

Beginning with the middle forties of the last century, they [Marx and En-
gels] examined fundamental problems of art as a form of ideology, eluci-
dating questions pertaining to realism, especially in the conditions of
bourgeois society, and analyzing the status of literature under the domination of capitalist relations. Although the works of Marx and Engels contain
truly profound observations concerning the opportunities Socialism opens
for the development of creative art, they naturally could not formulate a
finished theory on the development of art after the Socialist revolution and
the launching of the practical construction of Socialism. The historical
background of the nineteenth century could not provide the material for
any such theoretical generalization, and the two great thinkers concentrated on an analysis of the substance of art in the conditions prevailing
in class society in general and bourgeois society in particular.... And in
connection with this many general questions of aesthetics which Marx and
Engels dealt with in their time had to be subjected to a more profound
treatment in the light of the new situation.[50]

So the argument runs. One notes the narrow superstructural view
of art, which assumes, first, that art will undergo a metamorphosis in
close, mechanical response to changes in economic conditions, and
second, that this process can be directed by a single "theoretical generalization." Marx and Engels have been trapped in their own system, and dismissed as prisoners of their times. The losses implicit in
this view of culture include much that Marx and Engels valued: diversity of form, continuity of tradition, spontaneity of creation, and
universality of interest. Although his reasons are open to challenge,
Nedoshivin is right at least in noting the incompatibility between
classical Marxian and Soviet attitudes toward literature. "Shakespearean vivacity" must fare ill in the grim climate of official uplift
described in the following excerpt (typical of many) taken from an
editorial of the fifties:

Cultural advancement that leads to an abundance of spiritual values for
the people has always been regarded by the Communist Party and the Soviet Government as one of their major tasks. The great leaders of the Soviet
people, Lenin and Stalin, always attached exceptional importance to literature and the arts, emphasizing their immense part in molding the minds
of millions and accelerating the process of socialist development.

[50] G. Nedoshivin, "Lenin and Soviet Art," *Soviet Literature*, 1 (1952): 142–43.

To fulfill this mission every work of art, no matter in what sphere, must above all give expression to the advanced ideas of the times, to the genuine spirit of the people, it must correctly reflect the needs of society and respond to the hopes and aspirations of the masses, the real makers of history.[51]

The whole of the humanist heritage, so reverently regarded by Marx and Engels, is swept away in this flood of jargon. And all the ways art has discovered for exploring man's condition are reduced to a single formula. The same editorial points out that in order "to fulfill his mission the artist must produce works which help to bring out the finest traits of the Soviet character."[52] The final issue of this doctrine is the new Soviet man, his eye all agleam with official virtue. Marx and Engels have contributed nothing to this closed system with its single, predetermined outcome, not because of the limitations imposed on them by "class society," but because they shared few of the assumptions that support it.

It is Lenin who is credited today with the "profound treatment" of Marxian ideas on art which Soviet critics see as an extension beyond— and any outsider must see as a departure from—the original premises. The "principle of political partisanship" in literature, although it was ultimately to find more congenial sanctions in the theories of the radical democrats, was derived by Lenin from another area of Marxist theory. The Soviet Spartacus, whom Marx and Engels never foresaw, has Marxian blood in his veins. We must examine the choice Lenin made between the humaneness of Marxism's basic moral intentions, and the harsh ethic of the class struggle, which he was convinced was the only way to fulfill those intentions.

[51] "Soviet Literature and Art on the Upgrade," *Soviet Literature*, 12 (1951): 134.
[52] *Ibid.*

CHAPTER 9

Complete and Incomplete Men

❧❧❧

The Marxian view, after Lenin, that man is an historical creature whose social matrix is the only source of his grievances and aspirations serves an interest in manipulating him in those terms. But Marx and Engels themselves have a view of mankind far broader than considerations of malleability and manipulation: it involves a concept of human nature itself.[1] Their distrust of essences and fixities makes them reluctant to define such a vast and imprecise thing as human nature. But they cannot wholly avoid the matter, cannot, that is, assume that man's *only* identity through time is physical, or that he is, at any historical moment, *only* an aggregate of cultural traits; and they do make allowances for that entity which the British Marxist Christopher Caudwell has called the human "genotype," "man as he is born," "the common human creature."[2]

Venable suggests that, though it does not constitute a formal philosophical commitment on the matter, the use of the terms "human" and "human reality" by Marx and Engels acknowledges the existence of a common fund of traits, needs, and potentialities. They are not metaphysical essences, but they exist, nonetheless, as "relative historical constants, empirical common denominators, which emerge for sufficiently long periods of time to furnish the ordinary social meanings of nouns."[3]

[1] See Vernon Venable, *Human Nature: The Marxian View* (New York, 1946), Chapters 1 and 2.
[2] Christopher Caudwell, *Illusion and Reality* (London, 1946), pp. 124, 136.
[3] Venable, *Human Nature*, p. 24.

Marx and Engels have generally associated the term "human" with the generous ethical purposes that enclose the whole of their system. Venable has defined those purposes simply as "the amelioration of the human lot."[4] Engels is almost lightheartedly imprecise and undogmatic on this score: "The urge towards happiness is innate in man, and must therefore form the basis of all morality."[5] The entire apparatus of theoretical Marxism has presumably been created to serve this universal need of "the common human creature," and it is in this moral substratum that the Marxian views of art examined in the preceding chapter would seem to have their permanent roots. As Caudwell put it: "Art cannot escape its close relation with the genotype whose secret desires link in one endless series all human culture."[6] In the Marxian view, great art reflects the wholeness, the creativity, and the passion men enjoy at certain privileged moments in history. The artists themselves seem at times to have represented the supreme expression of this potential.[7]

Are there clues to the nature of the fully developed Marxian man which were not disclosed in the comments by Marx and Engels on specifically literary matters? He is characterized, in the first place, by a complete and active set of appetites, senses, and emotions, for which the fullest expression is sought through his relations with the external world:

Man adopts his all-sided being in an all-sided manner, in other words, as a total man. Every one of his *human* relations with the world: seeing, hearing, smelling, tasting, feeling, thinking, contemplating, willing, acting, loving; in short, all the organs of his individuality as well as the organs which in their immediate form are common to all.[8]

If these activities represent the common denominator of the human endowment, a rough measure of a society's worth may be taken by the degree to which men are permitted to exercise them. Again and again capitalism is condemned in precisely these terms by Marx and

[4] *Ibid.*, p. 26.

[5] Karl Marx and Friedrich Engels, *Selected Works* (Moscow, 1951), 2: 346.

[6] Caudwell, *Illusion and Reality*, p. 206.

[7] Engels said of Goethe: "[He] did not like to deal with 'God': the word made him uncomfortable. He felt himself at home only in the human, and it was this humanity, this emancipation of art from the fetters of religion that determined Goethe's greatness. In this respect neither the great writers of antiquity nor even Shakespeare are up to him." Karl Marx and Friedrich Engels, *Literature and Art* (New York, 1947), p. 80.

[8] *Ibid.*, p. 61.

Engels because it denies the fulfillment of this basic human minimum. The list of frustrating conditions is a familiar one: division of labor, the reign of money ("universal whore ... universal procurer of human beings and people"),[9] "naked, shameless, direct brutal exploitation,"[10] and so forth. Man's alienation from his full human potential, as it is brought about by these destructive forces, appears as a greater crime in their eyes than the immediate suffering inflicted by hunger, cold, disease, or overwork.

Marx and Engels clearly felt that the blight of alienation was much more virulent and widespread under capitalism than it had been in most, if not all, past historical epochs. At the heart of their indictment of the present system is a vision of man crippled, fragmented, shriveled by the conditions of his economic existence. Marx and Engels repeatedly point out that this unhappy, stunted creature represents an absolute decline in the density and richness of human experience, because of the reduction, through enforced and prolonged disuse, of his given human capacities.

A much truer measure of man's creative potential is found in the human giants of the Renaissance, for example, or in the ancient Greek heroes. The key motifs of human existence at its fullest were the wholeness and versatility of man's interests and achievements, and the grandeur of his claims on life. As a sketch of the Marxian human ideal, Engels's extravagant remarks on the man of the Renaissance are worth quoting at length:

It was the greatest progressive revolution that mankind has so far experienced, a time which called for giants and produced giants—giants in power of thought, passion, and character, in universality and learning. The men who founded the modern rule of the bourgeoisie had anything but bourgeois limitations. On the contrary, the adventurous character of the time inspired them.... There was hardly any man of importance then living who had not traveled extensively, who did not command four or five languages, who did not shine in a number of fields. Leonardo da Vinci was not only a great painter but also a great mathematician, mechanician, and engineer, to whom the most diverse branches of physics are indebted for important discoveries. Albrecht Dürer was painter, engraver, sculptor, and architect, and in addition invented a system of fortifications. ... Machiavelli was statesman, historian, poet, and at the same time the first military writer of modern times. Luther not only cleaned the Augean stable

---

[9] *Ibid.*, p. 34.   [10] *Ibid.*, p. 37.

of the Church but also that of the German language; he created modern German prose and composed the text and melody of that triumphal hymn which became the Marseillaise of the sixteenth century. The heroes of that time had not yet come under the servitude of the division of labor, the restricting effects of which, with its production of one-sidedness, we so often notice in their successors. But what is especially characteristic of them is that they almost all pursue their lives and activities in the midst of contemporary movements, in the practical struggle; they take sides and join in the fight, one by speaking and writing, another with the sword, many with both. Hence the fullness and force of character that makes them complete men.[11]

History does not repeat itself in the Marxian universe; there is no nostalgia in this admiration for Renaissance heroes, or any suggestion that these particular types would ever again be duplicated. But if epochs of great social metamorphosis provided the richest soil for large-scale individuals, there was a hope that the transition to socialism might produce men of equivalent *stature*, if not of identical qualities.[12] Marx also felt that these exciting periods of large-scale human figures were invariably moments of great art: "It has been observed that great men appear in surprising numbers at certain periods which are characterized by the efflorescence of art. Whatever the outstanding traits of this efflorescence, its influence upon men is undeniable; it fills them with its vivifying force."[13]

These high points of artistic and human greatness form an historical pattern which is distinct from the stages of social development. Let us note the major phases of the first process. It describes, in general terms, a steady decline from the Renaissance—the last stopping place, they felt, in modern history for the men of truly heroic stature—to the depths of the factory system, and then gives promise of rising again with the establishment of socialism's "truly human culture," to a level equivalent, at least, to history's previous high points. Their language is of particular interest because of the frequent connections it reveals between art, morality, and human dignity. Among their caustic remarks about the new aristocracy of sausage makers and button manufacturers, one characterization of the petite bourgeoisie sums

[11] *Ibid.*, pp. 23–24.
[12] See Engels's remarks on Dante, above, p. 124, footnote 21.
[13] A marginal note made by the young Marx in a copy of Johann Jakob Grund's *Die Malerei der Griechen*, quoted in Mikhail Lifshitz, *The Philosophy of Art of Karl Marx* (New York, 1938), p. 44.

up all the others, and measures one of capitalism's dominant personality types against Marx's standard of human worth:

If the decline of former classes—such as the knight, for instance—could furnish material for magnificent works of tragic art, the *petite bourgeoisie* naturally provides nothing but feeble manifestations of fanatical malice, nothing but collections of phrases and sayings in the manner of Sancho Panza.[14]

This wretched class was so spiritually bankrupt that Marx and Engels would not grant it even the pathos of its own descent. They returned to this thesis again and again. In one oft-quoted statement Marx sets the noble vision of man in Greek mythology against the antipoetic, antihuman conditions of capitalist institutions and technology:

Is the view of nature and of social relations which shaped Greek imagination and Greek [art] possible in the age of automatic machinery, and railways and locomotives and electric telegraphs? Where does Vulcan come in as against Roberts and Co.; Jupiter as against the lightning rod; and Hermes as against the Crédit Mobilier? ... Greek art presupposes the existence of Greek mythology, i.e., that nature and even the form of society are wrought up in popular fancy in an unconsciously artistic fashion.... Looking at it from another side: Is Achilles possible side by side with powder and lead? Or is the *Iliad* at all compatible with the printing press?[15]

Marx obviously feels that in these juxtapositions he is recording an absolute loss. But he would violate the logic of his theory of history if he proposed then to roll back capitalism's enormous advances in social organization and technology, or to create by some cultural alchemy a new mythology (Marx hated pseudo-classicism), or if he despaired entirely of the future of art. The only route open led forward, and history moved on it toward harmony and fruitfulness. As Marx and Engels saw it, capitalism at the height of its powers embodied an absolute contradiction on this matter of human fulfillment. While it had registered gains in many areas, gains unprecedented in human history, it had done so at tremendous costs, including the near death of art and the mangling of the human being. But in the very process, capitalism had generated the forces that would destroy it, and would, eventually, restore man to his true poetic dimensions. At this point the upward movement of the humanist phase is joined with

[14] Karl Marx and Friedrich Engels, *Sur la littérature et l'art*, ed. Jean Fréville (Paris, 1936), pp. 123–24.

[15] Marx and Engels, *Literature and Art*, pp. 18–19.

the process of social change. In *The Holy Family*, Marx describes the act of awareness by which the worker transcended his degraded situation:

Since the abstraction of all humanity, even of the *semblance* of humanity, is practically complete in the full-grown proletariat; since the conditions of life of the proletariat sum up all the conditions of life ... today in all their inhuman acuity; since man has lost himself in the proletariat, yet at the same time has not only gained theoretical consciousness of that loss, but through urgent, no longer disguisable, absolutely imperative *need*— that practical expression of *necessity*—is driven directly to revolt against that inhumanity; it follows that the proletariat can and must free itself. But it cannot free itself without abolishing the conditions of its life. It cannot abolish the conditions of its own life without abolishing *all* the inhuman conditions of life of society today which are summed up in its own situation.[16]

It may be said that the ethical impulse exposes itself in the early work as antecedent to all the later "scientific" justifications for the overthrow of capitalism. In any case the industrial worker by his destructive acts will point the way to man's discovery—or *re*discovery if we consider the glories of human achievement in the Renaissance as a kind of norm to *return* to—of his incalculably rich potential.

Marx and Engels diligently avoided precise predictions about the socialist future. But when they did occasionally permit themselves moments of visionary anticipation, their remarks, again, are in the humanist key. When he was still young, Marx felt that the first condition for conquering man's alienation was "the abolition of private property," which could not fail to result in the "complete emancipation of all human senses and aptitudes" and "the vindication of real human life." "Communism," he wrote, "is humanism brought about by abolishing private property"; it is "the real materialization for man of his being."[17]

Nearly all of their remarks on the Communist future are put not in terms of economic predictions but of the humanist ethic, and point unmistakably to the restoration of man's wholeness on something like the Renaissance scale. The ultimate *moral* principle of the Communist order, "from each according to his abilities, to each according to his needs," will be enacted when man will have eliminated all the contradictions that separate him from others and from his own poten-

---

[16] Karl Marx and Friedrich Engels, *The Holy Family* (Moscow, 1956), p. 52.
[17] *Literature and Art*, pp. 61–62.

tial capacities. The differences between city and country living conditions will be overcome, and the discrepancies in status and rewards
between the workers of hand and of brain will disappear as well. But
this is only the beginning. The effects of the division of labor presumably will disappear and the demoralizing cash nexus will be replaced by a truly human standard of value. Man will be brought into
a true unity with nature, with his fellow men, and with society. From
all this, man will emerge with a new creative individuality which will
be sustained, not contradicted, by the egalitarian collectivity in which
it will have its being. In contrast with other societies which are plagued
with the division of labor, Marx sketches this idyllic picture of man in
the future society:

In Communist society, where nobody has one exclusive sphere of activity
but each can become accomplished in any branch he wishes, society reg-
ulates the general production and thus makes it possible for me to do one
thing today and another tomorrow, to hunt in the morning, fish in the
afternoon, rear cattle in the evening, criticize after dinner, just as I have
a mind, without ever becoming hunter, fisherman, shepherd or critic.[18]

With the resolution of *all* the contradictions of capitalism in the
new order, art's emancipation will parallel the restoration of man to
completeness. Lifshitz interprets Marx to mean that the artificial separation between the fantasy of poetry and the harsh realities of daily
existence will disappear: "Communist society removes not only the
abstract contradiction between 'work and pleasure,' but also the very
real contradiction between feeling and reason, between 'the play of
bodily and mental powers' and 'the conscious will.' "[19] Marx himself
felt that the distinction between the professional artist and the laity
would disappear:

The exclusive concentration of artistic talent in a few individuals and its
consequent suppression in the large masses is the result of the division of
labor.[20]

If Marx intended to say that every man might be his own da Vinci,
he could hardly have made more extravagant claims. If he intended
less than that, he has still implied that art will somehow be made available to all in the grand redistribution of material (and spiritual) goods

---

[18] Karl Marx and Friedrich Engels, *The German Ideology*, ed. R. Pascal (New York, 1939), p. 22.
[19] Lifshitz, *The Philosophy of Art of Karl Marx*, p. 93.
[20] *Literature and Art*, p. 76.

and services. There is little reason to doubt in this connection that the vision of the "whole," "human" man, made free and enriched by the socialist revolution, was an effective agitational device. But the persistence with which this vision reappears at critical moments in his thought makes it difficult to dismiss the concept as the fabrication of a propagandist. It seems quite clear that this notion is the nearest thing we can find to an embodiment of the innermost ethical purposes of Marxian theory.

The image of the whole man—if there is an outline of him distinct enough to justify use of the term—would seem to offer another model for Soviet imitation. But the information about him is so general and so imprecise he can hardly be said to have an identity of his own. At his most distinct he combines the general virtues of a few Renaissance giants with less discernible resemblances to Marx's own Promethean image of himself. In his hypothetical existence in the Communist future this individual is least tangible, no more than a bundle of abstract qualities. This is hardly a usable image. It lacks the human immediacy of even the Russian radicals' diagram for the new man. The elements that are consistent in it are nevertheless interesting and worth recording as a standard for evaluating the Soviet view. The greatest stress is laid on his freedom from crippling inhibitions. His integrated many-sidedness guarantees a broad receptivity to experience and an equally great intensity and generosity in his response to it. Above all, he is conceived as a very large and autonomous *individual*, self-directed in his choices and acts. In the many ways he is associated with aesthetic and ethical universals, he is ill-suited to the expediencies of revolutionary action, and to the disciplined, self-sacrificing code that sustains it. If the whole man is the *end* of the process of social change, he is material of dubious value for the struggle that must precede that distant eventuality. He is the beneficiary of social change, not its maker. For the period of transition we must posit a different sort of human being—an *interim man*, who is a means toward an end, not an end in himself, a man who will accept all kinds of restrictions on his demands on life in order to make himself over, like Chernyshevsky's Rakhmetov, into history's instrument.

II

The Marxian Utopia, with its roseate vision of man, "whole, integrated, and free," has little connection with the actual moral dimensions of the operating Soviet hero. It has merely given us a standard for ultimate (and invidious) comparisons. It is the "realm of necessity," preceding the "realm of freedom," that concerns us now. We need only recall a few of the conditions which various Marxist thinkers have attributed to the final stage—the withering away of the state, the free and equal distribution of goods according to need, the change-over from the government of people to "the administration of things" —to realize how far Soviet reality is from this destination. In the Marxian design, the era of necessity has the character of a period of transition. In that term are included the years of prerevolutionary struggle, the revolution itself, and all the subsequent years of Soviet history, in which the iron requirements of necessity are defined (as Soviet spokesmen view it) by three primary conditions: the techno-logical lag, the economy of scarcity, and hostile encirclement. Our final question here is this: what clues are there in Marx to the nature of the interim man who has dominated these transitional years? The answers are not to be sought in the humane intentions which support the image of the whole man, but in the specific ethical imperative which Lenin and others have derived from them.

The Marxian imperative may be phrased in the Kantian idiom: "So act, that thy act forwards the historical process." Thus formulated, it is clear that every condition of the act is established by history itself, and by man's position in it. Class struggle is the central fact of history and the touchstone of all moral choice. Since one half of the warring universe, the proletariat, is the power behind history's forward thrust toward a saner, healthier future, and is the instrument which will destroy all obstacles in the way, the primary *ethical* obligation is to support the efforts of that class to free itself. These efforts are exerted in an atmosphere of ruthless, no-quarter conflict: "That man must fight, that there is no hope of human liberation without fight, is thus the very essence, the central command of materialist ethics."[21]

From the outset we are advised to expect the harsh stringencies of a military life. Venable has characterized this internal imperative of Marxian theory as an ethic of "action, pugnacity and partisanship."[22] Its initial premise of total commitment sets aside many of man's nor-mal ethical concerns: the personal as opposed to the class nature of moral problems, the responsibility for making *individual* choices be-tween complex alternatives, and the attendant agonies of doubt and

[21] Venable, *Human Nature*, p. 179.   [22] *Ibid.*, p. 204.

uncertainty that beset the individual who is unsure of history's direction, or of its intentions toward him.

Yet there is a concept of freedom in this moral doctrine, which insists that involvement in the simultaneous battle for the inevitable and the good is binding on all men who learn of its existence. This freedom, which depends on the "recognition of necessity,"

does not consist in the dream of independence of natural laws, but in the knowledge of these laws and in the possibility this gives of systematically making them work toward definite ends. Freedom of the will therefore means nothing but the capacity to make decisions with real knowledge of the subject. Therefore the freer a man's judgment is in relation to a definite question, with so much the greater *necessity* is the content of his judgment determined; while the uncertainty, founded on ignorance, which seems to make an arbitrary choice among many different and conflicting possible tensions, shows by this precisely that it is not free, that it is controlled by the very object it would itself control.[23]

It is a "law-abiding" freedom, then, based on a scientific kind of knowledge which dictates a *single* course of action to all who analyze history correctly. All other kinds of freedom are illusory since they do not hasten history toward its morally desirable ends. It is a freedom that is concerned exclusively with man's ability to act effectively, to apply the correct leverage to history, and to manipulate men and events toward those ends. In its concentration on this kind of efficacy whole areas of human experience are declared irrelevant: in exchange for the chance to act purposefully, the Marxian must accept an unlimited burden of restraints on his personal freedom as most men define it. Man is free when he acts in the only way possible. Man may feel that he is "free" to do almost anything—to act, to dream, to reject, to accept. But he is not free to do away with the objective world simply by closing his mind to it. Even when he "rejects" the world he is making a decision which has consequences on the balance of contending forces, merely by withholding his energies from active commitment. To act in concert with the embattled proletariat is the only truly compelling obligation of modern life; all others are illusory, immoral, or antisocial.

In this monolithic view of moral behavior, the most important moment is the act of "recognizing" the necessity. This act is informed by a number of elements, the first of which is scientific insight into the

23 Friedrich Engels, *Herr Eugen Dühring's Revolution in Science* (New York, 1939), p. 125.

laws of history and into the configuration of historical forces at any given moment. Secondly, it is presumed that this knowledge will dictate a rational course of action. Thirdly, there is a strong emotional component: men are impelled by their disgust and anger to act in accordance with their convictions. This assumption is based on the certainty that most men live in something close to absolute misery, that they are wretchedly and unnecessarily unhappy. Anger is stimulated and given focus by emotional exhortations to replace the intolerable present with a more rational future.

It is quite clear that an ethical imperative based on such a diffuse mixture of analytical, doctrinal, and emotional knowledge cannot be logically or universally binding. Marx and Engels were not particularly concerned with closing their system here. They felt that, so long as the analysis of society remained valid, and the fact of suffering dominated most men's experience, their own empirical findings would be confirmed. Men would, by one route or another, come to accept a concept of revolutionary duty similar to theirs.

The question arises: what place is there for a humane, questing literature in this schematically arranged universe, where virtue is made synonymous with disciplined, militant behavior, where each of the human actors is fortified with incontrovertible assurances of the justice of his cause? The first answer that comes to mind is that, except perhaps for a declamatory poetry like Mayakovsky's, there is none. This may in the end be history's answer, but it has been a surprisingly long time in coming. The delay has been a result of the writers' ability to preserve a vantage of their own, whether by privileged dispensation, or by calculated deception, which has permitted them to make their own comments on the human drama of history. What, then, are the proper subjects for a writer who sympathizes with Marxism, but wants to remain true to the traditions of his art?

Here Plekhanov's attempt to describe the formally binding element in the Marxian ethic is illuminating. In his schematic formulation of the problem of the hero in history, he says of the man who is sympathetic to the Marxian cause that "being conscious of the absolute inevitability of a given phenomenon can only increase the energy of a man who sympathizes with it and who regards himself as one of the forces which called it into being."[24] Plekhanov translates his idea into an algebraic formula: if the inevitable and desirable event A will

[24] George Plekhanov, *The Role of the Individual in History* (New York, 1940), p. 19.

be brought about by the sum of forces S at the time T, then the individual who desires A but does not add a, the force of his own energy, changes the formula to $S - a$, and A's occurrence will be postponed or blocked.[25]

However rudimentary and foolish this may seem (even to Marxists) it points to a basic distinction between two kinds of men. The writer in search of dramatic conflicts might confine his attention to the model revolutionary, the individual whose own energies are entirely identified with the historical demiurge. But he would probably find greater dramatic interest in the man who knows that A is inevitable but that he will not live to see it, or the man who discovers that A has been indefinitely delayed, or the man who finds that his work for A is wrecking his physical or mental health, blighting his emotional life, alienating him from treasured emotional ties, or destroying his moral image of himself. There is no answer to this problem in prerevolutionary Marxian thought, but the official Soviet solution is clear-cut: the man who is unable to submerge himself in the flux of history, who fails to "understand" its direction, who is paralyzed by a tension between his private and public life, or who for any other reason, except physical annihilation, becomes an honorable casualty of the revolutionary struggle is simply not interesting—not typical, significant, or true in the special sense those words have had in the Russian utilitarian tradition since Belinsky. Plekhanov's distinction contains grounds for excluding an enormous range of human experience, particularly of that anguished kind that revolutions cannot fail to create. There are the seeds, too, of a basic quarrel between the writer and the magistrate. Plekhanov's sinister little equation is extended to the writer himself, and he is compelled to identify *his* strength and skill with all other human and historical energies. There is, in fact, no *theoretical* obstacle in Marxism to the enforced submergence of the writer along with all other like-minded men. The protections against it are informal or pragmatic: the kind of respect for the writer expressed by Marx and Engels was also present in the background of many of the early Bolshevik intellectuals, of Plekhanov, Lunacharsky, Trotsky, and, though it yielded at crucial moments to political expediency, of Lenin himself. But beyond good taste, there is no formal stay against the iron logic of the Marxian argument.

What in the abstract are the human costs and rewards for the in-

25 *Ibid.*, pp. 19–20.

dividual who chooses to spend his life in the harness of history? It is clear that the man who accepts the restrictions of Marxian freedom surrenders most of the other kinds of freedom that Marx, himself, celebrated in the past and anticipated in the Communist future: freedom from violence, and from confining disciplines, freedom to explore the universe at leisure, and endlessly to amplify one's responses to it. But this discrepancy is in the nature of things, and to act as though one were confronted with a choice between the interim view of morality and its end product is to engage in self-deception. They come in an ineluctable sequence, never the second before the first, and so long as capitalism survives and Communism is not yet built, the realm of true human freedom exists nowhere on earth, not for the most privileged bourgeois individualist.

Even if there is no choice, will not the conscious historical actor, sure of his mission in the necessity of things, undergo terrible deprivations and find few personal rewards? Will he not pay a prohibitive human cost for his many acts of self-renunciation, and for the consequences of his obligatory hostility toward large sections of the human community whose crime, so far as he is concerned, is defined simply by their position in the system of property relations? Marx and Engels were willing to make no such admission. The chances of human fulfillment were certainly no less in a career of engagement than they were in an attitude of unconcern toward the daily ravages of the class enemy. And if it was a warrior's existence that was promised to the recruit, the very justice of the struggle would more than compensate for the wounds he suffered.[26] That the fight contained its own reward and was a surer road to human health than any kind of acquiescence in the order of things is suggested by Marx's view of the revolutionary in combat with his environment:

By ... acting on the external world and changing it, he at the same time changes his own nature. He develops the potentialities that slumber within him and subjects them to his own control.[27]

The distinction between the interim man and the whole man would seem to be very nearly lost in this view of the historical actor. Marx

---

[26] Venable gives his own version of the Marxian answer to this question: "The downtrodden, the expropriated, the dispossessed, feel revolution as emancipation, not as limitation, and in respect not merely to its ultimate outcome for humanity at large, but in respect to its daily act for the subjugated themselves." *Human Nature*, p. 189.

[27] Karl Marx, *Capital: A Critique of Political Economy*, ed. Friedrich Engels, trans. Samuel Moore and Edward Aveling (Chicago, 1906–9), p. 198.

apparently thought that man starts his journey back to wholeness from the very moment he begins to do battle with his environment. Actually, there was no reason for Marx to be particularly aware of the two kinds of men which are implied by the two distinct phases in his thinking about morality. The revolutionary awakening was just beginning. Why should he emphasize—if indeed he was aware at all of—the variety and intensity of the suffering that stretched ahead of the Marxian revolutionary at a time when Marx, himself, was only beginning to divine the direction the road took? He welcomed the forthcoming battle himself (his definition of happiness was simply "to fight"[28]), but he was never the director of an embattled revolutionary army, never responsible for its strategic disposition, for its discipline, or for its morale. The Communist future was unimaginably remote. For the practical strategist's approach to these problems we must turn finally to Lenin.

III

As the theorist of actual revolution, Lenin shifted the emphasis to the activist pole within Marxian theory more drastically than anyone had before him. His union of theory and practice tended unmistakably to put the former at the service of the latter, and to limit men's intellectual horizons to the immediately attainable future. All his energies were applied to systematizing and simplifying human experience in order to expose the controlling levers of history and to direct man's strength to the single task of pulling them. He also tried to prove to men that they had no obligation superior to that task. As indifferent to the formal categories of ethical theory as Marx and Engels, he nevertheless was the advocate of a strenuous, extremist, and exclusive moral doctrine. In the act of creating the Bolshevik Party apparatus he gave institutional form to the classical Marxian "ethic of action, pugnacity and partisanship," and established the principal conditions, perspectives, and goals of what has been considered ethical behavior ever since in the USSR. Everything he had to say about the function and organization of history's human instrument has a bearing on what was to follow.

One quotation contains a clear outline of the new heroism and the restricted conditions under which it would find expression:

[28] See the account of the parlor game he played with his children, in *Literature and Art*, p. 145.

And first of all the question arises: how is the discipline of the revolutionary party of the proletariat maintained? How is it tested? How is it reinforced? First, by the class consciousness of the proletarian vanguard 'and by its devotion to the revolution, by its perseverance, self-sacrifice and heroism. Secondly, by its ability to link itself, to keep in touch with, and to a certain extent, if you like, to merge itself with the broadest masses of the toilers. . . . Thirdly, by the correctness of the political leadership exercised by this vanguard, and of its political strategy and tactics, provided that the broadest masses have been convinced by their own experience that they are correct. . . . Without these conditions all attempts to establish discipline inevitably fail and end in phrasemongering.[29]

Most of the determinants of Communist behavior are contained in this passage: first of all, the overriding concern with discipline, and, together with that, the virtuous personal qualities that guarantee its maintenance and find their *only* expression as a function of it. It is a regime which makes unlimited demands on the adherent's allegiances, his time, and his energy, and welcomes the harsh asceticism, the hardened will, the habits of self-renunciation and self-limitation that this kind of discipline bespeaks. There is the notion, too, that there are two *kinds* of people, the leaders and the led, and that the Bolshevik is urged "to link" or "to merge" himself ("to a certain extent") with the masses so that he can most effectively exhort, agitate, persuade—in short, manipulate them toward predetermined ends. Though in its prerevolutionary statement this approach has a suggestion of man-to-man argument in it, the exchange is never based on the belief that all opinions have equal value. With the Party's accumulation of power, the essentially parental nature of this relationship became hardened and clarified.[30] The "vanguard" needed, and still needs, to know the temper and grievances of the masses, to make an informed estimate at any given moment of the "possible" (the art of which was and is their consuming concern) in their pursuit of goals which are not open to debate. The third element to note in Lenin's quotation is his definition of the nature of the truths in the name of which leadership is exercised. The key word is "correctness," with its overtone of scien-

[29] V. I. Lenin, *"Left-Wing" Communism, an Infantile Disorder* (New York, 1940), pp. 10–11.

[30] This is not to suggest that force simply replaced argument; agitation is still a primary activity of the Party member. The change that came with the revolution's victory can be summarized this way: before 1917 the Bolshevik leader hoped to persuade the masses to do what he wanted them to do; after 1917 he set out to persuade them to do what had been decided they *had* to do. He now had gained physical control over his adherents. Whether he used it or not, his relations with his followers were changed.

tific infallibility, and its implication that a single tactical doctrine is absolutely true—even if only for a short time—after which a new version of the *absolute but temporary* truths that govern the Communist's every utterance and action will be laid down. Of the ingredients that determine what is "correct"—and the place where that uncompromising word is defined is the actual locus of power—the grievances and expectations of the masses are one, the theoretical teachings of Marxism are another. But the dominant concern is political warfare of a merciless kind manifest in the constant use of the language of "strategy and tactics" with all it suggests of command and obedience, of maneuver and deception, and in the end, of course, of all the limitations a condition of warfare imposes on the whole human being.

War is the arena of virtuous behavior in this transitional phase, as Marx suggested, and it is not governed by rules of any kind. The combat is murderous, without quarter or scruple. Anything less would jeopardize the cause itself:

Everyone will agree that an army which does not train itself to wield all arms, all the means and methods of warfare that the enemy possesses, or may possess, behaves in an unwise or even in a criminal manner.[31]

Since the enemy's "vanguard" was the Tsar's secret, political police, the first occupants of the battlefield, it may be assumed that these unenlightened minions of the status quo established the moral climate in which the struggle took place. Bolshevik virtue was animated in the nature of things by murderous hostility, and armed itself with weapons of counterterror equivalent in effectiveness to every tactic of political terror the experienced and inventive political police could devise. There were other categories of weapons, of course—techniques of instruction, organization, and agitation, even the polite duplicities of parliamentary "struggle"—but the illegal methods, since they involved ultimate weapons, and were the determinants not of victory or defeat, but of survival or extermination, were central in the Leninist design.[32]

It often seems that Lenin had set aside forever the Marxian whole

---

[31] Lenin, *"Left-Wing" Communism, an Infantile Disorder*, pp. 76–77.

[32] The lawlessness of the Dostoevskyan rebel or of the Nietzschean "free spirit" lacks the Marxian revolutionary's grounding in history, but neither is irrelevant to the "illegal" situation of the Bolshevik at this time. Nietzsche's warning is in point: "He who fights with monsters should be careful lest he thereby become a monster. And if thou gaze long into an abyss, the abyss will also gaze into thee." *Beyond Good and Evil*, in *The Philosophy of Nietzsche* (New York, Modern Library), p. 87.

man in favor of the hardened political monolith. In occasional ac-
knowledgments, however, he indicates that he, too, is working in the
larger humanist scheme of Marxism, and that the self-limited human
instrument he desires *is* indeed only an interim man. There is an
echo of the Marxian classics in his assurance that the development of
genuine industrial unions will lead

to the abolition of the division of labor among people, to the education,
schooling and training of people with an *all-around development and an
all-around training*, people *able to do everything*. Communism is marching
and must march towards this goal, and *will reach it*, but only after very
many years. To attempt in practice today to anticipate this future of a fully
developed, fully stabilized and formed, fully expanded and mature Communism would be like trying to teach higher mathematics to a four-year-
old child.[33]

The interim man will presumably last, in Lenin's view, during the
"very many years" of tutelage, working as teacher, disciplinarian,
exemplar, foster-parent, and turnkey. As he pointed out more than
once, the human problem was at the heart of all the reasons that would
make the period of transition such a long one:

We can (and must) begin to build Socialism not with imaginary human
material invented by us, but with the human material bequeathed to us
by capitalism.[34]

By every indication, he regarded this "human material" as a sorry
lot, and the forging of a new image of man out of it was, for all the
Bolshevik optimism about the plasticity of human nature, a titanic
job during which the vanguard presumably would never abandon
its superior vantage.

Now, we may ask once more what fictional possibilities this individual presents to the writer. Or to put it more broadly: with the
world divided into the convenient black and white of a for-or-against
morality, with a narrow concept of political efficacy, always described
in military terms, as the governing standard of truth, what hope or
encouragement is there for literary truth? In the first place, it is legitimate, perhaps, to apply the Marxian thesis that man changes and
is changed by circumstances to the moral climate of the pre-October
Russian revolutionary. If it is true that a master circumstance of his

---

[33] *"Left-Wing" Communism, an Infantile Disorder*, p. 34. Note the parental image
at the end of the quotation.
[34] *Ibid.*

life is the battle with the secret police, then he must be equipped to meet them on their own terms. He must be inured to the harsh, secretive, austere, distrustful life of the underground conspirator and secret agent. He must be eternally armed against betrayal, by others or by himself. He must live, in a sense, "beyond good and evil," ready, on occasion, to lie, steal, or kill for his cause, to outrage his own moral sense, a greater sacrifice of self than any other deprivation he undergoes. In this climate it is not difficult to imagine that the nourishing flame of the world-historical purpose often flickers low or burns out, as it does in Gorky's brilliant story "Karamora" (1924),[35] about the moral disintegration of a Party member turned informer; or, on the contrary, grows to a fanatical white heat destructive of everything that comes near it. Necessity may be the road to liberation, but it is a harshly formative, if not actually disfiguring, taskmaster while one lives in its service.

There is the moral disease, contracted in underground struggle, when deception and violence begin to have a narcotic effect on men, and make addicts of them. Both revolutionary and police agent are susceptible, though they catch the sickness differently. The brutality of the fight perverts the revolutionary's idealism and turns it, mysteriously, into its opposite. For the police agent, a man with a job to do, it is simply one of the occupational hazards of his work. The moral diagnosis is the same whether Holy Russia or the socialist state is the ultimate object of allegiance, or whether the infected Communist is an underground conspirator or a colonel of the secret police.

Plekhanov's equation has already raised the question of the revolution's honorable casualties, the men who fail through doubt, or fallibility, or inner collapse. One variation could be added to the hypothetical situations that were suggested by it, perhaps the most tragic of all: the case of the man who accepts the obligation to hasten history, but disagrees about the means to accomplish it, who persists in his disagreement to the point of an open break, and then is destroyed because his acts are said to threaten history's instrument, the Party, with disintegration. The mere mention of modern candidates for this role—Trotsky, Bukharin, Radek—suggests the inappropriateness of this theme for Soviet writers. It might be said that Soviet literature will reach maturity when it is willing to produce a drama based on

---

[35] In Maxim Gorky, *Best Short Stories*, ed. Avrahm Yarmolinsky and Baroness Moura Budberg (New York, 1947).

the lives of one of these men. Not that Trotsky and the others are, necessarily, tragic heroes, but the Soviet refusal to see the pathos of its own power struggles is a measure of the immaturity of its art. The "death of kings" has simply been banned from the list of approved themes.

But it is not to the tragic deviant alone that the writer need direct his attention. Even the "adjusted" revolutionary must collect his share of scars, must at some time weigh the balance of costs and rewards in personal terms. Even the believing writer, who at the same time honors his craft as something more than an instrument of agitation, would, one would think, find fruitful sources of dramatic tension in the accumulation of experiences that go to make up that balance. And, though the costs and the scars have been emphasized here (because they are underplayed in most of the subsequent literature), certain rewards as well are available to the practicing revolutionary. In addition to the satisfaction of service and of power, there are moments of transcendent harmony and triumph when history's power galvanizes all its servants. Lenin had known the aesthetic experience of revolution:

History generally, and the history of revolution in particular, is always richer in content, more varied, more many-sided, more lively and "subtle" than even the best parties and the most class-conscious vanguards of the most advanced classes imagine. This is understandable because even the best vanguards express the class consciousness, will, passion and imagination of tens of thousands, whereas the revolution is made, at the moment of its climax and the exertion of all human capacities, by the class consciousness, will, passion, and imagination of tens of millions.[36]

This lyrical experience of communion is echoed, presumably, on a lesser scale in the local triumphs of a Communist's life, and must provide him with the memories to be treasured. A longing for the richness of the civil war experience created an ungovernable nostalgia in many Soviet citizens who felt that their lives had become meaningless in the details of peacetime routine, in the corruption of the New Economic Policy (NEP), or in the pointless dislocations of forcible collectivization.

All that we have said so far of the literary use of the revolutionary experience has assumed the existence of a large measure of freedom for the writer—sympathizer or not—to concentrate on its human as-

---

[36] *"Left-Wing" Communism, an Infantile Disorder*, p. 76.

pects, to see it wholly, and to rearrange it without falsification, according to the traditional properties of his medium. Now we must consider the final movement of encirclement, cutting off all escape: the direct application of the Leninist ethic to the writer himself. It is this potential, resident in the Leninist reading of Marx and Engels, that threatens to turn the writer into something they had never imagined—an engineer of the human soul, salaried, disciplined, and subject to dismissal, and worse, for faulty blueprints.

CHAPTER 10

Lenin and Gorky: The Turning Point

The people need heroes. GORKY

No fewer than six attitudes toward literature, some of them contradictory, have been discerned in Lenin's writings.[1] Soviet critics have had to make the most of these disparate views, stressing one at the expense of the others, but never moving beyond them.[2] Although, taken together, they indicate that Lenin sensed the fundamental antitheses between the Russian classical writers and the radical critics, his most consistent emphasis was functional, and his contribution to the utilitarian tradition is his declaration of the principle of outright political partisanship in literature. The most severely functionalist document in the Leninist heritage is his article "Party Organization and Party Literature," published in November, 1905,[3] which since 1932 has underlain all major efforts to subjugate literature to political interests.[4]

[1] See Stanley Edgar Hyman, "Christopher Caudwell and Marxist Criticism," in *The Armed Vision: A Study in the Methods of Modern Literary Criticism* (New York, 1948), pp. 168–208. These are: (1) "the attitude of simple functionalism, ... that art is a weapon in the class struggle and must be recruited to help make a revolution"; (2) "the analytic Marxist view that art reflects social reality but in many respects transcends both it and the creator's views"; (3) "a puritanic resistance to the sinfulness of art"; (4) "the tired businessman's philistine conception of art as a soothing relaxation"; (5) "the social utilitarian view that art is a form of wealth, to be made accessible to the masses under socialism like any other form of wealth"; and (6) "a number of reservations and hesitancies about the other five compounded of his own rich personal respect for the creative artist, devotion to tolerance and personal freedom, and a sense of humor."

[2] *Ibid.*, pp. 196–97.

[3] V. I. Lenin, *Sochineniia*, 4th ed. (Moscow, 1947), 10: 26–31.

[4] In his 1946 "Report" Zhdanov uses it to justify unprecedentedly narrow strictures

Many critics have questioned its significance on the grounds that it is so much a product of local circumstances that it had little influence at the time it was written, and less in later years.[5] Others have said that when he used the word *literatura* he was talking about the Party press, not about imaginative writing. Still others have challenged his credentials as a literary critic and have discredited the article on those grounds.

Of course, in an atmosphere where the uses of the past are confined to a selective, Talmudic referral to authority, ideas are validated differently than they are when their evolution is undirected and their worth established in competition with other ideas. Lenin's article is important for the literary future because it was Lenin who wrote it, and because of the immense authority it gained in the USSR. When the accredited contributors to a society's stock of wisdom are so limited in number, any theoretical redefinition by a major prophet like Lenin may take on a lasting magnitude out of all proportion to its intrinsic worth.

The question of the ambiguity of the meaning of *literatura* may be set aside here with the observation that, although the Russian word means both journalism and belles-lettres, the mere existence of uncertainty about Lenin's intentions is the most revealing point of all. Judging from several comments Lenin made on works of fiction it is quite clear that, when he was in his "functionalist" mood, he in fact made *no* distinction between the two kinds of *literatura*.[6] As to the range of the article's applicability, since we are not concerned with its "correctness" as a guide to Soviet literary policy, we note only that extravagant emphasis has been placed on it in modern times, most notably by Zhdanov in 1946. But, considered with respect to the continuity of the utilitarian tradition, the article has great significance. Even at his most tactical, Lenin was seldom unaware of theoretical matters, and the article may be read, despite all qualifications, as the most sweeping statement of the contempt for literature inherent in Soviet Marxism. There are familiar echoes from the Russian past, too, in Lenin's concept of literary partisanship, although here it is given

---

against the artist. He cites it as the next major moment in thinking about art after the radical democrats. See "Doklad o zhurnalakh *Zvezda* i *Leningrad*," *Literaturnaya gazeta*, 39 (September 21, 1946).

[5] Franklin Reeve has demonstrated that Bryusov, the poet, was very much alive to the significance and to the danger of Lenin's argument. Franklin Reeve, "Politics and Imagination," *American Slavic and East European Review*, 16.2 (April 1957): 175–89.

[6] See p. 174 for his "tactical" estimate of Gorky's *Mother*.

a narrowness and rigidity of statement that even the radical democrats stopped short of. The article takes on added significance from
the fact that it contains some recognition of the delicacy and complexity of the literary process, stemming, no doubt, from Lenin's intelligentsia background. Even in this inhospitable atmosphere the
opposition to the utilitarian trend receives reluctant recognition. At
one moment Lenin seems to propose that the best of the two traditions be fused, but he makes no serious effort in the end to resolve the
fundamental contradiction between them.

The emergence of the Party and its press from underground ille-
gality late in 1905 provided the local occasion for the article, which
poses the strategic question: now that the Party press has passed the
"cursed time of Aesopian language, of literary servility, of slavish
language, of intellectual serfdom,"[7] what use shall be made of the
new freedom? Lenin's answer touches on so many of the permanent
issues from the Russian past, his testament is so authoritative, so
characteristic of recent Soviet thought on these matters, that it deserves intensive analysis.

The first statement of his thesis is in absolute terms:

Literature must become permeated with Party spirit. To counterbalance
bourgeois morals, the bourgeois entrepreneurial and huckstering press, to
counterbalance bourgeois literary careerism and individualism, "noble
anarchism," and the pursuit of profits—the socialist proletariat must advance the principle of Party literature, must develop this principle, and
must establish it in reality to the fullest degree possible.[8]

Lenin leaves no doubt that this principle is entirely a function of political concerns. The degree of subordination it demands of literature
is, perhaps, unprecedented, short of certain anarchist prescriptions for
the abolition of the written word.

In what does this principle of Party literature consist? Not only that for
the socialist proletariat the practice of literature must not be a source of
profit for persons and groups, but that, in general, it must not be an individual matter, independent of the whole proletarian cause. Down with
non-Party writers! Down with superman writers! Literature must become
a part of the general proletarian cause, the flywheel and screw of a single
whole, of the great social-democratic mechanism, set in motion by the conscious vanguard of the entire working class. Literature must become a part
of organized, systematic, unified Social Democratic Party work.[9]

[7] Lenin, *Sochineniia*, 10: 26–27.   [8] *Ibid.*, p. 27.   [9] *Ibid.*

After this, there would seem to be little left to say. But Lenin anticipates the rebuttal he knows his opinions will provoke:

There will be ... hysterical members of the intelligentsia, who will raise a howl to the effect that such a comparison belittles, benumbs, "bureaucratizes" the free struggle of ideas, freedom of criticism, freedom of literary creation, and so on and so on. The fact of the matter is that such howls would only be an expression of bourgeois-intelligentsia individualism. There is no argument that literature, less than anything else, will yield to mechanical alignment, to leveling, to the supremacy of the majority over the minority. There is no argument ... that the guarantee of the greatest range of personal initiative, of individual inclination, the range of thought and fantasy, of form and content, is unconditionally necessary. All this is indisputable.[10]

There echo in this candid summary of the intelligentsia's probable objections the principal arguments made by Turgenev, Tolstoy, Chekhov, and others in defense of the free practice of their craft. Yet the original thesis still stands. He sees no contradiction in stating that

literature must certainly and necessarily become indissolubly connected with other parts of Social Democratic Party work. ... The organized socialist proletariat must look after all this work, control all of it, introduce into all its work, without a single exception, the living stream of the living proletarian cause.[11]

With this point established, Lenin remains responsive to the Hegelian rhythm, nevertheless, and endeavors to resolve the two propositions in a kind of synthesis. The problem is essentially an administrative one, he seems to say, and needs only patient attention to it by all concerned:

We are far from the idea of preaching any kind of uniform system, or solution to the problem by means of a few resolutions. No schematism can be considered in this area. ... The point is that our entire Party ... should be aware of this new problem, should state it clearly, and should undertake everywhere to solve it. Emerging from the captivity of feudal censorship, we do not want to go and will not go into the captivity of bourgeois-huckstering literary relations. We wish to form, and we will form, a free press not only in the police sense, but also in the sense of freedom from careerism ... also in the sense of freedom from bourgeois-anarchistic individualism.[12]

In the second half of this passage (from the word "Emerging ..."), and in the swift transition between the two parts of it, we are able to

[10] *Ibid.*, p. 28.   [11] *Ibid.*   [12] *Ibid.*, p. 29.

distinguish the essential *non sequitur* in all subsequent Soviet thinking about art—the deceptive key-change, the illegitimate merging of incommensurable orders of thought. Up to this point Lenin has been concerned primarily with the opposition between freedom and control as it concerns the functioning Party artist. Then suddenly, without warning, he has translated this antithesis into the terms of the unrelated *political* opposition between the bourgeoisie and the proletariat. With his transvalued definition of freedom he reaches the peak of his intellectual sleight of hand. For if we follow him to the end of his list of the negative freedoms it is impossible to avoid the conclusion that "freedom from ... bourgeois-anarchistic individualism" is, in essence, freedom from every right and privilege the artist has demanded for himself since ancient Greece, that it is, indeed, freedom from freedom itself. Bourgeois freedom is slavery; proletarian "control" is freedom.

But Lenin was not satisfied with this formulation of the problem. In his new version, however, he amplifies the specious key-change and uses it to carry him triumphantly out of the otherwise insoluble dilemma. He begins by restating the original antithesis in very similar terms. Continuing his argument from the remark about "bourgeois-anarchistic individualism," he observes defensively:

> The last words will seem to be a paradox or a joke on the readers. What! Some member of the intelligentsia, a passionate partisan of freedom will shout, What! You want the subordination to the collective of such a fine individual matter as literary creation! You want the workers to decide questions of science, philosophy, aesthetics, by a majority vote! You deny the absolute freedom of absolutely individualistic intellectual creation!
>
> Calm yourselves, gentlemen! In the first place we are considering Party literature and its submission to Party control. Each is free to write and speak as he pleases without the slightest limitation.[13]

It would appear then that all was well. Lenin recognizes the right of all writers who chafe at Party discipline to remove themselves from it and to write as they please. But he has approached the crux of the issue between the needs of the artist and the needs of an absolutist political group. In 1905 he could dispose of it with a pluralist solution, because there was no need at this time for him to face all the consequences of holding political power. If the opposition between these needs is absolute, Lenin felt free to say in 1905, let each go his own

[13] *Ibid.*

way. But there is a new note in his next formulation of the polarity between artist and revolutionary. He suggests that the freedom of choice he has just granted the writer is, itself, spurious; that this is a freedom only to write irresponsibly or dishonestly:

Every free union, among them the Party, is free to dismiss those members who make use of the Party label to preach anti-Party views. Freedom of speech must be complete. I am obliged to concede to you, in the name of freedom of speech, the full right to shout, to lie, and to write as you please. But you are obliged to concede to me in the name of the freedom of unions, the right to exclude or to break with people who talk this way and that way. The Party is a voluntary union which inevitably would disintegrate ideologically and then materially if it did not cleanse itself of members who preach anti-Party views.[14]

At this point there is a note of plain suspicion of the freely judging intellectual, but on the whole it is a reasonable statement of a more or less gentlemanly standoff, a reasonable statement for any political leader to make to freely committed followers. Though we know now that it is a provisional arrangement, one would think that it might have served as a final comment on the matter as things stood in 1905. Not so. Lenin is not content with this: the note of partisanship must be struck again, and the original thesis must be reestablished in its purity. The conflict between the classes is again superimposed on the issue of control versus freedom. His crude for-or-against morality rearranges the elements of the argument in such a way that all virtue and the only valid freedom are found to reside in the proletarian cause. By the same token, the freedom Lenin has just granted the dissident artist is found to be false, nothing but a mask for the "free" writer's status as a kept hireling of the class enemy.

Mister bourgeois individualists, we must tell you that your talk about absolute freedom is only hypocrisy. In a society based on the power of money, in a society where the mass of workers begs and a handful of the rich live like parasites, there cannot be real genuine freedom. Are you free of your bourgeois publisher, mister writer? from your bourgeois public which demands framed pornographic pictures from you ... ? Actually this absolute freedom is a bourgeois or an anarchist phrase.... It is impossible to live in a society and be free of that society. The freedom of the bourgeois writer, artist, actress is only a masked dependence on the money bag, on bribes, on banknotes.[15]

[14] *Ibid.*   [15] *Ibid.*, p. 30.

Lenin has abandoned all efforts to analyze the knottiest problem of all, and has retreated inside the political certainty that all who cannot be persuaded to be with you are unavoidably and implacably against you. All men are reducible in moral terms to their class allegiances, and their creative product can only be judged in those terms. At this point Lenin might have permitted himself the honesty Tolstoy showed when he faced the bitter fact that art and social change are, in a final sense, incompatible activities, and that if the latter is to gain absolute ascendancy, the former must be considered expendable. But Lenin wanted it both ways, and in the following pronouncement, with its sudden reversal of hitherto accepted meanings, there is a fateful setting of the future course of the Russian literary tradition. Socialists, he says, will unmask the "hypocritically free" literature of the bourgeoisie and will set against it "a truly free literature *openly* connected with the proletariat":

This will be a free literature because not profit or career, but the idea of socialism and a sympathy for toilers will win over more and more new forces to its ranks. This will be a free literature because it will serve not a sated heroine, not the boring "upper ten thousand" suffering from obesity, but the millions and tens of millions of toilers, who make up the flower of the country, its strength, its future. This will be a free literature impregnating the most recent word of humanity's revolutionary thought with the experience ... of the socialist proletariat. ...

To work, then, comrades! Before us is a difficult and new but great and noble task—the organization of a broad, many-sided diverse literature in close connection with the Social Democratic workers' meetings. All Social Democratic literature must become permeated with Party spirit ... only then will Social Democratic literature ... know how to carry out its duty, only then will it know how even in the framework of bourgeois society to tear itself loose from bourgeois slavery and to merge with the truly advanced ... revolutionary class.[16]

We have already noted the deceptive altering of the terms of the discussion. In a sense it proceeds out of the arrogance of the political revolutionary who insists—who, indeed, must insist—that his "made" universe contains not a portion of the truth or of virtue, but the whole of it, including the only meaningful definitions of freedom, and the only formula for creating a truly great literature. But this formula rests on the major fallacy in Soviet Marxian thinking about art: that art's worth is coterminous with its ideological value.

[16] *Ibid.*, pp. 30–31.

Much of the Soviet future is forecast in the final passage. First, there is the familiar idea that a "free," and presumably a great, literature, will express those qualities only through service to an idea and to the needs of the suffering masses. There is, in addition, the *mystique* of the *narod*, "the flower of the country, its strength, its future," the same *narod* which was, as Lenin repeatedly observed, such poor human material for social change that it had to be harnessed into a relationship of parental control so harsh that it was to require the indefinite suspension of many of the rights, privileges, and amenities of the most advanced civilizations. There is, too, the orientation toward the future, toward *should be* and *shall be*, conceived as the end of a long upward process of education, in which literature will be assigned a major share of the task of propagating healthy, correct, energizing ideas. Through the entire article runs the certainty that this will be best accomplished through "controls," exercised in the name of politically conceived goals.

On the level of theory, whether or not he realized it, Lenin has completed the encirclement of the free intellect. He has accomplished it simply by extending the ethical imperative of revolutionary Marxism to the artist, with no allowance made for his professional needs. The fact that there is no formal barrier in Marxian theory to the assertion of a principle of conscription[17] may now be translated into that other more ominous formula that neither Chernyshevsky, nor Lenin, nor, with few exceptions, the later Communist theorists have had the honesty or the perspicacity to admit, namely, that when the needs of revolution collide with the needs of art, the latter will always be denied.

In his thinking about art, Lenin has made an absolute choice within two sets of polar opposites that were isolated in the examination of Marxist theory. In the first place, he has clearly chosen future-oriented agitation over scientific investigation, and he has placed overwhelming emphasis on the harsh, one-sided command of interim revolutionary ethics as against the generous vision of man as a versatile, creative, many-sided creature—a vision implicit in the long-range Marx-

---

[17] It is true that in 1905 Lenin considered the writer a volunteer in the Social Democratic cause who was free to resign and "lie" for the bourgeoisie. But he has asserted the Party's right to control the writers who come under its discipline, has asserted the principle of political partisanship, as modern Soviet Marxists claim. In the one-Party state today the writer still has the "freedom" to refuse to accept controls, but it is a freedom that leads only to silence or obloquy.

ian perspective. Lenin is predictable in these choices since they are part and parcel of his pioneering changes of emphasis within the whole world of Marxism. He was a changer, not an interpreter, of the world, and, drastic as his emphasis was, the conclusions he drew in this article are not in the end surprising. But we must note, since he is unwilling to do it, the disastrous consequences for the poet or the philosopher in the advocacy of a standard of political efficacy as the ultimate measure of truth.

Lenin's article may be said to mark the junction of the two principal currents of the Russian revolutionary tradition as it is concerned with imaginative literature. The waters are muddy, it is true, and Lenin makes no explicit acknowledgment here of his dependence on the Russian radical democrats, but their accent is unmistakable in the article, particularly in the final prescription for a socialist literature. The concepts of service to an idea and to the masses, of orienting art always toward a better future, and of educating men explicitly in their social responsibilities are nowhere to be found in the classical Marxist writings on art. Since they have been present in the Russian tradition since Belinsky, there is every reason to attribute them to Lenin's native inheritance, to Chernyshevsky, above all. Finally, Lenin has made an unequivocal choice within another crucial set of polarities, this time not Marxist but indigenous, that of knowledge versus political utility as the principal end of literature, as these ideas were developed in the mid-nineteenth-century debate in Russia.

At the risk of imposing too great a symmetry on very complex material, it is possible to outline the general terms of the merger between Marxism and radical democratic thought, as it affects literature. The complicated apparatus of Marxian determinism, with its claims to confirmation in the process of history and in nature itself, with its documented analysis of social injustice, and its proposals for action (as Lenin derived them from Marx and Engels), all replaced or supplemented the vaguer notions of "progress," "natural truth," and the rudimentary critique of social decay in the thinking of the Russians. Both bodies of ideas rested on the concept of an upward moving, dialectically operated universe, which the partisans of both had learned from Hegel. Brought together, as they were, by this shared belief, radical democratic ideas about literature seem to have survived the Marxian reinforcement to their assumptions, without fundamental change. There was, after all, a vacuum in classical

Marxism on the matter of literature's role during the epoch of transition, which the Russian utilitarian theories were perfectly designed to fill. The wonder is that it took Soviet theorists so long to recognize the jigsaw neatness with which they fit together. Of course, early Soviet critics came into disturbing contact with the contrary, that is, the classical, or anti-utilitarian, trend in Marx's and Engels's remarks on art. Some of the critics may have been spellbound by the belittling designation, "pre-Marxist," which Plekhanov and others placed on the Russian radicals' ideas. Others may have inherited scruples from the classical past about controlling art and the artist as drastically as Chernyshevsky proposed. In any case, it was not until after 1932 that the prerevolutionary critics rose to a position of influence on a level with Marx and Engels. By 1946 they seemed to have gained absolute ascendancy. When the grand merger had been effected it became clear that the binding force between them was the supremacy of the activist, political ethic in both set of ideas.

Hegel to the contrary, history does not often organize itself into the form of dramatic tragedy. But if I may borrow the analogy, this moment (1905) deserves to be seen as one climax (albeit a hidden one) in the dramatic contest between the two factions within the Russian literary tradition, the moment of a fatal reversal of direction for the affairs of the protagonist, here thought of as the ideas of the classical tradition. Although it took years for this to become apparent, all else that follows is, in a sense, a denouement. The climactic moment was not apparent to the actors, but Lenin's article, together with Gorky's *Mother*, the novel that appeared a short time later as if to illustrate his doctrine, marks a watershed in the history of Russian thought. If these two documents announced the beginning of a new tradition, as postwar Soviet critics claimed, they also contained a veiled death sentence for the old. It may be that the sentence will not be carried out in the end, but for the trained ear in 1946 Zhdanov's "Report" had the ring of an epitaph.

II

Gorky had written to Chekhov as early as 1900: "The time has come when the heroic is required."[18] Gorky felt this generalized need throughout his creative life: he found dignity and defiance, tenderness and courage, wisdom and saintliness in the lower depths of Rus-

---

[18] Maxim Gorky, *Reminiscences* (New York, 1946), p. 99.

sian life. His lifelong moral quest took the form of a search for heroes. He seems to have projected his own intense, almost virginal, sense of moral purity outward into the crowds he moved through, in a constant search for the men whose strength, humility, and independence he could admire. His searchlight picked them out of the most unexpected places. His gallery of heroes is varied and colorful—tramps, thieves, prostitutes, hermits, smugglers—and, although it is always threatened by sentimentalism, few of the portraits are blurred by the playing down of compensating vices, or by minimizing the filth, corruption, or despair that framed the reflected glint of virtue. In the tension of these contrasts, Gorky's notes of human affirmation establish their veracity. The function of these unlikely heroes was a simple one: to provide reassurance that man's dignity survived all vicissitudes, that there was hope. Nilovna, the heroine of his novel *Mother*, described the nourishing effects of contemplating virtue in others, in the broad, extrapolitical terms that characterize most of Gorky's own search:

She knew men who had emancipated themselves from greed and evil; she understood that if there were more such people, the dark, incomprehensible, and awful face of life would become more kindly and simple, better and brighter.[19]

He did not limit his search to a single class, or look for a single set of admirable qualities through the range of castes and classes in Imperial Russia. He found a successful tragic design, for example, in the career of the energetic, self-made bourgeois who was destroyed by the wealth he had accumulated. In his autobiography he tended to celebrate all kinds of dissenters, from the Old Believers to the most extreme elements of the revolutionary movement. When his quest centered momentarily on the rising Social Democratic Labor Party in the first decade of the twentieth century, and his long, uneven affiliation with that movement began, the generative force of a new kind of literature was created. It did not matter that *Mother*, the single novel he devoted to this theme, had no sequel, or that he shied away from the treatment of revolutionary political virtue in fiction in later years. The novel's publication in 1907 crystallized and gave literary expression to the fateful tendencies Lenin's article promised. The dangers that are forecast by this event may be summarized as the

19 Maxim Gorky, *Mother*, trans. Isidore Schneider (New York, 1947), p. 248.

substitution of a programmatic, declamatory optimism for the un-dogmatic exploration of human life and suffering which had been the major preoccupation of the classical writers. The new novel promised, as Chernyshevsky had done in his novel, a way to end suffering. The issue of the positive hero becomes central again and is, according to the faction that welcomed the changes *Mother* initiated in Russian writing, the element that most solidly links the past with what is to come. In the novel's Bolshevik hero, Pavel Vlasov, we are told that Gorky

continues the tradition of classical revolutionary-democratic literature, which created a series of freedom-loving heroes ... but at the same time includes in it completely new material [so that] the image of Pavel Vlasov is the ancestor of the gallery of heroic images in Soviet literature: of Os-trovsky's Pavel Korchagin, the heroes of Fadeev's *Young Guard*, and a number of others.[20]

Mother contains two formulas often found in later Soviet fiction: the conversion of the innocent, the ignorant, or the misled to a richer life of participation in the forward movement of society; and the more important pattern of emblematic political heroism in the face of terrible obstacles. The first theme is embodied in the figure of the mother, whose life is transformed by affiliation with the revolutionary movement, and the second in the grim figure of her son, Pavel. Actually the two themes are interwoven, with Pavel acting as the principal agent in restoring his mother to a life of dignity and purpose. This relationship also illustrates the kind of inspiriting effect the image of Pavel is intended to have on the sympathetic reader.

Pavel's inspirational value derives from the moral qualities he dis-plays and the kind of purposeful activity in which he displays them. When courage, endurance, strength of will are exercised in certain kinds of tactically "correct" political behavior, during the May Day parade, for example, it is always a calculated effect he aims for. His later defiance of the Tsarist court reflects a public, not a private, emotion in the sense that it is not a personal defense, but an occasion to instruct the masses in the workings of the hateful system. Pavel acts on this, and on all other occasions, out of two supplementary kinds of knowledge that make up class consciousness: the abstract generalizations about society learned from his precious books, plus the documentation of working-class misery which is daily before his

[20] L. I. Timofeev, *Sovremennaya literatura* (Moscow, 1947), p. 52.

eyes. Thus equipped with emotion and knowledge, Pavel goes forth to permanent battle with the status quo.

This, at least, is the way we are asked to read the novel. It may be read quite differently, however. The novel's conflict is posed between moral absolutes and the writer's attitude toward the conflict is not that of an observer but of a partisan who is, himself, engaged in the bitter class warfare. In this rigid opposition there is no opportunity for the emblematic good man to move in the area between good and evil, or to be involved with, tempted by, or overcome from within by evil. He may reproach himself for lacking the endurance he needs to carry out the tasks history has set for him. He may search his soul to find the courage he needs. He may examine the reasons which brought him to his exposed position. But he will not question the position itself. Evil is tangible and external, and all man's resources are needed to combat it. Since, according to the formula in *Mother*, the good man is the most distant from evil, he cannot yield to it without forfeiting his position in the novel's moral hierarchy. Pavel's revolutionary colleague, the Ukrainian, Andrei Nakhodka, asks a question which is vital for the revolutionary and suggests at the same time a fruitful approach for the writer to the tensions of revolutionary activity. After he has confessed to the murder of a police spy, he asks, in effect, what crimes he will commit in the name of the revolution, what violations of his private moral code are permissible (or bearable) for the dedicated man.[21] But Nakhodka is too weak, too susceptible. He is a good-hearted follower, but not the leader Pavel is. In Pavel's eyes such questions have a certain validity, but they do not really concern *him*, and can always be resolved in the terms of his political-moral absolutes.

But the ease with which he does resolve them seriously challenges his adequacy as a literary portrait. He is, among other things, a fanatical moralizer and prophet. It may be argued that these qualities have been forced on him by the stringencies of his situation, or that they are inevitable costs of his kind of life. In any case they are there— we know because Gorky, perhaps unwittingly, shows them to us—to be accounted for, overcome, or read into any final assessment of his human worth. At the very least they are barriers to awareness, if not to action. By failing to record his hero's limitations fully Gorky has

21 See Gorky, *Mother*, pp. 140–50.

provided grounds for seriously questioning his human and literary judgment in this matter.

The politicalizing of Pavel's emotions is very nearly complete. The following rapture is brought on by uttering the introductory word "Comrade" to a crowd of listening factory hands:

When Pavel had thrown out the word to which he was meant to attach a deep and significant meaning, his throat contracted in a sharp spasm of the joy of fight. He was seized with the invincible desire to give himself up to the strength of his faith, to throw his heart to the people. His heart kindled with the dream of truth.[22]

Despite the extravagantly bad writing and the hints of psychological imbalance, this passage, together with many others like it, is important because it describes the deepest emotional satisfaction of the political man. When his mother argues that he should not expose himself to danger by carrying the banner in the May Day parade, Pavel answers: "I must do it! Please understand me! It is my happiness."[23] She is silent, and he continues in the vein of his grand political passion, hinting now at a taste for martyrdom: "You oughtn't to be grieved. You ought to rejoice. When are we going to have mothers who will rejoice in sending their children even to death?" Told by his mother that she speaks out of love for him, he answers: "There is a love that interferes with a man's very life,"[24] and then, later, "I want no love, I want no friendship which gets between my feet and holds me back."[25] When Nakhodka, whose humane awareness is in inverse proportion to his political effectiveness, reproaches him for his harshness, and for acting the hero in front of his helpless mother, Gorky the writer has brought to light a legitimate conflict of values. Pavel's pomposity, rigidity, and fixity of purpose, with their suggestions of sublimation and megalomania, are predictable consequences of his personality and of his way of life, as given. But Gorky the propagandist betrays his persuasive insight, a few moments later, by extracting a quick apology from Pavel. For the rest of the novel the insight is forgotten. Gorky's uncritical approval of Pavel is unmistakable as the latter grows into the most effective political leader in the area. Finally, when Pavel rises to speak at his trial, "A party man, I recognize only the court of my party and will not speak here in my

22 *Ibid.*, p. 68.
24 *Ibid.*, p. 138.
23 *Ibid.*, p. 137.
25 *Ibid.*, p. 139.

defense,"[26] he has become in his own eyes the selfless incarnation of the public cause, without doubts, hesitations, or concern for personal loss, and Gorky, having surrendered his control over the character, can only agree.

The matter of tension between private and public life appears constantly, but it is resolved with one exception in favor of the latter. Sacrifice and suffering are often mentioned but seldom shown, and never explored to any depth. Consider the example of the design for marriage which Pavel's wife outlines to his mother:

He's free at any moment. I am his comrade—a wife, of course. But the conditions of his work are such that for years and years I cannot regard our bond as the usual one, like that of others. It will be hard, I know it, to part with him; but, of course, I'll manage to. He knows that I'm not capable of regarding a man as my possession. . . . I love him very much and he me . . . we will enrich each other by all in our power; and if necessary we will part as friends.[27]

Gorky records this solemnly, without irony, or any sense that it is any less than what will be accomplished. The two women sit enclosed in each other's arms: "It was quiet, melancholy and warm."[28]

Nikolai, another revolutionary, whose marriage was broken up by the exigencies of exile and underground conspiracy, rationalized his loss in harsher terms:

Family life always diminishes the energy of a revolutionary. Children must be maintained in security, and there's the need to work for one's bread. The revolutionist ought without cease to develop every iota of his energy; he must deepen and broaden it; but this demands time. He must always be at hand, because we—the working men—are called by the logic of history, to destroy the old world, to create a new life. . . . No revolutionist can attach himself to an individual—work through life side by side with another individual—without distorting his faith; and we must never forget our aim is not little conquests, but only complete victory![29]

Only once does raw human experience force its way through the web of political rationalization. Nakhodka's anguish at his casual blow which turned out to be an act of murder bespeaks real inner conflict. He knows the conventional terms in which the crime can be justified, and he recites them with an air of conviction:

[26] *Ibid.*, p. 363.
[28] *Ibid.*, p. 381.
[27] *Ibid.*, p. 378.
[29] *Ibid.*

It so happens that we sometimes must abhor a certain person in order to hasten the time when it will be possible only to take delight in one another. You must destroy those who hinder the progress of life, who sell human beings for money in order to buy quiet or esteem for themselves. . . . If it happens sometimes that I am compelled to take their stick into my hands, what am I going to do then? Why I am going to take it, of course, I will not decline.[30]

He has the right, even the duty, to act in that way. But this explanation is only "logic," he says, it has nothing to say to the conscience:

I go against logic for once. I do not need your logic now. I know that blood can bring no results, I know that thin blood is barren, fruitless. . . . But I take the sin upon myself, I'll kill if I see a need for it. I speak only for myself, mind you. My crime dies with me. It will not remain a blot upon the future. It will sully no one but myself—no one but myself.[31]

The crime which is justifiable in public terms is nevertheless unacceptable to Nakhodka's moral sensibility. It is the most terrible and destructive act of self-renunciation the revolutionary can be asked to carry out, even though he believes, as he does it, that it is in the name of the time when "free men will walk on the earth" and "life will be one great service to man":

In your forward march it sometimes chances that you must go against your very self. You must be able to give up every thing—your heart and all. To give your life, to die for the cause—that's simple. Give more! Give that which is dearer to you than your life. . . . I will tear my heart out, if necessary, and will trample it with my own feet.[32]

Despite the congealed rhetoric, this is intelligible moral utterance, exposing grounds for the deepest division between the individual and his cause, including permanent banishment from the Utopia to come. One need not agree with his definition of the dilemma to see in this the germ of genuine tragic conflict, the real drama of the revolution's honorable casualties. Gorky does not develop it further. Pavel, who, with his mother, remains in the center of the stage, understands and sympathizes: "Andrei won't forgive himself soon," he says, "if he'll forgive himself at all." But he reduces it again to the comforting blacks and whites of the political morality which Andrei has for a moment seen through:

[30] *Ibid.*, p. 148.   [31] *Ibid.*   [32] *Ibid.*, pp. 148–49.

He killed a man unwittingly. He feels disgusted, ashamed, sick.... But they kill off thousands calmly, without a qualm, without a shudder of the heart. They kill with pleasure and with delight.[33]

And then, true to the basic cadence of the book, Pavel dissolves his doubts in the strain of political evangelism that disfigures so much of the novel. Addressing his troubled mother, he says:

If you felt the abomination of it all, the disgrace and rottenness, you would understand our truth; you would then perceive how great it is, how glorious.[34]

With this the mother's doubts are set at rest, and the episode is ended.

Gorky's optimism, at this time, about the revolutionary's capacity to endure hardship of all kinds, without moral damage, is summed up in some observations that the mother, by now a hardened revolutionary, makes to a comrade:

There's a great deal of hardship, you know. People suffer; they are beaten, cruelly beaten, and everyone is oppressed and watched. They hide, live like monks, and many joys are closed to them, it's very hard. And when you look at them well you see that the hard things, the evil and difficult, are around them on the outside, and not within.[35]

But even by the most ungenerous estimate, the virtues of monks do not contain Gorky's sense of human possibilities. It was this fact, perhaps, that prevented his ever again attempting a large-scale fictional treatment of the revolutionary movement.[36]

We are confronted here with problems already made familiar to us by *What Is to Be Done?* The hardheaded visionaries of *Mother*, like the self-confident new men in Chernyshevsky's novel, have their minds fixed firmly on the emergent future. They are struggling to forward a trend which, they are convinced, is both inevitable and infinitely preferable to the unbearable present. Gorky makes no attempt to hide his own partisanship in this contest. Completely identified with his protagonists, he is as committed as they are to the overthrow of life as it is, in the name of a compelling vision of life as it should be. But the question again arises: how can the conflict between future and

---

[33] *Ibid.*, p. 153.   [34] *Ibid.*, p. 154.   [35] *Ibid.*, p. 385.

[36] The dramatic use made of revolution in *Egor Bulychov* and *The Artamanov Business* is more characteristic of Gorky. In both works it appears at the very end as an offstage turbulence which implies that an impersonal vengeance has caught up with the sinful, doomed, but dramatically interesting merchants, whose end it announces.

present be dramatized within the confines of the realistic novel? Apart from the many "utopian" speculations in the novel, the desirability of the future can be suggested only indirectly, through the intensity of the characters' dedication to it. Otherwise the affirmative case must be set forth in declamatory assertions by the hero or his lieutenants. In spite of the endless, florid talk about the better world their personal struggle brings closer, what these men are fighting against is always more vividly realized than what they are fighting for. Their anger is thus better motivated than their invincible optimism. In a novel of repeated tactical defeats this assurance is communicated only by defiant speeches.

The source of their optimism is a political truth founded upon abstractions. That the historical force championed by Pavel and his comrades is somehow benign is an assumption outside the novel which may or may not be accepted by the reader. Gorky's abandonment of a more traditional novelist's vantage for overt political commitment, therefore, prejudices any claims the novel may have to universal interest. The novel of open political partisanship can be acceptable only to like-minded readers. The only possibility of reaching a more indifferent audience rests in the acceptability or credibility of the human material—above all, of the hero—in the novel. And we have seen, I think, that the partisan blight has effectively neutralized his (or their) appeal.

The general difficulties we have indicated—involvement with the future, motivation by doctrine, and this writer's close identification with his heroes and with their cause—have one marked effect on the texture of the novel: it is shaped, down to the smallest technical details, by the spirit of political evangelism. It is not only that the climax of the novel is declamatory (Pavel's speech before the court), or that all the characters' actions and utterances are shaped by political considerations. The dialogue often resembles a verbal exchange of newspaper editorials, written in the turgid rhetoric which also disfigures Gorky's pamphleteering. The expository passages, the dramatic passages, the physical descriptions of the characters and of nature are likewise permeated with evangelism. As the mother goes down under the strangling fingers of the police spy at the novel's end she shouts a slogan, "You will not drown the truth in seas of blood."[37] When Pavel has overcome her doubts about the essential justice of Na-

[37] Gorky, *Mother*, p. 402.

khodka's act of homicide, "The mother arose agitated, full of a desire to fuse her heart into the heart of her son, into one burning, flaming torch."[38] Class virtue manifests itself in the bodies, postures, faces, above all in the eyes of the characters. The eyes of the class enemy are muddy, bleared, or shifty, but, in the midst of his courtroom speech, "Pavel smiled, and the generous fire of his blue eyes blazed forth more brilliantly."[39] At times Gorky comes very close to self-parody: "You'd better put on something; it's cold," one character remarks; and the other answers, "There's a fire inside of me."[40] This is not simply bad writing but a striking example of the fusion of form and content. At the heart of the matter is Gorky's total partisanship. Under its influence all literary and human truth—even the truth of the physical universe—becomes subordinated to a single dogmatic view of political truth.

The history of this novel's reputation is voluminous. We may note only the major trend here: what was at first, in the opinion of critics, a very questionable piece of work is now considered the foundation of socialist realism. Lenin at his most functionalist is reported by Gorky to have told him while it was still in proofs:

Yes, I should hurry up with it, such a book is needed, for many of the workers who take part in the revolutionary movement do so unconsciously, chaotically, and it would be very useful to them to read *Mother*. "The very book for the moment."[41]

Gorky's biographer in English reports that Gorky himself was extremely displeased with it: "Gorky ... has come to agree with most of his critics, namely, that the novel suffers from weakness of characterization and too obvious didacticism."[42] His critics included many authoritative Soviet voices in the 1920s. Plekhanov and others found the novel schematic, sentimental, didactic, and ideologically false. The reversal of this generally held verdict coincided with the promulgation of socialist realism in 1932, with all that this meant for the setting of new standards of literary judgments on the leading personages in the novel. I. Bespalov's article on Gorky in the *Literary Encyclopedia* (1929) has this to say:

Most vividly developed in *Mother* are the mother, Andrei Nakhodka, and Rybin. Pavel is presented schematically and somewhat bookishly.[43]

[38] *Ibid.*, p. 154.   [39] *Ibid.*, p. 364.   [40] *Ibid.*, p. 239.
[41] Maxim Gorky, *Days with Lenin* (New York, 1932), p. 6.
[42] Alexander Kaun, *Maxim Gorky and His Russia* (New York, 1931), p. 557.
[43] I. Bespalov, "Gorky," *Literaturnaya entsiklopediya*, 2 (1929): 652. Bespalov goes

In later judgments Andrei's and Pavel's positions are generally re-versed. The Ukrainian is seen as a loyal, if fallible, lieutenant, but Pavel is the "first among equals." Timofeev's textbook for secondary schools notes Pavel's resemblance to Chernyshevsky's Rakhmetov, and praises his image as the incarnation of Bolshevik virtue. He is en-dowed with "will, intelligence," and "firmness of character." These traits in turn sustain his chief political attribute: "clarity of goal, readiness to surmount all obstacles for the achievement of this goal."[44] This judgment echoes scores of others, which find in Pavel a point of junction of the old and the new, the first successful image of the positive Bolshevik hero, and the first successful solution of all at-tendant creative problems. At the heart of these opinions is the as-sumption that the contemplation of Pavel's image by the reader will stimulate him to emulate the hero's actions and thoughts, and coin-cidentally to respect Pavel's position as a representative of Communist leadership.

Gorky knew that his approach to literature implied important de-partures from classical realism. In his letter to Chekhov about the need for "the heroic," Gorky exposed some of the thinking that under-lay this demand:

So there you go, doing away with realism. And I am extremely glad. So be it! And to hell with it! ... Everyone wants things that are exciting and brilliant so that it won't be like life, you see, but superior to life, better, more beautiful. Present-day literature must definitely begin to color life and as soon as it does this, life itself will acquire color. That is to say, peo-ple will live faster, more brilliantly.[45]

The "realism" that must give way to the "heroic" was neutral, he felt, hopeless, and rooted in the present, in life as it is; the "heroic" that was to replace it was not escapist, but functional, in that it was to quicken and change men's lives and set them in motion toward an unspecified vision of life as it should be. On the single occasion when this general feeling was translated into political myth-making, he invested the "color" and the promise in Pavel and the other Bolshe-viks. This lapse has been seized upon and made the theoretical basis of "socialist romanticism," the ingredient of socialist realism which

on to say that even though the core of Nakhodka's ideological views is anarchist in substance and Christian in form, he is a better propagandist and a more compelling literary figure than the "rationalist Pavel Vlasov." Ideological correctness has not yet become the sole measure of truth.

[44] Timofeev, *Sovremennaya literatura*, pp. 83–84.
[45] Gorky, *Reminiscences*, p. 99.

176 THE MARXIAN INCREMENT

directs the writer not to a general heightening of experience as Gorky originally intended, but to the celebration of the emergent future exactly as it is defined in the Party program and in the five-year plans. This is the obligatory step beyond the present, beyond reality, beyond realism, and beyond the empirical truth that the figure of the Soviet hero must express. Pavel Vlasov is valued as an *ideological* portrait, made up of hope, doctrine, and tendency as much as he is of flesh and blood. Thus the grounds for doubting his human validity are built into the very basis of the theory he stands on.

In a sense, Gorky and Lenin collaborated in this first demonstration of Soviet literary partisanship. Perhaps in Lenin's, certainly in Gorky's, case, it did not represent their only or their final thought on literature. But it set an example of the extreme prescriptive potential in Soviet Marxism, which, even at that time, had the critical inheritance of the Russian radical tradition solidly grafted onto it. It has provided primary documentation ever since for the most extreme applications of this theory to Soviet writing.

PART THREE

Toward Orthodoxy, 1918-1953

CHAPTER II

Leather Men

*People whose revolutionary class consciousness has already
grown into an emotion, an unbreakable will, has
become an instinct like hunger and love.* GORKY

Postrevolutionary literature makes it clear that the civil war is the
brightest and most fearsome experience in the memory of Soviet man.
Many who lived through its worst moments remained fascinated by
it and continued to value it for the intensity of its emotion, even as
they forgot the suffering, the brutality, and the suspension by all factions of minimal standards of human justice. Every man enacted the
private drama of his own expectations within the national tragedy.
Many found the revolution stillborn when the bloodletting finally
ended; others had been recast in its furnace, and never lost their taste
for the easy release of rage and violence. Many more went home
numb, hiding their psychic wounds and seeking relief in the cadences
of peacetime existence.

The Soviet Russian imagination has never ceased to regard those
years as the climactic moment of its own history, and has never found
a suitable substitute for it as a source, not simply of fictional material,
but of genuine spiritual adventure. Of the four later novels we shall
examine in a survey of the range of Soviet literary expression before
1941, two, *Road to Calvary* and *The Silent Don*, deal almost entirely
with the civil war, and in the other two, *Road to the Ocean* and *The
Making of a Hero*, civil war experiences have shaped characters and
situations which are explored in later years.

One finds in the early civil war novels a disorder and lack of control over the material which may be attributed to two factors: the
extraordinary resistance of the material itself, rich though it was, to

conventional literary organization; and a tendency on the part of the writers to celebrate violence, riot, and disintegration for their own sakes. Had they been disposed to make leisurely explorations of character, the moral conflicts, complex though they were in a certain sense (within the family, within the village, as well as between armies and social classes), were posed so absolutely and settled by such violent means—often by the blow of a saber—that they had few opportunities to do so. Few have succeeded as Sholokhov did in *The Silent Don* in assimilating the entire experience into a grand literary design.[1] In the early works about the civil war, the writers hewed close to a vein of personal reminiscence, accepted a broad standard of partisan virtue (although the departures from it are often the most interesting moments), and attempted a minimum of literary invention.

The Soviet writer has never been entirely free of doctrinal "guidance," but in the 1920s he worked under less pressure than he has at any time since. In 1925, government and Party formally declared hands-off in art, and the many unofficial literary groups then clamoring for supremacy exerted so much pressure from so many directions that they tended to neutralize one another. The views of these groups reproduced the spectrum of theories lying between the prescriptive and the exploratory extremes that have already been isolated in the Russian national tradition. Some of the schools, it is true, are beyond its limits: the formalists who considered the preoccupation with human value to be outside the proper concern of criticism; the Plekhanov-oriented "sociologists" whose "unmasking" of the class essence of past literary works was an academic, not a critical or creative, concern; the Mayakovsky-led experimenters with "the word," whose primary concern was with poetry. But within our spectrum the debate continued, between the On Guardists as the spokesmen for the harshest tendencies in the prescriptive aesthetic and the diffuse group known as the fellow-travelers, partially organized in the Serapion Brotherhood, whose spokesman was Alexander Voronsky.

Voronsky's aesthetic was one of the few theories of the Soviet era which was not *primarily* directed toward finding a place for art within

---

[1] Solzhenitsyn's sensational charge (see the *New York Times*, September 1, 1974) that the novel was written by a White Cossack officer, Fyodor Kryukov, and appropriated by Sholokhov as his own, has considerable *prima facie* plausibility: how did the young uneducated Sholokhov write so well and so persuasively about events he had never experienced? Scholarship will eventually settle the question of authorship; my judgment here concerns the literary merits of the published text, whoever wrote it.

the fixed and absolute limits of class warfare. From Tolstoy and Proust he derived the central assumption of his theory—that art essentially was a form of cognition, not of agitation:

Before everything else art is knowledge of life. Art is not the arbitrary play of fantasies, of feeling, of moods, art is not an expression of the subjective sensations, or experiences of the poet. Art does not set itself the goal ... of awakening "good feelings" in the reader. Art like science perceives life. Art and science have one and the same subject—life, reality. But science analyzes, art synthesizes; science is abstract, art concrete; science is directed to man's reason, art to his sensuous nature.[2]

Voronsky, an old Bolshevik himself, had, of course, to come to grips with the problems of the class-divided universe and of the relation between art and ideology. But his formulation avoided two extremes: first, the view that the artist tropismatically expresses the ideology of his class by virtue of his birth or of his class conditioning, and that this reflection is the most important element in his work; or, second, the view that the artist is obliged to become a conscious spokesman for the interests of the "advanced" class, the proletariat. The artist, as well as the scholar, reflects his findings through a "psychological class prism."[3] But his researches are undirected, are not valued simply because they reflect class interest, and their objective pursuit constitutes his first obligation to his class. Reality exactly as he discovers it to be is his primary area of operation.

This summary of Voronsky's views indicates that the non-prescriptive strains in the Soviet intellectual legacy found hospitality in the early days, and that accommodation was thought possible between two basic human activities, free investigation of the world and the making of revolution. It is not surprising that a majority of the most gifted writers drew together under the shelter of this doctrine. Variety in theme, frankness in treatment, and ambiguity in outcome are qualities that have often been noted in this early fiction. It is reasonable to assume that the more adventurous of the writers found support for their freedom of movement in Voronsky's rejection of narrow political claims made on them by the Proletkult–On Guard–RAPP axis.

In this air of relative nonconformity no single doctrine was preeminent, and no single design for the literary hero prevailed. In fact, the concept of the hero as an important structural device or didactic

[2] *Literaturnaya entsiklopediya*, 2 (1929): 313.
[3] *Ibid.*, p. 312.

instrument was not widely discussed in the critical debates of the time.[4] Trotsky and Voronsky, for example, both expressed dissatisfaction with the various images of Communists that had appeared in novels, but neither they nor anybody else proclaimed that the creation of the shining image of the Communist hero was a preeminent obligation of the Soviet writer. All factions were concerned with defining the nature of literature itself, and with making a literature worthy of the new epoch, whether a radically different one, a "proletarian" literature, or, if this was a daydream (as both Trotsky and Voronsky maintained), then a literature which incorporated the best of the past in its investigation of the new Soviet reality. The most explicit treatment of the hero problem is contained in the doctrine of "the living man," a very general notion which echoes the classical past in its overall injunction to show the Communist with all his faults and the class enemy with all his virtues.[5]

Whatever there is of interest on the hero is to be found in the literature itself. Free from hounding by any single omnipotent, critical group, the writers explored a number of disparate solutions. Non-Party writers like Fedin, Kaverin, and Olesha dealt sympathetically with the tragic "maladjustment" of the prerevolutionary *intelligent* who could not comprehend the disorder of a world in revolution. In this connection one occasionally finds discussions about "the superfluous man," but it had become clear by 1929 that this was a declining trend, that the new "new man," the Bolshevik, had established himself at the center of Soviet literature.

II

The most celebrated essay on heroism from these early years is Dmitri Furmanov's *Chapaev*, published in 1923, a book which has survived all doctrinal reversals, and is still established as a Soviet classic. Though it is usually classified as a novel, it is really a diary with the thinnest of fictional disguises—the author has simply changed

---

[4] A symptom of the general indifference to the matter is found in the brief entry under "Hero" in the *Bolshaya sovetskaya entsiklopediya*, 17 (1929): 451–52. Hero is defined as an ancient Greek concept which reappeared in the figure of the Christian saint, and as a device of neoclassic tragedy. In the *Literary Encyclopedia*, the problem is briefly treated under the heading "Obraz" (8 [1934]: 190–91). The treatment, which reflects the (then) new doctrine, socialist realism, also looks like a last-minute insertion in a long article, most of which echoes the ponderous terminology of Plekhanovist literary scholarship.

[5] See below, pp. 212–17.

his own name—and has all the immediacy and incoherence of history directly observed at a volcanic moment. Judged in terms of its fictional pretensions, it is episodic and formless. The war between Red and White is the background, but the real conflict, as it appears fitfully in the narrative of events, is between the attitudes that make for victory over the external enemy and the personal inadequacies and organizational shortcomings that threaten victory. There are two heroes, the legendary guerrilla leader, Chapaev, and his commissar, Klychkov (Furmanov). Their relationship, their initial antagonism and ultimate partnership, is the focal point of the human story and, at the same time, the source of a crude symbolism.

The distribution of skills and energies between the two heroes is as expected: Klychkov, the Party man, the "rationalist," is the guardian of policy and discipline, but he lacks the military skills and is not himself a primary source of revolutionary energy. His faith in his Party's knowledge of the laws of social change is absolute. His disciplined allegiance to those who are directing the process of change endows him with a self-assured wisdom in the name of which he focuses and manipulates the skills and energies of others. His work is leadership; he deals with men's attitudes, their morale, their understanding of the cause, and their allegiance to it.

Chapaev, the source of the book's color, embodies a different set of heroic virtues. His elemental strength, his colorful boasting, and his instinctive qualities of leadership recall the heroes of Russian folklore, or the strain of peasant anarchism represented in the past by Bolotnikov, Razin, and Pugachev, leaders of the great *Jacqueries* of the seventeenth and eighteenth centuries. The alliance between the two men, the commissar and the peasant guerrilla leader, which is central in the book, has extra significance because of the unintentional disclosure that their "partnership" conceals a subtle inequality which ends in the subjugation of one by the other.

Klychkov's premise—"that politics is the mainspring of the civil war"—defines his function and his personality as well. He is convinced that his work of inspiring troops, regulating human relations, expediting, planning, explaining policies, and imposing order on undisciplined emotion is the *sine qua non* of victory. Military skills are merely the techniques of the struggle; Klychkov manipulates the men who direct the strategy and fire the guns. "Political work" is the very heart of the matter:

The political department was like a huge sponge continually absorbing the innumerable reports, facts, and wealth of experiences that came pouring in from the various units and from the surrounding population; and then, having assimilated this experience—at all kinds of conferences, meetings, etc.—it would exhale it again, through the medium of its organizers and agitators, in the form of countless leaflets, proclamations, instructions, and directives.[6]

In the execution of his mission as one of the "torchbearers, mouth-pieces, teachers," of the revolution, Klychkov shows himself to be quick, flexible, determined, patient, ruthless, tactful, or deceptive, as the situation demands. He aims above all things to gain control over himself and over others. When his inner life is touched on, it is the story of the perfection of self-discipline, and of the systematic conquest of his emotions. In this respect, lapses from his standards of political virtue are more revealing than his adherence to them. His first hours under fire are spent in abject cowardice in the baggage train, far from the front where his duty requires him to be:

Oh! Shame, unspeakable, unutterable shame! It was bitter to realize that his heart had failed him in the first battle, that he had fallen short of his own expectations. Where had been the boldness, the heroism of which he had dreamed so much when he was still far from the front line?[7]

His steadfastness in subsequent engagements is not a result of the mere accumulation of experience. There is a quality of dogged self-improvement about his preparation for future battles:

He managed to train himself, as he had planned, to boldness and outward calm, to grasp the situation and cope with it quickly. But this training took time; like everyone else, he had to go the way that leads from open confusion and cowardice to befitting behavior in the presence of the enemy.[8]

He succeeds in rationalizing other disturbing experiences. On the day he signs his first execution order,

Klychkov was agitated and upset the whole day. He did not smile and joke, spoke little and unwillingly, and tried to keep by himself most of the time. But that state of mind did not survive the day; when he woke up next morning, no trace of it remained. This was natural. It would have been abnormal to let such a thing dwell for long on one's mind at the front,

[6] Dmitri Furmanov, *Chapaev* (Moscow, 1934), p. 205.
[7] *Ibid.*, p. 124.   [8] *Ibid.*, p. 127.

when, daily, hourly, heartrending, gruesome pictures followed one after the other, and the victims were not isolated, but numbered tens, hundreds, and thousands.[9]

Later he discussed the matter with his fighting companions. They agreed "that to cut down a human being ... to have him shot, or shoot him with one's own hand is a hard job at first for anyone, however strong his nerves and however hard his heart; it always makes him feel confused, ashamed, and remorseful."[10] But one "gets used to it," the sensibility is "blunted," and Klychkov reaches the comforting conclusion that "the destruction of an enemy, in whatever way it is done, becomes something almost mechanical."[11]

In the same way that he has conquered cowardice and squeamishness, he curbs his tendency to be swept away by the powerful, inchoate emotions of front-line comradeship. Under the influence of the egalitarian spirit, which sometimes persuaded front-line units to refuse individual decorations and to blur all distinctions of rank, Klychkov wrote a letter on impulse to his superiors to protest raises in pay for political workers in the Red Army. The impulse was an "incorrect" one—as indeed are most impulses in this austere political world—and his own comment on his indiscretion established the scale of values governing his behavior. His letter, he remarked drily, "displays more warmth of heart than reason."[12]

These incidents hardly yield a full-length portrait of the man, but they introduce patterns of behavior that are integral to the stereotype of the Soviet positive hero: the preeminence of conscious self-discipline, awareness of the public consequences of every private act, and a capacity to subordinate every personal emotion to the political program of the Party. Klychkov summarizes his growth after six months of war, and we note that his progress toward maturity has been progress toward austerity, discipline, and toughness:

Looking back upon these last six months, Klychkov, too, found that he could hardly recognize himself—so much had he grown up, acquired moral strength, been steeled by hardships, so simply and unhesitatingly had he come to tackle the solution of all sorts of innumerable problems which would have completely baffled him prior to his experience at the front. Only now did he feel the mighty influence of the hardships of war, the meaning of the front line as a school.[13]

[9] *Ibid.*, p. 281.   [10] *Ibid.*, p. 283.   [11] *Ibid.*
[12] *Ibid.*, p. 330.   [13] *Ibid.*, p. 401.

Klychkov's biggest achievement was the domestication of the "wild horse of the steppes," Chapaev himself. Chapaev was the "born leader" of the peasant masses, "heroic but raw," the expression of their "unlimited bravery, resolution, hardihood, unavoidable cruelty, and stern temper,"[14] the voice of "all the irrepressible and spontaneous feelings of rage and protest that have accumulated in the hearts of the peasants."[15] He was fearless, hot-tempered, credulous, illiterate, and an indisputable military genius. Klychkov's job was to tame this elemental force whose appeal to his own kind, the peasant rank and file, was far greater than the bookish commissar's ever could be, to funnel his energies into useful channels, and to preserve at all costs the myth that surrounded him. It was not only difficult, it was dangerous. Wild spirits of the steppes like Chapaev hated intellectuals, officers, and workers on principle, and were known to have "taken it into their heads to bump off their commissars."[16] Klychkov's job was not alone to direct a single gifted but wayward individual, but through him to harness a force in the revolutionary movement which was often skeptical about avenging its grievances against the Whites under Bolshevik leadership. Klychkov's dangerous and delicate task aimed at a goal that was central to the Bolshevik mission, the establishment of absolute control over all the energies released by October. Klychkov, who, for all the affection he felt for Chapaev, viewed him always from the condescending vantage of his superior education, approached the problem with a cunning sense of tactical manipulation. He had to establish himself as an equal in the exclusive fraternity of fighting men that surrounded Chapaev, and probe for the weaknesses in the leader himself. Before he had met him he had devised a plan that would guarantee him a superior vantage in all their dealings:

At first he would avoid conversations on military topics, in order not to show that he was a mere layman in these matters. He would turn the conversation to politics, because then all the advantages would be on his side. He would gain Chapaev's confidence, encourage him to speak quite frankly on all subjects, including intimate, personal peculiarities and minor details. He, Fedor, would speak mostly about science, culture, general education— and here again Chapaev would be reduced to the role of listener. And later —later Fedor would reveal himself as a brave fighter.[17]

[14] *Ibid.*   [15] *Ibid.*, p. 86.
[16] *Ibid.* ". . . not some contemptible . . . cowardly commissar but first-rate revolutionaries," Furmanov adds, "or they have suddenly gone over to the Whites with their whole 'spontaneous' detachments at their heels."
[17] *Ibid.*, p. 84.

To establish this version of himself and to avoid appearing sycophantic before the hero, Klychkov determined to set a tone of Bolshevik crispness: "He must at once establish simple and cordial relations, with a touch of the necessary rudeness."[18]

Long after he had undertaken his duties, Fedor stuck to his plan to bully Chapaev with book-learning. "Spiritual domination over Chapaev would surely 'curb' him, before setting him on the path of conscious struggle—not that of blind instinctive heroism, however colorful, riotous, and splendid that might be."[19] In that case Fedor would "hold all the cards and would draw him away from anarchy and incoherent thinking."[20] But then Fedor was overcome by one of those engaging lapses of discipline that give his diary a certain freshness even as he manages a moment later to stifle it with his sense of Bolshevik duty. In a wildly poetic moment it occurs to him that the "breaking" of Chapaev might, in itself, represent a loss to humanity:

Chapaev was a remarkable man, head and shoulders above the crowd— that was true; it would be as difficult to gain control over him as to break in a wild horse of the steppe—difficult but not impossible. But was it worthwhile, Fedor suddenly asked himself. Would it not be wiser to abandon the beautiful, original, and vital character to the will of destiny and leave it untouched? Let Chapaev sparkle with iridescent fire like a precious stone, let him brag and boast and play the bravo![21]

Why not? Klychkov's Bolshevik conscience gives him a curt answer. "The great struggle that was in progress did not admit of such frivolity."[22] Sternly, then, with programmatic earnestness, Klychkov embarked on his plan of conquest. The books given to Chapaev sapped his self-assurance by opening "new ways unknown to him, new explanations to everything."[23] But when this approach was not enough, when his role as teacher was not effective, Klychkov argued bitterly, resourcefully, and unfairly to curb Chapaev's "anarchist" tendencies. His personal triumph over the hero of the folk is, in the end, complete. The hero has become "wax in his hands." In the midst of a Chapaev tantrum, "Fedor saw that things were getting beyond a joke and decided to triumph over Chapaev as he always did by keeping a cool head."[24] These were the personal terms between them in the final stages of their relationship. It was a partnership, Furmanov insists, in which each handled his specialty: Chapaev, the essential

18 *Ibid.*, p. 85.   19 *Ibid.*, p. 152.   20 *Ibid.*
21 *Ibid.*   22 *Ibid.*   23 *Ibid.*, p. 175.
24 *Ibid.*, p. 374.

military business, and Klychkov, the control of policy and morale. But the partnership, for all the personal affection between them, conceals a hidden inequality, by the terms of which the Bolsheviks became custodians and manipulators of the Chapaev legend. They could not deflate it if they wanted to, because it exerted a personal appeal on the troops no slogans could match:

Chapaev's fame was wide, and this fame, it is true, was better deserved than that of any other man. Chapaev's division knew no defeat, and for this he was himself largely responsible. To infuse the whole division with one impulse, to make it believe in its invincibility, and to bear patiently, even to treat with scorn, the privations and hardships of campaigning, to choose fitting commanders, harden them, permeate and saturate them with his own impetuous will, gather them around him, and make them concentrate on a single idea, a single aspiration—the aspiration to victory, to victory, to victory—this was true heroism![25]

Yet, for all its temporary usefulness, the Chapaev legend was a primitive makeshift, "how magnificent all this was but how wrong, harmful, and dangerous."[26] Certainly it was not part of the ethos of the workers, and, if the future truly belonged to them, both the man and his myth were expendable:

Obviously he was the commander they needed at that time, a commander born of those peasant masses, incorporating all their peculiarities. When the masses grow up in wisdom and culture, the need for men like Chapaev will disappear. Even then for such troops as, say, the Ivanovo-Vosnesensk Regiment, his appeal was not powerful. His primitive speeches did not inflame the workers, who put sober reason above reckless bravery; they preferred discussion and meetings ... and spoke with Chapaev as equals instead of gazing at him with adoration and grinning from ear to ear.[27]

For that matter, the very basis of his reputation was open to challenge: "Not a few men were braver, better qualified to lead troops, politically maturer, but their names are forgotten."[28] It was the special hold he had on the imagination of his own kind that constituted his great value. His "personal bravery, gallantry, daring, and resolution"[29] expressed the quality of the peasants' heroism and were, because of their lack of "political maturity," doomed to extinction, as the solemn,

25 *Ibid.*, pp. 399–400. 26 *Ibid.*, p. 202. 27 *Ibid.*, p. 263.
28 *Ibid.* 29 *Ibid.*

pamphlet-inspired uplift of the Bolshevik workers became the governing morality of the land.

Furmanov's personal attachment to Chapaev, and his sense of the human differences between worker and peasant, between himself and the living legend he kept watch over, illuminate value conflicts that are later to be resolved unquestioningly in favor of the commissar's own arid kind of virtue. Chapaev's instinctive likes and dislikes, his genuine courage, and his scornful energy represent inchoate aspirations which expressed the real, uninstructed, perhaps unrealizable, needs of the Russian peasant mass. It is not just the difference between worker and peasant, or between the latter's illiteracy and the "culture" of Bolshevik pamphlets, that is at stake, but the tensions between the authentic grievances of the average Russian (statistically, a peasant) and the dogmatic, strategic solutions the Bolsheviks imposed upon them. Furmanov's exploration of these two "moments" of revolution (grievance and solution), despite its tendency toward the cut-and-dried Bolshevik answer, discloses a permanent and tragic problem in Soviet life.

At the end of the book Furmanov, in his matter-of-fact way, is quite skeptical about the myth he manipulated. He distrusted the extravagant emotion which surrounded Chapaev and saw the real hero of the future in his own dry image. Chapaev was the child, and he the parent. Although he had found great sustenance in the massive emotions of the civil war, and had admired Chapaev greatly, he found assurance in the fact that "our heroic days will pass, and people will call this mere romancing."

Yet the popularity of the Chapaev myth itself indicates that Chapaev was very much to the popular taste. A passage in a much later play, Afinogenov's *Far Taiga*, indicates the kind of currency the myth had, and raises, at the same time, interesting questions about the primitive expectations of the Soviet audience. A peasant girl in the play remarks to her sophisticated Communist visitor, Vera:

Glasha: I read about Chapaev once. That was exciting. But the ending was wrong. He's a hero, then suddenly he drowns. Why should a hero drown?
Vera: That's how it happened in real life.
Glasha: No, that's wrong. As I see it, he only pretended to drown. He went down to the bottom, then crawled quick over the bed, and

got out on the other side of the river. . . . That's the ending I've thought of.

Vera: No, Glasha dear, one has to die for victory too.

Glasha: Let the Whites die. Our Red Commanders must live on![30]

Concessions to folk expectations have contributed to the creation of a special literary formula. The extraordinary event, taken from life, and too improbable to be contained in a conventional novel or story, is recorded in literal detail. As a result, a kind of journalistic mythology replaces fiction. Boris Polevoi's *The Story of a Real Man* (1946), the account of a legless Soviet fighter-pilot in World War II, and Nikolai Ostrovsky's *The Making of a Hero* (1932–34), the disorderly memoirs of a Party primitive, are outstanding later examples of this Soviet genre. Although these best-sellers serve the interests of Party and state, it is hard to believe that official promotion alone could account for their phenomenal success. Bespalov reports, in his article on Gorky in the *Literary Encyclopedia*, that in spite of the novel's serious flaws, *Mother* has always been extremely popular with the workers themselves.[31] Too little can be known of the factor of public taste in shaping Soviet fiction for us to speculate further here. Its existence must be assumed, nevertheless, and kept in mind as an important, if uncertain, point of reference, in the formation of heroic images.

III

Although it uses few of the resources of fiction, Furmanov's *Chapaev* brings to light most of the dramatic constants in the major, heroic strain of Soviet writing. There is the political hero—tough, dedicated, self-controlled; there is the enemy—faceless, heartless, beyond the reach of pity or understanding; there are the masses—powerful, blind, long-suffering, requiring leadership, protection, and indoctrination; and there is the central dramatic design—the sorely tried leader, hemmed in by the demands of public policy, by personal privation, and set off by the solitude of leadership, summoning the resources in himself and in others to accomplish the task he believes history has set for him.

[30] Alexander Afinogenov, *Far Taiga*, in *Soviet Scene: Six Plays of Russian Life*, trans. Alexander Bakshy (New Haven, Conn., 1946), p. 227. Yuri Sokolov, the Soviet folklorist, describes many oral variants of the "Chapai" legend, with a variety of magical solutions similar to Glasha's above. See Yu. M. Sokolov, *Russki folklor* (Moscow, 1938), pp. 494–97.

[31] *Literaturnaya entsiklopediya*, 2 (1929): 645–66.

In Alexander Fadeev's *The Rout* (1927) these elements are organized into a coherent literary pattern. It does not differ in kind from
dozens of later Soviet novels, but achieves a certain plausibility by mut-
ing the note of political evangelism. The human material is thin, and
the situations are severely limited as a means of exposing character.
But Fadeev has concentrated on this dimension to the nearly complete
exclusion of political matters, and further has tried hard to remain
true to it.

The wanderings of a doomed company of mounted guerrillas in
the back country of the Far Eastern Maritime Provinces provide a
setting remote from the main revolutionary struggle. The novel is
organized around two human situations: the first is a political-sexual
triangle in which a shopworn but kindhearted camp-follower and
nurse, Varya, moves between two men, her "husband," Morozka, a
confused coal miner, and Metchik, an oversensitive, self-pitying intellectual. Varya's final reunion with Morozka, whose attitudes have
been clarified by the influence of the more steadfast of his fellow
miners, is intended to make a political point. Metchik is never able
to become a part of the unit, never perceives its inner human "mechanism," and expresses his intellectual's selfishness in a final moment
of cowardice that destroys the entire company. Varya's return to
Morozka is a return at the same time to the selfless fraternity of her
own kind, in response to a mystique of class solidarity.

The second situation, less schematic than the first, deals with the
inner drama of the company's leader, the hunched, "gnome-like" Jewish Communist, Levinson. He struggles to retain "control" over men,
over events, and over himself, and, what is genuinely refreshing, loses
out in a certain sense on all these scores. We cannot know Fadeev's
intention in this matter, but there is a suggestion, at least, that Levinson's "inappropriateness," because he is a Jew, and is physically deformed, implies that the leader is an isolated, special kind of being,
who is crippled in more than a physical sense. Levinson's solitude is
established as a primary condition of his existence. He is entirely cut
off from his family. At one moment of great fatigue he notes that
one of his troopers has the same beautifully rounded head as his son,
but a moment later the impression vanishes. The very fact that it
occurs to him represents a lapse in control, because of his delirious
state of fatigue.

Earlier, long before the crisis that ends in the unit's defeat, a letter from his wife, containing nothing but bad news, provokes Levinson to write a reply:

At first he was reluctant to break the circle of thought enclosing this side of his life, but little by little he penetrated it, his face softening; he covered two sheets with his small, scarcely legible handwriting, and in them were many words which few people who knew him would have expected from him.[32]

Then the "circle" is closed as Levinson gallops off to inspect the sentries, and is not opened again. He is cut off, too, by the nature of his detached guerrilla command from whatever spiritual nourishment he might derive from association with his political brotherhood. He is cut off, too, from his past. The only reference he makes to his childhood concerns the illusions which clouded his view of the world. There is a glimpse of the big-eyed Jewish boy, waiting in vain for the photographer's "pretty little bird" to fly out of the camera, and then mastering his disappointment, as he was to do on countless later occasions, when he had been deceived by false promises and attractive illusions. He had finally learned to distrust them all:

And when he was really convinced he understood what dangers and evils befall men because of these lying tales about pretty little birds ... and he realized how many of them spend their lives in fruitless expectation. ... No, he had no further need of those birds! He had relentlessly suppressed all sweet and vain regrets for them; he had crushed in himself everything that he had inherited from past generations brought up on these lying tales of pretty little birds.[33]

The most significant measure of his solitude is the distance separating him from his men. Levinson feels that an inscrutable façade and a cultivated air of certainty about all decisions, even when they are wild guesses, are indispensable for maintaining command over his volunteer crew. He needed to struggle remorselessly with his own weaknesses, but those he could not overcome had to be hidden:

From the hour that Levinson had been elected commandant, nobody could think of him in any other capacity. It seemed to each one of them that the

[32] Published here as *The Nineteen*, in *Russian Literature Since the Revolution*, ed. Joshua Kunitz (New York, 1948), p. 120. The suggestion that the Communist hero has a hidden family life in his off-duty hours has become a cliché of Soviet writing. There is a second and, one suspects, more accurate cliché to the effect that the married lives of Communists are very meager, indeed. Though it is always a secondary theme, it persists monotonously through subsequent Soviet writing.

[33] *Ibid.*, pp. 194–95.

distinctive thing about Levinson was that he was made to command the company. If he had told them how, in his childhood, he had helped his father in a second-hand furniture business, how his father all his life had dreamed of becoming rich, but was afraid of mice and played the violin very badly—all of them would have thought it a bad joke. Levinson never spoke of such things. Not that he deliberately avoided them, but he knew that everybody looked on him as an exceptional type of person. He realized his own weaknesses and the weaknesses of others; and he thought that, if one was to lead other people, one must above all make them aware of their weaknesses whilst suppressing and hiding one's own.[34]

This glimpse behind the hero's façade, of course, is never permitted his men. When the military situation is confused, Levinson's

whole attitude . . . was calculated to convey the impression that he understood perfectly how these things had come about, that he knew where they were heading, that there was nothing unusual or terrifying about them, and that he, Levinson, had long ago decided upon a safe, infallible plan for their salvation.[35]

Actually the exact opposite is the case: "In point of fact, not only had he no such plan, but he was completely lost, as perplexed as a schoolboy."[36]

The necessary deceptions of leadership, certainly not unique to Bolshevik guerrilla leaders, impose certain extra burdens on Levinson. The men of this detachment, with its nucleus of class-conscious miners, are not disposed to question their cause, but neither are they likely to consult it very often to find reasons for endurance. Levinson is made the custodian of their collective conscience, longings, and anxieties. But he does not doubt their steadfastness. It was rooted in an "instinct" as strong as self-preservation:

Because of this instinct every thing they had to suffer, even death, was justified by the ultimate cause, and without it not one of them, he knew, would have voluntarily chosen to die in the Ulahinsk *taiga*. But he also knew that this profound instinct dwelt in men under a thick covering of the commonplace, of the trivial necessities of daily life, and of all the cares and anxieties for one's own insignificant but vital being; they had all to eat and sleep, and the flesh was weak.[37]

Levinson and his lieutenants took on all these burdens, looking after the physical comforts, as well, of these simple partisans, "all of them conscious of their own weakness," as importunate as children.

[34] *Ibid.*, pp. 114–15.   [35] *Ibid.*, p. 116.
[36] *Ibid.*   [37] *Ibid.*, p. 161.

The parental responsibilities Levinson assumes have a sanction, Fadeev tells us, in the needs of "the children," who collaborate willingly in the manufacture of the myth of Levinson's infallibility. Under the pressure of events, however, his mask of mocking self-assurance is no longer adequate. An act of open defiance by one of his men is met by Levinson with his Mauser in his hand. They are volunteers, after all, in history's cause, bound to it by an instinct as strong as self-preservation. Strong measures are necessary to remind the errant one of his obligation. But such measures are costly:

When Levinson looked round at his men they were all staring at him in fear and with respect, but that was all. There was no sympathy in their eyes. At that moment he felt that he was a hostile force raised above the company. But he was ready to go on; he was convinced that this force was right.[38]

Defeat was in the air, morale had declined, Levinson had become harsher: "Every day unseen ties—ties which linked him to the heart of the company—snapped."[39] His authority came to depend more and more on the force of his will. As his words lost their effect, the premium on the toughness and rectitude of his personal example increased. He was in the forefront of all the fighting; he dreaded compromising the image of himself at the head of the column by dozing and slumping in the saddle. As the company moves blindly toward annihilation, the final contest begins between Levinson's "control" over himself and the weakness of his flesh, as his body disintegrates under the nervous and physical strain.

Levinson's is not the simple drive of class instinct. The combination of knowledge, doctrine, and emotion which powers every Marxian activist has an interesting configuration in him. Almost nothing is said of doctrine; there is very little in his behavior that is tactically motivated. On the one occasion when orders come from higher authority, Levinson rejects four of the five paragraphs as nonsensical, and proceeds to carry out the one he agrees with. There is no "political work" in his detachment, no agitation, pamphlets, commissars, or amateur theatricals. The morale problem of the men is solved, as we have seen, by Levinson's custodianship of their unarticulated aspirations and by the rigorous example of his own conduct. The source of his

[38] *Ibid.*, p. 163.   [39] *Ibid.*, p. 162.

own strength is to be found in a creed which has echoes in it of classical Marxian humanism, of the Leninist revision of that ethos, and of Chernyshevsky's—and many other Russians'—belief in the eventual appearance of a new kind of man.

A conversation with the self-centered Metchik provokes the central moment of speculation in the novel:

> Only with us... could such lazy and spineless creatures, so futile and worthless, be found; only in our own country, where millions of people have lived for centuries under an indolent sun, in dirt and poverty, ploughing with primitive tools, believing in a vindictive and foolish God—only in such a country, where there is so little store of wisdom, could they exist.[40]

Levinson is here echoing the ancient complaint of Russian men of conscience: Russia's tragic backwardness, above all her *human* backwardness, is the truest measure of her degradation. Belinsky's letter to Gogol in 1848 is as much the source of these thoughts as Marx's essays on the factory system. Levinson's goals and his deepest beliefs display the same double origin, recalling the dreams of the radical democrats a good deal more vividly, perhaps, than Marx's vision of the human creature restored to wholeness. We are close now to the heart of his credo:

> And Levinson was moved, because these were his deepest and most intimate beliefs; because the inner meaning of his life lay in overcoming this poverty and ignorance; because otherwise he would not be Levinson at all, but someone else; because he was urged by an overpowering desire, stronger than any other of his desires, to help create a new, fine, vigorous man. But how could one talk of a new, fine man when numberless millions of people still lived such wretched, poverty-stricken, primitive lives?[41]

For the interim man there is Engels's freedom and Lenin's activist ethic:

> "To see everything as it is, in order to change everything that is, to control everything there is"—Levinson had achieved this *wisdom*, the simplest and the most difficult a man can achieve.[42]

To overcome all enemies, to dispel all illusions, to surmount all obstacles, he has built his life around a core of revolutionary virtues: clarity of vision and inflexibility of will. If we recall the critique of the radical personality in the nineteenth century, these virtues are

[40] *Ibid.*, p. 194.   [41] *Ibid.*   [42] *Ibid.*, p. 195.

sources as well of his crippling alienation from his fellows. From time to time, like his predecessor, he needs to consult his vision of the future to find the strength to bear the unpromising and intolerable present:

He went on without caring where; the cold, dewy branches freshened his face; he felt a rush of unusual strength, which seemed to carry him high above the actual moment (might it not be toward the new man of whom he dreamt with all the strength of his soul?) and from this vast height, earthly and human, he mastered his enemy, his own weak flesh.[43]

Levinson is not the "new man" himself, as he clearly understands, but he sometimes senses his kinship with him. In preserving the mold of the leader, and passing it on to hand-picked successors, he feels that he is keeping alive the strain that will ultimately issue in the higher human type he dreams of. He carefully refrains from discouraging his assistant Baklanov, who imitates his every act, intonation, and gesture—even the physical movements that result from Levinson's bodily deformation. Baklanov will learn in his own time about the deception of leadership. It is more important to preserve the chain of virtuous being:

As a young man, Levinson had also copied those who instructed him, and they had seemed to him as admirable and right-minded as he apparently seemed to Baklanov. When he was older he understood that his teachers were not what he had supposed them, and he was none the less grateful to them. After all, Baklanov not only copied his mannerisms, but drew on his whole experience of life—his methods of fighting, of working, of living. And Levinson knew that the mannerisms would pass with the years, while the other things, enriched by his own experience, would pass on to new Levinsons and Baklanovs; and that, he felt, was important, that was as it should be.[44]

Levinson's "control," which depends on his own recognition and definition of necessity, is put to a number of minor tests. When it becomes "necessary" to poison a fatally wounded partisan, Metchik, indifferent to the "necessity," is horrified. Not Levinson, who, though troubled by the decision, falls back on his basic standard of virtue: "If it's necessary, it can't be helped . . . can it?"[45] This answer is made easier by the victim's concurrence in his own death. His men look away while an impoverished Korean peasant weeps at Levinson's feet,

[43] *Ibid.*   [44] *Ibid.*, p. 115.   [45] *Ibid.*, p. 168.

pleading to be allowed to keep his last pig. Levinson is affected, but necessity's answer is all he heeds. His men are starving.

These decisions have no aftereffects because history, after all, justifies them. But when his control is threatened by a set of overwhelming circumstances, Levinson is thrown into the ultimate conflict of the Bolshevik saint: his body and his nervous system are subject to relentless pressure, increasing until the breaking point is reached. What is engaging in Levinson's drama is the fact that he *does* break.

After a hideous night of pursuit through a forest bog, the battered column of partisans emerges with the daylight on a peaceful forest road, sparkling with autumn frost. Levinson's brain is reeling with fatigue (it is at this moment that the image of his son's head appears to him). He is conscious of a strong feeling of affection for his men but his control has finally deserted him:

He no longer led them, and it was only they themselves who were unaware of his powerlessness, and continued to follow him like a herd accustomed to its leader. And it was precisely this terrible thing that he had feared most of all in the early morning hours.[46]

When the Cossack ambush is announced by shots down the road, Levinson betrays his helplessness by two physical movements which pass unobserved:

He looked back helplessly, searching for the first time for support from others; but in the partisans' despairing, dumbly pleading faces, which seemed to melt under his gaze into a single face, pale, white, questioning, he read only helplessness and fear.... "Here it is, here's what I feared," Levinson thought, and he flung out a hand as though he sought something to hold on to.[47]

A glance at the simple, resolute face of his lieutenant inspires a last act of will and he leads his company deliriously to its doom.

At this moment Fadeev might have ended his epic, with Bolshevik virtue convincingly intact, and with a sense of men having died not badly for aspirations which, for all their incoherence, did them no dishonor. A handful, however, nineteen in all, survived, and through them Fadeev contrives a swift moment of catharsis, ending with the obligatory note of uplift. For a while, Levinson automatically enacts his role as leader before the surviving handful:

[46] *Ibid.*, p. 235.   [47] *Ibid.*, p. 238.

Levinson rode a little in front of the others, thoughtful, his head drooping. Sometimes he looked back helplessly, as if he wanted to ask something and could not remember what; he looked at them all with a prolonged unseeing stare, his glance strange and suffering.[48]

At last understanding dawns on him and with it the last shred of his Bolshevik control departs:

Levinson's eyes remained fixed for several seconds on the men. Then all at once he somehow collapsed and shrank, and everybody at once noticed that he had become weaker and much older. He was no longer ashamed of his weakness and he no longer tried to hide it; he sat huddled up in his saddle, slowly blinking his long wet lashes, and the tears ran down his beard.... The men turned aside in fear that they might lose control of themselves.[49]

Here again Fadeev might have ended his tale with the pathos of loss still uppermost, with Levinson reduced at last to his human dimensions, but more plausible because of it. But this unpretentious novel, not distinguished for its depth of insight or richness of character, yet sound enough up to this moment because of its response to the inner logic of its elements, must now proceed to its directed conclusion. This characteristic moment of the Soviet novel deserves a careful look. The standard mechanism is the verbal coda, presented most often in the form of a flat declaration of faith or belief. Fadeev relies rather on the transfiguring effect of a natural landscape, and thus approaches by indirection his final statement of affirmation.

Levinson is weeping uncontrollably, the others are silent when they finally ride out of the forest:

The forest came to an end in front of them quite unexpectedly, merging into the vastness of the high blue sky and the bright russet-colored earth bathed in the sunshine; the harvested fields spread out on either side.[50]

The valley is full of the voices and the movements of people, "resounding with a joyful, busy life of their own."[51] In the final poetic lunge, Fadeev reaches for the transfiguring note:

Behind the river, propping up the sky, rose the blue mountains, and from their sharp peaks, which seemed to grow out of the sky, a transparent foam of pinkish-white cloud, salted by the sea, poured into the valley, foaming and speckled like new milk.[52]

48 *Ibid.*, p. 242.   49 *Ibid.*, p. 243.   50 *Ibid.*
51 *Ibid.*   52 *Ibid.*

Levinson is delivered from his lapse into the human, as if by magic, and returned to his political matrix, and to his master image of control:

Levinson looked silently, with eyes which were still wet, at this vastness of earth and sky, promising bread and rest, at these distant people on the threshing-ground whom he would soon have to make his own—as near to him as were the eighteen men who followed him in silence. He ceased crying; it was necessary to live and a man had to do his duty.[53]

It requires care to decide what the grounds are for questioning this resolution. It is possible, of course, that this final paragraph is not a response to the formula but was intended simply as a conventional and rather noncommittal contrasting of a vulnerable character with the "eternal" aspects of life, in order to give Levinson a final poignancy. If this is so, the effect is certainly too abrupt—not deep enough (or relevant to what we know of Levinson) to be a religious experience—and not pointed enough to be ironic. We have not, after all, known Levinson very well. But that is the novelist's fault, in the end. And there are grounds within the novel for pronouncing its ending false. Levinson's abrupt recovery may be taken as a possible response of the politically obsessed personality, or it may be explained simply as a shallowness of affect on Levinson's part. But this is unkind to the image we already have of him. We have seen him stretched to the limit of his endurance, and we lack the evidence to term him any more than an ordinarily limited man, with ties to the nourishing commonplaces of human experience that have not yet been snapped. The "fault" and the violation of the material's logic are Fadeev's in the end. To suggest that "life" for Levinson involves a simple return to the political image of himself, or to imply that the prolonged suffering he has undergone can be assimilated through the restorative effects of nature, is to betray the integrity of his image. To ignore entirely the implication that if "life" means the repetition of what Levinson has just gone through, it forecasts a downward progress toward aridity, exhaustion, and death, is simply to write badly. Or it is to impose on the reader the dictum that the cause matters above all things and its casualties will be forgotten.

IV

The basic design of *Chapaev* and *The Rout* has remained a standard one. Scores of Soviet novels may be classified as variations of this

[53] *Ibid.*, pp. 243–44.

archetypal pattern. The degree of fallibility permitted the hero, or the amount of suffering inflicted on him, or the complexity of his dilemma may vary, but certain limits are never overstepped. All the writing in this vein is distinguished by the writer's identification with his protagonist and with his cause. Other attitudes toward the dominant political power are evident, however, in these early years. The writer who is not a committed partisan may fall under two other general headings: that of the detached but sympathetic observer, or that of the regretful agnostic. A fourth approach, that of open hostility, was proscribed even in those relatively unregulated years.

The other two approaches, rich at times in irony and ambiguity, naturally give rise to greater variety of character, and a richer choice of destinies. Interesting in this connection is Konstantin Fedin's *Cities and Years* (1926), which records the disintegration of an artist under the stresses of civil war, after a lengthy account of his private emotional life as a prisoner of war in Germany. Fedin's sympathy for his hero is evident in the long treatment of his adventures abroad. But the note of reproach in his final comment indirectly expresses Fedin's accommodation to the new regime:

And now we finish the story of the man who waited in anguish to be accepted by life. We contemplate the road along which he followed love's cruelty, the bloody and flowered road. He traversed it without once being splattered, without crushing a flower.... Oh, if he had been spotted once by blood, or had crushed a single flower. Then, perhaps our pity for him would turn into tenderness, and we would not have allowed him to die so frightfully.... But until the very end he could not act, not a single time. He only waited for the wind that would push him toward the shore he wanted to reach. That is why we can change nothing about his destiny.[54]

Unable to act, eaten away by his morbid sensitivity, one of the last of the superfluous men, he falls to pieces before the brutal choices of civil war. Fedin's independence as a writer is evident in the dramatic design he has allowed himself: the revolution is in no sense glorified, but it has the rightness of its inevitability, and the man who cannot accommodate to its rigors, when he falls before it, is neither honorable nor dishonorable, but a pitiable victim of it. This is a viable formula, it would seem, avoiding overt political statement, yet opening a certain area for the exploration of character. It was never to become a dominant pattern in Soviet writing, but it was to provoke an uproar, as

[54] Konstantin Fedin, *Goroda i gody* (Moscow, 1926), p. 376.

we shall see, when it turned up as the central dramatic design of Sholokhov's *The Silent Don*.

Isaac Babel's *Red Cavalry* (1926) displays none of the qualities of the official heroic strain, and if the writer's attitude to the cause verges on agnosticism, it is because he is indifferent to political loyalties while he records the savage human truth of Budenny's campaigns in Poland. A detached writer's intelligence, unconcerned with political testament, moving through the maelstrom recorded by Furmanov, turns up a strikingly different version of events. The antiseptic judgments, and the persistent political rationalizing of the solemn commissar, are replaced by artful revelations of the naked experience. The casual, gratuitous brutalities—looting, rape, murder—the curious fusion of revolutionary idealism and Cossack blood lust, of propaganda and obscenity, may contribute in the end to the making of a legend, but it would draw few recruits to the cause of the World Revolution.

In the absence of the didactic function, heroes, too, drop from view. High rank and political virtue confer no distinction in Babel's eyes. Biographies of commanders and common soldiers are set down with the same ironic detachment. Jews, Cossacks, Poles, priests, soldiers, whores, and agitators are equal possibilities for literary representation. If virtue is resident in men (and there is relatively little), it is not distributed according to men's external allegiances. The treatment of the conventional hero-types in other kinds of novels is directly challenged. The ex-herdsman, Pavlichenko, now a ranking Red commander, tells his story to Babel, and does not omit the account of the conscientious revenge he takes on his former landlord:

Then I stamped on my *barin* Nikitinsky. I trampled him for an hour or more. And in that time I got to know life through and through. With shooting—I'll put it this way—with shooting you only get rid of a man. With shooting you are letting him off, and it's too damned easy on yourself. With shooting you'll never get at the soul, to where it is in a fellow and the way it shows itself. But I don't spare myself, and I've more than once trampled an enemy for an hour or more. You see, I want to find out what life really is.[55]

It is unlikely that Babel intends "a slander" on Budenny's "glorious falcons." It may be said that he is a trifle too concerned with self-conscious literary effects—the tone of solemn philosophic inquiry, for example, with which Pavlichenko stamps the life out of his enemy.

[55] I. Babel, *Konarmiya* (Moscow-Leningrad, 1926), p. 75.

But the striking element in this and other episodes is the incomparable savagery toward the human person, part of the Cossack ethos as Babel, Sholokhov, and others testify. Perhaps a fourth of the book is concerned with similar studies in cold-blooded murder, often presented, for ironic effect, in the naively rationalized language of the murderer himself.[56]

The division commanders, all of them comparable in status, if not in ability, to Chapaev, present themselves to Babel in a very different light. When a new, young commander returns to his bivouac, blooded by his first successful cavalry charge, his naked thirst for glory has found an almost sexual fulfillment:

> I happened to see Kolesnikov that same evening, an hour after the Poles were wiped out. He was riding at the head of his brigade—alone and dreaming—on a chestnut stallion of great beauty. His right arm hung in a sling. Ten paces from him a Cossack cavalryman carried the unfurled banner. The leading squadron began lazily to sing obscene verses. The brigade stretched out dusty and endless, like peasant carts on their way to the fair. At the tail end of the column weary musicians were wheezing.
> That evening, in Kolesnikov's quarters, I saw the masterful indifference of a Tartar Khan.[57]

The only Communist identified as such is the "Ryazan Jesus," Galin, an editor of the First Cavalry Army's newspaper. In the course of the story he talks significantly to the self-pitying "I" of the story (presumably Babel himself) about the situation of the Party and the writer:

> You're a driveler ... and we're condemned to put up with you drivelers. ... The whole Party goes around in aprons smeared with blood and excrement. We are shelling the nut for you. Some time will pass. You'll see the shelled nut. You'll take your finger out of your nose then, and you'll sing of the new life in no ordinary prose. Meanwhile, sit still, driveler, and don't whimper.[58]

Besides suggesting Babel's own relations with the Party, the contempt in these words contains prophetic overtones about his own

---

[56] Patricia Carden's full-length study of Babel's fiction goes far beyond the single political question I have pursued here. She argues quite daringly that the violence in Babel expresses both a primitive hunger for justice and the impact of genuine art. See *The Art of Isaac Babel* (Ithaca, N.Y., 1972).

The two excellent collections of Babel material edited by his daughter Nathalie Babel tell us much that we did not know before about her father's life and art. See Isaac Babel, *The Lonely Years 1925–1939* (New York, 1964); and Isaac Babel, *You Must Know Everything* (New York, 1966).

[57] Babel, *Konarmiya*, pp. 60–61.   [58] *Ibid.*, p. 99.

tragic fate.[59] But the exposure of this friction is not the point of the sketch. While Galin talks the night through, the unit's washerwoman, whom he covets, is bewildered by his eloquence, and disappears with the cook. Babel's real concern is to expose with precision and indirectness the sexual alienation of the Communist:

And Galin talked on about political instincts in the First Cavalry Army. He talked for a long time, in a dead voice, but perfectly clearly. His eyelid fluttered over his wall-eye, and blood flowed from the lacerated palms of his hands.[60]

Doctrine is nowhere presented in its barefaced literal meanings. Babel, rather, uses it for ironic effects. The men repeatedly use their skin-deep indoctrination to justify their private Cossack tantrums. The platoon leader, who throws a woman smuggler off a troop train and then shoots her, describes it in a letter to the press: "So I took my faithful rifle off the wall and washed away that stain from the face of the toilers' land and the republic."[61]

A bitter wrangle over the ownership of a white stallion between two ranking officers ends with this letter of reconciliation, which resembles the work of the gifted Soviet humorist Mikhail Zoshchenko in its agile mockery of official jargon:

And I cannot be angry at Budenny's army any more. I understand my suffering in that army and I keep it in my heart cleaner than holy things. And to you, Comrade Savitsky, as a world-wide hero, the toiling masses of Vitebshchina where I am chairman of the revolutionary committee send you proletarian greetings—"On with the World Revolution!"—and hope that the white stallion will carry you for many years along soft paths for the good of the freedom we all love and the fraternal republics, on which we must keep a sharp eye in local government and on district units concerning all administrative matters.[62]

Nor is this a "slander." It is, rather, a device Babel frequently uses to effect those human exposures that are his main concern. It is the

---

[59] Babel disappeared five years after his speech at the Writers' Conference in 1934, a victim, presumably, of the political purges. He was arrested in the spring of 1939, and is believed to have died two years later.

[60] Babel, *Konarmiya*, p. 100. It is worth noting that in later editions of this work the final phrase ("... and blood flowed from the lacerated palms of his hands") has been deleted. Whether it was Babel or anonymous political editors who did it we do not know. Removal of this fleeting reference to Christ's stigmata deadens the sting of the story.

[61] *Ibid.*, p. 96.   [62] *Ibid.*, p. 133.

technique of the slow disclosure of a situation through the naive view of a participant who comprehends dimly (if at all) the consequences or meanings of what he is describing. The method, in the end, serves one of the most searching and tragic comments he hoped to make: that no one understood the events that were shaping or ruining their lives.

Only once does Babel venture close to a personal statement. In one sketch, the wise old Jew, Gedali, discusses the revolution's violence:

> But the Pole shot ... because he was the counterrevolution. You shoot because you are the revolution. But the revolution means happiness. And happiness doesn't like orphans in the house. Good men do good deeds. The revolution is the good deed of good men. But good men don't kill. It means bad people are making the revolution. But the Poles are not bad people. Who will tell Gedali where the revolution is and where the counterrevolution is?[63]

The stubborn, impractical simplicity of these remarks does not express Babel's "position" toward the revolution as much as it reflects his misgivings about the gratuitous sufferings he records elsewhere without comment. This book may be taken as representative of that tendency in Soviet literature which challenges that of Furmanov and Fadeev. Many of the situations it treats have been made familiar in the work of the Communist writers. But the final result is quite different. The freely judging sensibility has remained true to its traditional concerns, and the final result rings true to the classical inheritance in the most important sense: human truth eclipses and contains the political truth.

V

In a certain sense there is not a distinctive literature of the NEP period that can be set apart from the civil war writing we have been examining. There is, rather, the literature of the twenties, dealing with the present or with the immediate past, reflecting, in both cases, the relatively tolerant, pluralist solution to the literary "problem" that events had dictated and the Party had accepted.

There is, of course, a literature *about* the NEP, though even here distinctions are blurred. A novel like Leonid Leonov's *The Thief* (1927) is typical. The hero wanders through the thieves' underworld

[63] *Ibid.*, p. 47.

of the newly restored commercialism, driven by the need to expiate a Dostoevskyan sense of guilt. But the act itself, the murder of a White officer in a row over a horse,[64] occurred during the civil war. Problems of readjustment, of war neurosis, of guilt and nostalgia, all imply that the civil war is the dominant experience, even as it receded somewhat into the background. When the NEP ended in 1929, its particular flavor disappeared entirely from fiction, while the civil war remained a permanent point of reference for the literary imagination.

One novel, Fedor Gladkov's *Cement* (1924), reflects the prescriptive tradition in all respects, and at the same time moves it forward by adjusting it to the new social situation as it was defined by the problems of industrialization. The compliant literary imagination was now presented with a new set of conditions to work with: problems of factory administration, of construction, and of production. It is not surprising that in the majority of cases these conditions have, by their intrinsic dullness, defied the already inhibited imaginations of Party-oriented writers. But the mimeograph machine and the blueprint had replaced the machine gun and the cavalry saber as the instruments of social progress, and this fact took precedence over all others. In human terms, the literature of the time testifies repeatedly to the emotional wrench that the sudden transition from war to peace meant for "incorrectly" oriented believers in the revolution. The man who survived the shift and acquired the new virtues was the obvious candidate for heroism.

The return of its hero, the demobilized military commissar, Chumalov, in the first pages of *Cement* suggests a sequel to *Chapaev*. Tired and confused, he is confronted immediately by the challenge of finding his home town demoralized and in ruins. The key breakdown is in the cement factory where Chumalov had worked before the war. The rebuilding of this factory against a sea of troubles—bad morale, lack of materials, sabotage, Party bureaucracy, private emotional crises, and bandit attacks—is the main thread of Gladkov's story. Chumalov, as workers' representative on the Factory Committee, is the prime mover in getting the factory back into production.

The implacable partisanship we have already seen in *Mother* and *Chapaev* underlies the conflict in *Cement*. The shooting war is over but a spirit of mortal combat pervades the book. There is a sense of

---

[64] A study would show, I am sure, that horses were valued more highly than men.

not too distant menace, with survival itself always at stake. The external evil, however, remains below the horizon, and the immediate conflict in the book is between a secondary evil—all the obstacles human and material that block reconstruction—and the forces, principally human, which overcome the obstacles, solve the problems, and provide leadership for the recalcitrant, the demoralized, and the ignorant.

Cement has a quality of documentary authenticity which interferes at times with its didactic plan, and poses the question of the standards for selecting the hero from a gallery of potentially more interesting characters. Human inadequacy and moral failure appear in a variety of suggestive portraits. Many of these characters are Communists. One of the more arresting figures, Polia, her heart broken by the moral letdown of the NEP period and the ebbing of civil war fervor, utters the oft-quoted words about the difficulties of readjusting to the new situation:

I can't endure it, because I can neither understand nor justify.... We have destroyed and we have suffered—a sea of blood—famine. And suddenly— the past arises again with joyful sound.... And I don't know where the nightmare is: in those years of blood, misery, sacrifice, or in this bacchanalia of rich shop windows and drunken cafes! What was the good of mountains of corpses? Were they to make the workers' dens, their poverty and their death, more cheerful? Was it that blackguards and vampires should again enjoy all the good things of life and get fat by robbery? I cannot recognize this, and I cannot live with it! We have fought, suffered and died—was it in order that we should be so shamefully crucified? What for?[65]

This outburst exposes for a moment a real human situation, but it is politically harmful, so it is dropped. Polia is accused of "lyricism" (*sic*) and expelled from the Party. It is interesting, too, that Chumalov watches the purge with an attitude that is typical of his response to all human situations, "with the dull gaze of a stunned beast."[66] But his emotional illiteracy, brought out in his incomprehensible estrangement from his wife, never interferes with the solution of the production problem. His heroic credentials are, therefore, of the highest quality.

[65] F. Gladkov, *Cement*, trans. A. S. Arthur and C. Ashleigh (New York, 1929), p. 275.
[66] *Ibid.*, p. 276.

There are other glimpses of human interest: Chibis, the Cheka man, who is carrying an intolerable burden; Badin, the iron Communist and libertine; Shuk, the raging, inarticulate, and ultimately disruptive worker; Serge, the gentle, dedicated intellectual who is harshly expelled from the Party; Schramm, the self-seeking bureaucrat; and others. These people give promise of much greater complexity than the blunt Chumalov, and their lives would provide richer literary material than the prosaic matter of getting a cement factory into production. But they are set aside, or reformed, or forgotten by the novelist. The evidence of their fallibility is at the same time evidence of their inability to perform the paramount task, or to serve as models of emblematic Bolshevik behavior. Successful function within the terms of the Party program is the only criterion of selection. Chumalov is chosen because he contributes most to the survival of the new social order.

But, Gladkov suggests, this life of public dedication is not without its costs. Chumalov's attempts at reconciliation with his estranged Bolshevik wife show him inept and inarticulate in matters of private emotion. The idea that dedication to public matters might be the *cause* of his emotional inadequacies, or that his public life might be a form of sublimation, remains unexplored in the novel. But apparently it is an unimportant consideration, since private matters are lost sight of in the triumphant resolution of the social problem.

The socially efficacious solution of personal problems is illustrated in Chumalov's relations with Kleist, the old-regime engineer, whom he has ample reason to hate. When Kleist indicates his willingness to direct the reconstruction of the factory, Chumalov's forgiveness has a threefold social significance: it aids in the reconstruction of the factory, it opens the way for Kleist's redemption through constructive work, and it marks Chumalov's own abandonment of the fierce personal emotions of civil war. Confronted with such a definition of the public interest, Chumalov would have been guilty of antisocial behavior if he had acted to satisfy his personal revenge. As he says himself, "Not he, but everything mattered."[67] His success in safeguarding the collective interest is the test of his moral personality and the source of his heroism.

The sense of selfless participation, we are led to believe, is its own

[67] *Ibid.*, p. 278.

reward. The masses for whom Chumalov works share not only the increased prosperity and stability, but the credit for achieving it: "If I am a hero," Chumalov tells the assembled workers, "then you are all heroes."[68] Finally, we are confronted with the same kind of declamatory utterance, the inspirational coda, which we found in Gorky's *Mother* and elsewhere. Describing Chumalov's jubilation at the final triumphant ceremony, Gladkov tries to draw together the individual and the mass emotions and to suggest at the same time that private defeats are eclipsed in the public victory:

Unbearable rapture, and his heart was almost bursting from the flooding blood. The working class, the Republic, the great life they were constructing! God damn it, we understand how to suffer, but we also know the grandeur of our struggle, and how to rejoice.[69]

In conclusion, we are invited to rejoice with the chief architect of the triumph, to share his generalized feeling about the objects of his own loyalty, and finally to welcome the future which we are expected to believe is brought nearer through his achievements. Chumalov's experience is the most instructive; the failure of others is not treated sympathetically, because it is uninteresting. The nonconformist and the special pleader do not receive sympathy or deserve pity. To function successfully, whatever problem is set by the Party, is the virtue, Gladkov tells us, that comes before all others. This, in turn, explains the general function of this kind of novel. Representation of a problem successfully solved by human agency, it is assumed, will inspire all who confront similar problems. This is the fundamental aesthetic aim of all official Soviet art.

To the degree that the Soviet novel solves problems, it is analogous to a manual of technology. The hero is central to this aspect of Soviet fiction. He may expect assignment to any task the Party chooses for him. He will be invested with the virtues appropriate to the situation, including the correct *technical* approach to the problem, and his behavior will illustrate their correct application. The engineer, for example, has an engineer's virtues: caution, daring, boldness of vision, and attention to detail. The Polar aviator and the collective farm manager will each have his occupational *vertu*, too. But at the center of their beings will be the same catalogue of politically efficacious

[68] *Ibid.*   [69] *Ibid.*, p. 304.

moral qualities: loyalty, resourcefulness, steadfastness, vigilance, and, whenever they are called for, ruthlessness and intolerance.

Chumalov's emotional illiteracy calls attention, finally, to Yuri Olesha's novel *Envy* (1927), which discusses with extraordinary frankness the terrible human losses in the post-revolutionary years. Cast partly in the form of a debate, with both sides contained in an all-embracing ambiguity, the idiom sounds strange to the modern ear. The Communist spokesman, Babichev, has the attributes of a bourgeois *en caricature:* he is the smug, well-fed (with a roll of fat on the back of his neck) administrator of a large food trust. In his self-assured Babbittry this man symbolizes the achievements of the revolution as well as its losses. The insuperably high cost of this kind of progress, as Olesha sees it, is the atrophy of all the traditional human emotions. A spokesman for the doomed life of the heart, who calls himself "king of the rabble," outlines his position in a discussion with a barroom companion:

"...a whole series of human emotions is about to be eliminated...."
"Which, for example?"
"Compassion, tenderness, pride, zeal, love—in short, almost all those emotions which constituted the soul of man in the age which is now dying."
"I see."
"I take it you understand me. Stung by the serpent of jealousy, the Communist who can feel pity is a prey to persecution. The buttercup of pity, the lizard of vanity, the serpent of jealousy,—all this flora and fauna must be eradicated from the heart of the new man....
"...we know that the grave of a young Communist who has committed suicide is alternatively covered with wreaths and the curses of his colleagues. The man of the new world says: 'Suicide is the deed of a decadent.' But the man of the old world says: 'He must have committed suicide in order to save his honor.'
"Thus we see that the new man schools himself to scorn sentiments that are hallowed by poets and by the muse of history itself."
"So that is what you mean by the conspiracy of the emotions?"
"Yes, that is the conspiracy of emotions of which I am the leader."[70]

Without the old stock of emotions and cast of characters, he decides, there can be no heroes of any kind:

"...history is watching us with its dazzling glance through the eye slits of its mask. And I want to be able to say: 'This is the lover, this the am-

70 Y. Olesha, *Envy*, introduction by Gleb Struve (London, 1947), pp. 88–89.

bitious man, this the traitor, this the intrepid hero, this the faithful friend, this the prodigal son—these are the standard-bearers of great emotions now regarded as valueless and base. . . .' "

". . . it's so hard to find heroes. . . ."

". . . there are no heroes."[71]

---

[71] *Ibid.*, pp. 90–91. Much work has been done on Olesha since I read the novel in this way. Elizabeth Beaujour's precise and comprehensive definition of the properties of his imagination would subordinate to deeper and subtler concerns the political statement I have found in *Envy*, although my emphasis on the doomed hero remains apposite. See her *The Invisible Land: A Study of the Artistic Imagination of Iurii Olesha* (New York, 1970). William Harkins has proposed a startling—and certainly a nonpolitical—Freudian reading of *Envy* in "The Theme of Sterility in Olesha's *Envy*," *Slavic Review*, September 1966, pp. 443–57.

CHAPTER 12

Two Bureaucracies

When the revolution was abruptly resumed with the initiation of the five-year plans, literary debate came to an end; all but one of the quarreling groups of the twenties were dissolved, and their leaders were either "captured" or hounded into silence. Thus began the unprecedentedly grim hegemony in Soviet literature of the Russian Association of Proletarian Writers (RAPP). It was a time of nightmarish unreality. The complex problems of the written word were reduced to such crude constructions as "literary shock-workers," "wall-newspapers," "worker-correspondents," and "the dialectical literary historical method." Professor Edward J. Brown in his study of the period cites the following as typical of the slogans that filled the air: "For a Great Art of Bolshevism! Against the Varnishers of Reality! For the Hegemony of Proletarian Literature! Liquidate Backwardness!"[1] The atmosphere of frenzy and bickering, the endless "struggles," conferences, resolutions, and the back-alley warfare of literary politics—all suggest an Orwellian fantasy.

Yet, beneath these surface extravagances, the clash between two contrary theories of art went on, in a pattern the nineteenth century

---

[1] Quoted in Edward J. Brown, *The Proletarian Episode in Russian Literature, 1928–1932* (New York, 1953), p. 171. I would like to acknowledge my debt to this excellent study, and not alone because it confirms my hypothesis of the continuing competition between the two branches of the Russian realist tradition, in its detailed study of a critical moment in that conflict. It also finds coherent patterns in a confused period which my own researches, necessarily less thorough here than Mr. Brown's, might not have yielded.

has already made familiar. RAPP aesthetic theory was an unresolved mixture of elements taken from the arguments of its bitterest opponents, notably Voronsky and his "cognition" school; and of other, contrary elements which bespeak an agitational, world-changing view of literature. As Brown indicates, the combination of incompatible elements was a source of profound confusion in RAPP's theoretical pronouncements. His analysis of a pivotal statement by the RAPP leadership in October, 1930, leads him to this interesting conclusion:

The document ... is admittedly a strange and not entirely clear one. The reason for this lack of clarity is, I believe, that the leadership of RAPP is attempting to steer a middle course between the cultivation of literature as "cognition of life"—the understanding of art given to them by Voronsky —and the Party demand that it be cultivated as a handmaiden of the "class," as a means for "changing the world"—in practical terms, as propaganda for the Five-Year Plan. Though in its day-to-day leadership of Soviet literature RAPP was of course obliged to give weight to enforcing such a literary program, and therefore was forced to modify its literary theory and devise new literary slogans of a utilitarian character, yet the subsequent history of the organization indicates that in steering its compromise course the leadership continued to lean in the direction of "Voronskyism," and to resist the intrusion of utilitarian ideas which it could not absolutely reject.[2]

It is surprising to discover that the RAPP leaders emerge as the true, and very nearly the last, defenders of the classical Russian tradition. They made substantial concessions to expediency and they vulgarized what they defended, but they continued to speak for an essential fund of literary values, which included a notion of apolitical objectivity, an insistence, with qualifications, of course, on the author's right independently to judge of all he treated, and, what concerns us most, a demand for full human portraiture in fiction.

Characteristically, the RAPP leadership condensed these issues into two slogans: "Tear off the masks!" and "For a living man!" The first injunction is derived from Tolstoy's conception of art's essential work—the "removal" of successive layers of "coverings" which hide essential truths from the casual eye. The conception of art as an especially intense kind of vision was central to Voronsky's "cognition" theory, and had only to be stripped of its intuitive overtones and restated in the homely, violent language of the Bolsheviks (Lenin is

[2] *Ibid.*

credited with the expression "tear off the masks") to become the first principle of the RAPP aesthetic. It is true that the eye of the RAPP writer was directed by certain *a priori* notions that were not to be questioned: he worked in the interests of the proletariat, and the reality he was to explore was their new, confident, and expanding world. But his faith in the stability of that new reality was so great that it was expected to withstand and to profit from the most merciless scrutiny. The principal construction put on the slogan concerned its hostility to falsifying, embellishing—as the critics put it—to "varnishing," reality. Fadeev, who began his career as a literary bureaucrat in the higher echelons of RAPP, indicated the kind of emphasis the slogan should lead to:

The new style of proletarian literature is a stranger to any and all adornment of the truth; it is a stranger to all "illusions which exalt us"; it must and will be a style involving the most resolute, consistent, and merciless removal of all masks.[3]

Whatever *arrière-pensées* lay behind this statement, it bears an obvious relation to the classical cry for "the absolute truth." It may be argued that too many key positions had already been surrendered to one-sided political doctrines, or that the "unadorned truth" turned up by the writers would be put to too narrow a use—a kind of short-range, editorial self-criticism—to bear any important resemblance to the Tolstoyan canon. But, whether or not RAPP theorists had compromised the position they were defending, they went down under the assaults of the new "Leninist" activism in 1931 and 1932, as champions of the last patch of free ground open to the Soviet artist. Their assurance that *within* the compass of the assumptions he shared with the Party magistrates, nothing was exempt from the writer's skeptical attention, had threatened to "unmask" entire institutions or value systems, instead of their inadequate or dishonest human representatives. In 1932 a new set of masks was made and a new theory of adorned truth was devised which would guarantee them permanent inviolability. Socialist realism and its counterpart theory of embellishment, socialist romanticism, were to divert the writer's eye from the faults of the officially virtuous forever after.

The RAPP theory of character paralleled its approach to reality in

[3] Quoted by A. Selivanovski in *Oktyabr*, 5 (May 1929): 187. Selivanovsky goes on to say that Fadeev's formula is the only one which makes possible the "reflection of reality as it is."

general: it insisted upon absolute accuracy within the limits of a class-divided universe. It is typical of the RAPP compromise that it accepted a fundamental moral distinction between men as defined by the class struggle, and then insisted that the Communist and the class enemy be shown in their full "living" reality. Again the RAPP theorists' impatient emphasis is directed against simplification and idealization. Man is complex in himself, and is made more so in the historical process he reflects, they insisted, and proletarian literature defeated its own purposes when it ignored that fact. A quotation from the resolutions of the First Congress of Proletarian Writers betrays some of the confusion of their position:

The slogan for the presentation of the "living man" ... on the one hand correctly orients proletarian literature toward the reflection of contemporaneity, and on the other hand expresses the necessity of struggle with stereotypes, with schematic portrayal, with "bare poster art," and of development in the direction of showing forth the complex human psyche, with all its contradictions, elements of the past and seeds of the future, both conscious and subconscious.[4]

Some of the mysteries of human existence apparently transcended the limits of *class* psychology. But if virtue was still defined in class terms, it is clear that RAPP theorists had put themselves in a dangerously contradictory position. The "unmasking" of a "bad" Communist might indeed be psychologically sound, but the writer who did it always ran the risk of seeming to put the objects of the Communist's allegiances in question at the same time. For this reason it was soon decided with RAPP's overthrow that a "psychology" which did not blur the primary moral (class) distinctions—between good Communists and bad wreckers—would serve the agitational function in literature far better. In general, the "living man" theory sustained the following tendencies in characterization, all of which were to be challenged in the change-over to socialist realism: opposition to idealized, or, as it was to be called soon, "romanticized," portraits of Communist protagonists;[5] a broad standard of selectivity which not only permitted

---

[4] As quoted in Brown, *The Proletarian Episode in Russian Literature*, p. 78, from *Na literaturnom postu*, 8 (April 1927): 8.

[5] It is impossible to fix the line between true and false in this connection, since the most objective RAPP writer had made heavy commitments to the Communist cause. But I should be inclined to name Fadeev's Levinson as an index of the degree of fallibility permitted the "living man" hero. There are more drastic instances of Communist failure (suicide, breakdown, resignation, etc.) but they are extreme rather than typical. Fadeev's comment on the hero of Gladkov's *Cement* is instructive in this regard: "What

Communist failures, but sanctioned a wide range of non-Communist literary protagonists (so long as they were psychologically true to their class-conditioning); and a generally greater responsiveness to human truth as opposed to ideological truth.

The overthrow of RAPP, the Party's chosen instrument in literature, was carried out, of course, by the Party itself. The process of destroying RAPP occurred on two levels. Administrative liquidation by decree of the Central Committee of the Party on April 23, 1932, took care of one phase of the matter with dispatch. But a long period of undermining preceded its demise, and the inner ideological "struggles" that accompanied this process are of great importance in the Party's campaign to capture the literary imagination.

The offensive against Averbakh and other RAPP leaders was carried out by a little-known group called Litfront, which had formed within the parent body of RAPP. Its leaders were not famous or gifted men but they had the Party's cachet, by all accounts, and, in addition, were equipped with the message of the new "Stalinist" interpretation of Marxism-Leninism, which had first been hammered out in the philosophers' debates at two historic meetings in 1929.[6] All the consequences of this major doctrinal upheaval can only be outlined here, but it is clear that it affects literature at many points. This redefined Marxism was embodied in the word "Leninism." In general terms this meant a full and final turn to Marxism's activist, world-changing role in all spheres of human behavior. In the consequent devaluing of the determinist strain, all objective analysis of past phenomena in all intellectual disciplines became subject to "correction" according to Party-defined present and future needs. In psychological theory all aspects of environmentalism were done away with in favor of the new

---

character types have been represented in our literature? In the first place you all know the ... iron Communist in a leather jacket with an iron jaw....I believe this type reached its highest artistic expression in Gladkov's *Cement*.... But the weakness of Gleb Chumalov as a character is in this very quality. He is an incarnation of the mighty will of the working class to build socialism ... but he is not shown as a real human being: that's the weakness of the book. And now uncounted numbers of prolet-writers grind out their heroes on the model of Gleb Chumalov. And they are all as alike as two drops of water." A. Fadeev, "Na kakom etape my nakhodimsya," *Na literaturnom postu*, 11–12 (June 1927): 6. Perhaps a line can be drawn between Levinson and Chumalov, but the resemblances between them far outweigh the differences, it seems to me. The fact that both were placed on the permanent roster of Soviet heroism tends to support my contention.

[6] These credentials were not enough to protect Litfront later from the charge of "Trotskyism" which was also leveled at Voronsky, Averbakh, and many others after 1937.

doctrine of conscious, willed, goal-oriented behavior.[7] In education, "training" replaced conditioning, discipline replaced experiment, and indoctrination replaced instruction. In the realm of morality, the Leninist ethic, which had evolved in the prerevolutionary underground and, since then, had been imposed on every Party member, was extended to the entire population. The final measure of truth, the final touchstone of value, the final determinant of behavior were all declared to reside in Lenin's single, all-embracing term, *partiinost*. The word defies precise translation because its meaning is so alien to the English-speaking cultures, but the usual rendering, "Party spirit," will do if it is also understood to mean complete identification with the Party's interests. Derived from Lenin's theory of knowledge, it rests on the general proposition that whatever serves the Party is true, valuable, and legislative for all men. It is all-embracing, minutely intimate, and unlike other, similar codes of allegiance, it solicits not obedience, or reverence, or acquiescence, but the conscious, whole-hearted collaboration of every individual. From this Leninist-Stalinist complex of ideas there arose an official model for men, the New Soviet Man, whose image was expected, after 1932, to dominate imaginative literature.

The new values were not imposed on writers at once or without friction. But the initial attack on RAPP by the Litfront group in 1930 contained most of the key elements of socialist realism. The whole of the controversy was conceived as an opposition between Plekhanovism and Leninism. The RAPP leaders' unqualified commitment to Plekhanov's ideas brought them under fire on this point, and whatever support they had found for a contemplative aesthetic in Plekhanov's passive determinism was brought directly into question. Certain elementary distinctions Plekhanov had made between the properties of literary language and form and those of other kinds of discourse were likewise challenged. Voronsky's cognitive aesthetic, even in the cramped restatement that RAPP had given it, was declared anathema. The aim of art was no longer knowledge about the human mysteries, but guidance and inspiration entirely within the official canon of belief. A call for emblematic literary heroes—"heroes of labor" they were called in those early days—followed automatically from the enunciation of these views, and remained the central command to Soviet writers for decades.

---

[7] See Raymond Bauer's *The New Man in Soviet Psychology* (Cambridge, Mass., 1952), for the fullest account of this change.

The Litfront attack was centered on the two ungainly slogans we have already noted: "Tear off the masks!" and "For a living man!" Whose masks were to be torn off, it was asked, and in whose political interest were these indiscriminate exposés to be carried out? This kind of unmasking was a negative, pointless, if not actually dangerous, activity, the criticism ran, and had nothing to do with stimulating the great forward thrusts socialism was making. Preoccupation with "the living men" had led writers to concentrate entirely too much on the psychological problems of isolated men, and, it was pointed out scornfully, to set "eternal problems" above the far more important matters of socialist construction. The burden of these criticisms is summarized in the relatively mild article on RAPP in the *Literary Encyclopedia* (1935):

The slogan of the "living man," in favor of a psychological analysis of the heroes depicted, was complemented by another slogan, "for tearing off each and every mask," and with this RAPP's artistic program and its understanding of realism was exhausted. By concentrating writers' attention on the moods and feelings of the separate, isolated person, by demanding from writers the exposure of the conscious and unconscious movements of the soul, the RAPP theorists at the same time led the writers away from the paramount tasks of reflecting the objective processes of the socialist revolution.[8]

The writer goes on to explain in more detail what was wrong with this "psychologism." The slogan of the masks,

demanded of writers that they distrust the external conditions and actions of men, demanded the discovery in the heroes of contradictions, of duality, and in essence, of a lack of full-valuedness, from the point of view of certain abstract, moralistically colored criteria. Given such an interpretation the unmasking slogan was politically wrong.[9]

This, finally, is the point: the revelation of human complexity is politically harmful.

The administrative dissolution of RAPP was accompanied by a number of charges that had nothing to do with the leaders' theoretical "errors."[10] They were accused of a loyalty-test harshness toward

[8] "RAPP," *Literaturnaya entsiklopediya*, 9: 524.

[9] *Ibid*. RAPP's troubles arose in part from its misuse of the past: "RAPP was oriented primarily toward the work of L. Tolstoy, Flaubert, and toward psychological realism in general, and in the critical work of RAPP-ites an apologetic attitude toward the Tolstoyan method was expressed."

[10] Problems of literary *administration* are new to students of culture but they must be recorded with the same solemnity we accord to other matters marginal to the literary process. The real point, I suppose, is that in the USSR they are not marginal at all.

fellow-travelers, which cut those writers off from the literary world. The lower-level literary output RAPP supervised, the grotesque world of writers' shock-brigades, literary competitions, worker-correspondents, and wall-newspapers had proved, it was generally agreed, a complete failure. As administrators, then, the RAPP leaders had failed to fulfill the production plan, had misallocated their resources, and had produced work which served no agitational purpose—that is, goods of low quality. Yet these strangely confused men who had persecuted fellow-traveling writers of dubious loyalty had, at the same time, defended with mysterious stubbornness all that was left of the aesthetic those same writers expressed. The reformers of the literary line were to make the most of the situation: turning to all who had become disaffected by RAPP, the socialist realists offered them forgiveness and full restoration of status. At the same time they came forward with a scheme for an administrative apparatus that would enfold them forever in organizational and doctrinal commitments.

RAPP's final obituary was not written in the administrative decrees that dissolved it as an organization. Personal charges of "Trotskyism" were brought against many of its leaders five years later, and the history of RAPP has since been rewritten to prove that Averbakh and others were conducting a gigantic wrecking operation all the time. Voronsky, before this, had disappeared under the same charges, and it is odd to record that of all the traditions and values that went down with the purge trials, the last remnants of humanist realism, and the view of human complexity that accompanied it, were among the greatest casualties.

II

In the literary output between 1929 and 1932 the mood of dogmatic, sloganized arguments was not so insistently present as it was in criticism. Despite persistent efforts to lay hands on the imaginative product, the works of any value at all show no more than a partial response to the pressures that were exerted on them. Nearly all the novelists accepted the unpromising theme of industrial construction or agricultural collectivization (we may assume that this was a first condition of publication).[11] But the elements they worked with had not changed since the twenties, and when the works failed, as they often did, it was because the writers were unable to devise any more than clichéd

11 Though some RAPP critics, as Brown has shown, maintained that this was not so.

solutions to timeworn situations. The constants were: the fundamentalist for-or-against morality of civil war days; and the narrowly rigid and unchanging human situation of the virtuous Communist. The writer's relative freedom to explore could not withstand these negative pressures. None of this writing may be called a contribution to world literature; comparatively little of it acquired a lasting reputation even in the USSR. But it has great documentary interest at times, and there are moments of poignant revelation, and an occasional sense that the writer has touched on a rewarding human situation, even if he backs away from it, or imposes a finally spurious political resolution on it.

RAPP orthodoxy was never completely effective, nor was it completely binding on those who accepted it, nor did it automatically depress literary standards. Few of the works which have received favorable mention in foreign histories of Soviet literature were produced by writers who were members of RAPP,[12] yet Mikhail Sholokhov, the best-known Soviet writer at that time, was a full-fledged member. The most controversial and least orthodox book of the 1929–32 period, Libedinsky's *The Birth of a Hero* (1930), was written by one of RAPP's most devout communicants. One may conclude that the literary process went on somehow, under the impetus of its own inner vitality. It was increasingly harassed, to be sure, but behind the political clamor that passed for criticism there still existed that *relatively* tolerant standard of aesthetic judgment, inherited from Voronsky and, more remotely, from Tolstoy and the classical past. In this one particular the RAPP era differed sharply from what followed. It was the implacable central intolerance of the Zhdanov position that reduced Soviet literature to its post-1946 condition of *rigor mortis*.

A glance at a cross-section of the writing reveals ingenuity at least in the writers' struggles with the stereotypes. Valentin Kataev in *Time, Forward!* avoided the heavy melodrama of black-hearted wreckers and pure-hearted Communists by pitching his novel in a key of amiable satire. His hero, the Jewish engineer, Margulies, has exactly the right combination of temperamental qualities for his profession—caution, curiosity, and a calculated daring. As basic character traits they offer little to work with, but Kataev attempts to make these prosaic virtues palatable by investing Margulies with an engaging air of slovenliness and absent-mindedness. This does not represent invention on a high level, but few of the technician-heroes of the Five-

<hr />

12 See Brown, *The Proletarian Episode in Russian Literature*, p. 281.

Year Plan literature are granted even this degree of "embellishment." Polonsky's description of the dry, grim, effective, practical Communist is much closer to the image most writers worked with:

He runs the lathe, he carries a rifle, he directs the government, he does big deeds and engages in a work that may remain unnoticed. He builds plants and collectives, railways and blast furnaces. He destroys illiteracy, eradicates religion, banishes the dirt of ages, and uproots the advocates of private property. He loves work. He hates phrases. He is a soldier of the revolution. . . . He identifies himself with society. His aim is to understand the world in order to remold it. His personal responses are secondary. Social interests dominate over the egotistic. Indeed, his social and individual interests coincide. His life is broad and embraces a universe. . . .

The hero of our day . . . does not engage in sentimentality. He is a bit dry, somewhat hard, likes to stick to concrete facts. He is a realist. The unearthly, the unmaterial does not exist for him. He abhors idealism, mysticism and religion. He prefers dialectic materialism to metaphysics. He thirsts for knowledge so that he may destroy and create efficiently, and, of course, he lives a full, healthy personal life just because it is not the end of his existence.[13]

The writer confronted with this set of qualities may have recourse only to heavy melodrama.

In two notable instances the dehumanized world of the new industrialism was challenged to account for the casualties it was producing. Libedinsky's *Birth of a Hero* presents the value conflict between an older generation whose humane, questing radicalism is shown to be in direct collision with the schematic, shallow opportunism of the new generation, "the arrogant, superficially correct, self-assertive brittleness which gives way before everything obscure or elemental."[14] Ilya Ehrenburg, in *Out of Chaos*, sketched a similar opposition in the conflict between a young, self-educated humanist and the mindless, semiliterate technicians he is forced to live with, and defer to. It is Volodya's misfortune that he has discovered great literature and made a fatal commitment to it. The questions it puts in his head give rise to a mysterious estrangement from the status quo:

He was not an Onegin, or a Pechorin or a Bolkonsky. He was twenty-two. He did not remember the old life, nor did he long for its return. He studied in the department of mathematics. He could have been laughing as

---

[13] Quoted in Louis Fischer, *Machines and Men in Russia* (New York, 1932), pp. 262–63.

[14] Yurii Libedinsky, *Rozhdenie geroya* (Leningrad, 1930), pp. 183–84.

gaily as his fellow-students. What then prevented him? What spore was developing in him? Where lay the explanation of his tormenting irony—in historical materialism or the migration of souls?[15]

The "spore," Ehrenburg indicates, is an ineradicable knowledge of the cultural past and of the complexity of existence:

He did not explain Dr. Faust's boredom by the peculiarities of the period of initial accumulation of capital. When spring was in the courtyard and lilacs blossomed in the old gardens of Tomsk, he did not quote Marx. He knew that lilacs were more ancient than Marx. He knew that spring had come even in the days before the revolution. Ergo, he knew nothing. He was dense and illiterate.[16]

Volodya's sickness is incurable. But Ehrenburg blurs the conflict, conducts his maladjusted spokesman to a pointless suicide,[17] and shifts his own attention, in a typical gesture of accommodation, to the successful construction project. The novel ends in a rousing political speech.

Routine melodrama is the order of the day, however, despite these wayward examples and despite the embellishments disorderly writers like Pilnyak (*The Volga Flows Down to the Caspian*) and gifted writers like Leonov (*Sot*) attempted to impose on the given stereotype.

III

One novel of the period deserves a lengthier examination. Sholokhov is a writer of genuine attainments, and his study of the grim battle for collectivization, *Virgin Soil Upturned*, represents a maximum effort to write well, yet entirely within the official canon. The novel has become a permanent best-seller, and a textbook in the schools. Under the surface the essential dramatic situation reflects the same pattern that has been discovered in every other conformist Soviet novel. Davydov, the leathery worker from Leningrad, "a dry, hard chap," has accepted the Bolshevik mission of leading the unready and unwilling to a better life. Like all his kin, he has added to the

---

[15] Ilya Ehrenburg, *Out of Chaos*, trans. A. Bakshy (New York, 1934), pp. 68–69.
[16] *Ibid.*, p. 66.
[17] If Ehrenburg had been more than an agile journalist, he might have intended genuine irony in the reason he gives for the suicide: Volodya has spoken passionately in favor of Dostoevsky, and a young malcontent who heard him went out to the construction project and committed an act of sabotage. In the absence of a serious ironic intention, Volodya's guilt on this score is simply ludicrous.

role of the solicitous instructor—Lenin's "patiently to explain"—the capacity to pry, to goad, to deceive, and to punish. When he enters the Cossack village he has been ordered to collectivize, he directs his attention first to the hostile strangers he must manipulate in the name of their best interests:

He had been by no means a naive town dweller before he went to work in the country, but he had not realized all the complexities of the class struggle, its tangled knots and frequently secret courses, until he arrived in Gremyachy. He could not understand the stubborn reluctance of the majority of the middling peasants to join the collective farm despite the tremendous advantages of collective agriculture. He could not find the right key to an understanding of many of the people and their inter-relationships. . . . All the inhabitants of Gremyachy passed before Davydov's mental vision. And there was much in them that was incomprehensible to him, that was hidden behind a kind of impalpable curtain. The village was like a new type of complicated motor, and Davydov studied it intently and tensely, trying to understand its mechanism, to see clearly every detail, to note every interruption in the daily, incessant throbbing of this involved machine.[18]

He must persuade the unwilling Cossacks to act against tradition, belief, and instinct, in the name of a drastic redefinition of their own and of the nation's interest which has been decreed in distant Moscow. Acting out of his core of Communist virtue, he improvises the local virtues and techniques appropriate to the task, but it is the core itself, the combination of personal qualities and ideas, which enables this severely functional hero to gain mastery over any situation he confronts.

The doctrinal component of his sense of Party duty, apart from the general fund of Marxist-Leninist ideas, is contained in the directives he carries in his pocket. He quarrels with the district leaders on the correct interpretation to be placed upon them, but never questions their claims on his loyalty and energy. Doctrine provides the rational framework for every decision he makes, sometimes affecting the most minute details. When it has led Davydov's villagers to the point of revolt, his situation is miraculously resolved by the arrival of Stalin's new policy statement, "Dizzy with Success," which includes the magically successful order to decollectivize chickens. Davydov is saved

[18] Mikhail Sholokhov, *Virgin Soil Upturned*, trans. Stephen Garry (London, 1948), pp. 136–37. The novel was first published in 1932 and has served as a primary exhibit of the literature of positive heroes.

in the nick of time from the defeat of his plans, or from the unthinkable alternative of having to go against handed-down orders. The entire grotesque episode suggests that Davydov is the instrument of an all-seeing, infallible power, and that his faith in its policies will never betray him.

But Davydov is not merely the blind executor of policies drawn up by others, nor is he simply a technician or administrator. He is a leader, imposed from without on the men he is to lead, and in the forceful and flexible application of policy to the local scene he is forced to act in a number of painful and difficult human situations. In these decisions there is revealed in Davydov that perfect fusion of conviction with emotion that the nineteenth-century radicals had sought in their champion. In contrast to Davydov, both of his local Communist assistants come unstuck at the very point where the two elements are joined. Nagulnov, the overzealous "leftist," is carried away by the frenzied emotions he had acquired in the civil war and makes half-cracked decisions which threaten the success of the entire program. Such display of emotion is viewed as a kind of self-indulgence, and neither his years of loyalty to the cause nor the evident sincerity of his intentions is permitted to interfere with the punishment that is visited upon him. Davydov's rigid control over himself makes this kind of irresponsible outburst impossible in his case. But the furious emotion is in him, too, in the form of an inexhaustible fund of hatred for the old regime, the extermination of which he conceives as his world-historical mission. When Razmiotnov, his other assistant, breaks down and announces that he refuses to go on dispossessing kulaks and their families because it is no part of his work to wage war on children, Davydov erupts in a fury. "Did they ever weep over the orphans of those they killed?" he shouts at Razmiotnov, and exposes the deepest source of his energy in an account of the bitter suffering the old society inflicted on him in his childhood.[19] The emotion is there but it has been harnessed and put at the service of doctrine. When duty demands inhuman acts, Davydov's experience, generalized into the sufferings of his class, enables him to administer the awful individual injustices implicit in "class justice," without apparent damage to his own conscience.

The same subordination of personal emotion to the public interest, as he conceives it, determines his behavior in the novel's crisis. At its

[19] *Ibid.*, p. 84.

height, Davydov is attacked by furious women and beaten through the streets of the village while the men plunder the grain from the collective seed fund. One woman beats him with her fists in tearful, impotent rage, not because he is wicked, but because he is so inevitably and unshakably correct. When order has been restored, Davydov's speech is a model of Communist leadership. He instantly overlooks his personal humiliation, but exploits the Cossacks' guilt by telling them that the only expiation open to them is through support of the collective farm. An act of Communist forgiveness, like any other act, serves as a goad toward the desired social resolution.

Finally the question arises: What are the rewards and what are the costs implicit in Davydov's design for living? As always, in Soviet writing, the answer is less than adequate. We are never to find the full human exposure we might expect from the nineteenth-century writers. But enough hints are to be found that suggest that the negative features of the new man of the 1860s—the aridity, the one-sidedness, the blunted moral sensibility—have been duplicated in his Soviet counterpart. The calculus of his personal happiness and the means he uses to justify his life to himself must be set in this context of damage and deprivation.

The rewards are few enough. The uncertain pleasure of serving as history's instrument finds its expression in an occasional vision of the future. In a rare moment of introspection, Davydov discloses how bare and prosaic, yet how intensely felt, that vision is. A talk with a child has prompted him to speculate about what is to come:

We'll build a good life for them. Fact! ... In twenty years time he'll [the little boy] probably be plowing up this very earth with an electric plow. ... Machinery will do all the heavy work for man. The people of those days will have forgotten the smell of sweat, I suppose. I'd like to live till then, by all the devils. If only to see what it was like. ... You'll die ... brother Davydov, as sure as you're alive! Instead of descendants you'll leave behind the Gremyachy collective farm. The farm will become a commune, and then you'll see, they'll call it by the name of the Putilov locksmith, Semion Davydov.[20]

Davydov lives in great solitude. It is not the terrible metaphysical aloneness that Dostoevsky has inflicted on his rebels, but it is nonetheless complete and unrelieved. The instance of the woman who

20 *Ibid.*, pp. 345–46.

beats him because he is so infallible reminds us as much of his isolation as of his rectitude. He is unmarried. His shirt is dirty—so dirty that, as Razmiotnov points out, he "couldn't cut it with a sword."[21] But Davydov insists he will take care of it; an ex-sailor, he has learned to wash and mend his own clothes. His most outspoken display of personal emotion, which follows the receipt of a modest gift-box from his comrades in the Putilov Works in Leningrad, merely accents the austerity of his private life.[22] That the Soviet Communist's life is very often loveless is a cliché of pre–World War II literature. Sholokhov has given the cliché a special emphasis by exposing Davydov to a beautiful temptress, the wife of a Party colleague. Davydov is, indeed, tempted; he asks himself, "Am I a monk, or what?"[23] But, as always, public concerns crowd in on him. "Though he was attracted to Lukeria, he had feared that his association with her would undermine his authority."[24] His final, grudging acceptance of her favors gives rise not to a feeling of release but to new anxieties. Nor does it promise any kind of communion with the people he has been manipulating by involving him in the emotional substance of their daily lives.

The costs of his rigidly exemplary life are not counted out in full. There is no suggestion, for example, that his burden of duty is in any way increased by guilts arising from the injuries he has done to others in the name of that duty. We are left with the impression that his conscience is entirely contained within his concept of Party obligations. But it takes a small adjustment of the lens to see Davydov as his enemies might have done: ruthless, fanatical, limited, and remote, insulated against all the ordinary human weaknesses, yet protected against a true knowledge of his condition by the narrowness of his vision.[25]

[21] *Ibid.*, p. 162.
[22] *Ibid.*, p. 161. Davydov's comment: "A touching fact."
[23] *Ibid.*, p. 476.   [24] *Ibid.*, pp. 479–80.
[25] The second volume of *Virgin Soil* was completed in 1936, but was sent back to Sholokhov by the editors of *Novyi Mir* for revisions. Clouds of rumors have attended these revisions and the belated publication of the work in irregular serial form between 1955 and 1960. Two rumors suggest that Sholokhov may have contemplated a tragic end for Davydov—death in prison following his arrest in the purges, or, more remarkably, suicide. In the published text he is shot down by White Guard conspirators—an ending which Vera Alexandrova has properly described as "political melodrama"— and is mourned by the villagers who have come to love him. See her *A History of Soviet Literature* (New York, 1963) pp. 231–32; and Harrison Salisbury's article in the *New York Times*, September 1, 1974.

IV

The shift of power from one literary bureaucracy to another required more than two years—from RAPP's dissolution in 1932 to the grand inaugural fete of socialist realism, the First Soviet Writers' Congress, held in August, 1934.[26] The second event marked the end of a thorough process of overhaul, which resulted in complex readjustments in theory and practice. In all these decisions there is a consistent pattern of simultaneous release and constriction. Thus RAPP's harshness toward fellow-traveling writers was countered by the elaborate welcome extended to Babel, Olesha, and others whose cranky, individual approach had led them into estrangement and silence under RAPP. At the same time the foundation was laid in the protocols of the new Union of Soviet Writers for the most thorough administrative control (through a Party "fraction" and other devices) over writers yet attempted. On the level of doctrine there was a heady sense of release from the inanities of RAPP's agitprop activities. Yet the elaborate formulations of the new socialist realism concealed a theory of literature that was potentially far more restrictive than RAPP's assumption that art was a kind of passive cognition. In general, a sense of liberation and advance dominated the proceedings of the Congress and the succeeding years, at least until the purge trials sent new constrictive spasms through the entire social organism.

The fact that the controls were largely held in reserve in the early years may be attributed in part to the requirements of literary "foreign policy." RAPP's efforts in this direction had been concerned largely with enlisting pledges from foreign writers to sabotage their own armed forces in any impending attack against the USSR. An entirely new approach was inaugurated with the Popular Front strategy of the thirties. An air of tolerance toward the West and toward the past was designed to enlist the affiliation of foreign writers in terms far less bloodthirsty than RAPP's. Long, scholarly articles in the literary journals on Aristotle, Lessing, Hegel, and others affected to explore the aesthetic heritage for its possible relevance to socialist realism; Proust, Joyce, and Dos Passos became fixtures on the agenda of literary meetings. A minority of critics raised the disturbing question of the

---

[26] I have recorded some further thoughts on this meeting in "The First Writers' Congress: A Second Look," *Literature and Revolution in Soviet Russia, 1917–1962*, ed. Max Hayward and Leopold Labedz (London, 1963), pp. 62–73.

possibility of a tragic art within the framework of socialist realism. But these potentially liberating efforts had no lasting effect on the official doctrine because the doctrine's "purity" was in the custody of men entirely unconcerned in the end with literary values. The real legislators of socialist realism at the Writers' Congress were Radek and Zhdanov, and not Gorky, who simply managed, by a peculiarly tortured reading of the literary past, to find confirmation for the propositions laid down by the political magistrates.

Socialist realism does not require a lengthy exposition here. That has been done often enough in the West, both well and badly.[27] The juxtaposition of half a dozen authoritative utterances will show us all the central notions—service, optimism, selectivity, "romanticism" (orientation toward the future)—that result in the total politicalization of art.

Zhdanov defines the function of art in these familiar terms:

Our literature is impregnated with enthusiasm and heroism. It is optimistic, but not optimistic according to any kind of zoological, "interior" sensation. It is optimistic essentially because it is the literature of the rising class, of the proletariat, of the only progressive and advanced class. Our Soviet literature is strong because it serves a new cause—the cause of socialist construction.[28]

Here is the grim optimism of Hegelian history, and the related assurance that a literature which reflects history's unfolding will be a great one because it *serves* that process by publicizing it. In performing that service it cannot fail to be "tendentious because there cannot be in an epoch of class struggle a literature which is nonclass, nontendentious ... apolitical."[29] Here Zhdanov goes beyond the radical democrats in demanding that literature propagate not merely "healthy ideas," but specific political values. But the difference is merely in degree, not in kind, as far as the *fact* of commitment is concerned. Finally,

[27] A good analysis is Herbert Read's brief essay in *Art and Society*. His conclusions are worth quoting: "In effect, then, socialist realism is but one more attempt to impose an intellectual or dogmatic purpose on art. It may be that the actual circumstances of the moment—the revolutionary urgencies to which most intellectuals and artists subscribe—demand a temporary supersession of the primary conditions of a great art: that art, like much else, must be sacrificed to the common good. If this is so, let it be clearly recognized, and do not let us deceive ourselves into imagining that a great art can be created under conditions which both the history of art and the psychology of the artist prove to be impossible." Herbert Read, *Art and Society* (London, 1945), p. 133.

[28] *Pervyi vsesoyuznyi s'ezd sovetskikh pisatelei, 1934; stenograficheskii otchet* (Moscow, 1934), p. 4.

[29] *Ibid.*

literature departs from reality, involves itself in the future, and as the logical consequence of this (and all else we have noted), assumes its ultimate role as a vehicle for heroic "romanticism":

Socialist realism is the basic method of Soviet literature and literary criticism but this assumes that revolutionary romanticism must enter into literary creation as a constituent part, because the whole life of our Party, the whole life of the working class and its struggle consists of the combination of the grimmest ... practical work with the greatest heroism and most magnificent perspectives. Our Party has always been strong because it is united and combines ... practicality with a broad perspective, with a constant striving forward in the struggle for the construction of a Communist society. *Soviet literature must be able to show our heroes, be able to look into the future. It will not be a Utopia, for our tomorrow is being prepared by planned, conscious work today.*[30]

When we note that the only officially authorized views of the future are contained in the blueprints of the five-year plans, all area of creative maneuver is shut off on this point too. There can be only *one* kind of hero, performing *one* kind of work, with *one* kind of outcome: the politicalized technicians—from skilled worker to plant manager[31]—will work within the framework of the plan, and will fulfill its directives through the exercise of courage, initiative, self-denial, and the rest of the copybook virtues. The hero will perform a threefold function for the reader: he will inspire him to emulation, he will earn his respect as an admirable representative of political virtue, and he will, by linking the present with the future, provide magic assurance that the job can be done. Chernyshevsky's heroes were intended to have precisely these effects on the reader. The merging of the Leninist ethic with the Russian utilitarian aesthetic is publicly consummated at this moment. The elevation of the radical stereotype to the level of a nation-wide doctrine, binding on all writers, represents at the same time the "world-historical downfall" of the Russian classical aesthetic, at least on its native grounds.

The Writers' Congress went on to endless discussions *within* the limits of Zhdanov's introductory remarks. Bukharin, for example, developed an original thesis on the differences between the kinds of knowledge art and science provide, and then abandoned his distinc-

---

[30] *Ibid.*, pp. 4–5.

[31] Zhdanov defines the true heroes thus: "In our country the principal heroes of literature are the active builders of the new life: workers ... collective farmers, Party members, managers, engineers, Komsomols, Pioneers. Here are the basic types and the basic heroes of our Soviet literature." *Ibid.*, p. 4.

tions and rushed to the same conclusions Zhdanov had come to. The
most critical remarks were uttered by André Malraux, who spoke
briefly as a visiting dignitary. Behind a façade of compliments, he
complained that the world had yet to learn of the true inner nature
of the Soviet hero because the literature had failed to disclose it.[32]
Then he outlined the principles that underlay his own work, including, presumably, his revolutionary novels. Primarily, art helps men
live, he told the delegates. It is at once an act of "discovery," "invention," and "conquest" (above all of the unconscious), and he cited
Prince Andrei's revelation at Austerlitz in *War and Peace* as an
instance of all these functions. Art must be more than a photographic
documentation of external events. The challenge to Zhdanov's doctrine contained in these brief remarks was met only tangentially by
later speakers, although the irritation Malraux provoked is unmistakable in several of their comments. Certainly Malraux failed to
arrest the underlying movement toward agreement.

The principle of selectivity, the connecting rod between political
principles and their artistic representation, was discussed at length
by Radek. On the basis of standards of selection, controlled from outside the creative process, the all-important definitions of "the typical,"
"the significant," "the essential," "the true," "the correct," and "the
incorrect" are derived. Radek's remark is perhaps intended as an
answer to Malraux's charge of "photography." It does not meet the
substance of the charge, actually, and in its total effect moves art
still further away from Malraux's sense of its necessarily autonomous
functions. Radek's ideas, like Zhdanov's, are strongly reminiscent of
the Russian ideologies of the nineteenth century:

We do not photograph life. In the totality of phenomena we seek out the
main phenomenon. Presenting everything without discrimination is not
realism. We should select phenomena. Realism means that we make a
selection from the point of view of what is essential, from the point of
view of guiding principles. And as for what is essential—the very name
of socialism tells us. . . . Select all phenomena which show how the system
of capitalism is being destroyed, how socialism is growing, not embellishing socialism but showing that it is growing in battle, in hard work, in
sweat. Show how it is growing in deeds, in human beings.[33]

What the critics in the nineteenth century could only propose, an
all-powerful state could now dispose. This apparatus of manipula-

[32] *Ibid.*, p. 286.   [33] *Ibid.*, p. 373.

tion could lie dormant or could be applied to the literary imagination with any variation of pressures the magistrates felt to be necessary. Theme, character, scene, action, and resolution were all at the mercy of the policy makers. Thus Zhdanov's 1946 "Report" represented a particularly abrupt and severe tightening of the screws that had been there to turn since 1934. And it was the same man, of course, who was manipulating the controls on both occasions.

Gorky's journey through world literature was intended to prove that socialist realism is a culminating point in the history of art. As he traced its ancestry back through the nineteenth century and the Renaissance to its origins in folklore, Gorky injected his own moral standards into his curious literary judgments. Labor, to Gorky, is the fundamental condition of dignified human existence. Soviet society has made it the most honored function of human beings, hence the first source of heroism and dignity:

As the fundamental hero of our books we must choose labor, that is, man organized by the labor-process, which is armed here with the full power of technology, man in his turn making labor easier, more productive, raising it to the level of art. We must learn to understand labor as creativity.[34]

Folklore, which Gorky considered the most vital of all literary forms, he analyzes as principally concerned with the celebration of great feats of labor or craftsmanship. In an indictment as sweeping as Tolstoy's, he traces the slow disappearance of heroic feats of labor from literature and equates it with an overall decline in literary quality. The steepest descent he dates from Shakespeare and ascribes it to the growth of capitalism, which destroyed the creative relationship between man and his work, and brought about, thereby, a fatal degeneration of personality. The "superfluous" heroes of Russia's nineteenth century are some of the brightest images in the long record of decay, according to Gorky, but they provide at the same time the best illustration of the fatal results of ruling-class idleness. Soviet society has restored the creative relationship between men and labor which existed in pre-state society, has ended the sickness of individualism, and has created the basic condition for the heroic personalities which are to be recorded in the new era of world literature to be known as socialist realism.

[34] *Ibid.*, p. 13. Gorky's feeling about the virtues of labor resembles the Five-Year Plan mystique, but he held it long before the revolution. It is one of the points of his personal accommodation with the Bolshevik regime.

Gorky's celebration of labor in 1934 as a source of virtue and dignity is not new in Soviet life. What is new is his emphasis on what might be called "mythic realism." His remarks are the first authoritative recognition of the legendary quality in Soviet fiction we have already noted in the primitive response to the story of Chapaev. Gorky's advocacy of a hero image which is larger than life, on the scale of the folk hero, was reflected in very little of the critical writing which followed the Writers' Congress. It seems to contradict the widespread insistence on the averageness of the "typical character in typical circumstances" as it was applied to the standard Soviet hero. Gorky's models may voice the aspirations of the mass, but they are hardly typical characters, in any kind of circumstances.

I again direct your attention, comrades, to the fact that the deepest and brightest, the most artistically perfect types of heroes were created by folklore, the oral creation of the working mass. The perfection of such images as Hercules, Prometheus, Mikula Selyaninovich, Svyatogor... Doctor Faust... Ivan-durak, and finally Petrushka, who overcomes the priest, the policeman, the devil, and even death... all these are images in the creation of which reason and intuitive feeling and thought are harmoniously combined.[35]

In calling for a return to the hyperbole and fantasy of folk literature, Gorky may be reminding the makers of ideology of the survival of the folk imagination among large sections of the reading public. In any case, Gorky is clear about the manipulative value his "mythic" folklore-derived literature has for the ideologists:

Myth is an invention. To invent means to extract from a sum of real data its basic significance and to embody it in an image—in this way realism is achieved. But if we add to the significance of what is extracted from the real data... the desired, the possible and with these we complete the image we achieve that romanticism which is at the basis of myth and is extremely useful in that it contributes to the awakening of a revolutionary attitude toward reality, an attitude which in a practical sense changes the world.[36]

It is folklore, according to Gorky, that offers the most convincing example of that amalgam of present and future, of *is* and *should be*, which is at the heart of the new Soviet art. The lack of public response to Gorky's ideas at the Congress and later does not mean that the mythic component is absent from later Soviet writing. It is, on the contrary, very much present, but is deliberately concealed behind a

[35] *Ibid.*, p. 8.   [36] *Ibid.*, p. 10.

prosaic, "realistic" surface. The Soviet reader is expected to recognize some part of his own life in this fiction, and to respond in terms of personal action. The oversized figures of folklore might encourage complacency about the capacities of his champion. The fabricated myths of Soviet literature are functional in intention, designed to propel the reader into action, not to give him objects for remote veneration or passive identification.

CHAPTER 13

Four Novels

❦❦❦❦

Four novels that appeared in completed form in the years between the overthrow of RAPP and the beginning of World War II, Mikhail Sholokhov's *The Silent Don*, Alexei Tolstoy's *Road to Calvary*, Leonid Leonov's *Road to the Ocean*, and Nikolai Ostrovsky's *The Making of a Hero*, represent a cross-section of the writing in these years, and demonstrate the full range of possibility in Soviet literature. One of the novels, Sholokhov's, quite clearly goes back to the classical Russian tradition itself. Two of the novels, Tolstoy's and Sholokhov's, resist strict classification under the heading "socialist realism" because they were conceived and their early sections were published in the twenties. Leonov's and Ostrovsky's novels are authentic products of the era of socialist realism, although they differ radically in form, in approach, and in artistic worth.

These novels will be considered in a descending scale of literary value, since that has been the unmistakable direction of the historical trend. By this standard Sholokhov's novel must come first. Publication of its concluding sections in 1940 (the first chapters were published in 1928) raised a number of instructive issues because, although it was not generally admitted, Sholokhov had challenged every tenet of socialist realism in the tragic fate he devised for his hero. The most important aspects of the discussion of the novel in the USSR centered on the question: does the Soviet Union have "a right" to a tragic literature? The question is very much in point. Although they exist in attenuated and incomplete form, there are the elements of an

Aristotelian design in *The Silent Don*. The novel's hero, the gifted, humane, passionate Cossack, Gregor Melekhov, is a man of more than average human stature who is destroyed by superhuman forces he can neither comprehend nor control. His intellectual inability to understand history's movement cannot in itself be considered a tragic "flaw," though it does contribute to the blind sin of political affiliation with the Whites that is the external cause of his downfall.

But the basic terms of his collision with reality are moral. He prepares the way for his own destruction by a habit of impulsive decision which results in a sequence of temporary enlistments with both factions in the civil war. If this zigzag pattern of commitment were the product only of bewilderment, Gregor's destruction between implacable hostile forces would be productive only of a remote kind of pathos. But he is an assertive moral being, and beneath the inarticulated tangle of motives which produce his impulsive actions, there is a plain code of human decency and tolerance. A respect for the human person and a distaste for gratuitous acts of cruelty always underlie the other considerations—self-preservation, Cossack self-interest, love of the land—which motivate him. Acts of rape, looting, murder, or torture—committed by either side—are the determinants of his judgments.

He remains in a state of bewilderment to the end of his "strange and incoherent life,"[1] but at one moment he ventures close to an understanding of his dilemma. He had sought "one truth," he notes, which would embody his personal code and aspirations in political terms. But the world offered him "two truths," and neither fully comprehended the demands he made on life. A further step (which he cannot make) might have led him to reformulate the notion of truth's duality into the deeper division between human truth and political truth or between man in nature and man in history. Though Gregor is never permitted to know this, Sholokhov appears here to be suggesting that private moral judgment is sometimes irrelevant to the higher struggles of historical forces, and that in this fact there is genuine human tragedy.

Perhaps this is not Sholokhov's intention—and for it to be so the writer would have to betray the Communist in himself—but it is a defensible reading of the novel and it is possible to speculate about

[1] Mikhail Sholokhov, *The Silent Don*, trans. Stephen Garry (New York, 1946), p. 552.

its function in Soviet society. Despite the absence of positive affirmation at the novel's end, when Gregor returns home for a brief reunion
with his son, stripped of hope and aspiration, and prepared to meet
his fate at the hands of the Cheka, there is a strong sense of his final
reconciliation with a remote historical destiny, hence, with the new
revolutionary status quo itself. It might be imagined that this effect
could have a strict practical utility for the rulers of Soviet society, as
a solvent of doubt, unruliness, and grievance in their own population. If this were accepted as minimum compliance with the "social
command," the world might be entitled to expect the continued survival, at least, of the Russian tradition. But such "negative" effects are
not officially countenanced, and we must assume that the book's publication and great success are the results of a partial accident which
has been accepted because of Sholokhov's enormous popularity and
the unquestioned talent his novel exhibits.[2]

Sholokhov's novel does not deserve the designation "Tolstoyan"
which is often attached to it because it lacks the human density of
his predecessor's work. The very inarticulateness of Sholokhov's characters, and the unmitigated violence which engulfs all assertions of
moral worth, automatically deny it such depth of insight. But its
connections with the past call attention to one general question that
spans the century we have been concerned with. Ever since Chernyshevsky's clumsy attack on tragedy, there has been an obvious opposition between the affirmative and the tragic vision of experience. There
are not many explicit discussions of the matter in the Soviet era but
the problem is never absent, and occasionally it found its way into
print. Lunacharsky, himself a would-be playwright, raised the question in an article in the early twenties which discusses the tragic
formula Marx and Engels sketched in the correspondence with Lassalle,[3] the situation of the premature revolutionary whose tragedy
resides in his historical "inopportuneness." Trotsky, who felt that the

---

[2] Serial publication accounts in part for the bombshell effect the novel had. Apparently there was a widespread expectation that Gregor would be "converted," or at
least brought to a positive acceptance of the new regime. Such a resolution, of course,
would violate all that had gone before. The somewhat grudging Soviet acceptance of
the novel has taken two forms: first, that socialist realism is broad enough to encompass all the complexities of social struggle even when the outcome is tragic for individuals engaged in it; second, that Gregor's tragedy is that of a willful individualist
who "has cut himself off from the people," and therefore must die. L. I. Timofeev,
Sovremennaya literatura (Moscow, 1947), p. 311.

[3] A. Lunacharsky, "Mysli o kommunisticheskoi dramaturgii," *Pechat i revolyutsiya*,
2 (1921).

task of the "cultural revolution" was not the building of "proletarian" art but the creative repossession of the artistic heritage, remarked in *Literature and Revolution* that he considered dramatic tragedy the highest form art had ever achieved.[4] Gorky noted in his concluding remarks at the Writers' Congress that the impending anti-Soviet war should provide writers with material for great tragic works of art.[5] The problem of tragic resolutions was implicit in the approach of some writers in the declining trend in the twenties, and there had been a spate of articles in the mid-thirties on the question of "a Soviet tragedy." The matter came to a climax after the whole of Sholokhov's novel had appeared, but the final resolution of the question did not coincide with Sholokhov's formula. The fullest answer, as then formulated, is to be found in two earlier articles. One of these, entitled "Prometheus Liberated" (Marxism has set him free!), declares that there can be no tragedy in the USSR because man is now master of his own fate, is no longer at odds with his society, and fulfills himself through the collective's achievements.[6] The second article, "The Dramaturgical Principles of Aristotle," reviews Hegel's and Aristotle's theories of tragedy with some sympathy and understanding, and then attempts to readjust them to fit Soviet conditions.[7] The author focuses his attention on the catharsis, as the critical moment at which new truths are apprehended, and tinkers with its mechanism so that it yields the spectator not tragic reconciliation (through pity and terror), but political inspiration (through pity and respect). The politically motivated hero thus may die (without inner defeat, of course) and the spectator will emerge from the drama determined to fuse his will with the collective's as the hero had done up to the moment of his death. This is not to be taken seriously as a tragic formula since there is no real torment, doubt, or "stretching," only physical extinction, which the hero confronts unflinchingly.[8] And it has nothing to do in the end with Sholokhov, or the Russian past, or for that matter Hegel or Aristotle, or anyone who has thought seriously about tragedy.

[4] See Leon Trotsky, *Literature and Revolution*, trans. Rose Strunsky (London, 1925), pp. 240–45, for his discussion of tragedy.

[5] *Pervyi vsesoyuznyi s'ezd sovetskikh pisatelei, 1934; stenograficheskii otchet* (Moscow, 1934), p. 680.

[6] Yu. Yuzovsky, "Osvobozhdennyi Prometei," *Literaturny kritik*, 10 (October 1934): 113–39.

[7] I. Altman, "Dramaturgicheskie printsipy Aristotelya," *Literaturny kritik*, 10 (October 1935): 52–74.

[8] The title of one of the plays under discussion, Vishnevsky's *Optimistic Tragedy*, gives the game away.

II

Leonov's *Road to the Ocean* (1935) also ventures toward a tragic statement and then withdraws when it approaches the boundary between socialist realism and the larger world of art's undirected possibilities. Leonov is a gifted writer, literate in his craft, and aware of those possibilities which lie just beyond his reach. As a result of his knowledge of forbidden areas, Leonov is forced to expend a great deal of energy devising ingenious compromises between the requirements of the formula and what he might really like to say. Thus the two obligatory situations of the literature of industrialization, the exposure of the hidden wrecker-enemy and the celebration of the achievements of the Communist hero, are both in Leonov's novel, though they are disguised and set in the background. On the other hand, Leonov's pursuit of his genuine interests is clearly evident in the novel, and though he stops short of real tragic revelation, the work is permeated with a sense of the permanence, the dignity, and the value of human suffering.

His hero, Kurilov, is an old Bolshevik who holds high office in the Volga-Revizan railway, and has dedicated the whole of his life to the service of the cause. His life can be summarized, Leonov tells us, "in one infinite word: work."[9] The costs of this existence are fully acknowledged by Leonov, and more frankly than by any other Soviet writer of the time. Moreover, they are not presented as wistful sidelights on the character, as in Sholokhov's Davydov, but are brought into the foreground and incorporated in the hero's image as an ingredient of his greatness. Solitude and barrenness are the consequences of the dedicated, politicalized life, as we have come to know it. None the less so in Kurilov's case.[10] He is denied any intimacy with his subordinates whom he encounters primarily as incompetents, liars, or worse, and treats accordingly. His private life is equally solitary. Marriage has been a bleak, bloodless failure, and children have been denied him, first by the urgency of events and then by the prolonged illness of his wife. His two fumbling efforts to have affairs with younger women

---

[9] Leonid Leonov, *Road to the Ocean*, trans. Norbert Guterman (New York, copyright 1944, by A. A. Wyn, Inc., formerly L. B. Fischer Publishing Corp.), p. 4.

[10] Leonov is sometimes called "Dostoevskyan." The remark of one of Kurilov's colleagues suggests that his solitude has its origins in a rebellion against God similar to Ivan Karamazov's: "Atheism means ignoring God. But you negate him, fight against him, disrespectfully take the universe away from him." *Ibid.*, p. 463.

after her death are failures. Friendships with an odd crew of fellow-Bolsheviks and others, including "a poet and heretic" and an old steelworker, are the only nourishing relationships he has with other human beings, and they are denied him most of the time because of their physical separation. The quality of these friendships is conveyed in Kurilov's remarks at a birthday party that has brought them together. He is answering an earlier speech by the poet-heretic Kutenko, who has proposed a toast to the younger generation which will survive to populate the future, "which certainly neither you nor I will see!" Kurilov replies:

And so, Kutenko, in your opinion, socialism is for those who will survive. You even spoke of friendship from the point of view of our fate, rather than of our community of social interests. . . . But now, as I look at your faces, those dear familiar old beans, I see myself multiplied in them. All of you are fragments of my own life; that is because we made our lives together, guided by the same purpose. Each of you separately is my friend. I did not bring you together, I did not introduce you to each other, and yet you are each other's friends, too. And if I fall out of this circle, your friendship will remain unchanged. It binds you by an iron and rational discipline, it does not spoil or disintegrate—let us not even mention those who betrayed it! Of this friendship you should have spoken, not of the dead or the unborn ones, Kostia.[11]

Inadequate as these friendships are as a source of emotional sustenance, they are all that matters outside the cause. But the onset of death, which first announces itself by a sharp pain at the moment he finishes this speech, is to cut him off from whatever comfort these politically rationalized relations provide. Kutenko, it turns out, is right: Kurilov's work ends, the "community of social interests" loses its value for him, and he enters a more human plane of existence, from which he contemplates "the common human fate" and the immense irony that he will never live to see the future he has given his life to build.

In this new state he falls back on a strange, poetic, often incoherent apprehension of the place he and his society occupy in the perspective of history. He is oddly well informed about the human past. He is, for example, an occasional student of the history of religions, for the record he finds there of human fears and aspirations. At the same time he is a dreamer and a prophet. Large sections of the novel are taken up with his explorations, in fantasy, of Ocean, the city of the socialist

11 *Ibid.*, p. 100.

future. His effort to locate himself in history is the primary intellectual activity of his final months of life. Kurilov's own history is rooted, not surprisingly, in the Marxian view of progress, but there is a very un-Soviet awareness of the enormous human suffering that accompanies, and will continue to accompany, its unfolding.

Kutenko, the poet-heretic, has been right on another point, we are told, and has stated indirectly part of Leonov's design for the novel:

He had once been attacked for maintaining that the social maturity of a class in art is acquired through tragedy, and he assumed that the tragedy of the future might consist in biological extinction.[12]

Kurilov reenacts this "tragedy of the future" as he dies. But his fate has the other dimension indicated by Kutenko: the awareness generated in the tension between the imperfect present, in which he will expire, and the unattained future, which has called forth all the deprivations in his private life.

This is a most sympathetic recognition of the condition of the "interim man," and a complete transposition into Soviet terms of Marx's formula for the premature revolutionary, the man whom death forces to realize that he is a discarded means, not an end, whose personal claims on life are forcibly disconnected from the continuum of society's progress, since he is not ready to die and his aspirations are not yet realized in society.[13] Several images convey the sense of Kurilov's interim position. At one point he is described thus: "Kurilov, the great hunter, the seeker after human happiness, the man mountain, from the summit of which we see the future."[14] The girl, Liza, who is closest to him at the end of his life, and is most influenced by him as a human being, sees him in similar terms. "Yes," she says after his death, "he was like a bridge, and people passed over him into the future."[15] Kurilov sees himself and the men of his time in the process of development toward the new, whole man. He is as uncompleted as his society: "We ourselves are only rough drafts of giants, who in their own time will learn that they are only dwarfs."[16]

[12] *Ibid.*, p. 99.

[13] Leonov emphasizes this point by his extraordinary frankness about the dirt, disorder, and breakdown of Soviet life, and the vanity, dishonesty, and selfishness of the people Kurilov encounters. The present is indeed imperfect if not unbearable.

[14] Leonov, *Road to the Ocean*, p. 453.   [15] *Ibid.*, p. 362.

[16] *Ibid.*, p. 262. This image evokes Marx's vision of man restored to wholeness and may echo Trotsky's concluding words in *Literature and Revolution*: "The average human type will rise to the heights of an Aristotle, a Goethe, or a Marx. And above this ridge new peaks will rise."

Kurilov is engaged in striking the balance of his life in the months before his death, but as he counts out the human cost in full detail, he never brings himself to challenge the cause of it all, his allegiance to the revolution. He is finally more concerned with justifying than with questioning the value of his life. Here Leonov has missed the opportunity to transcend the tragic *fact* of death, and, by stretching Kurilov another degree, to comment on the tragic *nature* of experience. The novel ends, rather, on a note of muffled affirmation, although it is uttered in an atmosphere heavy with grief, and Leonov has swerved back at the last moment and by the skin of his teeth into the confines of socialist realism.

The positive, life-giving word is not pronounced by Kurilov himself but is communicated through the effect the example of his life has had on Liza. But Liza herself apprehends the meaning of his life through her own suffering at his death. The fact that maturity and self-mastery come to her through sorrow brings us finally to the matter of Soviet criticism of Leonov's novel. In general the reception was chilly. The consensus of a number of critics was that the novel was "abstract," "unreal," and "weak." One article represents the lowest common denominator of these opinions, and is very helpful in bringing to light, though in reverse, as it were, a number of my own general conclusions.

I. Grinberg devoted a large part of an article, called "The Hero of the Soviet Novel," to an attack on *Road to the Ocean* as an example of the way Soviet writers should *not* handle the fusion of the social and the human in Soviet experience.[17] Grinberg's principal objection is that Leonov seems dedicated to the pointless celebration of sorrow and suffering. Liza's path to understanding is a case in point. Because of his treatment of this and other situations the novel is denounced as

---

[17] I. I. Grinberg, "Geroi sovetskogo romana," in *Obraz bolshevika* (Leningrad, 1938), pp. 3–93. This book, an obvious response to the purge trials, is concerned with proving that loyalty to the Party of Lenin and Stalin is the noblest of *human* virtues. The qualities of Leonov's questioning individualist Bolshevik, Kurilov, prompt the speculation that if he had been real, he might well have ended in the dock with Bukharin, Radek, and others, from whose mold he seems, in some respects, to have been cast. Grinberg's definition of the monolithic Bolshevik "new man" contrasts sharply with Kurilov. It has the additional virtue of standing for hundreds of other such pronouncements. "The Bolshevik, the hero of our literature and of our epoch, is a man who is changing the world, an active man, strong-willed, whose actions are full of a high Leninist-Stalinist ideology, a man who grows in struggle, a man for whom the happiness of the whole people is a vital matter, the happiness of our beautiful and happy motherland, for the defense of which he has given, is giving, and is ready to give all his strength, abilities, and talents." *Ibid.*, p. 79.

"false."[18] But the implication is unmistakable that it is also harmful, and in this charge there is much that is instructive.

Kurilov has the "stamp of sorrow, the shadow of an undefined grief" on him. The young people in the novel are unhappy, too. As Leonov sees it, men's interest in their leaders is in the suffering the latter undergo in the name of the common cause. Even the Utopian future he sketches is marked not only by its joyousness, but by the purity and dignity of its grief.[19] All this is wrong, Grinberg insists, and partakes of a misguided "worship of sorrow," inherited from the diseased capitalist past. Leonov should be reminded that folklore from the most wretched periods is "optimistic" in its effects, and that the best of written literature from the past (he does not cite any) is distinguished by its message of hopeful joy about the human future. Leonov's misreading of the past has betrayed him into harmful practices:

All the harm the "soothers" and "glorifiers" of suffering bring is clearly seen.... It is necessary not to sing the sufferings, but to hate them, to destroy them, to struggle with them, it is necessary to show that the popular mass can deliver itself from them—and is delivering itself from them.[20]

The too frank recognition of suffering, quite apart from its celebration, might contradict the certain assurances that the removal of all known causes of human suffering was next on the Party agenda. Leonov had been misled, as had others, by relying too heavily on the classical past: "Some of our writers ... still think they can find the key to the new man by using the old traditions of the literature of

[18] Grinberg may be right in one sense. It is possible that Kurilov's extraordinary capacity for speculation and fantasy are a "falsification" of the literal human reality. It may be that by humanizing the Bolshevik, Leonov has sentimentalized him out of all recognition. It seems more likely that Leonov has dramatized his own idiosyncratic terms for making peace with the painful, disorderly revolutionary reality, and has projected them into the figure of the political commissar.

[19] Leonov, with Marx clearly in mind, says of the inhabitants of Ocean: "The people stood more erect, seemed more assured—whether because each one was aware of his neighbor at his side and did not fear him, or because the clean air of the new time did not contain the bacillus of falsehood.... I expected them to boast of the perfection of their social order and I should not have condemned their pride, but actually they took no notice of the social order. Here, man's natural state had at last been attained—he was free, he was not exploited, and he rejoiced in the work of hand and brain. But although everything was in reach—bread, work and fate itself—we often saw people with careworn faces. We understood that sadness dwelt among them, and that they, too, knew tragedy, though of a kind more worthy of man's dignity." Leonov, *Road to the Ocean*, p. 365.

[20] Grinberg, "Geroi sovetskogo romana," in *Obraz bolshevika*, p. 19.

suffering."[21] Leonov's sin is made perfectly clear, and his kinship with the tradition, as Grinberg remarks it, does him greater honor than his earnest but confused novel.

For the last time before 1941 we observe the two phases of Russian realism in conflict with each other; we may then draw a number of general conclusions about the all-out political attack on literature. Experience must be viewed optimistically at all times because the Party program offers nothing but joy, hope, and positive achievement. Suffering is irrelevant, uninteresting, and obstructive, whenever it is brought to public attention. In this way political agitation performs its final act of emasculation on the artist's traditional view of mankind. Let there be nothing but the solid joy of public successes. Let man be measured and known by this alone, and let him be ashamed of his broken heart—unless it can somehow be made to increase production. Whatever makes man suffer—his weakness, his illusions, his miscalculations, his progress toward senility and death, his commitments to unrealizable goals—is without efficacy and without general interest for that reason. Such is the burden of Grinberg's attack on Leonov's statement of the prevalence of human sorrow. Soviet man is not even to have his suffering as a measure of his joy. A blank-faced optimism, decreed by officialdom, is the only mood permitted him, encompassing his setbacks and illuminating his next day's triumph. Even his dreams must submit to the same kind of censorship. Kurilov's vision of Ocean is false and harmful when it is set against Klychkov's dream of controlling Chapaev or Davydov's dream of the happy kolkhoz meeting its production norms with the help of electric plows.[22]

Grinberg's attack on suffering is not the same as Chernyshevsky's repudiation of tragedy. But the same bleakly programmatic optimism and the same simplified, politicized view of man underlie it. Grinberg concludes his criticism of Leonov by quoting Gorky's definition of "complexity": "Complexity is the sad and deformed result of the ... disintegration of the 'soul' under the living conditions of petit-bourgeois society."[23] All else is clear, simple, unilinear, disciplined.

In the new Soviet Babbittry, suffering is simply inefficient, and when it does make itself felt it is seen as a phenomenon that can be reduced

[21] Ibid., p. 18.
[22] See ibid., p. 25; above, pp. 186–89 and p. 224.
[23] Quoted in ibid., p. 23.

or assimilated by ideological ministrations.[24] For the writer who is forced to abide by these definitions this is an irreparable loss. The image of man he is required to work with (and accept on his own terms) has a small, politically bound view of experience which is proof against all shocks. He cannot be dragged forth from his political casing and exposed to the temptations or trials of the human universe. He is limited, compact, smug, and unbreakable. The writer may acknowledge suffering but he may not show its effects. Deprived by his political masters of the "full awareness of suffering," he has lost a fundamental tool of definition and illumination.[25]

Leonov's world-view has one other important aspect: the heavy influence it shows of the humanist strain in the Marxian inheritance. The entire novel is set against the large perspective of men's progress toward wholeness, and the central dramatic situation of the inopportune revolutionary is translated into Soviet terms without major alteration from Marx's and Engels's correspondence with Lassalle.[26] The attack on *Road to the Ocean* by Grinberg and others suggests the growing estrangement in orthodox Soviet circles of the late thirties from those aspects of Marxism which bear most closely on imaginative literature.

III

The publication, section by section, of Alexei Tolstoy's *The Road to Calvary* spans the full era between the wars; the first volume appeared in 1920, the last in 1940. For this reason it is a laboratory specimen of the important changes in Soviet writing, most notably in the matter of the writer's control over his material. It may be that Alexei Tolstoy simply changed his mind, but it must be pointed out, also, that in

---

[24] A postwar Soviet novel had this to say on the question: "Great historical events are accompanied not only by general excitement, finding expression in elation or dejection of the human spirit, but also by suffering and deprivations far from the ordinary and beyond the power of man to prevent. For one who recognizes that the events taking place are part of the general movement of history, as well as for one who is consciously guiding the course of history, this suffering does not cease to exist any more than physical suffering ceases to exist when the disease causing it is known. But such a person reacts differently to the suffering than one who does not appreciate the historical significance of events, knowing only that life today is harder or easier, better or worse, than it was yesterday or will be tomorrow. For the former, the logic of history lends meaning to his suffering; for the latter, the suffering seems to have been imposed only to be suffered, as life itself seems to have been granted only to be lived." Konstantin Fedin, *No Ordinary Summer* (Moscow, 1950), pp. 9–10. The belief that there are political inoculations against the destructive effects of suffering is undoubtedly one of the positive sources of Soviet morale.

[25] See above, p. 84.   [26] See above, pp. 129–31.

doing so he has betrayed the vital interests of his profession and capitulated to the political invaders.

The novel has no hard center of moral purpose, nor any strong inner necessity of development. The mass of material might have been shaped to many ends; individual destinies, since they are not closely interlocked, might have been worked out in a number of ways. Only one thing is certain: the final solution Tolstoy did impose on the novel is extremely questionable, because it is introduced in the last third of the book in total disregard of what has gone before.

Despite its shortcomings, in its first two-thirds the work exhibits a number of the traditional attributes of the novel as an independent comment on experience. Tolstoy's interest in his material seems largely documentary. Thus, Part 1 stands as a vivid sketch of the St. Petersburg intelligentsia on the eve of the revolution; Part 2 is an attempt, like many others, to reflect the chaos of civil war itself. In his investigation on this not too profound level, Tolstoy has assembled a large group of sharply individualized characters, who embody, among other things, a number of contrasting attitudes toward the revolution. As an illustration of the variety of character and the honesty of presentation, consider Sapozhkov, the ex-Futurist, who fights on the Bolshevik side, but without illusions about the future: "The bourgeois world is vile, and it bores me stiff.... And if we win, the Communist world will be just as boring and grey, virtuous and boring."[27] In a disconnected speech he analyzes with pity and irony the dilemma of the pampered intelligentsia in the violence of civil war:

Our tragedy, my dear fellow, is that we, the Russian intelligentsia, have been cradled in the peaceful lap of serfdom, and the Revolution has terrified us out of our wits; it has given us a kind of vomiting of the brain. It's not right to frighten delicate people like that, is it? We used to sit in a quiet country arbor, with birds singing around us, and think to ourselves: Really, it would be very nice indeed to fix things up so that everybody would be happy.... What silly fools we are—serve the people indeed! It's a tragicomedy. We wept so much over the sufferings of the people that our tears ran dry. And when those tears were taken away we found we had nothing to live for.... It all comes from our gentle nurture; we're too squeamish, we can't understand without nice little books. ... In the nice little books the Revolution is described very attractively.... But our people simply deserts from the front, drowns officers, lynches the Commander-in-Chief, burns manors, hunts the merchants' wives on the railways, and digs their diamond ear-rings from all sorts of places under their petticoats. No, we say, we don't want to play with this nasty people,

27 Alexei Tolstoy, *Road to Calvary*, trans. Edith Bone (New York, 1946), p. 350.

there's nothing written in our books about such a people.... What's to be done? Shed an ocean of tears at home in our flats.... There's nothing left to live for. And so out of horror and disgust, some of us stick our heads under the pillow; others slink away to foreign parts; and those who are angriest take up arms.[28]

Sapozhkov is among the latter, though it is clear that he does so without hope, under a crushing and well-informed sense of his own and his country's doom. At the end of his tirade, Gymsa, the regimental security officer, enters and tells him, in a voice like the grinding of millstones, to keep quiet: "You've started your philosophical chatter again, your idiotic rigmaroles; hence I infer that you are drunk." Gymsa has just come from an execution. Sapozhkov says to him: "All right, I'm drunk. All right, shoot me!" To which Gymsa answers readily: "You know quite well I'd shoot you soon enough. If I don't it's because I take your fighting qualities into account."[29] Gymsa goes out a moment later and Sapozhkov mocks him:

Here's the whole secret: to give a straight answer to a straight question. ... Does God exist?—No. May one kill a man?—Yes. What is the immediate objective?—The world revolution.... Just like that, brother, without any high-falutin' emotions.[30]

If this episode reveals little else, it demonstrates that Tolstoy is still working from an independent vantage, from which he is prepared to consider ambiguities, to explore conflicting points of view, and to set humane considerations against political loyalties.

It is precisely this independence of judgment that is sacrificed in Part 3. The results are striking. Characters are interrupted in the more or less plausible drift of their careers, are hurried to improvised destinies, are hastily converted and refurbished as moral political beings. A highly questionable series of coincidences reunites separated lovers and scattered families.

That the blight of socialist realism is on the book becomes evident first when iron-jawed, clear-eyed Communists appear from nowhere and take over the direction of events. (Up to now the Communists have been indistinguishable as people from the other characters. These new men are of a higher moral order.) An imperturbable, pipe-smoking Stalin outwits Denikin at Tsaritsyn and crushes him, and the traitorous Trotsky issues orders which are properly disobeyed and unmasked.

[28] Ibid., pp. 351–52.   [29] Ibid., p. 353.   [30] Ibid., p. 355.

The disintegration of the entire fabric of the novel is clearest in the last ten pages. Two quite ordinary characters, who have been hurriedly made up on the model of positive heroes, are united with their wives in Moscow and troop off to a political meeting in the Bolshoi Theater. Before they go Roshchin, the converted White, talks intimately with his Katia:

Katia, our task is immense. We never dreamt that we would accomplish it. Remember, we often talked about it—the whirlpool of history, the destruction of great civilizations, ideas transformed into pitiful parodies of themselves—it all seemed so meaningless to us. Under the starched dress-shirt still the same hairy chest of the *pithecanthropos!* All lies! But now the veil has been torn from our eyes. All our past life was a lie and a crime! Russia has borne a new man and this man demands the right for men to live like men.... A dazzling light has fallen on the half-ruined arches of the past. Everything has a meaning; everything is governed by the same laws. We have found a goal, a goal every Red Army man knows. Katia, can you understand me a little better now? I wanted to give myself to you, all of myself, my darling, my heart, my beloved, my star.[31]

With such a political resolution fastened on the novel, it is not surprising that political rhetoric permeates even the lovemaking.

At the meeting Katia asks Roshchin: "Which is Lenin?" Roshchin answers:

Over there, in the black overcoat—he is writing quickly ... now he is throwing the note across the table. That's Lenin. And that thin one, with the black moustache, at the end of the row, is Stalin, the man who destroyed Denikin.[32]

Against this historical tableau, the two couples listen to a speech on the industrialized future and make their declaration of solidarity with Party, state, and the official blueprint of the future. Telegin, the engineer, engages in this dialogue with his wife:

Dashenka, I'm just wild to get to work again. If they build a network of electric power there is nothing we can't do. We have a devil of a lot of natural resources; once we get down to using them properly America can watch our smoke! ... We'll go to the Urals together, you and I.

Dasha takes it up:

Yes, we'll live in a log cabin with large windows, beautifully clean, with pearls of resin coming out of the wood. In the winter we'll have a huge fire flaming in the hearth.[33]

[31] *Ibid.*, p. 877.   [32] *Ibid.*, p. 884.   [33] *Ibid.*

Roshchin addresses his Katia in the same vein ("Can you see now how purposeful our efforts, all the blood we shed ... have become ... ? And this is happening here, in my country, and this is Russia!").[34] And there the novel ends. The banality of the situation has penetrated the emotions of the characters and the very texture of the language.[35]

We do not know whether Alexei Tolstoy made his surrender cynically or from conviction. In any case, he has provided a perfect case-study within the limits of a single work of the damages inflicted when rough political hands are laid on an imaginative work of more than average vitality. We may view this novel as marking one more instance of the conclusion of the long quarrel between the writers and the revolutionaries. The final consequences of Chernyshevsky's attempt to capture Russian realism are again made clear. Alexei Tolstoy's capitulation has this melancholy advantage.

IV

In our descent down the scale of literary value there is one more level we must plumb to bring the journey to an end. If we address some of the questions we have used before to one more novel, Ostrovsky's *The Making of a Hero*, we shall find, first of all, a sameness of pattern. But that is not all and that would not be reason enough for taking the trouble. We shall find, in addition, a progressive deterioration in insight and an increase in fictional disorganization that brings us finally to the level of juvenilia which Chernyshevsky first established as a norm in *What Is to Be Done?* We shall find final confirmation, too, of the close kinship between the heroes of the two novels, as psychological and moral beings. Finally, this novel set the standards for much of the writing that followed the Zhdanov blackout.

Pavel Korchagin, the hero of Ostrovsky's *The Making of a Hero*, carries the notion of the moral monolith to the limits of plausibility or beyond, to absurdity. To the extent that the novel is autobiographical, the author has sacrificed the essential remove from his protagonist

---

[34] *Ibid.*, pp. 884–85.

[35] It is comforting to discover that Grinberg is in complete disagreement with my evaluation of the two halves of the novel. He finds a lack of ideological clarity in the first two parts, and condemns them, therefore, as bad writing. In those sections of Part 3 which were published by the time he wrote his article, he found vast improvement on all levels. Grinberg, "Geroi sovetskogo romana," in *Obraz bolshevika*, pp. 80–86.

that enabled Sholokhov, for example, to exercise a measure of control over his Davydov, to trace the outline, at least, of his fallibilities, and to suggest that there are values in life not easily given up. For Korchagin the universe is completely demarcated into blacks and whites, according to his simplistic political morality. The bourgeois girl's lips twitch for cocaine; the Communists' eyes are clear and steady.

From the moment Korchagin joins the Komsomol, his only guiding principle is to serve: service is happiness; happiness, service. Since there are no other large choices, since there can be no question of moral fallibility, the only genuine tests he can undergo involve his capacity to stand physical suffering. Korchagin's body endures a severe beating in prison; in the civil war he incurs a hip wound, a head wound, a spinal wound, and a smashed knee; in addition, he contracts typhus, pneumonia, and rheumatic fever. When the cumulative effect of these afflictions proves to be paralysis and blindness, his "tempered" Bolshevik will responds to this ultimate challenge: he learns to become a writer and continues his life of service to the cause.

Korchagin's personal moral code is indistinguishable from the Party program. The habits of service and leadership in its name, we are led to believe, have become basic *character traits*. From this total absorption in Party work he derives whatever spiritual nourishment his intense if dehydrated nature requires. Thus powered, his actions are always successful (although it should be pointed out that the successes are never magically easy), whether he is tracking down a murderer on the frontier or discouraging kissing games among the youth. From his central fund of belief he, like Davydov and all the others, develops problem-solving virtues as required by the situation. He is endowed with technical skill, civic initiative, administrative subtlety, and military resourcefulness. As a leader he displays a range of qualities appropriate to the many roles he plays: patience, tact, indignation, courage, or, if the presence of the class enemy is sensed, intolerance and ruthlessness.

We must recall that we are always viewing Korchagin from within, as he justifies his own behavior to himself. No attention is paid to the likelihood that the people he manipulates or clashes with might regard him as a prig, a busybody, or a fanatic.[36] Since he is not seen at all

[36] An episode is revealing: "There was not much to learn, but these things were noted: Razvalikhin drinking and gathering all the rotters around him and keeping the better comrades out of things. Pavel reported all this to the Bureau. The other comrades ... were all for reprimanding Razvalikhin severely, when Pavel surprised them

from an outside vantage, we are only able to guess at the degree of the costs of his alienation from the rank-and-file members of the various communities he inhabits, or from the normal human experiences he has voluntarily forgone. We note, with a few exceptions, not the absence so much as the unimportance of friendship, love, or family ties. His personal attachments, such as they are, have an invariable political cast: they are with members of his own elite, or they are initiated, sustained, or ended on political grounds. In Korchagin's case, the question of rewards and costs must be changed to: What are the costs of *non*participation? As it happens, they are very nearly fatal. His deepest spiritual crisis is brought on by a doctor's decision that his multiple injuries have ended his usefulness to the Party. If he cannot serve it, life is without meaning and he has no alternative but to succumb to his wounds. But by overcoming the handicaps he wins through to a new kind of service, hence to a renewal of his life.

In this extraordinarily naive and incomplete human image the myth of the monolithic, functional, political man as it was first set forth in the nineteenth century has reached some kind of apotheosis. His author would have us believe that he has made the move from life as it is with its challenges, temptations, and ambiguities, to a fabricated, self-contained universe of ideology, and anchored himself within it. Doctrine has replaced life.[37] His activist political faith "permeates" his entire being as it does with Insarov in Turgenev's *On the Eve*, and like him, if he is denied participation in his cause, he will die. In the same way, Rakhmetov's bed of nails (in Chernyshevsky's *What Is to Be Done?*) forecasts Korchagin's terrible physical battering. By accepting the total commitment of the totally political man, Korchagin has placed himself beyond the last frontier of the human habitat. He does not, like Kurilov, accept death as a release from duty, but fights against it as an inexplicable nuisance. Both men are contemporaries and members of the same Party, but beyond that a world separates them. Their respective situations measure the gap between the old

---

by saying: 'I am for expelling him without the right to apply for membership again.' Everybody thought this much too severe, but Pavel said again: 'This scoundrel must be expelled.' " (Nikolai Ostrovsky, *The Making of a Hero*, New York, 1937, pp. 377–78.) He was.

[37] Consider this passage: "He was in a constant hurry to *live*; not only in a hurry himself, but anxious to urge others on too. . . . Often a light could be seen in his window late into the night, and people there gathered round a table—reading and studying. In two years they had worked through the third volume of *Capital*, and had gained an understanding of the delicate mechanics of capitalist exploitation." *Ibid.*, p. 377.

Bolshevik with his memory of other standards and other worlds, and the new Stalinist man who knows nothing but what he needs to know.

V

With this novel the work of the literary investigator would seem to end. Whenever Soviet writing descends to this level it is more usefully investigated by social scientists or propaganda analysts. If we turn over this kind of writing to them, certain tentative conclusions about the angle of refraction at which reality is reflected, about the inner workings of the literary mechanism, and about literature's function in times of social crisis may be useful. The hero, it may be assumed, will be a Party member on the level of tactical command, that is, where actual day-to-day leadership is exercised. The problem he is ordered to solve will doubtless be a widespread one, and the description of the problem will be a more or less frank account of some point of friction, breakdown, or disorganization in the social or economic structure. Or, if it is a story of new construction, the peculiar problems of terrain, technology, etc., will be carefully set forth.

Beginning on this level of *is*, the hero, by a process of engineering—human, technological, or administrative—lifts the entire situation to the level of *should be* and provides in that process minute instructions for the solution of similar problems. In addition to instruction there will be inspiration and the assurance of success provided everybody does what he should. In this last transaction with the reader, there is a kind of primitive process of wish fulfillment, as in the savage's war dance in which the imagined victory of the dance strengthens him for the next day's battle. But the Soviet citizen is not given magic assurances. His active, conscious, dedicated participation is an indispensable ingredient in the success of the project. The Soviet fictional dream does not endow him with false fantasies of his strength, but a moral blueprint accompanied by detailed instructions for its use.

The above description is a rough summary of the lowest level of Soviet writing as it existed on the agitational level in the days of RAPP, and as it has dominated the postwar years. It is a literature entirely shaped by didactic needs. And it is a literature which, I should say, is characteristic of a certain kind of crisis in Soviet life—not the crisis of event, such as the Nazi invasion, but the induced crisis or the crisis of anticipation in which invisible future menaces, imagined or real, are evoked to drive men to work. The latter is a time of the greatest constriction, regimentation, and coercion.[38] And it is reflected in the kind of fictional design I have just described. The hero, in this context, can be read as a kind of temperature gauge measuring the degree of crisis. When the crisis is considered greatest he will tend to be most infallible, most monolithic, most parental, most mythic, and most closely identified with the Party. As and if the crisis eases we may expect to see him resume more humane dimensions, although his quotient of virtue will probably be unacceptably high and unreal for Western readers for an indefinite period.

More rewarding here than a cataloguing of the virtues and vices of the positive hero, it seems to me, is a broad characterization of him as an *alienated* man, as that concept has been communicated by the great writers of the Russian past. There is a pathos in the fact that a tradition which has since its inception called for wholehearted engagement in history should play itself out with heroes who are disengaged from life, cut off even from a recognition of their own suffering. Soviet writers, with the few exceptions we have noted, will not, or are not permitted to, accord him that recognition.

The positive hero, unlike the estranged, "superfluous," or alienated man of the nineteenth century, is not rejected by, or denied participation in, society. The Soviet hero is promised fulfillment only through his acceptance of the institutions and values of his status quo. In the very act of conformity significant losses are registered.

He is, first of all, entirely politicalized, with his needs and aspirations defined by his political allegiances. Although he is expected to respond with *inner* enthusiasm to grandiose public goals, the real locus of judgment in these matters is outside his own conscience. He makes decisions, so to speak, but no choices. He lives in a world of rationalized deprivations, subsisting on reduced rations of love, friendship, and family happiness because, he is always told, of the terrible urgencies besetting his community. Finally, he is manipulated from

[38] Oddly enough, this is not necessarily so in wartime, when the enemy is tangibly present on Soviet soil and every blow against him is a socially useful act. The literature reflects this *relaxation* of attitude and exhibits a greater concern with the heroism and the human problems of the humble, non-Party citizens. There is no large body of war literature, partly because there was little time to write during the war, and partly because Zhdanovism ruled it out shortly after the war. But novels like Simonov's *Days and Nights*, Panova's *Train*, or Leonov's *Chariot of Wrath* exhibit a more than minimal concern with the problems of being human, and a consequent diminution of the political strain. Nation, army, state, and people are the objects of primary allegiance, not the Party.

above and in turn manipulates those beneath him: he lives in a hierarchy of these relationships.

Is his "incompleteness" envisioned as eternal? History will give the actual answer, of course, but we should note that the framers of the old and the new versions of his moral code did expect an end to his estrangement. The children, Chernyshevsky said, were to grow up in their parents' image. Few could belong to Rakhmetov's elite which would soon disappear, but, on a lower level, the number of new men was expected to increase by arithmetic progression, through the power of example, until they composed the whole population.[39] The extension of the Leninist ethic since 1930 to all levels of the population through every channel of communication seems to contemplate the same eventual reunion of the leaders and the led. Obviously, this "solution" raises additional troubling problems: the leaders, the exemplars, it should be remembered, are interim men. The life of the interim man has been long—it is a century since he was first conceived, more than fifty years since he inherited the Russian earth—but, in theory, at least, it is not expected to last forever. And if it ends, one wonders, will anyone remember how to live, as Marx hoped men would, as a "total man" in his full "human reality," "seeing, hearing, smelling, tasting, feeling, thinking, contemplating, willing, acting, loving"?[40] Or will the alienation of the incomplete, inopportune socialist man have become universalized? "Too long a sacrifice," as Yeats said in "Easter 1916," "can make a stone of the heart. / O when may it suffice?"

The pathos of the positive hero, as we have said, is that he does not know his sacrifice. Ostrovsky's novel *The Making of a Hero*, which with Chernyshevsky's *What Is to Be Done?* and Gorky's *Mother*, is recognized as a major work in the tradition, provides us with a classic instance. Ostrovsky's hero, Pavel Korchagin, is often linked with Rakhmetov and Vlasov, and he stands before us still as the most formulaic example of the new Soviet man, heading the company of latter-day heroes. By the same token he presents himself to us as the apotheosis of the politicalized man and the clearest example of the official literary treatment of the Communist "emasculate." The writer's attitude toward his hero's wound is central in the whole aesthetic tradition we have explored. Should it be celebrated, confronted, as-

---

[39] See *Chto delat?* (Moscow, 1947), pp. 55–56 and 191.
[40] Karl Marx and Friedrich Engels, *Literature and Art* (New York, 1947), p. 61.

similated, deprecated, concealed, or denied? If the governing type is Ostrovsky's hero, and not Sholokhov's or Leonov's, the question is closed. The fact that we know so much of the aridity of Korchagin's life suggests that Ostrovsky does not even know of his hero's deprivations. His identification with him is so thorough (in this case the novel is autobiographical) that the last pretense of fiction has evaporated. The hero's blindness coincides with the author's. It is as if we had been given a nihilist's view of Bazarov, or an atheist's view of Ivan Karamazov. The emasculated Myshkin goes mad, but the Soviet saint writes with abandoned admiration about himself.

The image of the hero as it has been cast from Belinsky to Zhdanov and the treatment of that image in literature have falsified the very values which the new man and the new literature were supposed to realize. The aesthetic of the radicals is self-defeating, if indeed it is not a contradiction in terms, when considered in the light of the tradition we have examined. It leads finally to the incomplete portraiture of incomplete men.

PART FOUR

Rebuttal III: The Dissident Vision

Zhdanov's freeze in 1946 made the simplicities of Ostrovsky legislative for all Soviet writing long after Stalin's death in 1953. The spokesmen for Thaw I and Thaw II rose to challenge the Zhdanov orthodoxy, which bent but never broke, recomposing itself in each instance with restatements, superficially changed, of the same musclebound doctrine. The forces of change advanced cautiously into undefended ground, and then were driven back when they approached some invisible boundary of the impermissible.

In "On Socialist Realism" Andrei Sinyavsky has made sport of all the clichés of the travesty-literature Zhdanovism nourished after the war. When he finds the climactic absurdity of this kind of writing in Leonov's *Russian Forest* (1953), he measures for us the decline of the promise still visible in *Road to the Ocean* (1935). Sinyavsky quotes Leonov's positive heroine, a brave girl pretending to collaborate with the Germans in World War II, who suddenly forgets her mission and throws off her impersonation: "I am a girl of my time.... Maybe just an ordinary girl, but I am the world's tomorrow.... Get up and show me where Soviet girls are shot!"[1] "We have here," Sinyavsky notes, "the straight and immutable determination of the positive hero raised ... to the second power.... Under no circumstances, even to further his task, does the positive hero dare so much as to look nega-

---

[1] Abram Tertz [pseud.], *"The Trial Begins" and "On Socialist Realism,"* trans. Max Hayward ("Trial") and George Dennis ("Realism") (New York, 1965), p. 179; *Fantasticheskii mir Abrama Tertsa* (New York, 1966), p. 422.

tive."[2] Has an excess of virtue led to self-defeat? Not exactly. Another Soviet citizen of much shakier loyalty, who is present at the interrogation, is galvanized into action by the purity of her example, shoots the German officer and sets her free. *Deus ex dogmate!* Clearly Leonov's earlier venturing toward tragedy has calcified into social allegory.

Other writers, from a safer, more "practical" position than Sinyavsky's, may also have sensed the bankruptcy of the positive hero. A maturing public may finally have rejected folkloric manipulation. In any case, the call for positive heroes is no longer the ultimate slogan of the socialist realists. In dropping the virtuous man, they might have recalled Gogol's weary words in *Dead Souls*:

> It's time at last to give the poor virtuous man a rest.... Because they have turned him into a horse, and there's no writer who hasn't ridden him, goading him with a knout and whatever comes to hand, because there isn't a shadow of virtue left, only skin and bones, because the virtuous man is no longer respected.[3]

At an optimistic moment in 1966, when *Cancer Ward* seemed close to publication, one critic saw a change—a succession in the line of heroes which would have connected the future with the best in the past. Speaking in Solzhenitsyn's presence at a Moscow writers' meeting, A. Borshchagovsky said:

> There is taking place an infinitely important inquiry into the nature of man as he is and not as he might be constructed.
>
> All of this we find in *Cancer Ward*. Remember how we kept on struggling everlastingly with the problem of the "positive hero" which really turned into a sort of curse.[4]

Cancer Ward was denied publication, and the exhausted, accursed man of virtue has had no official successor. His passing should be noted here, and his formal obituary deferred to some future history of literary mistakes. In any case, his disappearance represents no more than a tactical shift. Though he served as the keystone of a literary position for a century, his removal has not demolished the argument that created him. The official critics still excoriate his opposite number, the failed, alienated, superfluous or tragic hero; still call for a

---

2 "The Trial Begins," pp. 179–80; *Fantasticheskii*, p. 422.

3 N. V. Gogol, *Sobranie sochinenii v shesti tomakh* (Moscow, 1959), 5: 234.

4 *Solzhenitsyn: A Documentary Record*, ed. Leopold Labedz (New York, 1971), p. 62.

literature that cements the reader's loyalty to the benign present, to the still better future, and to the only means for getting from one to the other—Party leadership. And they increasingly deploy their resources to suppress, by argument or otherwise, the burgeoning literature of heresy. In pursuit of continuity as conflict, from Belinsky's later years to the present, I do not think the subtraction of the virtuous hero has altered the fundamental positions of the antagonists. The radical social determinist still attacks the free imagination; total politics still asserts total control over art.

Though doctrine finally prevailed in all tests of strength, the literary product of the thaws distinguished itself clearly from the official writing in its search for subject matter, forms, and language beyond the reach of politics. Apart from the explosion of interest in poetry, a modest corpus of prose works, largely in the shorter forms, aroused interest both there and here. Aksenov restored the genuine Russian comic voice; Kazakov worked in a Chekhovian mode of human disclosure; Tendriakov posed difficult moral problems outside official categories of thought. And there were others—Nekrasov, Nagibin, Bondarev. It was a movement, small in scope, moderate in promise, as admirable in intention as it was cautious in execution. These writers sometimes raised implicit questions which received fully amplified and explicit expression only in the greater literature of their underground contemporaries. But with this considerable achievement it did not establish a viable precedent, or win the right to grow and develop. One tends to speak of it in the past tense; most of its writers have fallen silent. The impermanence of the movement testifies to the transience of all the thaws, suggesting that they were never correctly read as a liberal trend, but are better understood as the result of bureaucratic decisions to loosen the screws in order to increase the quantity and elevate the quality of a failing literary "product." When the writers began to say the unsayable, and to move toward the heretical statements that issued from the underground, the screws were quickly retightened, editors were fired, resolutions were passed, and the *status quo* restored. At no time was the *legal* right of a free literature to exist seriously considered on any official agenda. The opposition between directed and undirected writing is absolute, I would conclude, not to be resolved by compromise, "liberal" measures, or the licensed relaxation of orthodox tenets. Solzhenitsyn has put it starkly:

"In the thirties, forties and fifties we had *no* literature. Because without *all* the truth there is no literature."[5]

Some Western scholars have proposed a theory of erosion, maintaining that the rigidities of a defunct doctrine will quietly give way under the pressures of active minds and forceful imaginations. There is some evidence to support this in literary commentary, particularly in scholarship, but the weakness of the doctrine has not inhibited the apparatus of physical oppression when the creative process itself is in question. It seems clear that tactical tolerance is not tolerance at all, that intellectual fatigue should not be taken for the weakening of political purpose, which summons the police when slogans fail.

Yet at certain euphoric moments the thaws seemed to promise greater and greater—perhaps total—freedom for all writers. Pasternak and Solzhenitsyn must have entertained the optimistic notion that their novels were a legitimate extension of the thaws when they submitted them for legal publication in the Soviet Union. There was considerable discussion in each case, much of it made public in the form of correspondence between editor and author, or transcripts of literary meetings. The successive rejections of these manuscripts (*One Day in the Life of Ivan Denisovich* is unique because of Khrushchev's imperial intervention in its behalf) have an accumulated significance. The rejected literature, driven underground by these decisions and forced into illegal channels to find its way to daylight, made it possible to draw the line between the permitted and the forbidden—the renewed battle line, in fact, between the two antagonistic forces of the Russian prose tradition. The outlawed works express an unlimited interrogation of the Soviet world's intellectual foundations with literary resources—breadth of thematic range, intensity of moral concern, complexity of structure, freshness of tone, language, and imagery —which make it clear we are listening to the full orchestral scoring of the great Russian writing. Political heresy and artistic mastery need not conjoin—indeed seldom do under the eye of eternity—but the Soviet bureaucrats' ban (quite right according to *their* lights) compels and confirms this special fusion of qualities in contemporary Russian cultural life.

[5] A. Solzhenitsyn, *Arkhipelag Gulag*, 3–4 (Paris, 1973): 619.

CHAPTER 14

Pasternak: "An Inward Music"

Pasternak's *Doctor Zhivago* is the first important work of the legal and illegal literary renaissance that followed Stalin's death in 1953. It was announced for publication in the USSR in 1954, and then banned after prolonged discussions in the Writers' Union. Pasternak has explored a traditional problem in the history of the Soviet novel— the nature and consequences of the October Revolution. His heretical conclusions on this score undoubtedly caused the novel's rejection.[1]

When Pasternak sent the manuscript abroad for publication he invoked an important tradition in Russian writing, that of the "smuggled" text, published abroad. Mere place of publication may seem remote from serious critical concerns, and the charge of heresy which propelled *Doctor Zhivago* and the principal works of Solzhenitsyn and Sinyavsky across their native boundaries threatens to limit criticism of the texts to political analysis. And yet, heresy—generated out of the novel's moral critique of the political system—is central to any reading of these works which would illuminate their design as well as their meaning. Read, as I propose, with close attention to the local meanings of heresy, read as we can guess Pasternak meant his contemporaries to read it, *Doctor Zhivago* nevertheless remains available for more timeless readings, as arcane religious utterance—as a gloss

---

[1] The rejection was blessed by several important literary figures. At a meeting of Moscow writers in October 1958, *Doctor Zhivago* was described as an "apologia for betrayal," and a resolution was passed asking the government to deprive Pasternak of Soviet citizenship, in effect, to excommunicate him. "Judgement on Pasternak," *Survey,* July 1966, pp. 134–63.

on the Book of Revelations, perhaps—or as a forest of coded symbols or a parable of the eternal situation of the artist.[2] My eye-level reading discloses a structural completeness and a related complexity of statement, which may be enriched by other readings but deserves full demonstration, I think, on intentional, expository, and didactic writer-to-reader grounds. I have taken my text from Pasternak's remark in an interview: "It seemed to me that it was my duty to make a statement about my epoch."[3] The elucidation of this statement, it seems to me, should precede other kinds of analysis.

Two vast constellations of ideas, attitudes, and values—intellectual, moral, and aesthetic—come into mortal conflict. One may be called the ethos of Revolution, the other the continuum of Life. At first these bodies of thought, or ways of taking experience, coexist more or less harmoniously in Zhivago's mind. As war and revolution progress, they become disengaged when Zhivago pursues a lonely personal existence, beyond the reach of historical events. In the novel's denouement they become re-engaged when the revolution, an anonymous menacing force, pursues and crushes Zhivago, who in his own eccentric person has come to represent the forces of life. Pasternak then attempts a counter-enveloping movement in the complex epilogue, in the rhapsodic words Lara utters over Zhivago's corpse, in the eventual coming to maturity—and to an understanding of what Zhivago stood for—of Zhivago's two lifelong friends after World War II, and in their faint premonition that a new freedom is to be felt in the air of Mos-

---

[2] I have not tried—or known how—to come to terms with Pasternak's cryptic remark in the novel, and possibly referring *to* it: "All great genuine art resembles and continues the Revelation of Saint John" (unless he is simply referring to the work of art as an epiphany, an exposing of concealed meanings). Mary and Paul Rowlands in *Pasternak's Doctor Zhivago* (Carbondale, Ill., 1967) have tried very hard, and failed, I think, but sometimes in a very fruitful way. In their Jungian evocation of myth and archetype and the racial unconscious, they have sought to show that it is a novel of "symbolic realism." Some of their discoveries are very persuasive, but many others are absurd, and the buried novel they claim to unearth is a rigid allegory about Russia and the Antichrist, far less compelling than the novel about recognizable men in recognizable history. Pasternak warned against this kind of symbol-hungry reading of his work: "I used religious symbolisms to give warmth to the book. Now some critics have become so wrapped up in those symbols—which are put in the book the way stoves go into a house, to warm it up—that they would like me to commit myself and climb into the stove." Quoted in Olga Carlisle, *Poets on Street Corners* (New York, 1968), p. 84. The Rowlands, it seems to me, have mistaken Pasternak's intentions: what is meant to illustrate a human, historical fact—a metaphor—they take as a statement of personal belief in deeper meanings which the represented circumstance symbolizes. Thus, the story of Christ and the Magdalene must be read as a vividly compressed way of describing the widening freedom of the human personality since the fall of Rome, not (as the Rowlands would have it) as a profession of faith in a supernatural causal process, attributable to the divine powers of Jesus.

[3] Carlisle, *Poets on Street Corners*, p. 88.

cow. By refusing publication, the Soviet government attempted a final extraliterary countermovement, which failed when the novel was published abroad and then filtered back into the USSR illegally.

The public confrontations in the novel do not present clear choices to Zhivago. No acceptable *political* alternative is ever visible to him. There are decent men among the Whites, but the grotesquely unjust social order they represent defends itself by terror and deceit, and generates its Bolshevik executioner in its own moral likeness. Zhivago's vision of the wholly lived life transcends the claims of all factions and the savage meaningless wars they fight among themselves. He stands apart from this struggle, but later, as the revolution gains the upper hand, he cannot avoid total engagement in the deeper conflict between the new politics and life itself, a conflict which impinges on language, art, morality, religion, theories of history, and culture in the broadest sense: all the ceremonies, institutions, and explanations men devise to ease their earthly situation. Zhivago defines and defends his view of these entities as he discovers that the revolution corrupts or destroys some aspects of each, ignores others, and proposes spurious substitutes for still others. Nothing of the revolution's total program except its initial grievances and its long-term aspirations—its ends—remains valid for him. The fanatical actions and doctrines that brought the revolution to power—its means—will apparently endure indefinitely, certainly beyond the span of his life. The interim men, who do not contemplate their own passing, will carry out their arrogant and misguided plans, as he sees it, at the expense of most of civilization's legacy. Alone, embattled and unknown, he must stand and fight.

His vision of the good life, derived from Christian mythology, is presented early in the novel. It recedes under the flood of historical and personal experiences in the novel's center, and then reappears, restated and amplified in the concluding chapters. Zhivago's mentor, his Uncle Nikolai, has devised a strange theory of history, which marks off stages as Marxism does, but defines them in wholly different ways. Modern history began with the example of Christ's life, miraculously acted out in the outworn Roman stage of history, "that tasteless heap of gold and marble,"[4] when men lived in coercive, conformist national units. Christ's example set man free as a moral being, made him "at home in history" (10, *10*), which Zhivago perceives as the "con-

---

[4] Boris Pasternak, *Doctor Zhivago*, trans. Max Hayward, Manya Harari, and Bernard Guilbert Guerney (New York, 1958), p. 43; Boris Pasternak, *Doctor Zhivago* (Ann Arbor, Mich., 1958), p. 44. References to these two editions hereafter are made in the text thus (43, *44*). I have changed the translation on several occasions.

tinuum of human effort," as "another universe, made by man with the help of time and memory in answer to the challenge of death" (66, 66). The perpetually mysterious adventure of mortality, "the riddle of life and death" (65, 65), repeats itself endlessly through time as the essential process of history, analogous, Zhivago decides at the novel's end, to the process of organic change in the vegetable kingdom. History is the intuited and continuing record of human experience, of how it feels to be human, in the largest of all realms: "Life, one, immense, identical throughout its innumerable combinations and transformations, fills the universe" (67, 68).

When its immensity and wholeness are experienced, the individual knows communion—akin to Walt Whitman's "knit of identity"—with true and immanent being, manifest most often in the details of ordinary life, of home and family, of street scenes, of the rhythm of weather and the cycle of the seasons. Life's immanent radiance and beauty are the subject matter of poetry, the recorded magic of ordinary existence: "Poetry is the prose of life." The poet, Zhivago, will apprehend this magic in the daily continuum of existence and record it in a language which will "call everything by its right name"; the words of this language, "the prose of life," will constitute poetic utterance, capturing the "wild enchantment of life" (75, 76), which is the chief end of Lara's existence. Art's involvement with being puts it in constant touch with death's riddle; art is a meditation on death out of which it creates new life. Art, then, touches the essence of man's involvement in the world; the beauty it discovers everywhere—even in the mutilated corpses Zhivago encounters in his medical work—answers the deepest human needs.

A doctrine which denies beauty, corrupts language, disfigures art and disconnects it from its roots is anti-human. Pasternak is close to his classical predecessors in setting a view of human nature resting on feeling and imagination against a schematic materialist ideology, or in this case, against the acting out of the ideology's inner potential in revolution and civil war.

Zhivago comes to this understanding in the course of the novel— the process of learning defines its central movement—as he is battered by public and private calamities. In the beginning, the coming revolution appears as a benevolent force, a healing wind, containing no hint of menace for his sense of himself in the world. Sympathetic characters support the revolutionary cause; a cavalry attack on unarmed demonstrators leaves no doubts about the moral savagery of the

Tsarist regime. Yet the revolution is not central in the complicated introductions of theme, idea, and character in the early chapters. None of the major characters is directly involved in politics; the revolution enters their lives from outside, an event to be observed and then endured, as is the war that precedes it.

Pasternak does not show Russian participation in World War I as a valued patriotic experience, as Solzhenitsyn will in *August 1914*. From Zhivago's doctor's-eye view we see it as a cataclysm of violence made peculiarly horrible by the mutilation the new weapons inflict. Zhivago notices two important signs of the corruption that accompanies violence in these war years: the decay of language in its public uses; and the disintegration of culture, of that shelter of values and institutions which make personal life possible. He analyzes two kinds of war journalism. One, written under the false mythology of the "people's soul," is characterized by "linguistic graphomania" and "verbal incontinence"; it is "a new version of Dahl[5] and just as bogus" (121, *123*). The other affects an impersonality of statement, a bare recital of facts cut off from human agency. Zhivago comments: "You can never say something meaningful by accumulating absurdities in your notebook;... facts don't exist until man puts into them something of his own, a bit of free human genius—of myth [*skazka*]" (121, *124*). These two war-bred affectations deprive language of its miraculous capacity to record experience. The disintegration of culture is a parallel process, begun in the war and accelerated by the revolution and civil war. Lara first feels its disorienting effect on the eve of the revolution:

> She had noticed a sharp change around her recently. Before, there had been obligations of all kinds, sacred duties—your duty to your country, to the army, to society. But now that the war was lost (and that was the misfortune at the bottom of all the rest) nothing was sacred any more.
> Everything had changed suddenly—the tone, the air; you didn't know what to think, whom to listen to. As if all your life you had been led by the hand like a small child and suddenly you were on your own, you had to learn to walk by yourself.... At such a time you felt the need of committing yourself to something absolute—life or truth or beauty—of being ruled by it in place of the man-made rules that had been discarded. (127, *129*)

Lara will find her absolute by being the mother of her daughter. If the death of a culture is like the loss of a parent, Lara will reconstruct

---

[5] V. I. Dahl, the nineteenth-century Russian lexicographer and folklorist.

that basic cellular matrix, the family, as a defense against chaos and a means of keeping her personal integrity. This Tolstoyan idea becomes an overreaching theme in the novel, the celebration of domesticity—of home and family as a way of preserving access to "life or truth or beauty."

II

Zhivago, an army surgeon, welcomes the first revolution in February because it promises an end to bloodletting. The further promise of the revolution is, at this moment, perfectly fused with his personal values. Early in their relationship, Zhivago tells Lara (while she, characteristically, irons) what the revolution means to him:

The war was an artificial break in life—as if life could be put off for a time—what nonsense! The revolution broke out willy-nilly, like a sigh suppressed too long. Everyone was revived, reborn, changed, transformed. You might say that everyone has been through two revolutions—his own personal revolution as well as the general one. It seems to me that socialism is the sea, and all these separate streams, these private, individual revolutions, are flowing into it—the sea of life, the sea of spontaneity. I said life, but I mean life as you see it in a great picture, transformed by genius, creatively enriched. Only now people have decided to experience it not in books and pictures but in themselves, not as an abstraction but in practice. (146–47, *148*)

This synthesis of the personal and the general, of life and history, of life and art, of Zhivago's and the nation's destinies remains fixed in his mind for a long time. Zhivago experiences a similar benign fusion in direct poetic terms, typical of Pasternak's own idiom as poet: "stars and trees meet and converse, flowers talk philosophy at night, stone houses hold meetings" (146, *148*). Man and nature commune by exchanging roles in an atmosphere of euphoria. But these moments of affirmation are punctuated by acts of violence, in a sinister rhythm, here and throughout the novel. In the Ukrainian town where Zhivago and Lara sense the promise of the February Revolution, the dapper young representative of the Provisional Government is shot down like an animal. Despite warnings against the foolhardiness of doing so, he has addressed a body of mutinous troops in the nearby forest. His reception is hostile, and as he leaves, alone, he is pursued by a group of faceless riflemen. In a final act of courage he climbs on a rain barrel to confront his pursuers but is brought down by an anonymous shot and falls, ludicrously, into the barrel. Much later, we learn that the shot was fired by Palykh, a member of the Bolshevik partisan band which kidnaps Zhivago and forces him to serve as the unit's surgeon. Palykh recalls this act as his initiation into a career of random killing, which has made him into an incarnation of the crazed violence released by the revolution. Palykh's first kill strikes Zhivago as ominous, but it does not yet threaten the synthesis of attitudes and perceptions which sanctions his loyalty to the revolution; when Zhivago learns of the final stages of Palykh's disintegration with the forest partisans, he experiences his final and complete alienation from the revolution.

His confidence in the future holds fast against other disturbing phenomena. With the ascendancy of radical politics between February and October, he notes the further deterioration of language, contrasting revolutionary speeches with "the yeast of life." Discussions of political strategy are expressed "in a torrent of words, superfluous, utterly false, murky, profoundly alien to life itself." Zhivago is ready to abandon language altogether:

Oh, how one wishes sometimes to escape from the meaningless dullness of human eloquence, from all those sublime phrases, to take refuge in nature, apparently so inarticulate, or in the wordlessness of grinding labor, of sound sleep, of true music, or of a human understanding rendered speechless by emotion. (139, *141*)

Later, in Moscow, he diagnoses abstractness born of revolutionary politics as another threat to the integrity of language: firewood has become "fuel supply," food, "alimentation." In these days of "the triumph of materialism," "matter has become a concept" (184, *186–87*).[6]

Zhivago is even more disturbed by the threat to morality and culture he senses in the climate of violence, generated equally in the theories of intellectuals and the atavisms of the people. When Zhivago leaves the provinces for Moscow, he shares a railway compartment with Pogorevshikh, a rich, intellectual dilettante who has been duck-hunting in the country. He is a disciple of the nineteenth-century anarchists, a modern apostle of universal destruction. An extremist in all things, his frivolity and shallowness remind Zhivago of Piotr Ver-

---

[6] Here Pasternak is touching on a question raised by other dissident writers: Marxist materialism conceals an idealist or theological core. As it changes from a radical critique to a coercive orthodoxy, it replaces concreteness with abstractions, and its language turns from particulars to essences.

hovensky, Dostoevsky's revolutionary monster in *The Possessed*.[7] However shallow and imitative his mind, his views trouble Zhivago, who longs, he says, for a return to peace and order. "That's naive," Pogorevshikh replies:

What you call disorder is just as normal a state of things as the order you're so keen about. All this destruction—it's a natural and preliminary stage of a broad, creative plan. Society has not distintegrated sufficiently. It must fall to pieces completely, then a genuinely revolutionary government will put the pieces together and build on completely new foundations. (164, *166*)

To counter his distaste, Zhivago, who is returning home to his wife and child after years of war, invokes here for the first time that private domestic world which will later become his fortress against revolutionary turmoil:

Three years of changes, moves, uncertainties, upheavals; the war, the revolution; scenes of destruction, scenes of death, shelling, blown-up bridges, fires, ruins—all this turned suddenly into a huge, empty, meaningless space. The first real event since the long interruption was this headspinning trip in the train, approaching his home, which was intact, which still existed, and in which every stone was dear to him. This was real life, authentic experience, the actual goal of all quests, this was what art aimed at—homecoming, return to one's family, to oneself, to true existence. (164, *167*)

Though the contrary forces are increasingly visible to Zhivago, the synthesis in his mind of revolution and life has not yet fallen apart. At a gathering of his oldest friends, most of them members of the intelligentsia, Zhivago defines the arrangement of elements in his mind in the late summer of 1917. He senses his growing separation from his friends, who have changed radically and modishly under the pressure of events. There is a terrible falseness in these changes, an intellectual irresponsibility which prompts Zhivago to conclude that the traditional Russian intelligentsia has ceased to exist, has, in effect, evaporated into idle foolishness. While the group dines luxuriously on vodka and wild duck (supplied by the nihilist Zhivago has

[7] Verhovensky is a reconstituted portrait of the historical figure Sergei Nechaev, who symbolizes for Russians of almost any persuasion the ultimate perversion of the revolutionary ethos. Solzhenitsyn, in his Nobel Prize speech in 1972, traced all the violence loose in the modern world back to that period: "Dostoevsky's 'Devils' who seemed a provincial nightmare of the last century ... are crawling through the whole world, including countries where they could not even have been imagined; the hijacking of airplanes, seizure of hostages, explosions and conflagrations ... signal their determination to ... annihilate civilization." *New York Times*, October 7, 1972.

met on the train), he takes note of their individual responses to the revolution. His childhood friend Misha Gordon asks light-mindedly: "Isn't it amusing?" Dudorov, a young scholar, has turned out fashionable books on Ivan the Terrible and Saint-Just, the most fanatical figure in the French Revolution. A woman talks fatuously about the virtues of the common people. Even Uncle Nikolai, his intellectual mentor, has become Bolshevized, welcoming the revolutionary effort to "get to the foundations" at whatever cost. Zhivago himself responds ambivalently in a drunken speech to the talk of his friends and to the historical moment. He perceives the revolution, however benign its ultimate promise, as a continuation of the bloodbath begun in the war, a flood of violence which will engulf everybody, including himself, until "killing and dying" will seem to be all that is going on. But it is useless to ask why such sacrifices are called for, and how such "tremendous" events take place: "What is truly great is without beginning, like the universe." For those who survive, the results will be benign; even if life and revolution have been split apart at this historical moment, they will be rejoined:

I too think that Russia is destined to become the first socialist state since the beginning of the world. When this comes to pass, the event will stun us for a long time, and after awakening we shall have lost half our memories forever. We'll have forgotten what came first and what followed, and we won't look for explanations of the unheard-of. The new order of things will be all around us and as familiar to us as the woods on the horizon or the clouds over our heads. There will be nothing else left. (182, *185*)

Revolution will have the authenticity of earth and sky, but at a cost—loss of memory, through shock, of how it came to be. This prophecy about Russian socialism may still be operative when its new "natural" era is faintly promised in the novel's final paragraph, even though Zhivago does not live to see it. It is possible that the novel's survival into that better time (outliving its hero and its author) is intended to correct for that amnesia, to remind people how bad it was for the blighted generations before life finally fused with the new order, the prerequisites for civilization with the institutions of the social system.

When the guests have left, a storm "clears the dusty, smoke-filled room. Suddenly the element of life became distinguishable, as apprehensible as electric currents, air and water, desire for happiness, earth, sky." For a moment Zhivago has sensed the life-giving alternative to the wordy attitudinizing of the intelligentsia, to the mysterious corruption that underlies it, and to the generalized confusion it bespeaks. And with this new clarity he understands that people have lost their bearings, their sense of themselves in the rush of unregulated and unpredictable change:

The people in the cities were as helpless as children in the face of the unknown—that unknown which swept every established habit aside and left nothing but desolation in its wake, although it was itself the off-spring of the city and the creation of city-dwellers. (184, *187*)

Habit here implies culture, morality, and whatever else anchors people in their communities. Deprived of that nourishing connection, they have lost contact with their own identities and become inauthentic: "They continued to deceive themselves, to talk endlessly." Dr. Zhivago occasionally pushes aside the lengthy medical administrative records he must keep to write in a journal he calls "Playing at People, a Gloomy Diary or Journal Consisting of Prose, Verse, and What-have-you, Inspired by the Realization that Half the People Have Stopped Being Themselves and Are Acting Unknown Parts." Zhivago keeps his own sanity through his work as a doctor, through his family, and through his continual experience of the natural world outside the windows of his office. He notes one late autumn day:

The sky is incredibly high, and through the transparent pillar of air be-tween it and the earth there moves an icy, dark-blue radiance coming from the north. Everything in the world becomes more visible and audi-ble. Distant sounds reach us in a state of frozen resonance. The horizons open, as if to show the whole of life for years ahead. (185, *188*)

These moments of clarity, of communion with genuine existence, permit Zhivago no personal optimism. "The doctor saw life as it was. It was clear to him that it was under sentence. He looked upon himself and his milieu as doomed." (184, *187*.) And though his sense of a personal doom has not broken his attachment to the process of funda-mental political change, he is unable to serve it. He felt helpless, "a pigmy before the monstrous machine of the future."

He feared the future and loved it and was secretly proud of it, and as though for the last time, as if in farewell, he avidly looked at the trees and the clouds and people walking in the streets, the great Russian city, struggling through misfortune—and he was ready to sacrifice himself for the general good, and could do nothing. (*Ibid.*)

This state of mind holds through the October Revolution. When the dictatorship of the proletariat is proclaimed, Zhivago welcomes it:

What splendid surgery! You take a knife and with one masterful stroke you cut out all the old stinking ulcers. Quite simply, without any nonsense, you take the old monster of injustice . . . and you sentence it to death. (194, *198*)

And this style of action has an honorable Russian pedigree:

This fearlessness, this way of seeing the thing through to the end, has a long familiar national look about it. It has something of Pushkin's uncompromising clarity and of Tolstoy's unwavering faithfulness to the facts. (195, *198*)

Zhivago sees the revolutionary experience at this moment in three different perspectives. Against the unmourned past, it appears as an overdue act of surgery. Against the distant future it looms as the fulfillment of a grandiose human dream. Against the painful present, it presents a more complex face—suffering, corruption, dislocation, violence, and death accompany the uprooting of the old and the laying of new foundations, but it also has the miraculous rightness of its inevitability. In these first hours of the new order, Zhivago is still able to muster justification for the timing of the revolutionaries:

This new thing, this marvel of history, this revelation is exploded right into the very thick of daily life without the slightest consideration for its course. It doesn't start at the beginning, it starts in the middle, without any schedule, on the first weekday that comes along, while the traffic in the street is at its height. That's real genius. Only real greatness can be so unconcerned with timing and opportunity. (195, *199*)

But as revolution gives way to civil war, the three perspectives in Zhivago's mind shift in importance. The past and future of the revolution are eclipsed by the catastrophic present, which finally forces Zhivago to realize that he must abandon his double allegiance to violent political change and the essential realms of being. Each excludes the other, and he discovers which he must reject.

He learns this slowly during the bitter winter of 1917–18, as he maintains a shaky balance of commitments. He comes to know the arrogance and ruthlessness of the Bolsheviks, "men of iron will in black leather jackets," "who overturned everything as their program commanded" (196, *199–200*). He experiences the new revolutionary order in the brawling disorder of a tenant-committee meeting. Yet cold, hunger, chaos, and corruption are not enough to destroy the ultimate promise of the revolution. When he meets former colleagues who reproach him for "working for *them*," he replies, "I do and ... I am proud of our privations and I respect those who honor us by imposing them on us" (197, *200–201*).

Delirious dreams brought on by a siege of typhus reorder the chief elements in Zhivago's mind, in a way that will reorient him in the world and direct him toward a different future. In his dream he is a poet, writing "what he should have written long ago and had always wished to write but never could." He is accompanied in the dream by a boy Zhivago recognizes as "the spirit of his death." But the poem his dream-self writes, called "Turmoil," is about the conquest of death, about the day between burial and resurrection, and the vain assault of "the black, raging, worm-filled earth" on "the deathless incarnations of love." The dream and the dreamed poem translate finally into a religious image:

Near him, touching him, were hell, dissolution, corruption, death, and equally near him were the spring and Mary Magdalene and life. And it was time to awake. Time to wake up and to get up. Time to arise, time to be resurrected. (207, *211*)

Pasternak has accomplished here a complex new crystallization of Zhivago's ideas, his moral commitments, his sense of his situation in history and in the world that transcends history. It is that kind of movement, with consequences in the conscious mind but roots in the subconscious, which Russian writers—better, perhaps, than any others—provide their characters through the flash of metaphor or the leap of self-analysis. These epiphanies are often precipitated by tiny events, which signal sudden, radical, but thoroughly prepared-for changes in direction.

Henceforth Zhivago refuses to acquiesce in his personal doom, foretold, as he had thought, by the revolution's violence; in effect, he withdraws the offer of self-sacrifice no one has heeded. In choosing to live, he has chosen love, and with it all else that now seems to him permanent and valuable in the world—nature, art, family, and freedom if he can find it. Death is present, but it is there to be overcome, a stimulus to self-definition through artistic creation. As we learn from all that follows, he will bear witness in his personal life to these values in the face of increasingly hostile circumstances. Mary Magdalene is merely named here, but we later learn that her act of wetting Christ's feet with her tears and then drying them with her hair marks the symbolic beginning of modern history—according to Uncle Nikolai, the era of personal moral freedom and free access to the wonders of existence which replaced Rome's tribalism. As love incarnate in the poem, as life, spring, and rebirth in the authorial interpretation of the poem, Mary Magdalene stands for all that matters to Zhivago in the novel and all that is threatened by the approaching apocalypse.

Zhivago's new state of mind takes him beyond the binary public choices then available; Reds and Whites contribute equally to the holocaust, and if the Reds' share increases as the novel develops, it is because their Marxist program of rational violence is in the ascendancy. Zhivago's direction is his own, and it is above all lonely (the rest have lost their moral identities or gone mad) because it is both apolitical and anti-political. Zhivago's formulation of the issues can win him no adherents. Nor does he try; Lara and he discover their harmony of interests without reference to any political doctrine. If his life is prophetic, beyond his influence on a few personal friends who rediscover him after he is dead, it is only because Pasternak has recorded—or invented—it, and so made Zhivago's experience into a public event.

When the Zhivagos leave the "Moscow Encampment" after his redefining dream, they try to step out of history into a life which touches the primary sources of being. Actually, they have started on a long process of wandering. The rest of the novel composes a pattern of journeys and encounters, traced by individuals, families, and armies in the chaos of civil war. People are brutally separated, magically reunited, and separated again. Zhivago's journeys form the main design of the narrative. He travels with his family to the Urals city of Yuriatin, thence to the remote country estate Varykino. He is kidnaped, then, by Red guerrillas, made to serve as the unit's surgeon, wanders with them through a bloody haze of violence, escapes and returns to Yuriatin—to Lara this time—and goes on with her to Varykino. He tricks her into leaving without him, as their world falls to pieces, and wanders across the moonscape of the ruined land, swarming with rats, to Moscow, where he contrives a marginal existence until his death. In this pattern, the central trio of episodes—the two sojourns at Varykino and the intervening involuntary tour of military duty—contain the heart of the novel. They offer alternating moments of war and peace, of life in history and life outside it. Zhivago's program for the full life is set in motion in the first visit to Varykino and frustrated in the second, the two visits marking the slopes of ascent and descent in his personal fortunes. The guerrilla episode dramatizes his disgusted and total estrangement from the historical arena, but more than that, it presents in vivid detail the destructive forces that are moving toward victory and will doom the second Varykino visit.

In the first Varykino episode, Zhivago is beyond the reach of the civil war and free to act out his scenario of the lived life, in rooted communion with the deepest realities—love, family, nature, and the free life of the mind. He cuts firewood, harvests a potato crop, and repairs the house. In addition, he keeps a diary, speculates on questions of biological theory, reviews his attachments to Russian literature, and leads a peaceful and active domestic existence in a pastoral setting. For this miraculous recreation of the ordinary, Tonya, his wife, is an ideal and beloved companion. In the second Varykino episode, wolves can be seen and heard across the snowy fields, supplies and firewood are in short supply, wild rumors foretell catastrophe. For this brief but heightened experience, Lara's fierce attachment to life enables them both to confront the apocalypse. Zhivago writes poetry, the fullest affirmation of his attachment to the world, at the moment when his own life is most clearly threatened.

He has already begun his relationship with Lara and entered the painful triangle which will torment him through all that follows, when the first Varykino episode ends and he is taken captive by the guerrilla band, the "Forest Brotherhood." With this body of Bolshevik irregulars, he penetrates to the heart of the revolutionary experience, witnesses hellish atrocities, discovers and diagnoses the revolutionary illness in the mad killer Palykh. He argues with his drug-crazed captor, the Red commander Liberius, translating his disgust into an analysis of the point of collision between the "rational" but senseless violence and its chief casualty, life itself:

And last—and this is the main thing—when I hear people speak of reshaping life it makes me lose my self-control and I fall into despair.

Reshaping life! People who can say that have never understood a thing about life—they have never felt its breath, its heartbeat—however much they have seen and done. They look on it as a lump of raw material that needs to be processed by them, to be ennobled by their touch. But life is never a material, a substance to be molded. If you want to know, life is the principle of self-renewal, it is constantly renewing and remaking and changing and transfiguring itself, it is infinitely beyond your or my obtuse theories about it. (338, 347–48)

Alyosha and Ivan Karamazov also confront the choice between "life" and "the meaning of life," between life simply lived and life reduced to the terms of the rational understanding. Now the terms of the choice are altered, and for Zhivago the choice is already made: life lived against life understood and made ready for reshaping. Life reshaped is life violated; the means have begun to destroy the end.

With this accumulated experience and knowledge, Zhivago escapes and makes his way back to Lara, who restores him to health and to life for their doomed but triumphant idyll at Varykino. Important ideas and motifs reappear here, with variations and amplifications wrought by the process of events, completing the novel's poetic design. When Zhivago passes a kiosk covered with Bolshevik proclamations forming a collage of gibberish, he takes note of the further decay of language. The Magdalene story is restated at much greater length while Zhivago is recovering from the typhus he has caught on his journey from the guerrilla camp. It is a cure for the beating he has taken, an agent of his healing. It marks, we recall, the historical moment when recognition was given to the free human personality, but its literal religiosity is less important than its action as a symbol for elementary human qualities fostered by centuries of civilization, qualities that make life livable, as prosaic as love, tenderness, and mercy—feelings Alyosha Karamazov would commend. A thirst for plain human decency lies close to the center of Zhivago's complaint, and deep in this dissident literature.

Lara's lament over Zhivago's body at the end (she finds him again only after his death) restates the great conflict the book has expressed through the dense web of historical experience, and, rhetorically, at least, promises redemption for Zhivago's suffering and defeat:

At last we are together again, Yurochka, and in what a terrible way God has willed our reunion. Can you conceive of such misfortune! I cannot, cannot. Oh, God! I can't stop crying. Think of it! It's again so much in our style, made to our measure. Your going—my end. Again something big, irreparable. The riddle of life, the riddle of death, the enchantment of genius, the enchantment of unadorned beauty—yes, yes, these things we understood. But the small worries of practical life—things like the reshaping of the planet—these things, no thank you, they are not for us.

Farewell, my great one, my kin, farewell, my pride, farewell, my swift, deep little river, how I loved your daylong splashing, how I loved to plunge into your cold waves. (502, 514)

This passage is analogous to the classical moment of tragic illumination, but opposite to it in the arrangement of its elements. In conventional tragedy, from Aristotle on, the world finally is "right," the
errant individual, whatever his stature, is "wrong." His suffering
endears him to us, finally, as it also teaches us it is time to separate
our fortunes from his, instructed as we are by his error. In Lara's
complaint, we are reminded that the dead and defeated hero is
"right"; the world's victory over him is permanently "wrong." Zhivago's suffering is ended by his death and redeemed only by Lara's
defiant interpretation of it.

In the second half of her lament, Lara describes the unbroken
physical and spiritual torment her life has been since her separation
from Zhivago. She goes on "speaking and sobbing in her agony,"
without relief or purgation. We are told that after the burial she had
begun to sort out Zhivago's papers, but is unable to finish because she
disappears—is, in effect, obliterated:

One day Larisa Feodorovna went out and did not come back. She must
have been arrested in the street at that time. She vanished without a trace
and probably died somewhere, forgotten as a nameless number on a list
that afterwards was mislaid, in one of the innumerable mixed or women's
concentration camps. (503, 515)

No words are spoken over her grave. There is no reconciliation, no
mediation of the confrontation. The actors are dead; the issues they
acted out are not resolved.

III

The body of the novel ends with this passage. The two epilogues—
the section called Epilogue and the twenty-five poems by Zhivago—
qualify the stark finality of the novel's "statement" as it applies to
an unverifiable future beyond the deaths of the two central characters,
but they cannot alter the meaning of its ending at the point where
its main narrative ends. What finally may be read out of it? Two
fictional lives have been lived out to a bitter conclusion. The evil that
destroyed them is faceless, implacable, victorious. Unmediated suffering engulfs every impulse toward the fulfillment of their human
potential; pity and terror remain unpurged.

Pasternak's "statement about my epoch," at this point, is much like
the statements of other writer-heretics. In the dramatic design we see

honorable individuals trapped in a society which is itself trapped in a failed prediction. Violence is generated out of the enforcement of what Zhivago describes as the "untruth [that] came down on Russia" (404, *414*), the generalized lie. People are forced "to live a life of constant, systematic duplicity" (482, *495*), a life that violates the individual soul as "you say the opposite of what you feel, ... grovel before what you dislike, and rejoice at what brings you nothing but misfortune" (483, *495*). Marxism, and its theory of history in particular, is the source of the imprisoning prediction, and of the hounding of Zhivago, who refuses to live its lie. In the stark finality of Lara's and Zhivago's end, the balance of forces is left unchanged, the reign of evil unchallenged. But in the novel's epilogic conclusion the primary effect of doom is mitigated by a secondary and countervailing effect of vindication, a kind of post-facto redemption. Pasternak picks up two threads from the body of the novel, Lara's defense, at Zhivago's death, of their way of life together, and the record Zhivago has kept of his own life. His marginal existence in Moscow after Lara's departure and his journey across a ruined Russia after something in him had "snapped" are largely veiled from us in the telling. But we do know he is writing down—and sometimes publishing—the fruits of his intellectual and imaginative experience. These are the "papers" Lara has begun to organize, just before her disappearance. They compose Zhivago's "book," which his friends Gordon and Dudorov are reading as the epilogue ends, contributing to their feeling of the new freedom which fills the air, of "tenderness" and peace and reconciliation.

These two friends have traced a long emblematic journey through the novel to reach this attitude. They have followed the path of the conformist intelligentsia, expressing its "political mysticism" (482, *494*) from their first modish acceptance of the revolution, rationalizing their constricted condition, including imprisonment. They are purged of this state of mind by long tours in the worst of Stalin's camps and revived by the renewed contact with the real world which World War II makes possible. They find freedom and truth in the rigors of war, rescue from the regime of the lie, an opportunity to rethink their lives and finally to come to terms with the ideas of their dead friend Zhivago. However we judge this as prophecy outside the novel—measuring it, for example, against the subsequent fates of our three writers—within the novel the record of Zhivago's existential resistance seems to promise a correction of error, the beginning, at least, of a process in which coercive, blueprinted change will give way to the flow of genuine history, hospitable to art, morality, and human individuality, a final vindication of Zhivago's values. He has survived in the thoughts and feelings of his friends—Pasternak's own definition of immortality—and the doomed end of his mortal life has been eclipsed by his survival in literature.

The full chordal effect of the novel's ending includes a further vindication from beyond the grave: Zhivago's twenty-five poems constituting a second epilogue. They are the record of his most intense engagement with life. The experience reported in the poem or the moment of its composition can sometimes be fixed in the text of the novel, sometimes not. Zhivago's poems repeat themes which are central to Pasternak's own poetic vision: the human is merged with the natural, particularly in the cycle of seasons; night, winter, and death are set against dawn, spring, and rebirth; lovers separate and reunite. Important moments in the life of Christ—the Nativity, the night in Gethsemane, the Crucifixion and Resurrection—are less familiar in Pasternak's work but are securely rooted in the novel's pattern of ideas and motifs. Mary Magdalene, whose relationship to Jesus symbolizes the origins of genuine human history in the novel, is the subject of the penultimate poem.

Taken as a whole, these poems express Zhivago's chief assertion of his identity, of his rooted being. Their appearance at the end of the novel "corrects" for his personal defeat and presents him to us as a tragic but finally redeemed figure. The ultimate meaning of his life is suggested in a theme announced in the first poem, "Hamlet," and repeated in the final lines of the last poem, "The Garden of Gethsemane." In "Hamlet" the poem's "I" appears on stage at the beginning of the play as the actor about to play the role. He pauses and tries to read the future in the buzzing darkness of the audience, "staring through thousands of binoculars." He asks his "Father" to release him temporarily from the play, though he cherishes its "stubborn design" and will act out the play to its determined end. The image of the controlling father here suggests Shakespeare directing the actor to play his part, the murdered King of Denmark commanding his son to avenge his death, and God ordering Jesus to enact his redeeming sacrifice. The poem's "I" has agreed to fulfill the creator's design, but he speaks out at the end: "I stand alone. All else is drowning in pharisaism. To live a life through—is not simply to walk across a field." In the concluding stanzas of the final poem the same summons to enact one's destiny and the same apprehensive obedience to the command are repeated. In this case, Jesus has paused at Gethsemane to examine the bitter difficulties of his situation: by now he is stripped of his divinity, reduced to human stature, "like us." He pleads with his Father "that this cup of death" might pass him by, but he realizes he is alone and when the summons comes, when the "book of life" has reached the "precious" page, it is clear that "that which was written must be fulfilled. Fulfilled be it, then. Amen." In the name of the "awesome majesty" of the "passing of the ages" he agrees, "I shall, in voluntary torments, descend into the grave." He foretells his resurrection and casts his future as overseer of history, of the drifting "centuries . . . coming for judgment, out of the darkness, to me."

The presence of this framing motif in the poetic epilogue suggests that it encodes and comments on an essential aspect in the novel itself. Zhivago cannot be directly or explicitly connected with Hamlet or Jesus. He is neither a doomed Messiah[8] nor a philosophical Renaissance prince, and as "author" of these poems, he surely knows it. But, with all proportions maintained, an analogue, less literal than symbolic, can be found. Zhivago is "alone," beset by Pharisees, and lives out his painful life in his own stubbornly individual way. There is no easily identifiable authority who is directing his destiny, nor is there any moment in his career when he ends his hesitation and, like Hamlet, begins to act out the controlling text of the play, or, like Jesus, resumes his progress toward Calvary. But he is in close touch with the doctrine of authentic history, spelled out by his Uncle

---

[8] A certain kinship is suggested in this description of Christ's transformation of the Roman world: "He came, light and clothed in an aura, emphatically human, deliberately provincial, Galilean, and at that moment gods and nations ceased to be and man came into being—man the plowman, man the shepherd with his flock of sheep at sunset, man who does not sound in the least proud, man celebrated in all the cradle songs of mothers and in all the picture galleries the world over" (43, 44). This colloquial Christ is the source of "an inward music" in man from which he has learned the secrets of both morality and art. "The beast who sleeps in man" has been tamed without threat of retribution by "the power of unarmed truth"; in Christ's "parables taken from life" man has learned to discover "the truth in terms of everyday reality," a description of the quest of the artist, who may assume that "the whole of life is symbolic" (42, 42). Zhivago has lived close to this nucleus of truths which Christ exemplifies.

Nikolai, and remains true to his own sense of himself, which has the dimension of a personal mission, undramatized by public enactment. Hamlet and Christ experience the power of fate in a single dramatic moment of decision; Zhivago makes a series of choices which gives the sense of a cumulative fatality: the decision to leave Moscow with his family, his desertion of the partisans, and the deception of Lara, which leaves him finally alone to confront the revolutionary Pharisees. His modest, unnoticed heroism leads to a defeat as complete in its reduced scale as that of his sublime predecessors, and a defeat which, like theirs, is redeemed by the telling of it.

CHAPTER 15

Solzhenitsyn I: Marx Proposes, Stalin Disposes

Like so many Soviet writers, Pasternak returned to the revolution and civil war to find the answer to a fundamental question. For the believer, the question is asked this way: what combination of political genius and human self-sacrifice brought us to where we are? "History" becomes hagiography (positive heroes) and apologetics, and celebration of a benign and infallible theory of change. For the dissidents and the disaffected, the question has an opposite import: what has been done to us, what curse was laid on us in October 1917? Explanation is sought in the sequence of events, in the ethos of the men who made it, or in the theory which they used to promote the sequence and justify it. Fiction written in this mode becomes a critical inquiry into the nature of history and of reigning historical theory, very much in the manner of Tolstoy's *War and Peace*. Pasternak asked these questions and provided, through Zhivago's life history, his diagnosis: we have suffered the unlimited release of violence and hatred through the agency of a mechanical theory of history which, for all it promises, is finally alien to human needs and purposes.

Solzhenitsyn is conducting a similar inquiry in a circuitous manner and on a much larger scale. His first three novels and his shorter works dwell on the later consequences of this historical process; his investigation of its point of origin has only begun with the publication of *August 1914*, the first of a multivolume investigation of the coming of the revolution and its aftermath, the completion of which, he has told us, is a lifelong commitment. In his total *oeuvre* as written and as projected, the penal system looms as his central concern, the sub-government that is the fruit of the revolution and the moral essence of the Soviet world. In his grand design, the volumes of *Gulag Archipelago* are the documented historical record, or the map, as the title suggests, of that unexampled prison empire, presented in a writer's language but without the range or the constrictions of fiction. Within this scheme, *One Day in the Life of Ivan Denisovich* is a kind of historical snapshot, a descriptive account in fiction of one day in the life of a humble man in one of the darkest corners of the prison universe. Solzhenitsyn's account, which marks the first time the inside of a concentration camp has been shown in a published Soviet novel, introduces the vast tale he has to tell. The full effect he desired was apparently gained by merely showing the routine of one day—and a "good" day at that. In the two larger novels *The First Circle* and *Cancer Ward*, a structure of argument is fused with the bare record of experience; characters dispute at length about the nature of morality, art, and history, and make vital personal decisions out of their feelings and thoughts on these questions within their constricted milieux—an elite prison for scientists and engineers (the *sharashka*) and the cancer wing of a major hospital.

II

In *The First Circle* a moral motto—in the form of a question: "If one is forever cautious, can one remain a human being?"—states a choice many of the characters must confront (3, 7).[1] The question implies corollary statements: he who remains human is certain to be punished; he who acts ethically invites extinction. The pressures the system exerts on individuals are catalogued in the worsening situations faced by the prisoners: prison regulations tightened and made nastier; the network of informers, in and out of prison, extended; the hierarchy of servile tyrants strengthened. Prison itself is a crystallization of the entire Soviet world as Stalin—a kind of mad Marxian emperor—has created it. Virtue resides in all the victims who resist, especially in the innocent prisoners who struggle to keep morally and humanly alive by drawing on rock-bottom resources within themselves. They struggle to make sense out of their crazy situation; they

---

[1] The two editions cited in the text are, in order, Aleksandr I. Solzhenitsyn, *The First Circle*, trans. Thomas P. Whitney (New York, 1968), and A. Solzhenitsyn, *V kruge pervom* (New York, 1968). I have changed Whitney's translation on occasion.

fight the implacable system to stay whole and to keep their human ties with the convict community and the world outside. Read this way, the clear-cut division between good and evil threatens to turn the novel into a minutely documented but dramatically static allegory. Such it is, to a degree, and such is the intractable world of the concentration camp that presents itself to the writer, as Terrence des Pres has persuasively argued.[2]

But Solzhenitsyn has found room to maneuver between these inflexible moral entities in the central confrontation of two characters. The first is Nerzhin, a physicist and mathematician, declared enemy of the system, author of a vast clandestine inquiry into the nature of history, and (no commentator has doubted it) a surrogate for the author, whom he resembles in biographical fact and intellectual disposition. The other is Rubin, philologist, literary parodist, and respected prison wit who, for all this, is a Communist, a believing Marxist accepting everything from the arcane arguments of the central doctrine to the hard realities of the present system—its rationalizations, its leaders, including Stalin, even the court that (through a mistake, he insists) has sentenced him.

Nerzhin is concerned throughout with thinking his way out of physical and spiritual imprisonment, with discovering the personal resources to resist humiliation, to make the right choice, no matter how painful. He learns and develops through the course of the novel, but in a single, a "positive," direction. When the choice presents itself, he survives morally by refusing to support the secret police research into new ways of entrapping the innocent, thus inviting transportation to a far harsher area of the vast Gulag Archipelago. His costly, perhaps suicidal, victory carries much of Solzhenitsyn's statement, and functions in the novel as the emblem of *human* resistance to Stalin's nearly perfect apparatus of dehumanization. But he covers a narrower range than Rubin, is less "interesting" fictionally than the man who never wholly comprehends his double allegiance—to art and culture and human spontaneity on the one hand, and to the rigidities of the system on the other.

By making Rubin a victim of the system, Solzhenitsyn excuses him from complicity in its day-to-day brutalities, grants him the leisure and freedom, paradoxically, to contemplate his circumstances, and

[2] Terrence des Pres, "The Survivor: On the Ethos of Survival in Extremity," *Encounter*, September 1971, pp. 3–19.

allows him to be a blood brother of the community of prisoners. His defense of conditions he considers inevitable exposes to debate and refutation the deeper rationales of the Soviet system. When he acts spontaneously, he loathes his wardens and lifts the morale of his fellow victims with marvelous flights of imagination mocking the grotesque injustices of their situation; when he falls into abstractions, he defends the entire cosmology that justifies their detention. "They were right," he is forced to say, "to put us in prison" (18, *19*).

The two sides of Rubin are presented early in the novel. Asked by a group of German prisoners at a Christmas party to review the December news, Rubin responds this way:

He was ashamed to review what had happened in December. After all, he could not behave like a non-Communist and abandon the hope of indoctrinating these people. And he could not try to explain to them, either, that in our complex age Socialist truth sometimes progresses in a roundabout, distorted way. Therefore he had to choose for them—for the sake of History, just as subconsciously he made such selections for himself—only those current events which indicated the main road, neglecting those which obscured it. (12, *14*)

This is, of course, a "correct" way to politicalize current history, exercising editorial selectivity by adapting the merely empirical to the invisible laws of history. But it is condescending—treating grown men in a tutelary way—and it leads to deception and to self-deception. Rubin dismisses the indecisive news about the unfinished Soviet-Chinese negotiations, passes over "the seventieth birthday of the Leader of the Peoples" (Stalin) as "positive," but less, perhaps, than news, and suppresses another event:

To tell the Germans about the trial of Traicho Kostov, where the whole courtroom farce had been so crudely staged, where correspondents had been handed, after a delay, a false confession allegedly written by Kostov in his death cell—that would have been shameful and would hardly have served the purposes of indoctrination.
So today Rubin dwelt mostly on the historical triumph of the Chinese Communists. (12, *14*)

That this version of the news is a lie his audience knows. One of them listens clandestinely to the German program of the BBC, and has told the others the full story of Kostov and much else besides. The lie is self-defeating in this small but representative instance. Whenever political questions arise, Rubin participates in this mystique of falsehood in the name of a higher if invisible truth. But the opposing side of his character is presented soon afterward when he accepts Nerzhin's invitation to listen to a broadcast of Beethoven's 17th Sonata, in D Minor. The music is suddenly cut off, but Rubin listens rapt while Nerzhin talks of the purity and serenity of the music; it should be called, he says, the "shining sonata." This communion recurs when Rubin, talking brilliantly about the final phases of the relationship between Faust and Mephistopheles, about the irony of Faust's situation as he dies blind and deceived, overturns the standard optimistic interpretation of official Soviet scholarship. Nerzhin's response identifies the contradiction in Rubin's nature: "Oh, Lev, my friend, I love you the way you are right now, when you argue from the heart and talk intelligently and don't try to pin abusive labels on things" (32, 32).

This cleft in Rubin between the political and the human makes the relationship with Nerzhin a kind of triangle with the unitary, self-directed Nerzhin at the apex. Nerzhin is repelled by the political side, attracted to the human, and bewildered by Rubin's shifts between them; he counts finally on the human as the deeper and ultimately predominate side of his nature. They argue about subjects Russians have always argued about, the nature of human nature and the nature of history, and as the character Sologdin puts it, "the great primordial questions of good and evil." As an intellectual, Nerzhin moves on his own track, free of handed-down ideas, entirely outside the confines of Marxism-Leninism. Soviet historians are such "liars," he tells Rubin, that amateurs like himself have to begin again to find out what has really happened in history. His own evidence, he says, will come from "stories I've heard in prison about real people" (33, 33). Nerzhin concludes from his prison experience that real happiness is to be found in adversity, under conditions very nearly the opposite to those usually invoked: from "incessant victory ... fulfilled desire, success ... and total satiety" come "suffering, unending moral pain" (33, 34). These ideas form part of an ascetic prison ethos which will enable Nerzhin to survive. Set against Rubin's Marxism, they describe an attitude of skeptical personalism, grounded in experience, like that of the classical Russian novelists who explored the world on their own, uncommitted to any system of thought, asserting their particularist vision against the closed systems of the social materialist critics.

Rubin calls Nerzhin's ideas idealist and metaphysical (as Nerzhin had anticipated) and attacks the self-indulgence and narrowness of his vision:

You prefer your personal experience to the collective experience of humanity. You're poisoned by the stink of prison-latrine-talk—and you want to see the world through that haze. Just because our lives have been wrecked...why should men change their convictions? (34, 34)

In Rubin's eyes, Nerzhin's philosophy lacks seriousness, dimension, the sense of vast orderly movements, of a governing causality. When Nerzhin asks Rubin if he is "proud to hold to [his] convictions," Rubin answers in Luther's words, *"Hier stehe ich! Ich kann nicht anders"*—grandiose (and somewhat inappropriate, but put there no doubt to remind us of Rubin's deeply serious and redeeming interest in German culture) and ironic because it describes Nerzhin's situation better than his own. Nerzhin tears into him, nevertheless, and Rubin's response brings to light a central intellectual issue of the novel. Nerzhin speaks first:

"Pigheaded fellow! That's what metaphysics is! Instead of learning here in prison, instead of learning from our real life—"
"What life? The bitter poison of failure?"
"—You've blindfolded yourself, plugged up your ears, assumed a pose, and you call that intelligence? According to you, intelligence is the refusal to grow!"
"Intelligence is objectivity."
"You—objective?...I've never known a person as lacking in objectivity as you."
"Get your head out of the sand! Look at things in their historical perspective....Natural law [*zakonomernost*]—do you understand the meaning of that term? Inevitable, conditioned, natural law. Everything follows its inevitable course. And it's useless to root around for some kind of rotten skepticism." (34, 34–35)

Note that it is Nerzhin, not Rubin, who preempts the term metaphysics, the standard Marxian term of abuse for "idealist" philosophies, which are seen as rigid intellectual constructs imposed on the world, divorced from the real historical process, designed, indeed, to arrest the forward development which Marxism defines and promotes. Nerzhin turns that precise meaning back on Rubin's Marxism, which, he implies here and elsewhere, has become a fixed structure of essences, as idealist as Plato's, obscuring the bitter realities of Soviet experience.

Rubin relies on two other talismanic terms in the Soviet Marxist vocabulary. The word *zakonomernost* (inadequately translated by Whitney as natural law) touches the heart of that system's description of the world and of itself. It means the lawful (in the scientific sense) regularity of a process, and it is used to describe the benign, ineluctable, and scientifically predictable historical process of which Soviet society is the beneficiary and exemplar. "Objective," as Rubin uses it here, means that which is known to be true after consulting the alignment of forces in the inner mechanism of the historical process. Objectivity, in this sense, and not as Nerzhin uses it, is a kind of revealed truth which often contradicts the apparent empirical truth. For a nonbeliever like Nerzhin, it is a form of mystification, justifying any act of political expediency by endowing it with semi-mystical validation. As deliberately and continuously misused by the society's governors, who consult and interpret the oracles, it is the ultimate source of the lie which pervades public and private life. We learn later that the term is used to disintegrate the traditional language of moral behavior and to falsify art in precisely the way Russia's classical writers feared that the Hegel-based ideologies of the radical critics threatened their own writing.

For Nerzhin, the physicist and mathematician, "objective" and "*zakonomernost*" invoke the rigor and authority of the natural sciences; he calls Rubin the least objective of men—a dogmatist, in fact—and tells him that "we, the scientific intelligentsia, have to study history ourselves," since the historians "don't write history; they just lick a well-known spot" (36, 36). The study of history, surely, is the purpose of Nerzhin's clandestine writing, and his manuscript a possible reflection in fiction of Solzhenitsyn's own *August 1914*. The novelist acting as historian recalls Tolstoy's inquiry into the fallacies of historical determinism in *War and Peace*. And we may see Rubin as the believer in scientific rationalism—extended into realms where it is impotent—a modern Bazarov or Ivan Karamazov compelled to live out the personal consequence of his faith.

When Nerzhin moves from theory to the fact of their imprisonment, Rubin responds, "What must be, must be. The state can't exist without a well-organized penal system." When Nerzhin speaks ill of its organizer, Stalin, Rubin bursts out: "He's the greatest. Some day you will understand. He's the Robespierre and Napoleon of our revolution wrapped up in one. He is wise. He is really wise. He sees far beyond what others can possibly see." Nerzhin answers characteristically, "You should believe your own eyes" (36, 35). Moments later personal concern replaces ideological bitterness when Nerzhin receives a menacing summons from the prison authorities.

Solzhenitsyn has shifted from the central premise of Rubin's philosophy, the benign inevitability of the historical process, to the immediate reality, the actual prison walls of Stalin's world. This ironic linkage of theory and practice is repeated throughout the novel; as intellectual statement and literary strategy, it is an important part of the design.

Rubin is aware of the contradictions in his own attitudes but is unable to bring them into focus or to resolve them. As he notes more than once, "All his life he had been rich in friends, but in prison it turned out that his friends were not like-minded persons and the like-minded persons were not his friends" (187, 166). At times he experiences the simultaneous presence of the two aspects of his nature in this paradoxical way; at other times he responds alternately to one and then the other. By the novel's end he has described a hesitant and irregular movement, not to a full resolution, perhaps, but to the brink of clarification.

Twice he responds fully to the human side of his nature. Challenged by his fellow convicts to stage one of his literary entertainments, he responds with a magnificent improvisation, impersonating a Soviet prosecutor arguing a charge of treason against the twelfth-century Kievan hero, Prince Igor, who was defeated by Asiatic nomads in a reckless campaign, then fraternized with his enemies.[3] Rubin's mockery of the Soviet judicial process in the parody trial is devastating, suggesting—and not for the first time in the novel—that the Soviet penal system is more barbarous than some of the worst in the history of penology.[4] Though he delights his audience (many of them play parts in his improvised drama), he suddenly breaks it off, depressed presumably by his spontaneous "betrayal" of his formal political beliefs.

[3] See p. 13 above, footnote 1.
[4] Consider the ironic "critique" one prisoner makes of the prison regime in the Chateau d'If where the Count of Monte Cristo was confined. It was deplorably lax, his fellow prisoners conclude, more like a Riviera vacation (312, 279). In the same vein, several prisoners discuss the girl-revolutionary who goes on a hunger strike when she is thrown in a Tsarist prison. She was treated decently then. Today, they point out, she would be force-fed intravenously.

Rubin swings farthest away from his abstract allegiances in a privileged moment he experiences when he walks across the prison courtyard very late on a winter night:

Here under the lovely cloudy night sky, smoky brown from the lights, feeling the innocent touch of cold little hexagonal stars on his warm face and beard, Rubin stopped and shut his eyes. He was filled with a sense of peace that was all the keener for being so brief—all the power of existence, all the delight of going nowhere, of asking nothing, desiring nothing, just to stand there the whole night long, blessedly, blissfully, as trees stand, catching the snowflakes. (419, *371*)

He hears a distant train whistle, "that special lonely-in-the-night, soul-seizing whistle which in our later years recalls our childhood because in childhood it promised so much." The moment continues: "If one could stand like this for half an hour, everything would go away, body and soul would become whole again, and he could compose tender verses about locomotive whistles in the night."[5] But he is in prison walking across the courtyard under guard, on his way to the sickbay for a sleeping pill. On his return the moment resumes its hold on him and yields its final fruit:

He breathed in the air which smelled of snow, bent down and grabbed a fistful of starry snow and rubbed his face and neck and filled his mouth with the weightless, bodiless substance. And his soul was at one with the freshness of the world. (420, *372*)

This experience of wholeness unites "body and soul," the adult with his childhood, the man with his matrix in the natural world, outside of history and beyond the reach of his political ethos. He feels restored by the "innocence" of the stars and the freshness of the world to artistic creativity, to the primal sources of morality, and, finally, to the fullness of the human side of his being.

III

Rubin does not live for long periods in this kind of communion with the world. In the chief moral action of the novel he acts in fatal touch with the opposite aspect of his being. This action concerns the secret police's efforts to arrest a diplomat who makes a clandestine

---

[5] Compare with Lenin's response to the Appassionata Sonata (see above, p. 101, footnote 3). What he regards as a fatal weakness, threatening his revolutionary mission, Solzhenitsyn presents as the way to salvation for his idealist Communist.

telephone call to a famous Soviet medical scientist, an old family friend, warning him not to give a sample of medicine to French colleagues he had recently met in Paris. The diplomat makes the call circumspectly and refuses to give his name to the stupid, uncomprehending woman who answers, but his voice has been recorded. At the end of the book he is arrested, imprisoned in the Lyubyanka, and initiated into the prison universe. Volodin, the diplomat, performs the act out of common decency, out of concern for the fate of an old family friend, who is himself acting out of the generosity common among international scientists. Volodin has acted, too, under the stimulus of the anachronistic moral vocabulary he had learned from his mother and out of his conviction that, frightened as he is, he will cease to be human if he is forever cautious.

These events—the telephone call and the arrest—frame the central action of the novel. A number of the scientists in the *sharashka*, including Nerzhin and Rubin, have been assigned to invent a way to classify and identify voice prints. Volodin's arrest depends on the perfection of this technique; the attitudes the scientist-convicts take toward this work—"discovering what makes a human voice unique" (20, 22) in order to arrest the unique human being it expresses— define them against the explicit moral criteria of the book. Nerzhin refuses to take part in any work which will result in the arrest of more innocent people and is transported finally to an unknown, but far worse, "island" in the "archipelago." Rubin works enthusiastically on the project, brings it close to perfection, and contributes substantially to the arrest of the innocent diplomat.

As Rubin listens to the recorded telephone conversation, his responses cover the full spectrum of his divided nature. He has been warned by two intelligence officers that he is about to hear a highly secret tape, involving the treasonable passing of scientific data to foreigners. "You are a prisoner, Rubin," the general in charge tells him. "But you were once a Communist and maybe someday you will be one again." Rubin suppresses the response he would like to make— "I am a Communist now" (194, *172*)—because of his contempt for the general. But it is as a Communist that he gets ready to listen with an appropriately cruel expression on his face ("One could never beg mercy from a person with such a face"). As he listens, his expression changes: "with every sentence Rubin's face lost its set, cruel expression and became perplexed. My God, it wasn't what he had expected at all" (195, *173*). The fixed abstract "emotion" induced in him by the political rhetoric begins to give way to a lively human and, in a sense, literary interest in the possessors of the unknown voices. "Rubin had to try hard to imagine the criminal, but he was haunted by that lady, whom, it seemed to him, he could very easily see, with luxuriant, dyed hair which was perhaps not even her own." This effort to visualize and to turn the voices into people leads Rubin into some homespun ethical speculations, thence to a judgment about the character of the "nervous, almost desperate" young man:

The most barbarous thing was that no reasonable person, with an unmuddled mind, could consider any medical discovery a state secret. Because any medicine which asked the nationality of a patient was not a medicine at all. And the man who had decided to telephone that booby-trapped apartment—he may not have understood the full danger—Rubin liked that reckless fellow. (*Ibid.*)

This chain of humane reflections is suddenly interrupted by the harsh "logic" of history:

But *objectively*—objectively that man who had wanted to do what seemed to him the right thing had in fact attacked the positive forces of history. Given the fact that priority in scientific discovery was recognized as important and necessary for strengthening the state, whoever undermined it stood objectively in the way of progress. And had to be swept away. (196, *173*)[6]

Having consulted the ultimate touchstone of judgment, Rubin loses the humane trend of his thoughts in a cloud of suspicion— "medicine could be a code word," there were many references to "foreigners," etc. He draws back for a moment when he considers the two "repulsive" police officials who were with him. They were the kind of "butchers" who had sent him to prison. But, in a characteristic impulse of misled selflessness, he thinks one "had to rise above one's personal feelings," "one had to rise above one's own wretched fate." Again the human opposes the political and loses out, "and though *these* two deserved to be blown up by an anti-personnel grenade here and now, one had to serve not them, but one's country, its progressive

[6] Kathryn Feuer has called attention to the centrality of this passage in her excellent analysis of Solzhenitsyn's attitudes toward Tolstoy: "Solženicyn and the Legacy of Tolstoy," *California Slavic Studies*, 6: 124.

idea, its banner" (196, *174*). Rubin remains locked in this sterile paradox until the completion of his work on the voice-print decoder.

At a climactic moment of Rubin's development, and of the intellectual conflict in the novel, he becomes engaged in a fierce argument with Sologdin, an extreme advocate of the ascetic prisoner imperative, "forge your inner self!" Sologdin challenges him to an intellectual duel, according to a prison camp ritual. He proposes a number of topics to the reluctant Rubin: the spiritual vitality of the Middle Ages, how should Dostoevsky's character Stavrogin (*The Possessed*) be understood,[7] "the significance of pride in a man's life" (381, *339*). Rubin dismisses them all but when Sologdin mentions "the three laws of dialectics," he traps Rubin by announcing that he accepts them and will "debate the premise that you yourself don't understand the three great laws" (382, *340*).[8]

The debate that follows challenges Rubin's views at a vital point. Earlier Nerzhin had mocked the lawful regularity of the historical process, seen as a constantly evolving struggle between positive and negative forces. At the end of that argument, Nerzhin had suggested that scientists should look into the big questions of history.

Sologdin also argues as a scientist but carries the critique even closer to the inner mysteries of the doctrine: he is now challenging the validity of the laws which make the process of history "lawful." Rubin has already defined the centrality of the laws of the dialectic: "everything else depends on them." Sologdin interrogates Rubin closely on the properties of these laws, aiming to show that Rubin does not understand them, but beyond that, that they are not universally applicable or valid. Proceeding Socratically, Sologdin demonstrates—on the basis of Rubin's admissions—that the negation of the negation, the third law of the dialectic, does not operate in every process; that in fact the governing metaphor, that of a sprouting seed, is misleading; that the laws apply in a totally different way to the

---

[7] Sologdin concludes his comment on the incapacities of literary scholarship this way: "Stavrogin! Svidrigailov! Kirillov! Can one really understand them? They are as complex and incomprehensible as people in real life! How seldom do we understand another human being right from the start, and we never do completely . . . that's why Dostoevsky is so great." The celebration of human mystery against the diagrams of social determinists, complexity of character against the certainties of false science—literary scholarship in this case—evokes again that enduring conflict at the heart of the modern Russian tradition.

[8] This debater's maneuver recalls Ivan Karamazov's acceptance of Alyosha's premise that God exists in order to demonstrate His incompetence.

organic and inorganic worlds; and that there is complete confusion about whether deductions can or cannot be made from these laws. When Sologdin pursues his inquiry on this last point—"If you deduce everything from those three laws"—Rubin cuts him off:

"But I've told you—we don't."
"You don't?" Sologdin asked in surprise.
"No!"
"Well then, what are the laws good for?"
"Listen," Rubin began to pound at Sologdin insistently, almost in a sing-song. "What are you, a block of wood or a human being? We decide all questions on the basis of the concrete analysis of specific information, do you understand that? All economic doctrine is derived from production figures. The solution of every social question is based on an analysis of the class situation."
"Then what do you need the three laws for?" Sologdin raged, oblivious of the quiet in the room. "You mean you don't need them?"
"Oh, yes, we need them very much," Rubin said quickly.
"But why? If nothing is deduced from them? If even the direction of development can't be ascertained through them, if it's high-flown empty verbiage? If all that's necessary is to repeat like a parrot, 'negation of the negation,' then what the hell are they for?" (384–85, 342)

The secret motor of history, indeed, of all "lawful" change (seen always as progress), seems to lie dismantled on the prison dormitory floor.[9]

Before Rubin can try to put the pieces together, Solzhenitsyn interrupts the argument. A prisoner who wants to sleep points silently at the informer in the group—this is dangerous talk. It goes on for hours elsewhere, in a prison corridor, but the reader is taken away, to observe Nerzhin pursuing *his* quest for the truth by posing the ques-

[9] One of the nine chapters excised, we now learn, from the published text is entitled "Dialectical Materialism—the Most Advanced World-View." It amplifies this criticism of "the philosophical bases of Communist ideology," this time by a mocking presentation of a Party official's speech on dialectical materialism at an annual event which the free workers of the *sharashka* are obliged to attend. Solzhenitsyn gains his estranging effect through every device of the comic monologue—the pretentious tricks of the stupid orator, dogmatic assertions fortified by puerile examples, disconnected exposition ending finally in a jumble of jargon—all set against the concealed boredom of the audience, which is jammed into a room as tiny and as cramped as the mind and the doctrine of the orator.
Although this chapter is numbered eighty-eight, it was not meant to appear after the eighty-seven chapters of the printed text. A subtitle to the chapter tells us that there are ninety-six chapters in the "full variant" of *First Circle*, suggesting that the nine missing chapters are to be inserted at various points in the narrative. This one, presumably, would recapitulate the ideological motif for a final time near the novel's end. See *Kontinent*, 1 (1974): 125–42.

tion the Russian intelligentsia has always asked itself: How should I feel and act toward "the people"? Worship them? Scorn them? Pity them? Or something less extreme? It becomes clear here that Solzhenitsyn's novel is a critical inquiry into the major preoccupations of Russian intellectuals since 1800. The concern with the philosophy of history and with the moral qualities of the *narod* are linked in that sense. Nerzhin occupies a middle ground, he says, between Rubin and Sologdin, not so much in the doctrinal sense, but as a relativist and empiricist between two absolutists. His findings on the moral qualities of the "people" are suitably pragmatic and measured. On balance the "people" are no better and no worse than others, but they are dramatically different. He learns from Spiridon, the prison janitor, of his wanderings with his family in World War II across battle lines and national boundaries, oblivious to all the categories of modern political life. He trusts only the truth of his own senses and the promptings of his own instincts, above all for the preservation of himself and his family. Nerzhin admires Spiridon but finds nothing vital to learn from him. He must "forge his soul" out of his own resources, he decides, thus aligning himself with Sologdin, the unqualified individualist.

When we rejoin the argument between the absolutists Rubin and Sologdin, hours and pages later, it has moved on from the validity of dialectic logic to questions of morality, a modulation which Nerzhin's intervening personalist speculations have prepared the reader for. We do not know all the steps, but note the direct passage, at least in our hearing, from philosophical premises to questions of moral behavior, skipping the intervening socioeconomic layers of Marxian theory.[10] When they begin to discuss ends and means, the quarrel becomes bitterly personal. Sologdin says:

And what really enrages me is the fact that inside you, you really believe in the motto ... that "the ends justify the means." Yet if anyone asks you to your face if you believe it, you deny it. (403–4, *358*)

Rubin makes a damaging admission as he defends himself:

I don't believe in it for myself. But it's different in a social sense. Our ends are the first in all human history which are so lofty that we can say they justify the means by which they have been attained. (404, *359*)

---

[10] We are told that the two debaters, out of our hearing, have covered the other two laws of the dialectic, "disturbing the shades of Hegel and Feuerbach" (402, *357*).

Sologdin, always insisting on the primacy of morality over politics, jumps on Rubin's distinction between private and public morality:

Morality shouldn't lose its force as it increases its scope. That would mean that it's villainy if you personally kill or betray someone; but if the One-and-Only and Infallible[11] knocks off five or ten million, then that's according to natural law [*zakonomerno*] and must be appraised in a progressive sense. (*Ibid.*)

Two moralities, public and private, mean no morality at all, since the first, which is false, dominates or perverts the second.[12]

Rubin answers Sologdin with more jargon, saying of the two moralities, "the two things cannot be compared! They are qualitatively different." Sologdin is infuriated by the talismanic use of language. (He has striven for years in prison to develop a "Language of Maximum Clarity" [135, *122*], eschewing most abstractions and all words of foreign origin.) His reply converts the debate into an exchange of personal abuse:

Stop pretending! You're too intelligent to believe that filth! No right-thinking person can think that way. You're simply lying! (404, *359*)

After swapping insults based on the intimate details they know about each other, coming close to a physical fight, they return finally to the dialectic. "But I know you! You'll hide behind dialectics, say that 'everything flows, everything changes,'"[13] Sologdin says. Neither

---

11 Stalin, of course. Solzhenitsyn's straight-faced use, as here, of these grotesque titles contributes to the tone of mocking exposé with which he and most of his prisoner characters discuss the official Soviet world.

12 Hegel is not invoked here, but this distinction between two moralities—one derived from history's purposes, the other from the private conscience—is defined at length in Hegel's Introduction to *The Philosophy of History*. They are not connected, and in any conflict between them historical morality always prevails. (See the epigraph, p. xxii, above).

13 This metaphor for the dialectic process, close to the heart of basic doctrine, is apparently familiar to all Soviet intellectuals. It is Engels's paraphrase of three "river" aphorisms by Heraclitus (described by Lenin as "one of the founders of the dialectic"). They are: (1) "Into the same river you could not step twice for other (and still other) waters are flowing" (XLI); (2) "To those entering the same river, other and still other waters flow" (XLII); (3) "Into the same river we both step and do not step. We both are and are not." See I. Bywater, ed., *Heraclitus of Ephesus* (Chicago, 1969); *Materialisty drevnei Gretsii*, ed. M. A. Dynnika (Moscow, 1955). Engels comments in *Anti-Dühring*: "This original, naive but intrinsically correct view of the world is that of ancient Greek philosophy, first clearly enunciated by Heraclitus: everything is and also is not, for everything *flows*, is continually changing, constantly coming into being and passing away." Friedrich Engels, *Herr Eugen Dühring's Revolution in Science* [*Anti-Dühring*] (Chicago, 1935), pp. 17–18.

character yields a fraction of his position to the other. But the confrontation does figure in the working out of Rubin's destiny, and·in the novel's resolution. Sologdin's assault on the sacred words prevails over Rubin's stereotyped defense, undermining his position in a way he is beginning to understand at the end of the novel. It resounds through all that follows and it contributes, too, to Solzhenitsyn's diagnosis of the doctrinal causes of his country's moral illness.[14]

At one cruel moment in their quarrel, Sologdin asks Rubin why he does not serve his jailers by informing, since he is in full doctrinal agreement with them. Rubin responds out of his humanity, with outrage.[15] But after the argument we learn that episodes of informing are centrally involved in Rubin's early attachment to the Party. When he was sixteen, a cousin, a member of an opposition group, had asked him to hide some fonts of type. He had kept the secret and served time in a Kharkov jail. Then, later, when he was editor of a factory newspaper, he was confronted with his involvement in that episode years before and told "to confess his shortcomings." His Party boss, a forty-year-old woman, speaks in Party-ese.

The Party! Can there be any thing higher than the Party? How can one answer the Party with denials? How can one hesitate to confess to the Party? The Party does not punish; it is our conscience. Remember what Lenin said. (413, 366–67)

Ordinarily fearless ("ten pistols pointed at his head would not have frightened Rubin"), he "could not in that red and black confessional lie to the Party." He tells all, and then is asked to sign a paper by a silent stranger wearing "yellow Oxfords." Surprised, Rubin asks him, "Who are you? You're not the Party." "Why not?" asked the guest, offended. "I'm a member of the Party, too. I'm a GPU investigator." (*Ibid.*) Rubin surrenders his conscience to the Party, which turns it over to the secret police. Until he recovers it, it would seem, he will

---

[14] The first sentence of the following chapter, devoted to the hunted diplomat, comments obliquely on the anti-human implications of dialectical materialism: "Relations between a man and a woman are always strange: nothing can be foreseen, they have no predictable direction, no law" (406, *361*). Life, again, envelops theory.

[15] Both agree that informing is an unmitigated evil. Throughout the novel it is the most tangible sign of the system's immorality. The network extends into every corner of public and private life, blighting relations between colleagues at work, between man and wife, parents and children, teachers and students, even between a doctoral candidate and her work. (Ashamed of the informer's role forced upon her, she feels unworthy to analyze the "human qualities" in Turgenev's "Hamlet and Don Quixote".) (272, *242*.)

be incapable of acting according to the ordinary dictates of the "lower," "private" morality.

But Rubin's surrender at that moment was not total or permanent. He feels ineradicable guilt over his participation in the mass starvation inflicted on the peasants and their children through forced grain collections. In the prison, where he will not inform on his fellow prisoners, he is asked by his jailers how he can call himself a Communist if he refuses to inform. He tries to clarify his anomalous situation to himself by casting himself as "tragic in the Aristotelian sense":

He had been dealt the blow by the hands of those he loved the most. He had been imprisoned by unfeeling bureaucrats because he loved the common cause to an improper degree. And as a result of that tragic contradiction, in order to defend his own dignity and that of his comrades, Rubin found himself compelled to stand up daily against the prison officers and guards whose actions were determined by a totally true, correct and progressive law. His comrades, on the other hand, were for the most part not comrades at all. Throughout the prison, they reproached him, cursed him, almost attacked him because they were unable to look beyond their own grief and see the Great Conformity to Natural Law [*zakonomernost*] behind it all. (409–10, *364*)

Rubin's situation certainly is not tragic as he sees it, or as we see it at this point in his development (just after the argument with Sologdin). The man who calls himself a tragic hero before his downfall, is not one. The tragic situation cannot be discerned until it is completed, and no one is worse qualified to define it than the hero while he is in the middle of it. His flawed vision of the world is precisely what he proclaims to be the truth at this moment: he remains locked in his illusion. While he is in this situation, he cannot know his error or foresee his downfall. (How would Hamlet have behaved, if he had known about those poisoned sword points?) Solzhenitsyn often teases Rubin in the novel, but here in his author's voice he supports him in his misconception: "He was all in all a tragic figure" (410, *364*). Actually, Rubin is locked in ambivalence, tense, frustrated, and bewildered. If he were to learn and move, he would experience a downfall, a saddening experience for the spectator, perhaps, but not a tragic one, because he would not have acted in error, according to the alignment of moral values in the novel. Presumably he would respond in full to the human side of his being, and in full knowledge confront the malevolent force all the others do battle against. If destroyed, he would end defiant, intact, a "survivor" in Des Pres' sense —and destroyed for that reason, responding finally to the deepest rhythms of the novel.

What does happen to Rubin is mislabeled as Aristotelian, but it does display a clear literary strategy. Throughout the novel Rubin remains suspended between the Laws of the Dialectic and the snow-filled night in the courtyard, responding simultaneously or sequentially to the pulls of both, but surrendering wholly to neither. There is a process of change beneath consciousness: Rubin learns "without noticing it" (323, 289). The intellectual battering he takes from Sologdin, Nerzhin, and others, the visible deterioration of the world he defends, set against the unwavering strength of his attachments to others, to art, to imagination, and to private morality effect a re-alignment of forces within him, a *preparation* for a change we do not see completed in the novel.

Rubin's "Project for Civic Temples," which he turns to after Solog-din's wounding arguments—"they hurt because he knew there was some justice in them" (416, 369)—fits the view that change is imminent, perhaps immediately offstage. His project is designed to fill the same cultural and moral vacuum his fellow prisoners have discovered in Stalin's Russia. He is in unacknowledged agreement with his opponents that the absence of moral standards dehumanizes the entire society; it would take a small adjustment of his thought, a recognition of the source of this condition, to make that agreement complete. His critique is implicit in his proposals for reform. He has asked himself whether it is "more important . . . to improve public morality than to build the Volga-Don Canal or Angarastroi" (*ibid.*). Rubin proposes to build Civic Temples in dominating sites all across the Soviet Union, to be used for the celebration of state holidays and for "lending ceremonial dignity to acts of marriage, naming the newborn, entering adulthood and mourning the dead." Ritual will be important; all sorts of aesthetic effects will be achieved: scents, melodious music and singing, the use of colored glass, stage lights, wall painting. "Indeed, the whole architectural ensemble of the temple must breathe majesty and eternity." The temple attendants would be chosen from those "who enjoyed the love and trust of the people because of their own irreproachable, unselfish, and worthy lives." Rubin denies that he is "simply proposing to revive Christian temples without Christ," but his project as presented is indistinguishable from a laicized church.

Solzhenitsyn is teasing Rubin here, but his irony goes further. He compels his character unwittingly to amplify the central critique of the novel by identifying the great deficiencies of a civilization derived from Marxist premises: deficiencies in ethical consciousness and in respect for culture in the most primary sense, as the ceremonial marking of the major milestones in a human life, both customarily centered in churches. Rubin's naivete, separating him from his fellows, is signaled by his intention to present his project to the Central Committee for its approval, an action which would certainly complete his disillusionment, suggesting again that events may soon change his mind in an implied epilogue to the novel.

Rubin's reflections on morality are immediately followed by his epiphany in the prison courtyard, when he experiences his total membership in the human world. On arising after his complicated sleepless night, he plunges into a frenzy of work, "forgetting his liver, his hypertension pains, feeling refreshed after the exhausting night, not hungry although he had eaten nothing since the night before" (502, *442*). He "was soaring aloft on the wings of the spirit," in a euphoric spasm of dedication to the solution of the voice-print problem, a strange misapplication of his recent spiritual discoveries. The taxing day of work produces a solution to the technical problem but none at all to the moral problem, which grows ever more confused. The list of suspects has been narrowed down from five to two. Rubin works on, not only to catch the guilty one, but to save the "one [who] is not guilty" (508, *447*). Rubin is talking to Oskolupov, the ranking police officer in charge of the project, "an out-and-out dolt," in Rubin's still-bifurcated view, but "also a high government official and ... a representative of those progressive forces" he is still willing to serve. He is stunned by Oskolupov's response: "Not guilty? ... Not guilty of anything at all? The security organization will find something; they'll sort it all out." He finds some comfort in the fact that he has saved three lives, but he has learned that Oskolupov would have arrested all five, or more, without hesitation. Rubin's work has been "trampled on." The euphoria passes, his devotion to the cause has taken another shocking blow and is visibly crumbling:

The passion of dedication which had burned for so many hours was extinguished. He remembered that his liver and his head ached, that his hair was falling out, that his wife was growing old, that he had another five years to serve, and that all this time they kept pressing on and on in a wrong direction. Now they had defamed Yugoslavia. . . . Rubin's map of China was pinned up on the wall, the Communist areas colored with a red pencil.

The map was the one thing that cheered him. Despite everything, despite everything, we are going to conquer. (508-9, *448*)

Rubin hangs on, but it is clear that he is slowly coming unstuck from his Communist faith. Solzhenitsyn's teasing relationship with Rubin may be operative here: when will China, the last grip he has on his position, betray him, too? And, as a Jew, he cannot remain indifferent to the rising tide of anti-Semitism. Solzhenitsyn has again prepared for the last phase of Rubin's disillusionment, through actual events that will occur beyond the novel's time span, in that same implied epilogue.

But when Rubin wakes up after his orgy of work, the description of his physical condition comments precisely on his spiritual paralysis. He lies unprotesting in the cold draft from the window opened by "his antagonist" Sologdin as part of his ascetic program of physical conditioning. Putting on his padded jacket and fur cap with the ear flaps down, he covers his head with his blanket and ignores the morning uproar, "trying desperately to prolong the scheduled hours of sleep" (554, *489*).

He is clearly refusing to recognize changes in his state of mind which have already taken place, but when he finally gets up, he is again set in significant motion. It is the day of the "transport," that fateful moment in the life of the prisoners, and Rubin's responses are the final comment on his fate. He makes his characteristic literary-historical reference, above the despairing clamor that follows the announcement of the transport, shouting, "A historical day at the *sharashka*! The morning of the execution of the Streltzy." The author notes that "his performance in no way meant that he was cheerful about the prisoner transport. He would have joked just as boisterously about his own departure. Nothing was so sacred as to restrain him from his own brand of commentary." (557, *491*.) His remark is not brilliant, but it is sympathetic to the prisoners, associating them with the execution by Ivan the Terrible of his personal bodyguard, and it is the spontaneous personal signature of the human Rubin that we read in the farewell scene.

Nerzhin has faced the consequences of his refusal to help the police. He has prepared himself for the hell he is being sent to, has chastely ended his flirtation with a female guard, has flushed his manuscript "in the needle-fine hand" down the prison toilet, and has asserted his human dignity in the tiny frame permitted him by compelling the prison authorities to live up to two minor regulations. While he prepares, he says goodbye to Rubin. Together they sort out Nerzhin's books, and then at the moment of farewell Nerzhin says:

"Listen, friend, ... for three years we haven't agreed once, we've argued all the time, ridiculed each other, but now that I'm losing you, maybe forever, I feel so strongly that you are one of my most—most—"
His voice broke.
Rubin's big black eyes, so often sparkling with anger, were warm with tenderness and shyness.
"So that's all in the past," he nodded. "Let's kiss, beast." (566, *498–99*)

No mention is made of the chief moral issue between them, the contrary positions they took on the pursuit and arrest of the innocent diplomat. We must assume that the issue is eclipsed, forgiven perhaps, or relegated to the past. The kiss takes on an aspect of absolution, and true to the rhythm of the book, and of this tradition, the human once more envelops the political.

IV

Solzhenitsyn's imaginary journey early in the novel into the office and into the mind of Stalin, the architect of the prison society, amplifies the arguments that are fought out between the prisoners. As Balzac mapped his society—its classes, occupations, *moeurs*—with respect to the power and consequences of money, Solzhenitsyn has mapped his with respect to the power and consequences of its governing doctrines. Money and ideas are the respective agents of moral corruption. The "visit" to Stalin introduces in crystallized form the principal issues, themes, and ideas, much as the episode of the Grand Inquisitor does in *The Brothers Karamazov*. Here it is the master ideas of Marxism, the great synthesizing concepts, the points of junction between different realms of being, the "explanations" of the way the world works which are central to Solzhenitsyn's design. We see Stalin as suspicious, vengeful, paranoid, and megalomaniacal, but we see him licensed in his acts and attitudes because he is privy to the secrets of history. He is both "principal" and "agent," acting without any moral or human restraint on his behavior, but always guided by the "science" of history. The position where these laws are consulted and decoded is the seat of power in the Marxist system: government by oracular revelation always permits the high priest to impose his own visions on the governed. Stalin has filled this void at the top with his own personality, and his monstrous acts are his own. But, Solzhenitsyn seems to be saying, it is not just that there is a fatal correspondence between *this* tyrant and *his* doctrine; it is rather that there is no stay anywhere in the Marxian metaphysic against the capricious exercise of total power, with all the consequences we are shown in the novel.

The mystique of orderly historical development is at the center of Stalin's ruminations on his achievements, on his plans for the future, and on his many frustrations. He has modified the work of "the founders" and corrected Lenin when forward movement required it. People are the chief obstacle. Lenin was wrong when he thought cooks could govern; a cook is a cook and governing is a high calling, carried out best by one leader. Stalin knew the people loved him, but they were full of "shortcomings"; it was "the people," after all, who had retreated in 1941 (89, 83). He has suffered a great deal for human progress, but, late at night, he has a deep sense of failure. "All his life things had never worked out. They had never worked out because there were always people who interfered." (90, 83.) He had found ways to remove human error from the path of inevitable progress; the exile of whole peoples constitutes his chief "theoretical contribution" to the vexed nationalities question. The restoration of the death penalty, he tells his brutal lieutenant Abbakumov, who has begged him for it, would perform a useful "educational function."

History's mission calls him again and again to act against inexplicable human recalcitrance by striking at the flesh of the misled. *Zakonomernost*, as we have seen it defined in the argument between Nerzhin and Rubin, takes the place of custom, law, and morality in determining millions of human destinies. In the final version of his mad ruminations, Stalin imagines himself crowned Emperor of the Planet. This fantasy foretells the promised outcome of the "final struggle," the end of the merciless binary war between progressive and regressive forces within the historical process, acted out in the struggle between hostile classes, between ideologies, and between nations embodying different "social systems."

It is acted out, too, in the heart of a progressive revolutionary order, where the new social arrangements had not yet affected the minds of all their beneficiaries. Every fragment of the world and every individual consciousness is fitted into the Manichean struggle between light and darkness. Elementary mistakes call for elemental measures. Execution will cure the worst offenders, harsh imprisonment will re-make the minds of the rest, or, if that fails, reduce them to one or another kind of non-function. The measurement "for us or against us" can be applied to anything or anybody, any issue, any pattern of behavior. Total war will issue in total victory, but until that time the "interim" emotions—Stalin's repertory of suspicion, hatred, fear, bru-tality, and vengefulness—must dominate the Soviet people, and what-ever other peoples he is called upon to rule. This paranoid family of feelings is inseparable from the Marxist logic summed up in the brutal Russian question *Kto kogo?*, literally "who whom?," with "beats" understood to be the missing verb. From this marriage of per-verse emotion and simplistic logic is derived the society's system of values, its social policies and institutions, all crystallized in the prison system itself, a travesty of a civilization.

The aging tyrant takes up a point of doctrine, hoping to make one more lasting contribution to the body of theory. It is the standard Marxian metaphor of base and superstructure, which he proposes to clarify for future believers, as the Pope might undertake to clarify the doctrine of the Assumption. He has decided to intervene in the lin-guistics controversy of 1949–50, centering on the question of whether language is determined by stages of historical development, as all other aspects of culture are, or whether it is somehow exempt, perhaps neutral in the class struggle as tools are or, like a rifle, taking on historical significance according to who points it at whom. He moves through a muddle of Marxist jargon:

> If language is a superstructure, why doesn't it change with every epoch? If it is not a superstructure, what is it? A base? A mode of production?
> Properly speaking, it is like this: modes of production consist of pro-ductive forces and productive relations. To call language a *relation* is impossible. So does that mean language is a productive force? But pro-ductive forces include the instruments of production, the means of pro-duction, and people. But even though people speak language, language is not people. The devil himself knows—he was at a dead end. (97, 89)

We are shown the process of composition, moving back and forth from actual sentences quoted from Stalin's text to the thought processes of the writer at work, all in a tone of murderous mockery which spares neither the man nor his doctrine. Stalin finds himself stuck on a fine point of theory regarding the essential relationship between base and superstructure. He jots down a phrase, "The superstructure was created by the base *for the purpose of* ..." (99, 90), unaware, as Solzhenitsyn says, "of the angel of medieval teleology smiling over his shoulder," and equally unaware, I might add, of the anthropomorphic tendency to animate abstractions.[16] Solzhenitsyn's targets are precise. He is ridiculing here the Marxian description of the connection between history and culture.[17] The base-superstructure formula accounts for the behavior of entire cultures, the being-consciousness formula for the behavior of individual men, seen as members of classes. Each implies the other and both repeatedly draw Solzhenitsyn's scornful attention in and out of his novels. He has explained the bitter despair in which he wrote the unpublished play *Feast of the Conquerors*: "It bears the stamp of desperation of the camps in those years when man's conscious being was determined by his social being."[18] If this doctrine is valid only in the brutish conditions of concentration camps, it is clearly inadequate to account for the higher functions of consciousness. And when it is converted from an historical description to an enforceable doctrine in the hands of an all-powerful leader, it violates human beings, extinguishes morality, and sterilizes culture.

This complex of ideas and feelings functions in *The First Circle* much as Ivan's rational arrogance and intellectual skepticism do in

[16] "It is no accident," as Stalin might say, that Andrei Sinyavsky chooses this same sentence to illustrate the religiosity of the official Soviet mind. He says of it, in "On Socialist Realism": "Suddenly, from the pages of scientific treatises and scientific investigations there resounds the voice of the great religious Mystery," and then quotes more of the sentence than Solzhenitsyn does: "The base creates the superstructure so that it can serve the base." Abram Tertz [pseud.], *"The Trial Begins" and "On Socialist Realism,"* trans. Max Hayward ("Trial") and George Dennis ("Realism") (New York, 1965), p. 159. Stalin's complete sentence reads: "The base creates the superstructure precisely in order that it may serve it, that it may actively help it to take shape and consolidate itself, that it may actively strive for the elimination of the old moribund base, and its old superstructure." J. Stalin, *Marxism and Linguistics* (New York, 1951), p. 10.

[17] The full operative passage from the Patristic texts is found in Marx's "Preface" to the *Critique of Political Economy*: "In the social production of their life, men enter into definite relations that are indispensable and independent of their will, relations of production which correspond to a definite stage of development of their material productive forces. The sum total of these relations of production constitutes the economic structure of society, the real foundation, on which rises a legal and political superstructure and to which correspond definite forms of social consciousness. The mode of production of material life conditions the social, political, and intellectual life in general. It is not the consciousness of men that determines their being, but, on the contrary, their social being that determines their consciousness." Karl Marx and Friedrich Engels, *Selected Works in Two Volumes* (Moscow, 1951), 1: 329.

[18] *Solzhenitsyn: A Documentary Record*, ed. Leopold Labedz (New York, 1971), p. 104.

The Brothers Karamazov, spreading to the far corners of the novel, animating dramatic conflicts, provoking arguments, influencing important decisions, appearing and reappearing to shape the documentary matter of the novel. It is explicitly present in the part of the novel concerned with the doomed diplomat, Volodin, and his wife's family, the Makarygins. The senior member of the family is a high-ranking military prosecutor, who "is unwaveringly firm" (234, *209*). Solzhenitsyn here extends his moral cartography to a broad area of the Soviet establishment, to a literary lion, for example, who consoles himself that he can still tell "1/32 of the truth" (360, *321*); to an authoritative literary critic, who is an expert at accommodating to official norms; and to a number of high-ranking military jurists, who tell us that in "a Party matter," all scruples are scrapped, that the actual conduct of judicial affairs is controlled not by statutes but by a secret "little file" (364, *324*).

The sympathetic figure in this group is Makarygin's daughter, Clara, who first confronts the consequences and then the causes of this corruption in art and morality. She has already been deadened by her work as a graduate student in literature:

Gorky was correct but somehow ponderous; Mayakovsky was very correct but somehow awkward; Saltykov-Shchedrin was progressive but you could die yawning if you tried to read him through; Turgenev was limited to his nobleman's ideals; Goncharov was associated with the beginnings of Russian capitalism; Leo Tolstoi came to favor the patriarchal peasantry—and their teacher did not recommend their reading Tolstoi's novels because they were very long and only confused the clear critical essays written about him. (236, *210*)[19]

In this travesty of a university education, an entire literary tradition is flattened out by the clichés of Marxian class analysis, in which social being determines and devitalizes the writers' consciousness. "They studied a kind of literature which dealt with everything on earth except what one could see with one's own eyes." She recalls the study group where they discussed Louis Aragon, Howard Fast, and Gorky's influence on Uzbek literature while she thought of the wild and evil vitality of the Tashkent bazaar nearby.

Clara tells Lansky, a rising young establishment critic, about the injustices she has seen at the *sharashka,* where she works as a "free

---

[19] The essays are Lenin's five short pieces on Tolstoy. They dominated Tolstoy scholarship during the entire Stalin era, but here, in Solzhenitsyn's mocking recapitulation of the literary curriculum, they take the place of Tolstoy's fiction.

employee." If innocent men are arrested, she says, that means that those who arrested them "can do whatever they want." Lansky invokes the touchstone of historicity, in order to envelop and neutralize her aggressive critique:

"No," he said softly but convincingly, "not 'whatever they want.' Who 'wants' anything? Who 'does' anything? History. To you and me that sometimes seems terrible, but, Clara, it's time to get used to the fact that there is a law of big numbers. The bigger the scope of an historical event, the greater the probability of individual errors, be they judicial, tactical, ideological, economic. . . . The essential thing is to be convinced that the process is inevitable and necessary. Yes, sometimes someone suffers. . . . Wisdom lies in accepting the process as it develops with its inevitable increment of victims." (246, *218*)

Thus, individual moral authority is short-circuited by delegating all responsibility to the higher purposes of a personified history, in effect, to Stalin, who alone is authorized to consult and interpret the pulsations from the Demiurge. Clara, who is beginning to understand what it means to stand on the ground of the "lower" morality, responds indignantly and personally, "The law of big numbers should be tried out on you." Her alienation from a false and falsified literature has become a moral awakening, touched off by her vivid sense of injustice and her disgust at official rationalizations. An incipient love affair with a prisoner, a tough, hustling street kid, has given these new thoughts a specific human reference.

Her inevitable confrontation with her privileged, bemedaled father centers on the relevance of the law: "social being determines consciousness";[20] on the incompatibility of "history" and "justice"; and, as her father says, on her habit of dwelling on "every kind of *untypical* occurrence." When he invokes "the Party of the working class" in an argument about the prisoners, she answers angrily, "Never mind the speeches, Papa":

You call yourself the working class! You were a worker for two years, ages ago, and for thirty years since you have been a prosecutor! Some worker you are, you don't even have a hammer in the house. A worker who won't go near a car without a chauffeur! Being determines consciousness—that's what we're taught, isn't it? (367, *327*)

[20] Kathryn Feuer has suggested that the Makarygin family has its roots in Tolstoy. If we note that Sinyavsky's Prosecutor in "The Trial Begins" quarrels with his son over many of the same things, we may paraphrase the opening sentence of *Anna Karenina*: The unhappy families of Soviet Prosecutors *are* all alike.

Clara here invokes Lenin's celebration of the working-class ethos to criticize Stalin's regime, but she is moving away from Marxism and toward Nerzhin's position through her initiation into the tensions and questions of the prisoner's world. In addition, she invokes Marx's law to attack her father's privileged and hypocritical position, but she misquotes it. Her father corrects her, "Yes, *social* being, you little fool! And *social* consciousness," and misquotes it, too. Clara uses the doctrine to disparage her father, but she also discredits the doctrine itself: it certainly bears no relation to his career. In this connection, we may note Nerzhin's bitter reply to the artist Kondrashev-Ivanov, who had said, "No camp should break a man's spiritual beauty."

Perhaps it should not, but it does! . . . You don't know how they break us there. People go in, and when they come out—if they come out—they're unrecognizably different. Yes, it's well known: being determines consciousness. (256, 227)[21]

Resistance to this regime is the essence of moral behavior. The entire prison apparatus is designed to enforce a process that has not developed as it should have: decades of Soviet social being have not produced Soviet consciousness. The drastic measures institutionalized in the system require two transactions of each individual, as summed up by Nerzhin: "In exchange for seven ounces of black bread they demand of us not only our spiritual harmony, but also the last remnants of conscience." It is quite clear that the doctrine of social being and consciousness lies at the very foundation of the entire prison system. Resistance to physical imprisonment must extend to the doctrine that sanctions it, if "harmony" and "conscience" are to be preserved intact.

V

The similar conflicts in the Makarygin family and in the Rubin-Nerzhin and Rubin-Sologdin confrontations bind together the levels of contrapuntal structure in this *roman à thèse*, and rest on a single dramatic pattern: the intellectual and moral battle between the Marx-Stalin axis and the lonely, self-defining individual, in and out of

21 Nerzhin's alteration of the formula should probably not be taken as a misquotation, as it is with the Makarygins. It may suggest his distaste for the formula in its broadest sense. There is reason to believe that in his own thinking Solzhenitsyn might reverse the order to "consciousness determines being," if he did not reject the idea altogether.

prison. Minor characters amplify these ideas at a distance from the dramatic center, filling in remote corners of the moral map. Both central and marginal characters clarify Solzhenitsyn's discursive intentions, and call fully and finally into question the widespread interpretation of his work as an attack on Stalinist "distortions." Georg Lukács has argued that in his novels Solzhenitsyn has sought to rescue Marxism and socialist realism from Stalin's crude versions of both: that he remains a loyal Marxist-Leninist as man and writer.[22] But there is no suggestion in the novel that Stalin has misused or perverted Marxian ideas. The protestant impulse to return to ancient texts in order to cleanse the doctrine of impurities is nowhere visible. In a number of backward flashes we are shown both the high idealism of the early years and its steady decline. One prisoner, a former Party member, had been arrested in the "Industrial Party" trials in 1930, and has survived by sheerest accident into the present. The violation of his and his comrades' integrity has permanently stunned him, but he remains immured in the past and has nothing to say to his fellow prisoners about his former idealism.

There is one hiatus in *The First Circle*'s structure of argument: Lenin's precise relation to the Marx-Stalin axis which dominates the novel. On several occasions Leninist ideas do serve as a *point d'appui* for a critique of Stalin's practices. Nerzhin tells of his youthful distaste for Stalin's language:

Listen, when I was a little boy, I started to read his books after reading Lenin's, and I couldn't get through them. After a style that was direct, ardent, precise, suddenly there was a sort of mush. Every one of his thoughts is crude and stupid—he doesn't even realize that he always misses what's important.... All that pretentiousness, the didactic condescension of his proclamations, drives me mad. (36, 35)

Direct, ardent, precise as against mush—a comparison of personal styles, but in a field, language, which Solzhenitsyn values as a chief attribute of civilization. Characters talk at length about style, literature, linguistics, often seeing language as an index of moral value.

---

[22] One is at a loss to account for Lukács's willful misreading of texts that are available to all of us. He reverses meanings at will, omits points that refute his argument, and turns the novels into precisely what they are not. One is compelled to speculate on the decline, just before death, of an able critic, or on the final bankruptcy of a method, or on a combination of the two. See Georg Lukács, *Solzhenitsyn*, trans. William David Graf (Cambridge, Mass, 1971).

It is central to the book's symbolism that the work on voice prints is a violative inquiry into the unique properties of each man's speech. But the contrast between Lenin and Stalin does not extend far beyond this single vital area.

On the moral plane, it is true, "Leninist purity" is invoked several times in a critical contrast with the gross inequalities and privileges of the Stalinist era. Clara mentions it in her attack on her father's parasitic situation. It is brought up, most significantly, by an old Bolshevik, Radovich, formerly a Serbian member of the Comintern. He is alive after years spent in hospitals and a career of total discretion since his release. His presence doubtless fulfills part of Solzhenitsyn's map-making intention. He is that representative of the Bolshevik past, now in a disinterested position because he is retired, who might be expected to make the case for the pre-Stalin Communist cause. In a long conversation with his lifelong friend Makarygin, he is critical of the present regime on several scores. Like arguing bishops, they cite texts—Plekhanov, Engels, Feuerbach. And they fence over contemporary events and public accounts of them; "I suppose you believe the Americans are dropping potato bugs from airplanes?" Radovich asks Makarygin. The old Bolshevik invokes the Leninist strictures against rank and privilege; in support of Clara's argument he inveighs against Makarygin's "bourgeois rot": "Look at what you have become." Finally, he comes close to a total break with his friend over Soviet vilification of Yugoslavia. But we are warned before this discussion not to expect any sign of genuinely creative dissidence in it. Though Radovich varies from the mold, and Makarygin warns him to be silent in the presence of a high-ranking third party, the author prejudges all we are about to hear:

In actual fact, even if Radovich had let himself go, he had nothing so terrible to say. He was a Marxist, flesh of their flesh, blood of their blood, and he held orthodox views about everything. However, Stalin's entourage was more violently allergic to minute differences of tone and shading than to completely contrasting colors, and for the slight deviations that distinguished Radovich from the others he could have been immediately liquidated. (363, 323)

He is in mortal danger, but for no good reason, certainly from the vantage of Solzhenitsyn, who finds in Radovich's position no source of moral renewal. At the end of the argument with Makarygin, Radovich escapes into a cloud of outdated Marxian fantasy:

The capitalist world is doomed by . . . contradictions. And, as everyone in the Comintern predicted, I believe firmly that we will soon witness an armed conflict between America and England for world markets. (370, 329)[23]

Lenin is not even an important part of this old veteran's nostalgia. In the world of the novel, Marx proposes and Stalin disposes, and Lenin is very nearly excluded as an influential historical figure. We see Lenin as a stylist and as the symbol of moral idealism in the early days of the regime, but not as a revolutionary theorist, or political actor, or builder of the new order.

One other reference in the novel suggests that Solzhenitsyn will separate the personal from the political dimension when he finally confronts Lenin in history, as he must, in one of the sequels to *August 1914*. In a discussion with Nerzhin, the romantic artist Kondrashev-Ivanov has this to say about Russian art, landscape, and character:

Understand one thing: the public has been fooled by Levitan.[24] After Levitan we've come to think of our Russian nature as low-key, impoverished, pleasant in a modest way. But if that's all our nature is, then tell me where all those rebels in our history come from: the self-immolators, the mutineers, Peter the Great, the Decembrists, the "People's Will" revolutionaries. (256, 227)

Nerzhin agrees excitedly, "It's true," and adds to this company of fanatics the names of Lenin and Zhelyabov, idealistic assassin of Alexander II. The painter completes his thought: "Our Russian nature exults and rages and doesn't give way before the Tartar hooves!" We cannot predict the Lenin scenes in the sequels to *August 1914*, but we can guess from these earlier suggestions that Lenin will be set in a national frame and represented in markedly "romantic" colors.[25]

[23] Isaac Deutscher traces the history of this Comintern thesis. It was formulated by Trotsky and accepted by the Politburo in the 1920s and repeated by Stalin as late as 1930. Deutscher, *Stalin, A Political Biography* (New York, 1960), p. 410.

[24] I. I. Levitan, nineteenth-century landscapist.

[25] The dissident writers have been very reticent about Lenin. Pasternak names no historical Bolsheviks in *Doctor Zhivago*. Lenin's name appears in Sinyavsky's work but never in a central position, not even in the short destructive history of the Soviet regime he includes in "On Socialist Realism." Only Vassily Grossman's anguished essay-novel *Forever Flowing* (*Vse techet* in Russian, again from Engels out of Heraclitus) raises questions about Lenin, proposing that he is a divided man—plain, aescetic, compassionate on the one hand, ruthless, domineering, and vengeful on the other. Grossman, *Forever Flowing* (New York, 1972). In *Gulag Archipelago*, Solzhenitsyn's approach is low key and documentary. He shows Lenin's complicity in the formation of

There is an upwelling of evil at the end of *First Circle*: new, savagely cruel prison regulations are issued; anti-Semitism makes its appearance as the Doctors' Plot takes shape; the apparatus of informers moves into the foreground. Nerzhin and others are borne away on this malevolent tide, "transported" to unknown corners of the prison empire. They are taken through Moscow in paddy wagons disguised as meat trucks; the word meat is written in four languages on the trucks' panels, and a fatuous, fellow-traveling French correspondent reports that "the provisioning of the capital is excellent" (580, *511*). Prisoners concealed in a meat truck—the lie perpetuated at home and abroad—recalls the prisoner's question that opens the novel: "May I ask what age we are living in? Numbers on human beings? ... Is that ... *progressive?*" Men begin as numbers and end as meat, and each image is set against the language of lies that has reduced them.

the penal system and in the spread of terrorism as a political tactic through precise quotations from his Collected Works. His explanation in Zurich that he had cut a chapter on the sacrosanct figure of Lenin from the text of *August 1914* in the hope that Soviet editors would publish it puts his own reticence in a new light. See the *New York Times*, December 4, 1974. It may be that others of the nine excised chapters in *First Circle* treat Lenin more fully, but at this writing we have not yet had the direct confrontation.

CHAPTER 16

Solzhenitsyn II: "Just Like That!"

Cancer Ward interrupts Solzhenitsyn's life work—his quest for the meaning of Russian experience since August 1914—and detains him, as *First Circle* did, in the personal and the contemporary. Both novels show men struggling to survive in conditions of gross adversity, confined in institutions, in one case for political reasons, in the other for biological reasons, but threatened in both with pain, indignity, mutilation, or death. The literary strategies are similar: a complicated but straightforward linear development—multilayered like many nineteenth-century novels—without experiments in time or perception or other modernist intricacies. Narration is rough-and-ready as measured against the strictures of the "well-made novel," more in the manner of Tolstoy in *War and Peace* than of Flaubert in *Madame Bovary*; authorial presence is strongly felt, attitudes toward characters are easily detected, the narrating voice is openly judgmental on occasion. Moral protagonists are highly visible—and some bear autobiographical labels—but they are not charged with the telling of the story. That is done by an authoritative author-narrator (there is no need to distinguish between the two), who hovers near his protagonists and reports on their thoughts and feelings, but moves away freely into other characters or upward toward omniscience. In both novels, these narrative properties serve the mode of documentary expose, in which the voice of the teller affects to show the readers hidden truths, to instruct them through shock, and thus to provoke them through indignation, to a new understanding of the world.

The norms of judgment are moral throughout both novels; the "system" called into question, or subverted, has failed because it is bound together by a texture of lies, enforced by organized brutality. Prescriptions for change, such as they are, envision the restoration of a moral foundation to society's institutions. If this requires *political* changes in the arrangement of these institutions, it is left as an unexplored inference to be drawn elsewhere and by others from the moral critique. In this important way, traditional in the history of the novel, Solzhenitsyn seeks to avoid the shallow, and to him irrelevant, charge of political disloyalty.

Both novels confine a large, varied group of strangers within institutional walls; the characters explore and expose one another's lives, and each major character confronts a personal crisis forced on him by his confinement. *Cancer Ward*, of course, differs from *First Circle* as a hospital differs from a prison. The walls of the hospital are a symbol of mortality; each character is required to react to the possibility of his own arbitrary and premature death. In Solzhenitsyn's prisons, characters undergo a similar act of enforced self-definition, but their primary antagonist is man, the arbitrary fate they face is man-made, the pressure for unequivocal moral choice is sharper.

II

Yet the concentration-camp experience is vitally represented in *Cancer Ward* by the protagonist, Oleg Kostoglotov, who observes and interrogates the extra-prison world he is experiencing for the first time in many years. His total response is a reflective critique of the moral quality of the post-Stalin Soviet world. He is not an intellectual —he is more "innocent" than Nerzhin in that sense—but as a long-time prisoner, and former worker and army sergeant, he, too, represents that special ethos of prisoners who have "survived," who have gained a precious freedom from material needs by owning nothing and have graduated into a kind of moral elite. His critique is expressed in a number of raging arguments with fellow patients who for one reason or another defend the system. The biggest quarrel, forming part of the novel's climax, concerns a new variation on a familiar theme: social being, which determines consciousness, is in turn determined by social genesis—by the class one is born into—as the doctrine is translated into Soviet practice. Given the *kto-kogo* mentality of class struggle, birth alone determines the moral worth or legal liability of individuals, in effect, the guilt or innocence of whole classes. When the patients discuss a Party member who stole Party funds and built himself a villa, they diagnose it as another case of "bourgeois mentality." Oleg's moral instincts alert him to the false-hood and the menace in this phrase:

Why, it's human greed, that's what it is, not bourgeois mentality. There were greedy people *before* the bourgeoisie and there'll be greedy people *after* the bourgeoisie. (405, 342)[1]

Rusanov, the Stalinist careerist and chief target of Oleg's attacks, de-clares, "If you dig deep into such cases you'll always find bourgeois social origins." "Nonsense," Oleg replies, and then drops his bomb-shell: "That's not Marxism. It's racism!" He still regards this doctrine as a departure from Marxism, not a consequence of it, but when he translates bourgeois morality into greed, replacing Party jargon with the language of ordinary moral discourse, he is repeating the char-acteristic envelopment of the doctrinal by the human. He does not propose his own definition of the relations between social origin and "mentality," but seems rather to ask for a purge of the false language in order to end the acts it licenses.

By linking "social being" with Nazi "blood" theory, he has merged the opposites of an unquestioned polarity in the Soviet value spectrum. Rusanov is outraged and the ward explodes. Oleg bursts into the pungent obscenities of camp language, the idiom of his real exper-ience, as shocking to his respectable ward-mates as his ideas are. Before a fight breaks out, the discussion moves on to privilege and inequality, when Oleg contrasts Lenin's dream of a revolution by and for equals with the moral squalor of Soviet reality.[2] He is sup-ported unexpectedly in the argument by Shulubin, a strange, owl-like character, an enigmatic onlooker until now, who quotes the Party's famous April Theses (1917), which translated Lenin's egali-tarian views into policy. Shulubin's quiet, authoritative voice changes the tone of the dispute and brings it to an end, but reveals nothing about himself or his personal convictions.

A later meeting in the hospital garden between Oleg and Shu-

---

[1] The editions cited in the text are, in order, Alexander Solzhenitsyn, *Cancer Ward*, trans. Nicholas Bethell and David Burg (New York, 1969), and A. Solzhenitsyn, *Rakovyi korpus* (Paris, 1968).

[2] The discovery of this contrast seems to mark a precise stage in Solzhenitsyn's view of the process of disillusionment.

lubin illuminates the moral and intellectual issues for Oleg, resolves undefined tensions in his mind, and sends him toward his destiny with a measure of clarity. Shulubin brings an educated mind to bear on the issues Oleg gropes to define through his experience and his moral impulses. Oleg has hesitated, according to prisoner etiquette, to approach this misshapen, suffering recluse because "the camps had taught him that people who say nothing carry something within themselves," but when Shulubin invites him to sit down on a park bench they talk. They compare their cancers, and Oleg wonders who is worse off: "For instance, I might conclude that I've led an extraordinarily unlucky life, but how do I know? Maybe yours has been even harder." (432, 363.) He reviews his misfortunes, not only the war and the labor camps, but "no higher education, no officer's commission, exile in perpetuity ... and one more thing, cancer." They agree to call it "quits about the cancer" in their sympathetic competition, and then Shulubin makes his case to a responsive Oleg: "The man with the hardest life is the man who walks out of his house every day and bangs his head against the top of the door because it's too low." With this image, he introduces his experience of the universal lie and the individual life lived out according to its dictates. Shulubin constructs a pattern of parallel violations, in which his forced acquiescence in the lie is shown to be as painful and as destructive as the other's physical suffering:

You people were arrested, but we were herded into meetings to "expose" you. They executed people like you, but they made us stand up and applaud the verdicts as they were announced. And not just applaud, they made us demand the firing squad. *Demand* it! (432, 364)

Shulubin has more to say about the obscene unanimity required of everybody at the risk of their lives. Oleg is sympathetic: "People like you who understand what was happening, who understood early enough, suffered searing agonies." But, he adds, "those who believed were all right." "Who believed?" Shulubin asks. When Oleg acknowledges that he believed—"until Finland"—Shulubin continues his bill of indictment in a cascading rhetoric (suggestive of Ivan Karamazov's accusation of God) as he lists what a man would have to believe in order to remain a believer:

Suddenly all the professors and all the engineers turn out to be wreckers, and he believes it! The best Civil War divisional commanders turn out to be German and Japanese spies, and he believes it! The whole of Lenin's old guard are shown up as vile renegades, and he believes it! His own friends and acquaintances are unmasked as enemies of the people, and he believes it! Millions of Russian soldiers turn out to have betrayed their country, and he believes it all! Whole nations, old men and babies, are mown down, and he believes it! Then what sort of man is he, may I ask? He's a fool. But can there really be a whole nation of fools? No, you'll have to forgive me. The people are intelligent enough, it's simply that they wanted to live. (434, 365)

The resolution of the intellectual, psychological, and stylistic tensions in this passage points toward moral self-condemnation. Shulubin quotes three lines from Pushkin about the only judgments history can make about any man "in our vile times": "Either tyrant or traitor or prisoner!"[3] There is no room in the line for "fool," Shulubin points out; he has never been a tyrant or a prisoner, but before he labels himself a traitor, he returns to the question of comparative suffering: "Do you think that sort of life was easier than yours? My whole life I've lived in fear, but now I'd change places with you." Oleg finds Pushkin too rash and Shulubin too harsh, but still sympathetic, he refuses to pronounce judgment.

Shulubin then moves from his and the nation's *experience* of lying to what might be called the *theory* of lying, by invoking Francis Bacon's four categories of deception and self-deception, the four ways men "pollute experience with prejudices." These are symbolized in *The New Organon* as the four idols—of the tribe, the cave, the market place, and the theater—all described by Bacon as opening the way to the "false notions which are now in possession of the human understanding, and have taken deep root therein," and "so beset men's minds that truth can hardly find entrance."[4]

Shulubin does not define the idols of the tribe or the cave, which

---

[3] Shulubin is quoting Pushkin's poem "To Vyazemsky" (1826). The full text of the poem follows, with the quoted portions in italics: Tak, more, drevnii dushegubets, / Vosplamenyaet genii tvoi? / Ty slavish' liroi zolotoi / Neptuna groznogo trezubets. Ne slav' ego. *V nash gnusnyi vek* / Sedoi Neptun zemli soyuznik. / *Na vsekh stikhiyakh chelovek— / Tiran, predatel' ili uznik.* (So, the sea, that ancient murderer, / Ignites your genius? / You praise with your golden lyre / The trident of the dread Neptune / Do not praise it. *In our vile time* / The hoary Neptune is an ally of earth. / *In all the elements man is / A tyrant, a traitor or a prisoner.*)

This poem was sent in a letter to Prince P. A. Vyazemsky in response to his poem "The Sea." It refers to the rumor, later disproved, that N. I. Turgenev, one of those accused in the Decembrist conspiracy, had been arrested in London and brought back to Petersburg by ship. See A. S. Pushkin, *Polnoe sobranie sochinenii* (Moscow, 1956), 2: 31, 437.

[4] Francis Bacon, *The New Organon and Related Writings* (New York, 1960), p. 47.

stand for humanity's capacity to be deceived or to deceive itself.[5]
He merely names them, but Oleg's response is vivid and characteristic:
he takes Bacon's metaphors literally and pictures the cave "smoke-
filled, with a fire in the middle, the savages roasting meat, while in
the depths of the cave there stood, almost indiscernible, a bluish idol."[6]
When Oleg asks Shulubin what the idols of the theater are, the following dialogue ensues:

"The idols of the theater are the authoritative opinions of others which
a man likes to accept as a guide when interpreting something he hasn't
experienced himself."
"Oh, but this happens very often."
"But sometimes he actually has experienced it, only it's more convenient not to believe what he's seen."
"I've seen cases like that as well. . . ."
"Another idol of the theater is our over-willingness to agree with the
arguments of science. One can sum this up as the voluntary acceptance
of other people's errors." (436, 366)[7]

[5] To convey the full resonance of Solzhenitsyn's reference, I present Bacon's initial
definition of both idols: "The Idols of the Tribe have their foundation in human
nature itself, and in the tribe or race of men. For it is a false assertion that the sense
of man is the measure of things. On the contrary, all perceptions as well of the sense
as of the mind are according to the measure of the individual and not according to the
measure of the universe. And the human understanding is like a false mirror, which,
receiving rays irregularly, distorts and discolors the nature of things by mingling its
own nature with it.
"The Idols of the Cave are the idols of the individual man. For everyone (besides
the errors common to human nature in general) has a cave or den of his own, which
refracts and discolors the light of nature, owing either to his own proper and peculiar
nature; or to his education and conversation with others; or to the reading of books,
and the authority of those whom he esteems and admires; or to the differences of
impressions, accordingly as they take place in a mind preoccupied and predisposed
or in a mind indifferent and settled; or the like. So that the spirit of man (according
as it is meted out to different individuals) is in fact a thing variable and full of
perturbation, and governed as it were by chance. Whence it was well observed by
Heraclitus that men look for sciences in their own lesser worlds, and not in the greater
or common world." *Ibid.*, pp. 48–49.
[6] One member of the Writers' Union exhibited the same simplicity of mind at a
meeting to censure Solzhenitsyn in 1967. Aleksei Surkov, poet and ranking literary
bureaucrat, was puzzled by one of the idols: "And then there is that idol in the
theater square, even though the monument to Marx had not yet been erected at that
time." In his rebuttal, Solzhenitsyn politely corrected Surkov, but did not dwell on
the scene's Gogolian inanities. See *Solzhenitsyn: A Documentary Record*, ed. Leopold
Labedz (New York, 1971), pp. 115, 121. These mistakes, in and out of the novel,
are made possible by Solzhenitsyn's use of the Russian cognate for the Latin *idolum*.
The 1935 Russian edition of *Novum Organum* is closer to the correct meaning of
idolum, which is translated as *prizrak* (phantom), the preferred meaning in the sixteenth century according to the Oxford English Dictionary. See Frantsisk Bekon,
Novyi Organon, ed. G. Tymyanskii, trans. S. Krasilshchikov (Leningrad, 1935). One
wonders what text Solzhenitsyn had at hand.
[7] In Bacon's language: "Lastly, there are Idols which have immigrated into men's
minds from the various dogmas of philosophies, and also from wrong laws of demon-

Shulubin's accurate but limited reading of Bacon emphasizes the credulity of the receiver of false ideas, rather than their sources, which Bacon says are not innate, but learned: "...nor do they [the Idols of the Theater] steal into the understanding secretly, but are plainly impressed and received into the mind from the playbooks of philosophical systems and the perverted rules of demonstration."[8] To pursue this definition, Shulubin would be obliged to challenge the system and all the means of implanting it, but he aims only to strengthen Oleg's sense of the validity of his own experience, not to instruct him in the falseness of a philosophy, which, he indicates later, he rejects at its roots. In this sense, the most important of Bacon's aphorisms concerns the idol of the market place, which Shulubin brings into sharp Soviet focus:

The idols of the market place are the errors which result from the communication and association of men with each other. They are the errors a man commits because it has become customary to use certain phrases and formulas which do violence to reason. For example, "Enemy of the People!" "Not one of us!" "Traitor!" Call a man one of these and every one will renounce him. (436, 367)[9]

In this paraphrase of Bacon's argument, Shulubin has validated Oleg's instinctive revulsion against the use of false language—his spontaneous translation of bourgeois mentality into greed—and has shown that false language gives operative force to destructive impulses, to the insensate infliction of suffering.

The use of Bacon's aphorisms at this climactic moment in the novel

---

stration. These I call Idols of the Theater, because in my judgment all the received systems are but so many stage plays, representing worlds of their own creation after an unreal and scenic fashion. Nor is it only of the systems now in vogue, or only of the ancient sects and philosophies, that I speak; for many more plays of the same kind may yet be composed and in like artificial manner set forth; seeing that errors the most widely different have nevertheless causes for the most part alike. Neither again do I mean this only of entire systems, but also of many principles and axioms in science, which by tradition, credulity, and negligence have come to be received." Bacon, *The New Organon*, p. 49.

[8] *Ibid.*, p. 58.

[9] Bacon's text: "There are also Idols formed by the intercourse and association of men with each other, which I call Idols of the Market Place, on account of the commerce and consort of men there. For it is by discourse that men associate, and words are imposed according to the apprehension of the vulgar. And therefore the ill and unfit choice of words wonderfully obstructs the understanding. Nor do the definitions or explanations wherewith in some things learned men are wont to guard and defend themselves, by any means set the matter right. But words plainly force and overrule the understanding, and throw all into confusion, and lead men away into numberless empty controversies and idle fancies." *Ibid.*, p. 49.

clarifies the "statement" Solzhenitsyn would have the novel make. He seems to share Bacon's desire to define the idols of false notions in order that the "human understanding may the more willingly submit to its purgation and dismiss them."[10] He appears to join Bacon in celebrating the inductive method, the resolute attention to the particularities of experience—in Solzhenitsyn's view, the life histories of real individuals—in order to demonstrate "that all theories should be steadily rejected and dismissed as obsolete."[11] One larger irony in the history of thought is suggested by his reliance on *The New Organon*. Bacon's eloquence was directed primarily against the dogmatic cosmology of the medieval Church—"for many ages men's minds have been busied with religion and theology"—though he inveighs against all "systems." He asks for a clear mind, attentive to the actual contours of experience, resistant to all dogmas, all *a priori* assumptions and assumed conclusions, all false applications of systematic certainties.[12] It may be that Solzhenitsyn is asking for the same Renaissance view of the world, to oppose a cosmology as hermetic and coercive as the medieval Church's view of itself and the world, now manifest as a spurious scientism.

Bacon's Soviet editor points unwittingly to that irony when he justifies his own work because Bacon's "short, brilliant aphorisms ... set forth the materialist world view of the bourgeoisie in the epoch of primary capitalist accumulation in England."[13] In its opposition to scholasticism, the editor says, Bacon's work celebrates "the increase of man's power over nature," presumably by mastery over the world as it really is. Solzhenitsyn and other dissidents seem often to be asking for an empirical, pragmatic, particularized way to break out of the Marxian cosmology that encloses *them*. If all radical reformers, like the editors of the French *Encyclopédie*, for example, call attention to the actual configuration of things as against the superstitious, the handed-down, the falsely classified, all the givens of an "idealistic" system, then Solzhenitsyn's and his colleagues' critique of their world *does* coincide in this sense with Bacon's, Voltaire's, and Diderot's, and, ironically, with Marx's. *Ecrasez le nouvel infâme!*

Shulubin turns to personal confession in order to continue Oleg's program of instruction in the meaning of his experience. He begins the review of his own history with an atmospheric reference: "and

---

[10] *Ibid.*, p. 59.
[12] *Ibid.*, p. 59.
[11] *Ibid.*, p. 58.
[13] Bekon, *Novyi Organon*, p. 4.

over all idols there is the sky of fear, the sky of fear overhung with gray clouds" (436, 367). Fear governs the process by which his career has diminished, his intellectual range has shrunk, and his moral substance has disintegrated. He has "bowed low and kept silent" to save his skin, which is now "a bag of manure"; his wife is dead, and his children are alienated. His error—and his crime—are that he is still alive.

He traces his course: "Bolshevik in 1917, university lecturer in historical and dialectical materialism and other subjects," and then the long record of acquiescence and decline. He has bowed, retreated, confessed, renounced. He accepted the doctrines of Lysenko, "an ignorant agronomist," several times gave up his job under pressure, and reached bottom when he burned books—"into the stove with all your genetics, leftist aesthetics, ethics, cybernetics, arithmetic" (438, 367). But he notes that his complicity, his intellectual acquiescence, had begun many years before: "Had I not declared a quarter of a century earlier from my chair of dialectical materialism that the relativity theory was counterrevolutionary obscurantism?" (438, 368.) Again, moral corruption is traced back to basic doctrine. He dismisses himself as "a little man," but where were the others, Krupskaya, or Ordzhonikidze, "an eagle of a man"? Why did no one stand up and object publicly?

Shulubin does not doubt that "capitalism was doomed morally before it was doomed economically, and that was a long time ago. . . . If private enterprise isn't held in an iron grip, it gives birth to people who are no better than beasts." (440, 370.) Socialism is not to blame for Russia's recent suffering, but rather the foundation it has been built on. Again, the fallacy of social being is brought into focus:

We thought it was enough to change the mode of production and people would immediately change with it. But did they? The hell they did! They didn't change a bit. Man is a biological type. It takes thousands of years to change him. (*Ibid.*)[14]

[14] Bazarov, for one, in *Fathers and Sons*, utters this truism of the social materialisms in a conversation with Anna Odintsova, the object of his unexpected passion: "We know approximately what physical diseases come from; moral diseases come from bad education, from all the nonsense people's heads are stuffed with from childhood up, from the deformed state of society in a word. Reform society, and there will be no more diseases." Bazarov, of course, is not in the Kremlin, enforcing this dictum. Odintsova has had Oleg's insight about the persistence of ordinary human qualities. "And you suppose," she asks Bazarov, ". . . that when society is reformed, there will be no more stupid or wicked people?" And she is not uttering this thought from a con-

Shulubin has no more to say about the biological as opposed to the social roots of moral behavior, nor does he bother to distinguish between his own notion of genetic origins and the Soviet view of the class provenance of morality, which Oleg has called racist. He does, however, call attention to the mysterious presence of "evil," which is seen throughout the novel as ubiquitous and deep-rooted, whatever its source. For Shulubin it can be controlled only by a truly human socialist order.

He examines several foundations for that order and rejects them all. "Democratic" socialism is superficial, because it is defined only by the way it comes into being. Material abundance is an inadequate foundation for any kind of society, "because people sometimes behave like buffaloes, they stampede and trample the goods into the ground." Hatred is no better than greed as an emotional base, "because social life cannot be built on hatred."

After a man has burned with hatred year in, year out, he can't simply announce one fine day, "That's enough, as from today I'm finished with hatred, from now on I'm only going to love!" No, if he's used to hating, he'll go on hating. (*Ibid.*)

Love must replace hate, but "Christian" socialism is no better. Shulubin points out that parties bearing that label crawled out from under the Mussolini and Hitler regimes after World War II. In Tolstoy's earlier ventures in this direction another failure was registered:

At the end of the last century, Tolstoy decided to spread practical Christianity through society, but his ideals turned out to be impossible for his contemporaries to live with, his preaching had no link with reality. (441, *371*)

His own solution refers to another aspect of Russian traditional culture, though he includes Tolstoy among his references:

I should say that for Russia in particular, with our repentances, confessions, and revolts, our Dostoevsky, Tolstoy and Kropotkin, there's only one true socialism and that's moral socialism. That is something completely realistic. (*Ibid.*)[15]

---

centration camp. I. S. Turgenev, *Polnoe sobranie sochinenii* (Moscow-Leningrad, 1964), 8: 277–78.

[15] We cannot know whether or not these ideas and those that follow are Solzhenitsyn's own. It may be that through Shulubin he is trying to suggest other answers to closed questions as part of Oleg's education. But for the student of explicit political

The religion of powerful emotions, rather than any code of "practical behavior," must somehow form the base of what Shulubin goes on to define at length:

We have to show the world a society in which all relationships, fundamental principles and laws flow directly from morality and from it alone. Moral demands must determine all considerations: how to bring up children, what to train them for, to what end the work of grown-ups should be directed, and how their leisure should be occupied. As for scientific research, it should only be conducted where it doesn't damage morality . . . where it doesn't damage the researchers themselves. (*Ibid.*)[16]

Happiness, he says, is a false goal, "an idol of the market place in the literal sense"; mutual affection and sharing constitute the only grounds for moral behavior. Oleg asks what the material base will be for this new kind of socialism: "There has to be an economy. . . . That comes before anything else" (442, *371*). Shulubin cites Solovyov to argue that the economy itself must be built on a moral basis.[17] The

---

ideas, he has named here and in the text that follows Vladimir Solovyov, N. K. Mikhailovsky, and Prince Peter Kropotkin as possible sources. Shulubin asks Oleg if he has ever read Kropotkin's "Mutual Aid Among Men" (referring no doubt to his *Vzaimnaya pomosch, kak faktor evoliutsii* [Moscow, 1918]), in which it is argued that mutual aid is more important than struggle in the survival of species. Socialist or populist or anarchist, none of these Russian thinkers is a Marxist.

[16] Raymond Williams is troubled by what he calls this "dangerous passage— dangerous, I think, because it seems to a non-Marxist, Western socialist to ask an impossible backward turn of the world-wide movement toward human betterment." "Cannot theory of an advanced kind," he asks, "coexist with the most absolute, willed and unwilled, failures of human recognition, of the kind that here . . . is the first of all values?" Williams has missed Solzhenitsyn's point. It is not a question of coexistence (or not); it is rather that the "theory of an advanced kind" has *caused* the failures, both willed and unwilled, of human recognition. Shifting from the novel's record of experience to its explicit ideas, Williams explains his question as a disagreement: "If Solzhenitsyn believes that this kind of close, absolute human recognition was more present in the 'ethical socialism' of the nineteenth century than in the 'Marxism' which for sound economic and political reasons seemed to surpass it, I for one think he is right, though I doubt whether we could recover the recognition by going back on the historical insights; we would have to go on from them, and that is where many of us, in very different societies, now are and move." Williams seems to be saying that Marxism, that "body of historical insights," is usable and incorporable in the new stages of a general upward movement; whereas Solzhenitsyn, through Shulubin, seems to be saying that Marxism has so drastically misinterpreted the natures of man, history, and civilization that it looms as the major obstacle to that movement. For all the sensitivity of his effort to understand, Williams risks classification under Solzhenitsyn's anathema word "progressive," his collective designation of all Westerners who stubbornly refuse to see the truth about the Soviet world. See Raymond Williams, "On Solzhenitsyn," *Tri-Quarterly*, Winter-Spring, 1972.

[17] Here Shulubin seems to be repeating Solovyov's ideas on the proper relationship between morality and the economy in a healthy society. See, for example, "Morality, Politics and the Meaning of Nationality," in *A Solovyov Anthology*, S. L. Frank, ed. (New York, 1950).

Soviet world is stood on its head; materialism is dismissed, and moral consciousness, presumably, will determine social being!

Lukács says of this long episode that it is not "realized" fictionally, and that it is impossible to know where Solzhenitsyn stands with respect to these ideas.[18] Perhaps. But neither judgment takes full account of the complex intention Solzhenitsyn appears to be working out beyond the mere expression of an intellectual position through a sympathetic character. The encounter of the two men forms a climax in Oleg's process of self-definition, hence a climax in the conceptual structure of the novel itself. The two men end in close mutual understanding, Oleg's moral instincts enriched by ideas that illuminate and extend his own. The intellectual and the ordinary citizen have been brought together, and at the same time two great areas of suffering, inside and outside the prison camps, have been made intelligible to each other. Oleg's alienation is eased when he learns of suffering that parallels his own. Two large segments of Solzhenitsyn's moral map have been joined at this moment, when the men walk off together, Oleg supporting his crippled companion. Earlier, Oleg has commented on a misunderstanding with a former prison guard, "If decade after decade no one can tell the true story, each person's mind goes its own separate way. One's fellow countrymen become harder to understand than Martians." (458, *385*.) The opposite occurs in the long scene between him and Shulubin, and we come to realize that Solzhenitsyn is showing us one of the chief purposes of his art beyond indignation. The two men share, clarify, and ease their painful experiences, and offer the same opportunity, through the agency of the novel, to all who read it. Understanding, purgation, communion enlarge the aesthetic purpose beyond arousing indignation about false ideas, the mere dismissal of "the idols." All victims are invited to rally, to take counsel among themselves, to come to terms with their experience by sharing it, and thus to contribute to the restoration of the national conscience.

In Oleg's final encounter before his release, Solzhenitsyn fills another blank space on his map of Russia's suffering, and extends his definition of the special healing function his own work is meant to accomplish. The woman he meets is much like him; they are fellow Leningraders and have experienced parallel suffering. They

[18] Georg Lukács, *Solzhenitsyn*, trans. William David Graf (Cambridge, Mass., 1971), p. 75.

recognize in a flash that they are both victims, though in different ways, of the savage penal system.

Elizaveta, polite, efficient, thoughtful and reserved, is an orderly in the hospital, performing the dirtiest work. She is gently bred— "there had been lilac and lace in her life and the poetry of the symbolists" (479, *401*). She tells her story: the whole family arrested ("As for who was punished because of whom, I haven't any idea"); her daughter dead in exile; her husband, once a flautist in the Leningrad symphony, arrested, released, exiled, rearrested, and sent to the camps; she herself an exile, waiting now for the overdue semiannual letter. They talk about Leningrad, about the sequence of mass deportations, about how little they cared at first. When the nobility was moved out en masse, they remember, "We bought their pianos." Oleg listens sympathetically and gives one piece of advice, directly informed by his talk with Shulubin. She has hesitated about telling her eight-year-old son the truth about their lives. Oleg is unequivocal: "Burden him with the truth!" (478, *400*.)

Oleg had been full of his own misery before he listened to Elizaveta. But now that "another person's misery had rolled over him and washed his own away" (480, *403*), he experiences a kind of catharsis. Oleg's two encounters suggest a nationwide experience of communion, based on the harshest fronting of the truth, and a great outpouring of compassion, in which, to paraphrase Dostoevsky, each responds to the suffering of all, and all to the suffering of each.

Elizaveta reads light French novels, she says, because they offer a hermetic world that does not pretend to address itself to her experience and, therefore, cannot falsify it as "our writers" do.[19] Even when they have tried to tell the truth, they "have ignored those who are alive and suffering today" (479, *401*). Even the tragic literature of the past fails to bear on her experience: "Aida was allowed to join her loved one in the tomb and to die with him," but *she* cannot find out anything about her husband, not even where he is. Even *Anna Karenina* is a kind of deception for Elizaveta's generation because, as she points out, the terms of existence have changed and a new kind of literature is called for:

Children write essays in school about the unhappy, tragic, doomed, and I-don't-know-what-else life of Anna Karenina. But was Anna really un-

---

[19] Here she overturns the conventional experience of many Russian literary heroines, who read French novels to extend their knowledge of the world by learning about romantic love.

happy? She chose passion and she paid for her passion—that's happiness! She was a free, proud human being. But what if during peacetime a lot of greatcoats and peaked hats burst into the house where you were born and live, and order the whole family to leave house and town in twenty-four hours, with only what your feeble hands can carry. (*Ibid.*)

Beyond tears, as she is beyond tragedy, Elizaveta's eyes "could still flare up with a tense dry flame—her last curse upon the world" (*Ibid.*). She describes the final twenty-four hours in her house, selling her things to passersby, to black marketeers; her daughter at the piano "for the last time to play Mozart. But she bursts into tears and runs away."

So why should I read *Anna Karenina* again? Maybe it's enough—what I've experienced. Where can people read about us? US! Only in a hundred years' time? (*Ibid.*)[20]

It is Solzhenitsyn, of course, who has responded to her questions: her exchange with Oleg Kostoglotov is shared with the world.

III

Oleg is released, strengthened by this encounter too, but his first free day in town is bewilderingly difficult. His cure has desexed him, leaving him with the capacity to have sexual longings but not to fulfill them. Similarly, his years in prison and in the hospital have deprived him of other important aspects of his capacity to live a normal life. He knows he has not been granted a new life, only an extension,

---

[20] A character in Carlo Levi's *The Watch* defines Tolstoy's irrelevance when his novels are set against *l'univers concentrationnaire*: "You can keep your novels and your characters, those optimists and socialists, they're monsters.... Your Bezukhovs, your Levins, along with their Katyas and Natashas! After they've been conscience-stricken thousands of times, they decide in the end to get fat, to make children, work on their farms, farms of some thousands of acres, of course. It takes a war for them to achieve these happy results: Moscow in flames, Napoleon! Millions of people must go to pieces, beautiful women throw themselves under trains, all for their sake.... They don't have any value in the novels, nor do the novels have any value. Just caprice and falseness.... What sort of novel do you want after Auschwitz and Buchenwald? Did you see the photographs of women weeping as they buried pieces of soap made from the bodies of their husbands and their sons?... There you are... your *tranche de vie*—a piece of soap." Carlo Levi, *The Watch* (New York, 1951), pp. 64, 70–71.

Raymond Williams has understood very well that survival is the key to Solzhenitsyn and his novel: "In getting beyond pity, in his roughness, irritation, anger, laughter —Solzhenitsyn is honest, emotionally, in an exceptional degree. He stays with his people and with what is happening to them because in a deep way he is one of them, not an observer or a mirror, but a man in this collective, a surviving individual in this surviving, decimated group. It is the survival of the people, under so heavy an experience, that comes through as a value in the surviving, articulate, bitter and compassionate man." Williams, "On Solzhenitsyn," p. 331.

an "extra ration." Yet he enters the city at dawn as if it were "the morning of creation" (485, *406*). He is enchanted by the minutiae of existence: streets, passersby, courtyards, shashlik on a grill, a flowering apricot tree. Then confusion sets in, gradually eclipsing his sense of wonder; aspects of social existence are strange, even estranging. He waits for the opening of a department store and rushes in with the crowd, participating, without realizing it, in "the buffalo stampede" Shulubin has warned him about. Consumerism—literally, the idol of the market place—disgusts him. In the midst of this mob he sees himself in a mirror and realizes that he is not at all the jaunty young man he has imagined himself to be: he is awkward, disheveled, aged, out of place in the world of ordinary men.

He goes to the zoo, thinking he will be more at ease with the animals, but makes another disquieting discovery. The caged animals call up image after image of imprisoned men; he is haunted by his prison memories, disoriented by them because they usurp his daily perceptions. At the zoo he is shocked by a crude sign to the effect that a rhesus monkey was blinded when a visitor threw tobacco in his eyes. This image of gratuitous and inexplicable evil haunts him through this, the final day.

He has been invited by his friend, the woman doctor Vega (one of several dedicated and sympathetic medical figures), to stay with her after his release. He is delighted and bewildered by the invitation, wondering what it means, whether or not he can accept. The first time he goes to her house she is not there, but he is repelled by her hostile landlady and a snout-nosed neighbor with a coughing motorcycle, above all by the heaps of airing bedding which bespeak the solid respectability of "stable, tested experience" (514, *430*) from which he feels forever excluded. The second time, stimulated by the graceful Nilgai antelope in the zoo who resembles Vega, he buys violets for her but stops halfway to her house, finally realizing his total incapacity for such a relationship. Then, as a result of all he has experienced that day, he heads for the railroad station, on his way to the remote Central Asian village where his elderly friends live. He has settled for less, reduced his expectations, acknowledged his crippled condition. In the station he finds a situation he can handle: the standard Soviet battle for a place on the train. He knows all the tricks, remembers railway transport in the prison system, and is able to bring the real world and his spectral prison memories into a manageable relationship, the negative memory simply reinforcing the relative relief he feels in the train that will take him home. This integrating experience, modest and low key but entirely appropriate to his sense of his condition, is further strengthened by a memory from his pre-prison days: he recalls in detail an ingenious victory he had won over the train-boarding system in Stalingrad in 1939. When he fights his way into the relative comfort of an upper luggage rack, he makes a comfortable nest for himself with a practiced hand. His stretching out is told in a Hemingway rhythm, ending, "It was good to lie down. Good." In his relative felicity he has for a moment come to terms with all aspects of his condition: his illness, his imprisonment, his present afflictions, and his modified aspirations. Suddenly this moment of stasis is shattered. The novel ends with these words:

> The train shuddered and moved forward. It was only then that in his heart, or his soul, somewhere in his chest, in the deepest seat of his emotions, he was seized with anguish. He twisted his body and lay face down in his greatcoat, shut his eyes and thrust his face into the duffel bag. . . .
> The train went on and Kostoglotov's boots dangled toes down over the corridor like a dead man's.
> An evil man threw tobacco in the Macaque Rhesus's eyes.
> Just like that! [*Prosto tak!*] . . . (532, *446*)

Oleg has shut his eyes and hidden his face to avoid the tobacco in his own eyes, exhibiting at this freighted moment the defensive reflex of the victim. But victim of what? The word is "evil," but its sources and purposes are mysterious. The childish, handwritten sign in the zoo had said: "The little monkey that used to live here was blinded. An evil man threw tobacco into the Macaque Rhesus's eyes." Standing before the sign, Oleg had been struck dumb. The act was shocking but inexplicable. "Why? *Just like that!* Why? It's senseless! Why?" But he had noticed one thing:

> What went straight to his heart was the childish simplicity with which it was written. This unknown man, who had already made a safe getaway, was not described as "anti-humanist," or "an agent of American imperialism"; all it said was that he was evil. This was what was so striking: how could this man be simply "evil"? (506, *424*)

Again, through the agency of language, the human envelops the political, as "greed" replaced "bourgeois mentality," "evil" replaces the current jargon of vilification. But further questions remain. The victim was helpless, the perpetrator unknown, his motives mysterious.

The evil act was as sudden and violent and arbitrary as cancer and summary arrest, but its source is still unclear. The phrase "just like that" (*prosto tak!*) provides a clue. It appears once more between its first occurrence in Oleg's thoughts as he reads the sign about the rhesus monkey and its use as the concluding words of the novel. In the zoo he had moved to the section where the predators were kept. They were "prisoners," too, but they reminded him of the camp gangsters. Then:

A little further on he spotted "Mr. Tiger" [Stalin].[21] His whiskers—yes, it was the whiskers that were most expressive of his rapacious nature. But his eyes were yellow. . . . Strange thoughts came to Oleg's mind. He stood there looking at the tiger with hatred.
In the camps, Oleg had met an old political prisoner who had once been an exile in Turukhansk. He told Oleg about those eyes—they were not velvet black, they were yellow.
Welded to the ground with hatred, Oleg stood in front of the tiger's cage.
Prosto tak! Prosto tak!—Why? (507, 425)

Evil is not in Stalin, not in the tiger, but it works through both—a force of nature, it appears, an attribute of the realm they both inhabit. The human includes the bestial, but both are part of nature. In his discussion of evil, Shulubin has already told us that "man is a biological type."

Oleg's venture into the world has been told in two intricate chapters entitled "The First Day of Creation" and "And the Last Day." Oleg uses the first phrase to convey his sense of the wonder of life, as he explores the awakening city. The second may be read as the completion of that process, the final resolution of the tensions in the novel, and the ultimate formulation of the results of Solzhenitsyn's inquiry into experience. We do not know how explicitly we are to set this episode against the story of the creation in Genesis; certainly, Oleg's destiny, as he works it out, is to settle for less, and move toward

---

[21] Two passages in *First Circle* make it clear that "Mr. Tiger" is Stalin. In the exploration of Stalin's mind, Solzhenitsyn refers to "his exile in Turukhansk" (90, 83) and associates Stalin's peculiar eyes with the worst of his actions: "Stalin was terrifying because he did not listen to excuses, made no accusations; his yellow tiger eyes simply brightened balefully, his lower lids closed up a bit—and there, inside him, sentence had been passed, and the condemned man didn't know; he left in peace, was arrested at night, and shot by morning." (102, 93.) According to Deutscher, Stalin spent four years, from 1913 to 1917, in the province of Turukhansk in northern Siberia. See his *Stalin*, pp. 123–25.

a kind of rest, the prescribed activity for the last day of creation. Then this new, hard-won equilibrium is threatened by a recurrence of the mysterious terror he has felt in the zoo. The novel appears to end on a discord, but the two emotions—the sense of felicity and the spasm of terror—form a kind of final synthesis, a total image of the way the world is.[22]

The menace of sudden violence, we realize, has been present in the novel from the beginning. It is explicitly present in a letter Oleg receives from the aged couple, his neighbors in exile, telling him of the savage, unexplained killing of their dog. It is no less present, though more abstractly, in the random assaults of cancer, and in the many incidents of violence done by men to other men: the arrests, torture, executions, and the deliberate campaign of moral castration testified to by Shulubin.

Dostoevsky often argued in his novels that rational systems of thought provided rationalizations for the release of man's most vicious instincts. Solzhenitsyn has brought this notion to bear on his own time. If human felicity is forever threatened by the natural cruelty in man, the Marxist-based social system has built a civilization which —because of its premises about man, culture, and history—cannot protect the defenseless. In fact, it is not simply that there is no stay against evil; the system, through its dehumanizing ideas and language, not only permits, but institutionalizes, its tiger-leap.

[22] Lukács prescriptively criticizes the end on several counts. Solzhenitsyn has erred by making his hero a "plebeian," representing nothing significant on the Soviet social diagram, instead of a Party member who would draw conclusions from his experiences and set about to correct the conditions that gave rise to them. (A positive hero!) He has understood much about Stalinism; "nevertheless, objectively, his whole critique confines itself in the last analysis to the damage done to the integrity of individual human beings." (*Prosto tak!*) Oleg, then, merely represents Russia's violated humanity, and since all hope for rejuvenating the Soviet system is discredited in the novel, the novel itself is discredited. Lukács's misreading is monumental, but, given his premises, inevitable. He embraces everything Solzhenitsyn rejects, and in doing so, asserts his counterclaim that the political ought to envelop the human.

CHAPTER 17

Solzhenitsyn III: Positive Colonels and a Tragic General

Solzhenitsyn has told us in the Afterword to the Russian edition of *August 1914* that he is returning to a lifelong project, begun in 1936, which he had interrupted because he was distracted as a writer by "particular events of his own biography and the density of contemporary impressions."[1] This novel moves forward in Solzhenitsyn's literary development and backward in historical time. We now approach from the historical "rear" the novels we have looked at, and begin to follow the process which has brought about the nightmare conditions we have already read about. As one fascicle, or fragment (Russian *uzel*), of an immense work which Solzhenitsyn says he may not finish in his lifetime, *August 1914* presents itself as an indeterminate fraction of an unfinished literary whole. All we can discuss with certainty is the action within the fragment—in this case a full description of a single historical event, the rout of the Imperial Russian Army by the Germans in the Battle of the Masurian Lakes at the opening of World War I. This complex event, told in intricate detail, follows a pattern of rise and fall—from the optimistic Russian offensive into East Prussia to a climactic reversal of direction, thence to the total destruction of the Russian Army and the suicide of the commanding general.

---

[1] A. Solzhenitsyn, *Avgust chetyrnadtsatogo* (Paris, 1971), p. 572. "The Afterword to the Russian Edition Published Abroad, 1971" is not included in the English edition, Alexander Solzhenitsyn, *August 1914*, trans. Michael Glenny (New York, 1972). Page references will be made, as before, to the English edition first.

This fragment contains much that is realized fictionally within its boundaries, but much else is announced as motif clearly intended for later development. We can identify the threads in the incomplete carpet, but we can only speculate about the figures in the final weave. We recognize ideas, images, and themes already encountered in earlier novels about later stages of historical development; others appear to be new, appropriate to the earlier period in history, or products of his later thinking.[2] His novels, both written and projected, will form an historical circle as he moves from the present back to the past, and returns once more to the present.

When his total corpus becomes available, Solzhenitsyn's reliance on the Russian literary tradition will doubtless prove to be very complex. I have suggested an affinity between Solzhenitsyn's tiger image in *Cancer Ward* and Dostoevsky's notion that when a schematic doctrine is fastened on a human mind it will suppress the redemptive, life-giving resources in the human personality and release the forces of violence. But we cannot label Solzhenitsyn Dostoevskyan; he differs from Dostoevsky in too many ways. And this particular likeness is less the result of influence, perhaps, than a similar response to a similarly harmful doctrine: Marxism's *zakonomernost* has the same disintegrative effect on the moral sensibility as Chernyshevsky's "laws of nature" (*zakony prirody*) in *Notes from Underground*. There is much more of Tolstoy in *August 1914* but, despite his tangible influence as historical novelist, battle writer, theorist of strategy, and philosopher of morality and history, it is no more accurate to call Solzhenitsyn a Tolstoyan, or to speak of a submissive dependence. Solzhenitsyn's relation to Tolstoy is at once closer and less subservient than these terms suggest. He seems to be measuring himself against the last great figure in the Russian past as a successor—and a very critical one—rather than as a disciple. The writer as a "Second Government" describes each man in his time. We are witnessing, I think, the passing on from the nineteenth to the twentieth century of the view of Russian literature as a center of moral power: Solzhenitsyn has chosen to succeed Tolstoy in role but not in doctrine.

[2] We do not know when Solzhenitsyn conceived or wrote any part of this cycle. The texts in both languages bear the dates 1969–70, and the Afterword in the Russian edition is dated 1971. He has told us he started work on it when he graduated from school in the 1930s. We have seen Nerzhin, his fictional counterpart in *First Circle*, working on such a manuscript in "his needle-fine hand," though he flushed it down the toilet before he was transported.

Tolstoy himself appears in a brief early scene. A young disciple, Sanya Lazhenitsyn, contrives to meet Tolstoy in the woods at Yasnaya Polyana, with a burning question to put to the old "Sage." Shyly he asks, "What is the aim of man's life on earth?" Tolstoy says "what he has said a thousand times before: 'to serve good, and thereby to build the Kingdom of Heaven on earth.'" When Sanya asks how he is to serve—"does it have to be through love?"—Tolstoy answers: "Only through love." Sanya, disappointed, asks more questions: Is love that strong in all men? Shouldn't there be some "intermediate stage" between the present and the era of "universal good will"? Won't his teaching otherwise be "fruitless"? Tolstoy replies without a moment's hesitation: "Only through love! Nothing else. No one else will discover anything better." (18, 23.) His answers to Sanya's insistent questions show him as a dogmatic, impractical old man with a mind long closed. We recall Shulubin's comment in *Cancer Ward* that Tolstoy's teachings were out of touch with reality, and must assume that Tolstoy is here being dismissed as a moral philosopher, condemned by his own stale words. As Sanya leaves his mentor behind in search of new answers, he reverses the stages of Tolstoy's evolution from patriotic soldier to Christian pacifist anarchist. He is caught up in the national surge of emotion in 1914, joins the army, goes to war, and serves well at the Masurian Lakes.

In battle Sanya takes a small part in Solzhenitsyn's extensive testing of Tolstoy's views of military history, in which the behavior of armies in battle is described on a Tolstoyan scale, using Tolstoyan techniques to demonstrate an anti-Tolstoyan thesis. For all the complexity of national wars, courageous, decisive, intelligent, well-equipped, up-to-date professional officers are able to follow the course of action on the most complex battlefield and to control its outcome. The Russians are defeated, not because they lacked such men, but because the high command has systematically excluded this group from its highest ranks in strategic planning or combat command. Tsarist corruption—nepotism, favoritism, intrigue—guarantees the promotion of stupid, incompetent careerists. The Germans, better equipped, better trained, and better led, cut the blind, shambling, archaically equipped Russian army to pieces. Tolstoy's generals make plans and decisions, but mysterious currents of morale flow through the army, and determine the outcome when Kutuzov picks them up on the antennae of his intuition. Solzhenitsyn's generals make plans and decisions, and currents of information flow (or do not flow) through the army's reconnaissance and communications network, and form the basis of correct (or incorrect) decisions resolutely (or irresolutely) made by competent (or incompetent) commanders.

II

The differences between Solzhenitsyn and Tolstoy are more than a quarrel about the operational capacities of modern armies. There are philosophical differences as well. In Tolstoy's war, men do not make history, because when they try to make rational decisions they act blindly in a world determined by intricate and unknowable networks of causal process. In Solzhenitsyn's war, technology and intelligence make it possible to overcome the blind push of events and to arm the will of energetic, well-trained commanders. In the battle of the Masurian Lakes the performance of individual units—Army corps, divisions, battalions, and companies—reflects to some degree the character and competence of their leaders. It is part of Solzhenitsyn's polemical point that Blagoveshchensky, the most cowardly of the Russian corps commanders, quotes Tolstoy's aphorisms on the passivity of successful generals as he orders a retreat which opens the entire Russian right flank.[3]

The one military genius in this campaign, the German general Von François, acts decisively—against orders—takes carefully calculated risks, and stamps his enormously vain personality on the entire battle by a daring enveloping movement. (In demonstrating that men can "make history," Solzhenitsyn may be preparing the way for his presentation of Lenin.[4]) For Solzhenitsyn, men are free to act in discrete historical situations if they can pragmatically master the configurations of that situation. But there is no theory of history which explains the past in a manner that points the inevitable way to the future. His admirable men in this book are engineers or professional soldiers, who do what they set out to do because they act within the given, measurable data.

The nature of history is the chief subject of this multivolume project. Solzhenitsyn is far from ready to present his findings, but he

---

[3] Tolstoy's theory of war is mocked throughout. A spontaneous "Tolstoyan" attack is repulsed in blood; two energetic colonels, the backbone of Solzhenitsyn's army, complain bitterly that the high command's faith in the "spirit" of the army has caused them to neglect vital questions of military technology and organization. Not only is Tolstoy wrong; his ideas have weakened the Russian army.

[4] If Solzhenitsyn releases the chapter on Lenin which he omitted from the published text this question will be clarified.

does lay the foundations of his inquiry, beyond the question of the mechanics of battle. A number of statements by authoritative characters establish the negative premise that history as a whole is not to be understood as a scientific diagram, susceptible to rational analysis, hence to rational prediction. Solzhenitsyn's images for the historical process, like Pasternak's, are organic: "History grows like a living tree and ... reason is an ax: you'll never make it grow better by applying reason to it" (411, 377). Varsonofiev, a philosopher and obvious authorial surrogate, shifts his metaphor as he continues:

If you prefer, history is a river; it has its own laws which govern its flow, its bends, the way it meanders. Then along come some clever people who say it's a stagnant pond and must be diverted into another and better channel: all that's needed is to choose a better place and dig a new river bed. But the course of a river can't be interrupted—break it off only an inch and it won't flow any longer. And we're being told that the bed must be forcibly diverted by several thousand yards. The bonds between generations, the bonds of institutions, tradition, custom, are what hold the banks of the river bed together and keep the stream flowing. (*Ibid.*)[5]

When Sanya, the same young man who has left Tolstoy behind him, asks where he should look for the "laws that govern the flow of the river," Varsonofiev answers, "It may be that they are unknowable. At all events, they are not to be found on the surface, where every busy little half-wit casts around for them. ... The laws of the perfect human society can be found only within the total order of things. In the purpose of the universe. And in the destiny of man." These ultimate laws may be discovered in later volumes; here Solzhenitsyn merely prepares the ground for the argument between those who would maintain the banks of history's river and those who would blast them. Solzhenitsyn rejoins Tolstoy in the crucial insistence on the "bonds between generations, the bonds of institutions, tradition, custom," and—one should add—the nation. Whether history's motor is

[5] Michael Glenny, the translator of the English edition, suggested in a lecture at Columbia in the fall of 1972 that Varsonofiev is modeled in part on the Russian philosopher Nikolai Berdyaev, and that these ideas reflect his *The Meaning of History* (New York, 1936). Certainly some of Berdyaev's critique of Marxism's tendency to reduce history to one dimension, the economic, is reflected here. Berdyaev says that once that reduction is made, "everything else appears to be secondary, contingent and superficial. Religion, spirituality, art, human life itself, all are presented as the merest accidents of matter in movement and devoid of substantial reality" (p. 10). All these activities, it may be assumed, are part of Solzhenitsyn's river bank, and part of what will be lost when the revolution imposes its mechanistic regime on Russia. The apparent echo of Berdyaev here directs attention again to the prerevolutionary Russian alternatives to Marxism.

unknown or unknowable, these guiding entities guarantee its organic flow.

The "busy little half-wits," we come to realize, are the Russian intelligentsia, unpatriotic, disoriented by false theories, fatally susceptible to ideas of violent revolution. A most unfavorable composite portrait of this group is created out of a variety of types; they are the antagonists of the engineers and regular soldiers, and of Solzhenitsyn's own views, which are not hard to identify. They all share a "scientific" reading of the past joined with apocalyptic, utopian expectations for the future. Marxism takes its place in this series as the most recent of a number of variations on a single theme—the fusion of scientific certainty with revolutionary grievance and aspiration. The emblematic Bolshevik Lenartovich differs in doctrine, but not in ancestry or ethos, from other representatives of the widespread revolutionary climate. "For some reason, all Russia felt that these dangerous revolutionaries had right on their side" (53, 55).[6]

The continuing tension between contrasting views on history comes into clear focus in a long discussion between Olda Androzerskaya, a young professor of medieval history, and a group of university students. One, an aggressive leftist, asks Olda why she buries herself in "the useless gloomy Middle Ages" (547, 502). When the professor answers, "If you reject the Middle Ages, the history of the West collapses, and the rest of modern history becomes incomprehensible," the student responds with the standard intelligentsia view: "But practically speaking, the history of the West, and everything we need to know about it, begins with the French Revolution." When another student adds, "with the Age of Enlightenment," the young professor answers:

The Enlightenment is only one branch of Western culture, and perhaps by no means the most fruitful. It grows out of the trunk, not from the root.... The spiritual life of the Middle Ages is more important. Mankind has never known a time, before or since, when such an intense spiritual life prevailed over material existence. (548, 503)

The incredulous students, who think of Roman Catholic "obscurantism" and the Inquisition, ask a typically utilitarian question: how will the study of "papal bulls... help to emancipate people... help

---

[6] It is the author's voice speaking here. And in this statement: "The feeling among educated society was that it was everyone's duty to aid the cause of revolution, a sacred obligation to the exploited people of Russia" (53, 54).

progress in general?" Olda answers that history is not politics, not opinions but sources. When she argues for independent scholarship, the increasingly hostile students ask: "But what if your conclusions conflict with the needs of present-day society? ... All we need today is an analysis of the contemporary social environment and material conditions." Olda's answer echoes all else we have come upon in Solzhenitsyn on social being and consciousness and on the revolutionary expectations of all materialist determinisms:

That would be so if the life of the individual really were determined by his material environment. It would be much easier then: the environment is always at fault. So all you have to do is change it. But apart from the environment there is also a spiritual tradition, hundreds of spiritual traditions! There is, too, the spiritual life of the *individual*, and therefore each individual has, perhaps in spite of his environment, a *personal* responsibility—for what he does and for what other people around him do. (548, *504*)

These words, which recall Shulubin's in *Cancer Ward*, call the revolution into question before it happens, and constitute a prophecy we have already seen fulfilled in the earlier novels about the postrevolutionary world. The doctrine of social being, put into effect, will destroy both culture and conscience.

The professor invokes the "spiritual" aspects of culture; several of the military episodes emphasize national traditions. One long battlefield episode brings together two emblematic figures. Colonel Vorotyntsev represents patriotic military virtue and serves as Solzhenitsyn's observer and spokesman, approaching in his rectitude and effectiveness the stature and posture of a positive hero. The other, the Bolshevik Sasha Lenartovich, represents the quintessence of the radical intelligentsia tradition. He is intelligent, well educated, and well indoctrinated, and has an impeccable revolutionary pedigree, reaching back to the radical democrats of the mid-nineteenth century: an intellectual mother who transmits the materialist tradition, an uncle who was executed for terrorism. His mind is totally politicalized and polarized: "Sasha measured people, events, books by one yardstick: did they contribute to the emancipation of the people or to the consolidation of the state" (538, *493*). He is appalled to find himself in the Imperial Army, fighting the wrong war; he wants to save himself for the genuine one still to come (he is no coward). In fact, the Bolshevik aphorism "the worse the better" (140, *134*) has persuaded him that history would be best served if the Russians were defeated.

In his encounters with fellow soldiers he is skeptical, aloof, alienated from their minds, values, and goals. He has briefly known the comradeship and exaltation of battle, in a minor victorious engagement, but his principles reassert themselves, and he deserts. As he wanders toward the rear the front has broken, and he joins a small pick-up group of retreating soldiers and officers, commanded by Vorotyntsev. The soldiers have burdened themselves with the body of their former commander and with a wounded lieutenant, who is carrying the colors of the defeated regiment wrapped around his body. The colonel is a stranger to the men, but he is able to take command and lead them to safety through his knowledge of military traditions, of peasant thought and customs, and finally of Russian religious ceremony. Through this kind of cultural knowledge, which enables him to move in rhythm with his compatriots, he understands why they feel they must carry the two heavy litters. Lenartovich cannot understand, and objects both on grounds of principle—it is "sheer superstition" and the wounded lieutenant is certainly a member of the Black Hundreds (anti-Semitic reactionaries)—and on grounds of physical discomfort when he is asked to take his turn in carrying the corpse. The colonel has sized him up and will not answer his provocative questions with "routine army claptrap." His response is clipped and strategic. To Lenartovich's first objection, Vorotyntsev replies by asking what weapons he has for breaking through the German encirclement that night. When Lenartovich objects specifically to carrying his political enemy on a stretcher, Vorotyntsev contains his temper and answers "almost absent-mindedly: 'At a time like this, Ensign, party political differences are just so many ripples in the water'" (487, *446*). The ensuing exchange contains the familiar enveloping movement:

Party politics ripples? Astounded, Sasha tripped and almost dropped his pole. He could think of several answers, but decided that attack was the best defense. "What about international politics, then? Is that just ripples in the water? It's because of that that we're fighting, isn't it? In that case, what differences mean anything at all?"
"The difference between decency and indecency, Ensign," Vorotyntsev snapped back. With his free ... hand he lifted up his map case, snapped it open, and glanced down as he walked, now at the ground underfoot, now at the map. (487, *446*)[7]

[7] Though doctrinal positions are reversed, there are similarities between the colonel's handling of Lenartovich (down to the snapping map case) and a multitude of positive heroes in their dealings with the confused, the recalcitrant, or the dissident—Klychkov's control of Chapaev, for example. (See above, pp. 183ff.)

Nation over party, reality ("the map" and "the ground underfoot") over abstraction (international politics), finally the moral over the political. Basic priorities are established, and the colonel has won the conflict between them. Lenartovich's "defeat" is recorded in a heavily underlined scene. The colonel, in the tactful exercise of his authority, has chosen a quiet and beautiful spot to bury the dead commander. One of the peasant soldiers recites the Orthodox burial service in a "deaconish voice" over the grave, and the bareheaded handful take part in a profoundly Russian ceremony. "Unseen behind them, never joining in the responses, with a twisted smile of pity, yet with head bared, stood Lenartovich" (492, *451*).

Confrontations between revolutionaries of all parties and patriotic apolitical professionals recur in the nonmilitary episodes, forming an essential part of the structure of argument. One such encounter takes place between two middle-aged engineers and two youthful Socialist Revolutionaries. At stake, among many other things, is the validity of revolution as the way to the future. The engineers deplore the incalculable and senseless destruction resulting from violent change, and define an apolitical ethos of growth through technology, suggesting that Russia in 1913 has reached an economic take-off point into unlimited economic development. Political violence will wreck this opportunity; indeed, all politics seem irrelevant to them. An earlier comment by Colonel Vorotyntsev places this matter in a perspective which clarifies the argument and, possibly, the grand design of Solzhenitsyn's entire project. He discusses with a fellow colonel the backwardness of Russian arms, and his thoughts on progress are described by Solzhenitsyn:

Only that closed fraternity of General Staff officers, and perhaps a handful of engineers as well, were conscious of the fact that the world, and Russia with it, was moving invisibly, inaudibly, and imperceptibly into a new era; that the entire oxygen content, its rate of combustion, the mainspring pressure in all its clocks—had somehow changed. All Russia, from the imperial family down to the revolutionaries, naively thought that they were breathing the same old air and living on familiar ground; only a handful of engineers and officers were gifted with the perception to sense that the stars themselves had moved into new conjunctions. (113, *110*)

True progress will be charted by the new technical mastery of the physical universe, a trend visible only to this "handful." The monarchists and the revolutionaries are locked in an obsolete struggle begun a century earlier, each, in a sense, validating the other's existence. In this perspective, Marxism appears as the final version of an archaic European current of thought, the search for a scientific utopia, and as the last doctrinal mutation of the Russian revolutionary ethos. Genuine science, for those gifted enough to sense it, has asserted itself against the spurious sciences of history and of society. A victorious revolution would arrest this technological metamorphosis, for at least the length of time it took to clean up the destruction and heal the wounds.

At this point, the differences between the views expressed here and those of Tolstoy are very nearly complete.[8] Industrial growth is no part of Tolstoy's vision of a Christian agricultural commonwealth, in which each person lives close to the earth, practicing preindustrial handicrafts, turning away from cities, emptying his own slops. The menacing trains in *Anna Karenina* move through the novel as symbols of blind fatality, hostile to human purposes, themselves alien products of Western technology.

III

Solzhenitsyn has found Tolstoy archaic on most of his prescriptions for human betterment. As he put his book together, however, Solzhenitsyn was profoundly impressed by the old "Sage" as a writer, and in no sense can he be said to leave Tolstoy behind here, or, indeed, to measure up. Both *War and Peace*, the obvious model, and *August 1914*, seen as either fragment or whole work, exhibit a laminated structure, alternating episodes of war and peace, or front and rear. In both there is a heavy quotient of abstract ideas and discursive argument, an unembarrassed authorial presence, commenting, arguing, and judging. Flaubert's exasperated comment on *War and Peace*, "Mon Dieu, il prêche," could apply to both. Essays on military history, large lumps of researched material, unconcealed philosophical reflections interrupt the flow of invented characters and events and

---

[8] Since he wrote *August 1914*, Solzhenitsyn has lost his personal enthusiasm for a technocratic future, which he sees as a false dream learned from the West. In *Letter to the Soviet Leaders* (New York, 1974), he confronts the environmental crisis as spelled out in the language of the Club de Rome, responding fully to its message of imminent cataclysm. Misled by the Western cult of progress, he writes, industrial civilization, including Marxist Russia, has "choked, and is on its last legs" (p. 21). The optimism of his engineers in 1914 nevertheless remains valid as an apparent historical option at the time, above all as an attractive alternative to violent revolution.

the chronicle of families, including the author's own, in both cases. But this crude catalogue of similarities hides the real differences.

Setting aside the smaller formal questions, I would locate the essential difference in the choice of genre: *War and Peace* is an historical novel, *August 1914* an animated historical chronicle. If *War and Peace* illustrates Tolstoy's views on history, it also exists as a complete work of fiction. *August 1914* risks credibility as fiction in order to set the historical record straight, but runs the further risk of failing to persuade on either plane of discourse. In Solzhenitsyn's work to date, the documentary and the researched—the effort to reproduce the historical event—transcend and order the development of characters and the working out of personal destinies. Tolstoy achieves a more exact balance between war and peace, between military event and personal development, and never loses sight of his characters' intricate movement toward maturity; what they learn on the battlefield becomes part of what they are and what they grow to be. Solzhenitsyn's invented characters, so far, are eyewitnesses and participants—hence aids to the chronicler—who seem to learn what the event has to teach them but, aside from the abstract questions some of them ask, are not (not yet at least) presented as complex characters, facing complex choices. Colonel Vorotyntsev bears certain resemblances to Prince Andrei, especially when Tolstoy's character serves as aide-de-camp to Kutuzov during the Austerlitz episode. As agents of the high command, both move intelligently across the battlefield, discerning what actually is going on, intervening when they can to direct the action in an effective way. Both are independent minds, students of behavior, critics of their superiors. But Andrei's experience on the battlefield looms largest as a phase of his personal development: the conquest of military vanity, the sensing of the absolute, the beginning of his willed movement toward death. Vorotyntsev is a monolith of military virtue, troubled slightly by a fading marriage, but otherwise totally engaged in observing the battle, reporting on the military mess the Russian commanders make of it, in the hope that his report to the Grand Duke will eliminate the incompetent commanders and archaic practices which caused the Russian defeat. He yearns, as Andrei never seriously does but Soviet heroes do, to serve as an instrument of history. As a fictional character, he is too much the instrument of the documented event and the author's will to instruct.

This is an illuminating distinction, I hope, not an invidious one.

Solzhenitsyn himself recognizes the line between novel and battle report, and knows which side this work belongs on:

Without allowing any more scope to one's imagination than what can be learned from precise data, preferring historians to novelists as sources, we can only throw up our hands and admit it once and for all: no one would dare to write a fictional account of such unrelieved blackness; for the sake of verisimilitude, a writer would distribute the light and shade more evenly. But from the first battle on, a Russian general's badges of rank came to be seen as symbols of incompetence; and the further up the hierarchy, the more bungling the generals seem, until there is scarcely one from whom an author can derive any comfort. (In which case, there might appear to be some consolation in Tolstoy's conviction that it is not generals who lead armies, not captains who command ships or companies of infantry, not presidents or leaders who run states or political parties—were it not that all too often the twentieth century has proved to us that it *is* such men who do these things.) (381–82, *350*)

It is clearly not just the gloomy story of national disgrace that distinguishes *August 1914* from *War and Peace*. The "precise data" of *August 1914* and Solzhenitsyn's disagreement with Tolstoy about what controls events *require* that he write an animated history, not a novel. There *is* no consolation to be found in Tolstoy's conviction. In fact, he is one of the architects of the debacle, and Solzhenitsyn is driven further away from fiction by the need he feels to demonstrate Tolstoy's error.

Beyond the difference in intentions, the two writers chose different kinds of military situations as raw material for their works. In *War and Peace*, after initial defeats in the West, a patriotic national army, united around Tsar Alexander, drives Napoleon off the Russian land. There is a long interval of peace between the two campaigns. And at the end of the novel peace has returned and there is a general resolution of personal and historical tensions. When we leave Pierre, he may or may not have joined the Decembrist conspiracy, but ripeness and understanding have "enveloped" him and his family. In Solzhenitsyn's chronicle, a brave but badly led Russian army invades East Prussia and is driven out in disarray by the competent, quick, sometimes brilliantly led German army. At the center of the Russian effort is the corrupt, obscurantist Court, radiating a fatal infection outward into the high command of the Army. We know—because this is essentially a work of history—that the apocalypse which is being generated in the events we have just witnessed lies directly ahead. If the engineers fail—and we know they will—Russia will be fought over by the arrogant revolutionaries, with their arid doctrines, and by the malevolently incompetent minions of "this stinking monarchy" (582, 536), pious, self-serving, and fiercely stupid. When at the end of this first act, Vorotyntsev's mission of reform is eclipsed in incense and ikons, the shape of events foretells historical calamity which the artist may not be able to dramatize, but the chronicler must struggle to record.

Solzhenitsyn has not completely accomplished the classical movement of envelopment. The moral has eclipsed the political, perhaps, but character has not eclipsed doctrine—with one remarkable exception. He has employed his full novelist's powers with respect to one character—oddly enough, the historical Samsonov, the commander of the Russian expeditionary force. Samsonov's complex thoughts and feelings, the play of his personal qualities, his sense of patriotic obligation, his profound religious beliefs are imagined too subtly and deeply to permit him to fit into the scheme of the book's intellectual argument. As he acts less and less effectively against the encroaching disaster he consults his faith for strength and understanding. When the full dimensions of his defeat are borne in upon him, he moves among his defeated troops sorrowfully and guiltily, and the two sides of his mind begin "to slide ... apart" (315, 290). He escapes from his escort and retreats into the forest, where he takes his own life, "a dying creature of the forest" (469, 430). Here, on a truly Tolstoyan scale, Solzhenitsyn has created a human experience which eclipses the historical event.

CHAPTER 18

Andrei Sinyavsky: Conclusions

Much of Russian literature, I have suggested, is concerned with its own right to exist, its authors' right to write it and present it to an audience. The men, ideas, or institutions threatening that right are given fictional form, from the distant menace of Bazarov's positivism in *Fathers and Sons* to the quite tangible police and prisons in Soviet dissident literature. Our three writers include images of the closed system they have been forced to live in, yet as very different men they emphasize different aspects. *Zakonomernost*, social being, base-superstructure, and *kto-kogo?* paranoia—the rock-bottom premises of Marxism—are identified by all three, but shown to exert their malevolent influence in different ways. If they agree in defining the family of ideas that locks the system, each tends to stress a different area of deprivation: for Pasternak it is poetry, for Solzhenitsyn morality, and for Sinyavsky religion. The perversion of ends by means is a thematic common denominator in their distinctly personal artistic designs. In search of common patterns with individual variations, I find Sinyavsky, as the most alienated, the most despairing, and the most extreme in the expression of his condition, the most useful for precipitating my conclusions.

The total output of each of the three men may be divided into works published at home and those smuggled out and published abroad, but Sinyavsky has established a more complex literary identity; five separate "voices" can be distinguished in his work before his arrest. Two are "legal": the voice of the established Soviet scholar, contributor of the article on Gorky, among others, in the *History of*

Soviet Literature,[1] and that of the critic of modern poetry, celebrating the achievement of Pasternak and Mayakovsky, and belittling Evtushenko's, always striving to put the new poets, after Stalin, in nourishing contact with the genuine Russian tradition. Three other voices, under the pseudonym Abram Tertz, are "illegal": the voice of the savage critic of his own culture in the essay "On Socialist Realism"; that of the "writer"-narrator of stories and one short novel, some of them political satires, others fantasies in an existential vein; that of the morose religious reflections in *Random Thoughts* (1966).[2] Since the complex disguises and stratagems needed for the "legal" voices blunt the full force of his mind, I will discuss only the Tertz canon, counting on the candor of the smuggled literature as the fullest expression of his vision, soon to be amplified, no doubt, by the manuscripts he has brought with him into exile.

Pasternak and Solzhenitsyn oppose organic metaphors taken from nature to the fallacious symmetries of historical materialism. Sinyavsky has no alternative to propose. All history is governed by a fatal rhythm which invariably defeats human aspirations. Men posit a noble goal, then devise means to achieve it which not only defeat the original purpose but turn the original goal into its moral opposite. The leaders of the Catholic Church devised the Inquisition to realize their dream of building the divine order on earth. In Soviet experience the reversal of intentions is explicit and awful:

So that prisons should vanish forever, we built new prisons. So that all frontiers should fall, we surrounded ourselves with a Chinese wall. So that work should become a rest and a pleasure we introduced forced labor. So that not one drop of blood be shed, we killed and killed and killed.

In the name of the Purpose we turned to the means that our enemies used: we glorified Imperial Russia, we wrote lies in *Pravda* (Truth), we set a new Tsar on the empty throne, we introduced officers' epaulettes and torture.... Sometimes we felt that only one final sacrifice was needed for the triumph of Communism—the renunciation of Communism.

O Lord, O Lord—pardon us our sins![3]

[1] *Istoriya russkoi sovetskoi literatury* (Moscow, 1958–61). This three-volume work contains articles by Sinyavsky on Gorky, Bagritsky, and the literature of World War II, and a minor contribution by Svetlana Alliluyeva, Stalin's daughter.

[2] All the smuggled works except *Random Thoughts* (*Mysli vrasplokh*; New York, 1966) are contained in *Fantasticheskii mir Abrama Tertsa* (New York, 1966).

[3] Abram Tertz [pseud.], *"The Trial Begins" and "On Socialist Realism,"* trans. Max Hayward ("Trial") and George Dennis ("Realism") (New York, 1965), p. 162 [hereafter cited as *The Trial Begins*]; *Fantasticheskii*, p. 411. "We" in this passage reflects one of Sinyavsky's ironic strategies in the essay. Affecting to answer a query put by a curious Westerner, the responding "we" speaks at times as a bewildered believer whose extravagant defense of the Soviet world has just the opposite effect.

In the story "The Trial Begins," the same perversion of ends by means is explored in a variety of situations in private and public life. The unfailing pattern is summed up in a vivid image. The three virtuous characters, who end up in a concentration camp, dig up an ancient dagger fashioned from a Christian crucifix, designed presumably to defend the true faith. The Jewish abortionist Rabinovich notes the ironies the object symbolizes:

A nice place they found for God—the handle of a deadly weapon. . . . God was the end and they turned him into the means—a handle. And the dagger was the means and became the end. They changed places. . . . In the name of God! With the help of God! In place of God! Against God! . . . And now there is no God, only dialectics.[4]

Sinyavsky has no alternative to propose to the interlinked materialisms, dialectic and historical. They seem to be a new set of masks for an ironic demon, rooted in human foolishness and credulity, who reappears periodically but never changes. In the views expressed before his exile, Sinyavsky has retired from history and from hope, unlike his fellow heretics who have seemed to retain a shred of confidence in the ultimate comprehensibility and possible benevolence of the historical process.[5] Pasternak suggests at the end of *Doctor Zhivago* that life and history are moving toward each other, ending the unnatural separation imposed on Russia by the Bolshevik blueprint makers. Solzhenitsyn's lifelong inquiry into recent Russian history must rest on the assumption that the process will ultimately reveal its pattern. It is also hard to imagine that Solzhenitsyn's fictional protest-by-exposé does not imply a hope for improvement: the elimination, for example, of literary censorship or the abolition of the penal system, and finally a rectification of the society's governing ideas.[6] Sinyavsky's pessimism seems to permit no such hopes. He has moved from belief in "the Purpose" through a devastating critique of his former faith to a stark despair, impatiently awaiting death and the next life, living out the time in total solitude—or so one would conclude from the last works to reach the West before his arrest, *Random*

---

[4] Tertz, *The Trial Begins*, pp. 127–28; *Fantasticheskii*, pp. 275–76.

[5] His "escape" to France and to the literary life may have relieved Sinyavsky's metaphysical despair, expressed most completely in *Random Thoughts*.

[6] The drastic measures he proposes in his *Letter to the Leaders*—dissolution of the Soviet Union into its ethnic components, extinction of the "ideology" which has caused so much harm and now threatens disaster, demotion of the Communist Party and the removal of all Party members from the public payroll—all seem to point in this direction.

Thoughts and "Pkhentz," his remarkable fantasy on interplanetary life. This state of despair is accompanied—but not relieved—by a strong belief in the omnipresence and omnipotence of God. Sinyavsky's full final vision suggests his alienation from humanity, his sense that he is alone and trapped—in history, in the flesh and on earth.

This condition is starker than that of Solzhenitsyn's prisoners or Pasternak's battered eccentric, but Sinyavsky's journey to despair covers familiar ground and leads to familiar discoveries. He said at his trial that his views were idealistic, a heresy, of course, and the real reason, probably, for finding him guilty.[7] How and when he shed the obligatory "materialism" of his milieu is a personal question that cannot be answered from his published work; where that materialism comes from, how it has affected the artistic and moral quality of Soviet life, and the cruelty and absurdity of its manifestations are all vividly dramatized in the body of his work. The revolution and the civil war occurred in a blaze of fierce and generous emotions. In the relentless, heedless struggle, men carried—and poets recorded—grandiose dreams of human possibilities. This "romanticism" was slowly done to death by the onset of the mechanical, rationally planned technological order, as the indicated way to the classless and want-free utopia. The goal that justified all measures is no longer the noble dream of the revolutionaries; it has been corrupted and invalidated by the means used to achieve it. The religious purpose of historical materialism has gone the way of all the others. Because of a deep internal confusion, inevitable in a religion disguised as a science, a strange pseudo-literature has been generated. It is religious in its commitment to the socialist utopia, realist in its way of recording the texture of experience. The requirements of the purpose, working against the actual record of things, have confined literature to a set of suffocating conventions and euphemisms. The vast reach of Russian realism has perforce to be shrunk to the binary scheme of progressive-regressive. Gorky was helpful, before the revolution, in devising the formulae for the new literature. He fixed the label petty bourgeois on the superfluous heroes of Russian realism, and then extended the concept

far and wide and cast into it all who did not belong to the new religion: property-owners, large and small, liberals, conservatives, hooligans, hu-

[7] *On Trial: The Case of Sinyavsky (Tertz) and Daniel (Arzhak)*, ed. Leopold Labedz and Max Hayward (London, 1967), p. 192.

manists, decadents, Christians, Dostoevsky, Tolstoy. Gorky was a man of principle. . . . He knew that all that is not God is Devil.[8]

The partisans of the new religion, under Gorky's helpful program of simplification, became saints, positive heroes. These personifications of virtue represent, in Sinyavsky's view, the crowning disfigurement of Soviet literature:

The growing strength of the positive hero is shown not only in his incredible multiplication—he has far surpassed other kinds of literary character in quantity, put them into the shade. . . . His qualitative growth has also been remarkable. As he approaches the Purpose, he becomes ever more positive, great and splendid. He also becomes more and more persuaded of his own dignity, especially when he compares himself to contemporary Western man and realizes his immeasurable superiority. . . . The poet runs out of words when he tries to describe this superiority, this incomparable positiveness of our positive hero.[9]

Sinyavsky joins his two fellows in isolating, defining, and deploring the consequences of the "who-whom?" polarized mind of Marxism-Leninism, and the brutal warlike logic that flows from it. Experience rendered into art in this world is run through a mill: it is categorized, binarized, and allegorized. Language is rigidly stereotyped, thought and language corrupt each other, and literature becomes a series of falsified reports, purporting to be "real," derived finally from a schematized historicity. All three writers have noted this process in their characteristic ways.

If there is any future for Russian writing, Sinyavsky sees it as "a phantasmagoric art" drawn from Poe, Chagall, Dostoevsky, and Hoffman and based on hypotheses, not false certainties or exploded "purposes." All his own fiction suspends causal reality at some point in pursuit of the truth via the absurd and the grotesque. Some soar farther from the world of time and space than the others, ranging from the distortions of political caricature to the controlled improbabilities of science fiction. In the short novel *Lyubimov*, fantasy acts to compress and recapitulate the October Revolution in the history of a small northern town. An ambitious bicycle repairman, Tikhomirov, seizes power in a coup d'état from the central Soviet authority. Sinyavsky said in his trial that in some details he meant to burlesque Khrushchev in the person of the illiterate usurper, Tikhomirov, who acts

---

[8] Tertz, *The Trial Begins*, p. 192; *Fantasticheskii*, p. 430.
[9] Tertz, *The Trial Begins*, pp. 177–78; *Fantasticheskii*, p. 421.

out a scenario drawn from the lives of many Russian rulers. Tikhomi-rov seizes power armed with the teachings of two books, Engels's *Dialectics of Nature* and an Eastern book on the mystical powers of the human will. As the established ruler, he assumes Tsarist preroga-tives—the semiliterate narrator is promoted to "court scribe"—and the society under him snaps into its traditional hierarchical shape. He governs through a fog of Marxist jargon and the play of his massive willpower over the credulous Russian populace. He literally contains the regime within his mind, willing an invisible belt around the town to protect it from the punitive expedition sent by Moscow. When things go wrong and his mind wobbles under a succession of shocks, the new society wobbles too, disintegrates, and falls to the robot tanks from the "Center." A central source of strength in his mind is his superstitious faith in the power of science, replacing older and more nourishing forms of belief. He makes his pious old mother recite an antireligious catechism:

"There is no God," she articulated, her eyes bulging and her speech punc-tuated by pauses and gulps as if she were having hiccups. "No God. No prophet Elijah, they've shot him. Thunder is electricity.... No angels in heaven. No cherubim."[10]

The act of retaining an ancient form of discourse but reversing its sense suggests an underlying continuity. Seen this way, the story re-produces the rise and fall of the revolutionary ethos, based on a naive faith transferred uncritically from religion to science, which is then extended to account for the history of society. But the heart of the story's meaning is to be found in its complex narrative structure. One narrator is the town librarian, "the court scribe," whose mind is a hodgepodge of undigested books, whose narrative wanders off into flights of folkloric fantasy. His pen is directed by a second narrator. (Guided writing is nothing new in Russian life.) At times they struggle for control of the manuscript, and the loser snarls his angry comments in the footnotes. The controlling narrator is a ghost, a composite figure who spans the period from Nicholas I to the present, and clearly represents the spirit of the *Westernized* intellectual no-bility. His name, Proferansov, suggests games of solitaire—*préférence* —in countless Frenchified drawing rooms. He is a dilettante who cor-

---

[10] Abram Tertz [pseud.], *The Makepeace Experiment*, trans. Manya Harari (New York, 1965), p. 119; *Fantasticheskii*, pp. 348–49.

responds with Lavoisier and Tolstoy. And he is a confirmed crackpot who conducts endless solitary experiments in search of the Philosopher's Stone, the single key to all questions, the all-enclosing system of thought. His experiments invariably misfire through miscalculation, and this, we realize, is exactly what has happened in *Lyubimov*. Proferansov is conducting an experimental seizure of power. It is he who has directed Tikhomirov's coup d'état, we learn, and he is writing a report on the experiment through his dim-witted assistant narrator, also named Proferansov. Earlier, in the NEP period, he had become disillusioned. He has been overheard shouting into an imaginary telephone: "Hello, hello, call Lavoisier, ask Trotsky—who will restore love to the human heart? Who will encompass the mysteries of creation at a glance?" The Bolshevik effort has failed to solve the great unknowns of existence, but he has not given up hope: "We've miscalculated.... But the city of Lyubimov will make its mark." When that experiment fails in its turn, as we learn from the story it does, the foreground narrator comments, "How often we perish through miscalculation ... !"[11]

We are witnessing in capsule form the enactment in its special Russian pattern of the cruel historical joke that bedevils mankind. The old ghost expresses a hunger for certainty, fed by superstition among the uneducated and, in a not unrelated way, by total systems of thought among the educated. Both live in expectation of miracles, the advent of the Absolute. Proferansov the elder disappears from the city of Lyubimov when his experimental regime collapses, but we do not doubt that he will reappear—the deathless spirit of Russian credulity.

Each of the writers has named different moments when the Marxist-Leninist system slammed shut—historically, or in their own lives, or in the lives of their fictional characters. Dr. Zhivago welcomes the February days, the mingling of life and history, and hangs on to his hope through the brutalities of post-October, until he leaves Moscow with his family. Solzhenitsyn—and his character Nerzhin—trace their loss of faith back to the Industrial Party Trials in 1930, an event which coincided with their intellectual coming of age. The characters in *Cancer Ward* disagree: Oleg believed "until Finland"; Shulubin asks how anyone *could* believe after the onslaught against truth begun

---

[11] Tertz, *Makepeace*, pp. 141, 142, 143; *Fantasticheskii*, pp. 362, 364.

during the 1930 trials. Looking to the period before his birth, Sinyav-sky has expressed a literary nostalgia for the exploding emotions, re-corded in poetry, of the early years of struggle. The icy rigidities of planned development and channeled feelings ended that romantic period historically, but in his own life, if we read autobiography into his essay on socialist realism (and "The Trial Begins," the story smuggled out at the same time), the Marxian cosmology apparently evaporated for him toward the end of Stalin's life in 1953. These dif-fering experiences of disillusionment are joined in one unanimous historical judgment: an unqualified condemnation of the prerevolu-tionary intelligentsia's role in preparing men's minds for revolution. Proferansov's feckless experiments in search of a secular Absolute render fantastically the dogmatic rationalism, promising the apoc-alypse, which is part of the mental equipment of all factions of the left-of-center intelligentsia.

In *August 1914*, Solzhenitsyn is at great pains *not* to distinguish between radical doctrines, attributing the same immoral consequences to all of them. Zhivago turns away in disgust from the unnatural radical enthusiasms of his intellectual friends on the eve of October. We pursue two of them, Gordon and Dudorov, in a trajectory which, as we have seen, takes them from their original enthusiastic acceptance through a phase of routine apologetics during the 1920s, until the second incarceration in a camp reorders their thinking; at the end of the novel, they have become reconciled with the late Zhivago's view of the organic interconnection of life with art, with history, and with nature. Pasternak is more forgiving than the other two, but his treat-ment of the intelligentsia joined with Sinyavsky's and Solzhenitsyn's constitutes a charge of *trahison des clercs* on a massive scale. This is the most direct and tangible sense we have of their kinship with the classical writers as *they* opposed with the full force of their art the radical democrats, ancestors of the architects of the prison society.

Dostoevsky's conviction that the doctrines he opposed were evil was reinforced by his distrust of the Western mind. The various revo-lutionary ideologies have Western origins—and Dostoevsky was there to note the arrival in Russia of some early versions—but they seem to have taken a Russian form to some degree, at least, in the eyes of the contemporary dissidents. Solzhenitsyn's image of Tsar and revolu-tionary locked in anachronistic struggle suggests the domestication of the imported radicalism, though he places a Western label on Marxism when he calls on his leaders to abandon it. Sinyavsky has no more confidence in genuine science than he does in pseudo-science—he is a romantic in many senses—and he is, of the three, the most distant from the Western intellectual tradition. But he presents the fatal marriage of science and superstition as a purely Russian accomplishment.[12] Nothing in Pasternak's critique of those who would "remake life" indicates that the alien origin of their ideas is the source of error or corruption—at one point he invokes Darwin against Marx. Attitudes toward the West, expressed among the three in authorial statement or in the dramatization of ideas, range from selective admiration through unconcern—general indifference to or ignorance of Western civilization—to considerable antipathy. Solzhenitsyn's technocratic tendency in *August 1914* causes him to admire the extraordinary efficiency of the German Army. (One of his engineers dreams of the great prosperity that would result from an era of Russo-German economic collaboration.) And yet he has a particular loathing for the gullibility of Western "progressive" apologists for the Soviet regime, made vividly real in the wicked legend convicts invent about Mrs. Roosevelt's visit to a Soviet prison in *First Circle*.[13] It is the unwitting complicity in Soviet lies that Solzhenitsyn mocks here and elsewhere in the novel, which ends, as we recall, with the French correspondent's misreading of Soviet reality. Whatever its sources, the doctrinal evil has sunk deep roots in native soil.[14]

Sinyavsky, of the three, is most outspoken in his distaste for Western

[12] The power of scientific prediction Marxists claim in historical matters is mocked in his story "The Icicle." His grubby narrator, who has been cursed with the gift of clairvoyance, is put under "creative arrest" and compelled to work with a tough old colonel of the MVD on the Soviet timetable of world conquest. They wrangle over the dates for taking Madagascar or liberating Australia. The point of the critique seems to be contained in this remark: "anything accidental is quite inevitable once it's been foretold." The "accidental" or the desired—the wish to conquer the world, for example—will apparently be fulfilled by the muscle of those who believe the prediction. See "The Icicle" in Abram Tertz [pseud.], *Fantastic Stories*, trans. Max Hayward and Ronald Hingley (New York, 1963); and "Gololeditsa" in *Fantasticheskii*.

[13] The unknown author of this prison folklore has chosen Mrs. Roosevelt out of the blue to represent Western credulity. (One wonders if his source was Westbrook Pegler.) There is irony in realizing that Mrs. Roosevelt in her defense of human rights in the United Nations frequently clashed with Soviet representatives. Solzhenitsyn has said in his Nobel Prize acceptance speech that the Declaration of Human Rights is the "best document" the U.N. has produced in the twenty-five fruitless years of its existence. *New York Times*, October 7, 1972.

[14] We should recall that since the appearance of *August 1914*, he has formulated a more "pastoral" or Slavophile attitude, deploring the stench of pollution and Russian subservience since Peter to Western ideas, including Marxism and the mystique of industrial growth. See his *Letter to the Soviet Leaders* (New York, 1974).

values. In "The Trial Begins," his Westernized dilettante Karlinsky, a collector of snuffboxes and pornography, is concerned only with his own welfare. His end, the conquest of the Prosecutor's beautiful and totally self-centered wife, is pursued by all the means of seduction, including a clever—and mocking—use of the Hegelian dialectic to demonstrate that all knowledge is genital. His end evades him as he labors impotently in her bed, enacting once again the ironic movement —through perverse means to reversed ends. We learn elsewhere in Sinyavsky's work that the self-referring individual of the West is the corrupted product of the historical movement between Catholicism and socialism, symbolized by the Renaissance, when the human ego broke through Christ's self-effacement. The age of individualism came to its inevitable perverted end when it produced the Superman. The doctrine of freedom of choice simply masks the maneuvering of self-serving egos and, applied to religious preferences, is meaningless. Man does not choose God, God chooses him, and once he is chosen, he must obey God as a dog obeys his master.[15] Sinyavsky's antipathy for these standard Western attitudes is matched by an absence of references to Western writers or thinkers. Picasso alone among contemporary Western figures has earned his enthusiastic approval.[16] Indeed, in all three writers, one senses no vital dependence on that vast movement of intellectual growth which might include, among many others, Pascal, Locke, Montesquieu, Rousseau, Kant, Schopenhauer, Mill, Darwin, Nietzsche, Freud, and, for that matter, Marx himself. In Sinyavsky's case, it may be that his bruising encounter with Marx's false scientific "religion" has caused him to repudiate the entire tradition in an attitude of revulsion.

Whatever their attitudes to the rest of the world, all three writers are continuously preoccupied with Russia—her people, language, customs, folklore, history, and religion—to the exclusion of the unknown or irrelevant West. Cultural isolation, as hermetic under Stalin as it was when Ivan's Third Rome shut out the Renaissance, may have contributed to this self-absorption. The trouble and suffering are in Russia, it would appear, and native solutions must be found for native problems. Pasternak, trained by a neo-Kantian professor at the University of Marburg, has little to say about the West in Doctor Zhivago, but his hero's refusal, under the worst of circumstances, to accompany his wife and child into exile, celebrates a quality of rootedness often

15 Tertz, Mysli vrasplokh, p. 50.
16 I. Golomshtok and A. Sinyavskii, Pikasso (Moscow, 1960).

expressed by Pasternak himself in his lifetime, and by the other two writers, as well, before their unwilling exile. Solzhenitsyn's characters consider the alternative answers prerevolutionary Russian thinkers had proposed to the national dilemmas. In *First Circle*, we recall, Nerzhin tests the intelligentsia's traditional preoccupation with the moral qualities of the *narod* by exploring the instinctive, sub-historical existence of the janitor Spiridon. The episode resembles Pierre's rejuvenating encounter with the peasant Karataev in *War and Peace*, but Nerzhin, unlike Pierre, concludes that he has little to learn from this emblematic representative of the people (again we see Solzhenitsyn repudiating Tolstoyan views). Thrown back on himself as a man and as a Russian in his search for moral wisdom, he defines an attitude which may be expressed Socratically: Know God and create thine own self. Spiridon is no repository of wisdom, but he makes his contribution to the novel's moral commentary with a cryptic proverb: "The wolfhound is right, and the cannibal is wrong."[17] He has clarified in his own way the troubling kinship between the animal and the human: man and beast may perform the same kind of animal actions, but contrary standards apply. And in his own idiom Spiridon has joined the brotherhood of articulate resisters.

Spiridon's portrait is one instance of a steady effort to define the national self, to inventory national resources of the spirit, in the work of all three writers. We note Pasternak's effort to fix his poet-hero with respect to the Russian literary past, his agonized protest against the corruption of Russian language and Russian morality after 1917. He has given an important symbolic position to an old peasant soothsayer who interprets important events in her ancient peasant language. Sinyavsky's estimate of the Russian character is deliberately set against Western values, and shot through with his morbid irony. The apparent vices of the Russian people turn out to be their actual virtues. They are drunkards and thieves, but drink nourishes their perpetual expectation of miracles and expresses their constant preference for vodka over the worse evils of sensuality—sex, he says, is "a festival in a cesspool."[18] As inveterate thieves, they demonstrate an admirable contempt for private property. But they are not capable of generating a complete culture, only a heresy to trouble Europe; they require strong rulers to keep them in place or to set them in motion.

---

17 Aleksander I. Solzhenitsyn, *The First Circle*, trans. Thomas P. Whitney (New York, 1968), p. 401; A. Solzhenitsyn, *V kruge pervom* (New York, 1968), p. 356.
18 Tertz, *Mysli vrasplokh*, p. 67.

These judgments on the Russians are ironic—almost perverse—overturning the standard nineteenth-century worship of peasant virtue, but they express no desire to reform or civilize the Russians, least of all to Westernize them. They may appear condescending, but we should recall Sinyavsky's summer walking trips through the north, his fascination with proverbs and other folk expressions, and his cherished collection of ikons, which indicate his great admiration for the Russian people.[19] If there is contempt mixed with admiration, it merges with the despairing self-contempt one senses in the voices of most of his narrators, and perhaps in his own, if we can ever be sure we are hearing it correctly through his many masks.

At the end of *Lyubimov*, the usurper's old mother forgets her atheist catechism and travels to a distant church "at the edge of the world" to consult an aged priest. He recites a long, eloquent prayer in an ancient ecclesiastical language, asking mercy for all sinners. In the story this recital of simple Christian attitudes is surely meant to redress a moral imbalance, to correct for the harebrained scientism of social experiment and the arrogance that supports it. It has this countervailing aesthetic function, but it is noteworthy as the only time Sinyavsky's religious views find overt expression in his fiction.

The old priest's prayer is meant to correct for evil deeper than any rooted in environmental causes. All three writers hold similar views on evil's origins, and each would surely associate himself, in his own terms, with Dostoevsky's crucial statement of the meaning he finds in Tolstoy's *Anna Karenina*:

It is clear and intelligible to the point of obviousness that evil in mankind is concealed deeper than the physician-socialists suppose; that in no organization of society can evil be eliminated; that the human soul will remain the same; that abnormality and sin emanate from the soul itself, and finally, that the laws of the human spirit are so unknown to science, so obscure, so indeterminate and mysterious, that, as yet, there can be neither physicians nor *final* judges, but that there is only One, He who saith: "Vengeance is mine; I will repay, saith the Lord."[20]

19 For biographical information, see *On Trial: The Case of Sinyavsky (Tertz) and Daniel (Arzhak)*. In *A Voice from the Chorus*, a collection of excerpts from letters written to his wife from prison, he continues his exploration of the lore and language of the folk.

20 F. M. Dostoevsky, *The Diary of a Writer*, trans. Boris Brasol (New York, 1949), 2: 787. The Biblical quotation (Romans 12:19) is the epigraph to *Anna Karenina*. I have substituted the King James version for Brasol's translation and made other changes.

In a crucial personal illumination that came to him in prison, Solzhenitsyn discovers a similar incompatibility between the properties of human nature and radical theories

The superficial definition of evil held by the "physician-socialists" is not only ineffective, in this traditional literary view; put into effect, it releases evil in concentrated form. Although there are grounds for calling each of our modern dissidents a Christian (Pasternak valued the great myths of Christianity at the very least), none proposes religious doctrine as a specific antidote to evil or uses his work to propagate his faith. The religious dimension in their work allows for mystery, for the not-yet-known and for the inexplicable, and it provides the perspective of centuries of human experience and culture.

Turgenev's Bazarov acts out the part of the physician-socialist in *Fathers and Sons*. The target of his "scientific" critique—most of the values Russians live by—weathers his attack and outlives him. Bazarov's professed atheism is not the measure of his miscalculation; nor is Christ, onstage or off, any part of Turgenev's countervailing force. Bazarov's error is the repudiation of culture, both "high"—art and the aesthetic sense—and "low"—love, work, and the family—however modestly both are represented in the novel. And both are at stake when Arkady gently removes a volume of Pushkin's poems from his father's hands and replaces it with Friedrich Büchner's *Kraft und Stoff* (1855), a major articulation of the theory of "materialistic monism," comparing nature, man, and mind to the properties of a steam engine.

This gesture reminds us of the true nature of the opponents in the mid-nineteenth-century battle between the writers and the materialist critics, and it suggests what has happened, less gently, to Russian culture since 1917, when a materialistic reductivism usurped the ground where art normally grows. If our three dissident writers join forces in common advocacy, it is to reestablish the conditions without which literature cannot exist, to validate their inalienable right to write. This

---

of social change: "On rotting prison straw I felt in myself the first tremor of virtue. It gradually came clear to me that the line which separates good and evil does not pass between governments, or classes, or parties—it passes through each human heart, and through all human hearts. This line is mobile, it fluctuates within us as the years pass. Even in the heart embraced by evil, it preserves a small bridgehead of virtue. Even in the most virtuous heart, there is an ineradicable fragment of evil.

"Since then I have understood the truth of all the religions in history: they fight against the evil in man (in each man). It is not possible to expel evil from the world, but it is possible to shrink it in every man.

"Since then I have understood the lie of all the revolutions in history; they destroy only the bearers of evil who are their contemporaries (and in their indiscriminate haste, the bearers of good as well)—so that they take on evil itself (much magnified) as part of their legacy." *Arkhipelag Gulag* (Paris, 1974), 3-4: 602–3.

right, as they have shown by the example of their work, includes the entertainment of plural or open or ambiguous answers to questions of morality, metaphysics, religion, art, and epistemology, and implies restoration of the ground of genuine civilization. All three argue for the cleansing of literary Russian and demonstrate it by their own command of fresh, vigorous, and expressive styles. The joint assault on materialist historicity *within* their works constitutes at the same time an appeal to be read and interpreted by other standards. The discovery, made by all three, that a politicized morality is no morality at all argues for a restoration of the standard vocabulary of moral behavior that has always been an integral part of the Russian literary language. Though their work has this dimension of reformism, they do not go further toward social or political advocacy—no further, in fact, than their predecessors in the nineteenth century. Emphasis and scale have changed, but the central problem remains the same. Individuals, then, were seized with false doctrines which alienated them from their full humanity. The doctrines destroyed them or they were rescued from them. In the imagined worlds of these contemporary writers, the entire nation has been seized by the false doctrine (a small, fanatical, misguided minority has become an all-powerful state); the individual clings to his humanity, his sanity, and his integrity, and triumphs if he remains morally intact.

The Western reader's sense of "old-fashionedness" is caused in part, I think, by Russia's arrested intellectual development in Stalin's Fourth Rome; these writers are fighting an anachronistic battle from the nineteenth century against the extension of scientistic systems to areas of experience not susceptible to scientific reduction, against the closing of systems around not-yet-known or unknowable areas of experience. We think of Bazarov's destructive denial, in the name of positivist doctrines, of the emotional half of his being, of Raskolnikov's suicidal assault on his own moral instincts in the name of rationality, of Bezukhov's identification of determinism as the mortal enemy of human spontaneity. Or we remind ourselves of Dickens' mockery of the utilitarians in *Hard Times*, or of Flaubert's savage assault on his vulgarized age in *Madame Bovary*, and against the pieties of revolution in *The Sentimental Education*. Only Russian writers, it appears, are still required to do battle with these venerable enemies of human wholeness.

These three men are writers, and they are Russians, and they are true to their tradition. Their subject matter is the human; their bed-rock foundation is morality. If they propose any design for the future beyond the elimination of the evils they catalogue, it is a world which, in Chekhov's words, is built on "freedom from violence and false-hood, no matter how they are manifest,"[21] a world anchored in mercy, privacy, and dignity. This program for changing the quality of moral life, we must remember, is expressed in other impressive works of fiction, of poetry, and of memoirs—the full dissident corpus—defining the meaning of the nation's suffering.

The literature, then, asserts more than its right to exist and affects more than the quality of its day. It forms a continuum, Sinyavsky has said since his departure from Russia, that incarnates the nation's in-tegral being. Literature kept him alive in prison; it has kept Russia alive through the "blood-dimmed" centuries.[22] It is the nation's "living memory," Solzhenitsyn said in his Nobel Prize speech, its means of communing with itself through time, of establishing its own unique identity, but, beyond that, it is part of "the one great heart" of world literature, the only way humanity has "truly to know itself."

[21] Letter to A. N. Pleshcheev, dated October 4, 1888, in A. P. Chekhov, *Polnoe sobranie sochinenii* (Moscow, 1944–51), 14: 177.

[22] See Hélène Zamoyska, "Andrei Sinyavsky Arrives in Paris," *Encounter*, Novem-ber 1973, pp. 63–65; and Nicholas Bethell, "Andrei Sinyavsky: Thoughts of Eternity in the Face of Modern Pressures," *The Times* (London), November 21, 1973.

Index

Index